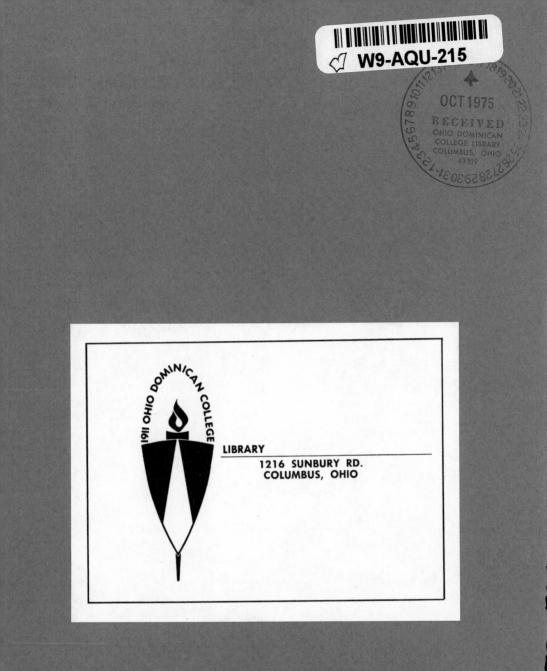

W. B. Yeats and Georgian Ireland

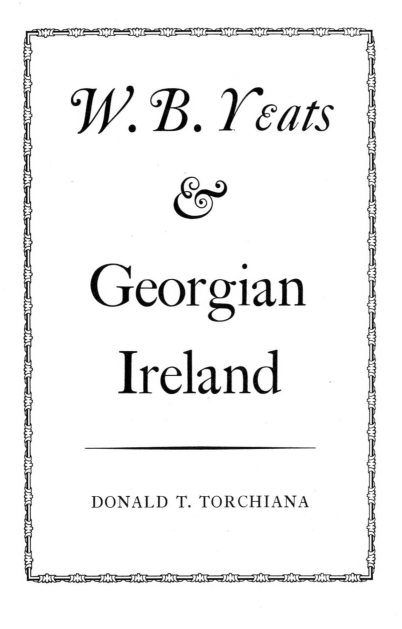

W. B. Yeats

&

Georgian
Ireland

DONALD T. TORCHIANA

Northwestern University Press

EVANSTON 1966

MATERIAL FROM THE FOLLOWING WORKS is reprinted with permission of The Macmillan Company of New York, Macmillan & Company Ltd. of London, and Mrs. W. B. Yeats: William Butler Yeats, *Wheels and Butterflies;* copyright 1934 by The Macmillan Company; copyright renewed 1962 by Bertha Georgie Yeats. *Variorum Edition of the Poems of W. B. Yeats,* eds. Peter Allt and Russell K. Alspach; copyright 1940 by Georgie Yeats. Various poems in William Butler Yeats, *Collected Poems;* copyright 1906, 1919, 1924, 1928, 1933, 1934 by The Macmillan Company; copyright 1940 by Georgie Yeats; copyright renewed 1934 by William B. Yeats; copyright renewed 1944, 1946, 1952, 1961, 1962 by Bertha Georgie Yeats; copyright renewed 1956 by Georgie Yeats. *The Autobiography of William Butler Yeats;* copyright 1916, 1936 by The Macmillan Company; copyright 1944 by Bertha Georgie Yeats. *Purgatory,* in *The Collected Plays of W. B. Yeats;* 2nd ed.; copyright 1952. W. B. Yeats, *Explorations,* selected by Mrs. W. B. Yeats; copyright 1962 by Mrs. W. B. Yeats. W. B. Yeats, *Essays and Introductions;* copyright 1961 by Mrs. W. B. Yeats.

MATERIAL FROM THE FOLLOWING WORKS is reprinted with permission of the publishers: *The Letters of W. B. Yeats,* ed. Allan Wade; The Macmillan Company of New York and Rupert Hart-Davis Ltd.; copyright 1954. William B. Yeats, *Letters to the New Island,* edited with an introduction by Horace Reynolds; Harvard University Press; copyright 1934 by the President and Fellows of Harvard College and 1962 by Horace Mason Reynolds. J. B. Yeats, *Letters to his son W. B. Yeats and others 1869–1922,* ed. Joseph Hone; Christy & Moore, Ltd., 1944. *Lady Gregory's Journals 1916–1930,* ed. Lennox Robinson; Putnam & Co. Ltd., 1946. *W. B. Yeats and T. Sturge Moore Their Correspondence 1901–1937,* ed. Ursula Bridge; Routledge & Kegan Paul Ltd., 1953. *The Senate Speeches of W. B. Yeats,* ed. Donald R. Pearce; Indiana University Press, 1960.

To
RICHARD ELLMANN
JEREMIAH MURPHY
CURT A. ZIMANSKY

Acknowledgments

M Y GREATEST DEBT is to Mrs. W. B. Yeats. Her generosity, encouragement, and friendship made this book possible. Otherwise, my chief indebtedness is to two old friends, my colleague Professor Glenn O'Malley, and Desmond Kennedy, Assistant Keeper of Printed Books in the National Library of Ireland. Professor O'Malley read my manuscript in its early stages, suggested major changes, and saved me from many errors. Mr. Kennedy was unstinting in tracking down or checking difficult sources and constantly made available to me his detailed knowledge of Irish life and history.

I have also been helped by several libraries and their staffs: Northwestern's Deering Library, the Newberry Library, the New York Public Library, and the British Museum. Most of all, I am indebted to the National Library of Ireland. It is a great pleasure to acknowledge my deep gratitude to Dr. R. J. Hayes, Director, and his staff. I was especially helped by Patrick Henchy, Keeper of Printed Books; Ailfrid MacLochlainn, Assistant Keeper of Manuscripts; Michael Hewson and Gearóid MacNiocaill, Assistant Librarians; Michael Breen (Newspaper Room), Leo. A. Cleary, and Herbert Frew, Library Assistants; and William Buckley, Attendant. The

National Gallery of Ireland, Bord Failte Eireann, the Irish Folklore Commission, and the United Arts Club also have my gratitude for offering me help and service in Dublin.

For aid in writing this book I also wish to thank Dr. C. P. Blacker, Ernest Blythe, John Chichester, Mrs. Bryan Cooper, Commander E. F. P. Cooper, C. P. Curran, S. Dunin-Markievicz, Oliver Edwards, Lady Gore-Booth, Gabrielle Gore-Booth, Harrison Hayford, the late Joseph M. Hone, Richard M. Kain, Edward Keene, Patrick Kennedy, T. J. Kiernan, Mrs. A. G. Larson, Eoin Linnane, Thomas MacGreevy, Captain D. A. MacManus, Ethel Mannin, Dermot Malone, E. M. Mills, Nora Niland, Peadar O'Donnell, Eoin O'Mahony, K.M., Mario M. Rossi, Richard Shakespeare, Dr. Thomas Wall, the late Ernest R. Walsh, Terence de Vere White, Sir Harold Williams, and Mrs. Hermione Wilson.

I am also grateful to Macmillan & Company Ltd., London, the Macmillan Company of New York, Oxford University Press, Harvard University Press, Indiana University Press, Routledge & Kegan Paul Ltd., Faber and Faber, Putnam & Co. Ltd., and Rupert Hart-Davis Ltd. for permission to quote materials from their editions of Yeats's work.

Portions of chapters IV and V have already appeared in *Modern Philology* and the *Newberry Library Bulletin*.

A Newberry Library Fellowship, grants-in-aid from the Committee on Research of Northwestern University, and a Fulbright lectureship in American literature at University College, Galway, permitted me to do the research necessary to complete my work.

I have dedicated this book to three men who gave me, respectively, the opportunity, the time, and the training to write it.

D. T. T.
Evanston
February 1965

Contents

Introduction   xi

Note   xv

Chapter One   3
   NOR MAY I LESS BE COUNTED ONE

Chapter Two   36
   THE TREES ARE IN THEIR AUTUMN BEAUTY

Chapter Three   85
   THAT ONE IRISH CENTURY THAT ESCAPED FROM DARKNESS
   AND CONFUSION

Chapter Four   120
   IMITATE HIM IF YOU DARE

Chapter Five   168
   BURKE'S GREAT MELODY

Chapter Six   222
   GOD-APPOINTED BERKELEY

Chapter Seven   266
   GOLDSMITH LURES AND WAITS

Contents

Chapter Eight   279
    I WOULD . . . GLADLY SING THEIR SONG

Chapter Nine   340
    STUDY THAT HOUSE . . . STUDY THAT TREE

Index   367

Introduction

DURING THE LAST TWENTY YEARS or so of his life, W. B. Yeats felt a close identification with Protestant Ireland, particularly with its eighteenth-century heritage. Throughout these years he reread, commented on, and wrote extensively about Swift, Burke, Berkeley, Goldsmith, and Grattan. He had long before championed the revolutionary tradition of Georgian Ireland by citing the heroics of Lord Edward, Tone, and Emmet as worthy of a modern Irishman's regard. But from the time he entered the Irish Senate, Yeats more and more stressed the importance of the conservative and intellectual tradition of the Protestant Ascendancy for the new nation. I consider both these traditions in this book but follow Yeats in emphasizing the second, especially as he saw it exemplified in the careers of Swift, Burke, and Berkeley.

Like all students of Yeats, I am indebted to T. R. Henn's opening chapter, "The Background," in *The Lonely Tower*. There Henn has established the essentially Protestant, rural, rigidly stratified culture of the declining minority that Yeats was born into. This book will show his rebellion against Protestant Ireland, his return to it, his glorification of its golden age, and his continuous disappointment in its weakness and hesitation. And, of course, I shall stress the glorification. Moreover, I see Yeats's identity with the Protestant nation as primarily intellectual, only partly social, and hardly at all religious. In his indifference to the dogmas of the Church of Ireland, he differed little from most Irish Protestants. Yet his celebrating the careers of Swift, Burke, and Berkeley was a living, important, and repeated preoccupation of Yeats's last two decades. For this reason I have chosen to describe in detail the importance of these men, and others, to Yeats in the daily round of his chores as poet, man of letters, Senator, lecturer, and denizen of the world of affairs. This focus has also led me to decline any thorough review of the culture of Georgian Ireland itself, paramount as it was to Yeats in his last years. The late Constantia Maxwell, for one, in her *Country and Town in Ireland Under the Georges* and *Dublin Under the Georges* has summed up that achievement beautifully. In short, with Henn's opening chapter in mind, I have decided to put my stress on Yeats first and Georgian Ireland second.

His blood tie to the Anglo-Irish eighteenth century excited Yeats more and more in these decades. In the early pages of *Reveries over Childhood and Youth* we see him pointing to ancestral associations with Marlborough, Sarsfield, Goldsmith, Major Sirr, and Emmet. Later, in his Introduction to *The Words Upon the Window-pane,* Yeats admits that there is a large element of truth in John Corbet's boasting of Georgian Ireland, "Everything great in Ireland and in our character, in what remains of our architecture, comes from that day . . . we have kept its seal longer than England." In the same year that he wrote this play, Yeats exclaimed in a letter to Hone, "I want Protestant Ireland to base some vital part of its culture upon Burke, Swift and Berkeley." Earlier he had hoped that Catholic Ireland too might heed his call, sensing in Kevin O'Higgins an ability and leadership that Swift and Burke might have admired. Accordingly, the nine chapters of this book accent the beginning and the flowering of Yeats's excited discovery of past Protestant greatness.

The first chapter deals with his enchantment and later disillusion with the patriotic literature and ideals of nineteenth-century Ireland. Here I also examine his early concomitant dislike and subsequent ambiguous admiration for the old Protestant Ascendancy. The second chapter reviews Yeats's friendship with the Gregorys, concentrating on his admiration for the traditions of life and art at Coole that had seemed to have come down from the days of Arthur Young's *Tour*. Chapter III concludes introductory matters by attempting to define what in eighteenth-century Ireland's Protestant culture so attracted Yeats. This chapter also outlines Yeats's hopes for directing modern Ireland's attention to this Anglo-Ireland, and then considers what he took to be her rejection of it. The next four chapters examine Yeats's enthusiasms for Swift, Burke, Berkeley, and Goldsmith. Chapter VIII surveys the uses to which Yeats put the theme of Georgian Ireland in his poetry. Finally, the ninth chapter concludes the book with an analysis of *On the Boiler* where, in the play *Purgatory*, Yeats seems to have reached some rather grim conclusions on the progress of modern Ireland since the French Revolution and the Union.

In tracing this enthusiasm for Georgian Ireland—a hardheaded one as I hope to show—the reader will encounter a number of curiosities. One is Yeats's tendency to play down or hold back mention of his Anglo-Irish identification, modern or Augustan, in his final draft of poems or in his own collected works. Typically, *Pages from a Diary*, published in 1944, contains more on these matters than any work published during his life. Thus I have searched out uncollected essays, reviews, speeches, interviews, and unpublished material to show the importance of an element in his background that might *appear* to be relatively unimportant. He probably realized that too obvious an emphasis on Protestant Ascendancy culture in his work might limit his national audience and baffle his wider audience outside Ireland. An analogy may be possible in the similar difference between the dogmatic Milton of the *De Doctrina* and the universal Milton of *Paradise Lost*. Yet, as with Milton, Yeats's local and private thoughts also exerted a tremendous pressure on his finished work.

A second curiosity is of a different order, yet it also hinges on the difference between history and poetry or fact and myth. Quite simply, Yeats is not always accurate in his reading of Irish history. His interpretation is richly biased, highly imaginative, yet strangely fair.

His history is a poet's history, more prejudiced and more objective than that of most historians. His praise and condemnation of the Protestant Ascendancy in his Introduction to *The Words Upon the Window-pane* are cases in point. Moreover, while the title of the book ought to cover the years between 1714 and 1830 strictly speaking, I have frequently stretched the years to cover the Protestant Ireland that goes back to the Battle of the Boyne, and then reaches down as far, in Yeats's way of thinking, as the building of Lissadell, and even to Famine times and the death of Mary Hines. On the other hand, Yeats sometimes hints strongly that his interest really stopped with the dissolution of Grattan's Parliament and the Union. In any case, I frequently stretch matters or focus on seemingly trivial material or push my theme a bit too far in reading a poem—all in an effort to show the steady force on Yeats of that momentary brilliance of Protestant Ireland.

This Protestant, aristocratic, eighteenth-century side of Yeats is not a popular one. I am sure he knew it. Thus the book has its perils. In America it may suggest that Yeats was a Fascist. In Ireland it may confirm a long-held suspicion that Yeats was hostile to the Gaelic Catholic nation, that is to say to most of Ireland. In England it may suggest his final apostasy from a tradition of intellectual enlightenment made available weekly in the pages of the *New Statesman*. All these charges are probably wrong. However, they represent in the aggregate the charges usually brought against the Anglo-Irish. Thus I would hope to show, after the example of Brian Inglis in *West Briton*, that Yeats, in taking upon himself the heritage of Georgian Ireland, was being most characteristically Irish. For, in holding up that golden age, he pointed to the critical, detached, and passionately cold intellect that is Protestant Ireland's distinctive contribution to Irish life. And, in a larger view, those who consign this side of Yeats to the ash heap of Fascism, anticlericalism, and reaction may also be forgetting that by turning to the eighteenth century of his forefathers he was turning to thinkers like Swift, Burke, and Berkeley who had been among the first to react against the loosening of the ties that bound men to God or to other men.

$\mathcal{N}$ote

THE FOLLOWING ABBREVIATIONS have been used in the notes:

Autobiographies   W. B. Yeats, *Autobiographies* (London, 1955).

"Autobiography"   Unpublished first draft of Yeats's *Autobiographies*, written in 1916–17.

Essays and Introductions   W. B. Yeats, *Essays and Introductions* (London, 1961).

Explorations   W. B. Yeats, *Explorations*, selected by Mrs. W. B. Yeats (London, 1962).

Henderson   W. A. Henderson, "The Abbey Theatre and Irish Plays," a collection of press clippings in the National Library of Ireland.

Holloway   Joseph Holloway, "Impressions of a Dublin Playgoer," a manuscript diary and collection of press clippings in the National Library of Ireland.

Hone   Joseph Hone, *W. B. Yeats, 1865–1939*, 2nd ed. (London, 1962).

Hugh Lane   Lady Gregory, *Hugh Lane's Life and Achievement, with Some Account of the Dublin Galleries* (London, 1921).

Lady Gregory's Journals	Lady Gregory, *Lady Gregory's Journals 1916–1930*, ed. Lennox Robinson (London, 1946).
Letters	W. B. Yeats, *The Letters of W. B. Yeats*, ed. Allan Wade (London, 1954).
Mythologies	W. B. Yeats, *Mythologies* (London, 1959).
On the Boiler	W. B. Yeats, *On the Boiler* (Dublin [1939]).
Our Irish Theatre	Lady Gregory, *Our Irish Theatre, A Chapter of Autobiography* (New York and London, 1913).
Pages from a Diary	*Pages from a Diary Written in Nineteen Hundred and Thirty*, selected by Mrs. W. B. Yeats (Dublin, 1944).
Senate Speeches	W. B. Yeats, *The Senate Speeches of W. B. Yeats*, ed. Donald R. Pearce (Bloomington, 1960).
Variorum	W. B. Yeats, *The Variorum Edition of the Poems of W. B. Yeats*, eds. Peter Allt and Russell K. Alspach (New York, 1957).
Wheels and Butterflies	W. B. Yeats, *Wheels and Butterflies* (London, 1934).
Yeats and T. Sturge Moore	*W. B. Yeats and T. Sturge Moore Their Correspondence 1901–1937*, ed. Ursula Bridge (London, 1953).

Since first editions of *Wheels and Butterflies* and *On the Boiler* are readily available, they are used in the footnotes rather than *Explorations*, where only the prose from these volumes is gathered. All poetry quoted, unless otherwise cited, is taken from the *Variorum Edition*. Unless otherwise noted, all unpublished materials are in the possession of Mrs. W. B. Yeats, © Mrs. W. B. Yeats, and may not be reproduced without written permission from her or from her heirs and executors. To simplify matters, this material is indicated without italics or quotation marks. In quoting from Yeats's unpublished papers, I have silently regularized his spelling and punctuation when his meaning would otherwise have been unclear.

W. B. Yeats and Georgian Ireland

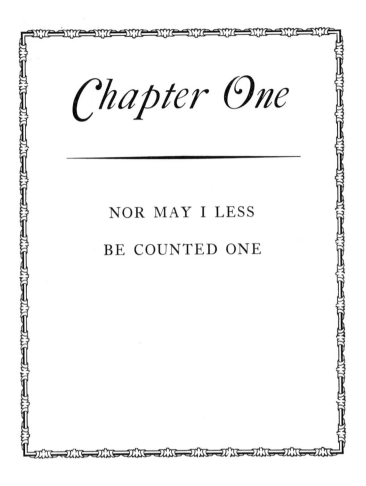

Chapter One

NOR MAY I LESS

BE COUNTED ONE

I

AT THE HEIGHT of his enthusiasm for Protestant Ireland of the eighteenth century—"that one Irish century that escaped from darkness and confusion" [1]—Yeats looked back to earlier days when his allegiances had been otherwise:

> . . . I turned from Goldsmith and from Burke because they had come to seem a part of the English system, from Swift because I acknowledged, being a romantic, no verse between

1. *Wheels and Butterflies*, p. 7.

Cowley and Smart's *Song to David,* no prose between Sir Thomas Browne and the *Conversations* of Landor.[2]

Thus Yeats had early rejected Georgian Ireland for the romantic Ireland of the nineteenth century. But his later hatred of nineteenth-century Ireland was not simple apostasy or the trailing of a Protestant coat that his severest critics assert. For Yeats's love of the romantic Ireland of his youth was always a qualified love as, in fact, was his later hatred. When, after the Treaty, he came to celebrate the golden age of Protestant Ireland, he was never blind to the ultimate failure of the Georgians, their responsibility for the Union, and, finally, their guilt in spawning a nineteenth century which had opened the flood gates for the "filthy modern tide."

As a professed romantic, however, Yeats in the eighties and nineties had found himself at home—sometimes uncomfortably so but nevertheless at home—with the lyric singers, stern orators, and militant nationalists of a resurgent Ireland. He threw in his lot with a national, political, and cultural self-assertion that glorified Gaelic Catholic Ireland. That was the real Ireland.[3] The romantic revival of Irish literature in English would by and large be a return to Gaelic folklore.[4] It was the fairy Ireland which Yeats romantically idealized as lighthearted and happy before the Famine. As a nationalist, he could set this Ireland as a pattern for the future and contrast it tellingly with the civilization of her oppressor, England:

> What is this nationality we are trying to preserve, this thing that we are fighting English influence to preserve? It is not merely our pride. . . . If you examine to the root a contest between two peoples, two nations, you will always find that it is really a war between two civilizations, two ideals of life. . . . Ireland will always be in the main an agricultural country.

2. *Ibid.*
3. TS. of lecture given in New York during 1903–4.
4. "The Message of the Folk-lorist," *The Speaker,* 19 August 1893, pp. 188–89. A good introduction to Yeats's own use of folklore is to be found in Russell K. Alspach, "The Use by Yeats and Other Irish Writers of the Folklore of Patrick Kennedy," *Journal of American Folklore,* LIX (October–December 1946), 404–12.

4

Industries we may have, but we will not have, as England has, a
very rich class nor whole districts blackened with smoke like
what they call in England their "Black Country." I think that
the best ideal for our people, an ideal very generally accepted
among us, is that Ireland is going to become a country where, if
there are few rich, there shall be nobody very poor. Wherever
men have tried to imagine a perfect life, they have imagined a
place where men plow and sow and reap, not a place where
there are great wheels turning and great chimneys vomiting
smoke. Ireland will always be a country where men plow and
sow and reap. . . . We wish to preserve an ancient ideal of
life.[5]

Right down to the death of Parnell, Yeats had praised Irish
writing, while being careful not to overestimate its literary value, for
its faithfulness to this patriotic ideal. At the age of twenty-four, he
noted the lack of a short book on Irish literature since Thomas Moore
and even suggested that he himself write it.[6] His intention, baldly
stated, was to "be systematically political or national . . . throughout the thing." [7] Partly, of course, this was Yeats's studied attempt
to fly in the face of the Ireland he considered academic and
obsequious to England. Yet he was not unacquainted with the
grimness of Irish rural life or ignorant of the toil of "real labourers
and potato diggers and potheen makers and cockle pickers," realities
whose presence he praised in Carleton and the absence of which he
condemned in Miss Barlow.[8] The new Irish writing could not be a
mere imitation of Thomas Davis and the *Nation* group.[9] It must
return to earlier sources. Only the unlikelihood of a Gaelic-speaking
Ireland made Yeats content to capture the Gaelic tradition in
English.[10] For this reason, he decided to combine what he took to be
the best of nineteenth-century literary Europe: a polished romantic

5. TS. of lecture . . . 1903–4.
6. *Letters*, pp. 133, 146, 201.
7. *Ibid.*, pp. 146–47.
8. "Irish National Literature," *Bookman*, August 1895, p. 139.
9. "The Irish Intellectual Capital: Where Is It?" *United Ireland*, 14 May
1892.
10. "The De-Anglicising of Ireland," *United Ireland*, 17 December 1892.

technique, seen in the work of the French symbolists and the Rhymers, and a content of ancient Irish lore and tales that would feed the national imagination.[11] Three days before Parnell's death, Yeats was quoted as saying that his work in the Young Ireland League was meant to rid Ireland of "ignorance and bigotry and fanaticism" whether Home Rule came or not.[12] He would reshape the modern Gaelic spirit in life and letters by artfully recalling it to its earlier sources.

Yeats's choice of nineteenth-century poets to praise and to pattern himself after is well known; for after putting himself in the general patriotic tradition,

> Know, that I would accounted be
> True brother of a company
> That sang, to sweeten Ireland's wrong,
> Ballad and story, rann and song;

he cites names, with an appropriate rider, that insure his kinship:

> Nor may I less be counted one
> With Davis, Mangan, Ferguson,
> Because, to him who ponders well,
> My rhymes more than their rhyming tell
> Of things discovered in the deep,
> Where only body's laid asleep.

But more striking is the fact that, aside from his quickened romantic absorption in Spenser, Blake, and Shelley, Yeats went out of his way to admire specific romantic traits in most nineteenth-century Irish writers such as those cited above. Not surprisingly, we also find him lauding qualities in these writers which he later discovers in his eighteenth-century pantheon.

For instance, he highly praised William Allingham, the poet of Ballyshannon, for evoking a local rather than an abstractly national feeling. His ability to catch the fleeting and obscure life of small

---

11. "Hopes and Fears for Irish Literature," *United Ireland*, 15 October 1892.
12. "The Young Ireland League," *United Ireland*, 3 October 1891.

seaboard towns of the West of Ireland was, understandably, dear to Yeats:

> He has expressed that curious devotion of the people for the earth under their feet, a devotion that is not national, but local, a thing at once more narrow and more idyllic. He sang Ballyshannon and not Ireland. Neither his emotions nor his thoughts took any wide sweep over the world of man and nature. He was the poet of little things and little moments, and of that vague melancholy Lord Palmerston considered peculiar to the peasantry of the wild seaboard where he lived.[13]

This romantic Ireland was still bardic and lived in a ballad age; so Yeats might also praise Ellen O'Leary for writing poetry for "a country where the populace are strongly moved by great fundamental passions."[14] At their best, poets like Ferguson, Katharine Tynan, and Allingham not only reproduced the beauty of the Gaelic poets but, as became romantic poets, were themselves sources of melody and light.[15]

Besides the local and fundamental passions Yeats also cherished what Pater called "strange beauty." This quality Yeats found in a poet like Mangan, who might in his gift resemble Poe or Baudelaire: "All the great poems of the world have their foundations fixed in agony" was Yeats's comment on Mangan's lyric "Nameless."[16] The intensity of a fated existence, not a weakness of will, gave a quality to his misery that made Mangan and his work exclaim to Yeats, "Look at me—I am so strange, so exotic, so different."[17] Beauty born out of misery was also part of the bardic fire that leaped from the true Irish character no less than from the best Irish poets of the century:

> Sir Samuel Ferguson, I contend, is the greatest Irish poet, because . . . his poems and the legends . . . embody more

13. "William Allingham," *The Poets and the Poetry of the Century*, ed. Alfred H. Miles (London [1892]), V, 211. See also "Irish Literature. A Poet we have Neglected," *United Ireland*, 12 December 1891.

14. "Ellen O'Leary," *The Poets and the Poetry of the Century*, VII, 449.

15. *Letters*, p. 253.

16. "Clarence Mangan," *Irish Fireside*, 12 March 1887, p. 169.

17. *Ibid.*, p. 170.

7

completely than in any other man's writings, the Irish character. Its unflinching devotion to some single aim. Its passion. . . . And this faithfulness to things tragic and bitter, to thoughts that wear one's life out and scatter one's joy, the Celt has above all others.[18]

Not the least among these romantic Irish traits Yeats chose to celebrate was indigenous, inward emotion. Startling revelation of it might transform a reader or an audience. So Maud Gonne, in a speech which displayed "throughout the wild sweetness of an Æolian Harp upon which the winds play," had reduced a French audience to tears over the woes of Ireland.[19] Thus too, the ancient soil of Ireland, properly sung, might provide the impetus for long-forgotten feelings even though the poet lacked depth; an example was R. D. Joyce:

> I hold Joyce to be the poet of all the external things that appertain to the barbaric earth—the earth of hunters and riders, and all young people; the poet of armour and hunting, of hounds and horses. That he was in no way a singer, also, of man's inner nature, of the vague *desires*, though it takes from his stature as a poet, makes him so much the dearer to many worn with modern unrest. In seeking to restore the young world, long faded, he has restored to us for an instant our childhood.[20]

There was an Irish literary tradition—Yeats once called it "the golden chain of Irish literature"—which was continued, not started, by the writers of '48.[21] It had been taken up in English by writers such as Allingham, De Vere, O'Grady, Ferguson, and Todhunter after the deaths of Davis, Carleton, and Mangan.[22] It was a literature

18. "The Poetry of Sir Samuel Ferguson," *Irish Fireside*, 9 October 1886, p. 220. See also "The Poetry of Sir Samuel Ferguson," *Dublin University Review*, November 1886, p. 923.

19. "The New 'Speranza,'" *United Ireland*, 16 January 1892.

20. "The Poetry of R. D. Joyce," *Irish Fireside*, 4 December 1886, p. 348.

21. "Dr. Todhunter's Irish Poems," *United Ireland*, 23 January 1892.

22. *Idem.* See also "Irish National Literature," *Bookman*, July 1895, pp. 105–7.

various enough but essentially of the soil of Irish land or Irish spirit, in either case a spur to primeval emotion. Only by this grounding could these poets and those before them be said to have "created a great movement out of the very heart of the people." [23] The poet's deep, inward impulses and his nationality were ideally one. So Carleton's intensity and "inbred fatalism" seemed to Yeats in these years part and parcel of Carleton's authority as a historian:

> The history of a nation is not in parliaments and battle-fields, but in what the people say to each other on fair-days and high days, and in how they farm, and quarrel, and go on pilgrimage. These things has Carleton recorded.[24]

And even new poets like AE, Nora Hopper, and Lionel Johnson could act as refining elements on the poet who tended to be too exclusively national or political, because "they touch our deepest and most delicate feelings, and believe that a beauty, not a worldly beauty, lives in worldly things." [25]

A few years later, while summing up romantic Ireland and systematically pointing out the limitations of these nineteenth-century poets and others in his much revised introduction to *A Book of Irish Verse*, Yeats nevertheless defended his selections in a phrase: ". . . no Irishman living in Ireland has sung excellently of any but a theme from Irish experience, Irish history, or Irish tradition." [26] There can be little doubt what "Irish" meant in this context.

II

Seemingly to underline his approval of the romantic Celtic revival, Yeats in the same pages began a long attack on contemporary Protestant Ireland. In doing so, he was hitting out at the vestiges of

23. TS. of lecture . . . 1903–4.
24. "William Carleton," *Stories from Carleton* (New York and Toronto [1889]), p. xvi.
25. "Three Irish Poets," *A Celtic Christmas* (Christmas Number of the *Irish Homestead*, December 1897), p. 8.
26. "Modern Irish Poetry," *A Book of Irish Verse*, rev. ed. (London, 1900), p. xxix. The 1895 Introduction makes the same assertion.

the Ascendancy of Penal days. His specific target was Trinity College, even then, under Dowden, Lecky, Mahaffy, and Tyrrell, basking in the glory of its illustrious eighteenth-century graduates. The passage is instructive in its condemnations:

> Trinity College, which desires to be English, has been the mother of many verse-writers and of few poets; and this can only be because she has set herself against the national genius, and taught her children to imitate alien styles, and choose out alien themes, for it is not possible to believe that the educated Irishman alone is prosaic and uninventive. . . . An enemy to all enthusiasms, because all enthusiasms seemed her enemies, she has taught her children to look neither to the world about them, nor into their own souls where some dangerous fire might slumber.
>
> To remember that in Ireland the professional and landed classes have been through the mould of Trinity College or of English Universities, and are ignorant of the very names of the best writers in this book, is to know how strong a wind blows from the ancient legends of Ireland, how vigorous an impulse to create is in her heart to-day.[27]

This attack, in some senses lifelong, was especially characteristic of the peppering Yeats gave Trinity in his early years. Trinity, apparently a mortmain from the previous century, summed up for him all that was uncreative, alien, aloof, and vulgarly English in Irish upper-class life. During the nineties, certainly, Yeats could see only apathy, cynicism, sterility, and bitter enmity within Trinity's imperturbably gray Georgian walls. She was the enemy of what Yeats named Ireland's "agrarian revolution" and the subsequent literary revival. In leveling this charge against Trinity in 1892, Yeats clearly pits romantic enthusiasm against what he takes to be something very close to Augustan complacency:

> As Dublin Castle with the help of the police keeps Ireland for England, so Trinity College with the help of the schoolmasters

---

27. *Ibid.*, pp. xxix–xxx. See also George Moore, *Ave* (London, 1911), p. 150.

keeps the mind of Ireland for scholasticism with its accompanying weight of mediocrity. All noble life, all noble thought,
depends primarily upon enthusiasm, and Trinity College, in
abject fear of the National enthusiasm which is at her gates, has
shut itself off from every kind of ardour, from every kind of
fiery and exultant life. She has gone over body and soul to
scholasticism, and scholasticism is but an aspect of the great god
Dagon of the Philistines. . . . Let us not sentimentalize over
her, but let us grant her all that she has, her mathematics, and
her metaphysics, and then acknowledge that a tractarian movement, or a single poet of the rank of Arnold or of Clough even,
were more than all these things, for not out of any logic mill,
but out of prolonged and fiery ardour and an ever present
consciousness of the overshadowing mysteries of life, emerges
the soul of man and the heroic heart.[28]

And at the end of the century, while roasting Dr. Atkinson of Trinity
for his ill-tempered belief that "all folk-lore is essentially abomi-
nable," Yeats lashed out at all such academics, for the most part
English or Protestant Anglo-Irish, in much the same spirit:

The academic class in Ireland, because the visible enthusiasm of
the time threatened its interests or the interests of the classes
among whom it dined and married, set its face against all Irish
enthusiasms in the first instance, and then, by perhaps slow
degrees, against all the great intellectual passions. An academic
class is always a little dead and deadening; and our political
rancours may long have made our academic class even quicker in
denial than its association with undeveloped minds, and its
preoccupation with words rather than ideas, with facts rather
than emotions, made unavoidable; but I am persuaded, from
much that I have heard and read, that it only came to its full
maturity of bitterness in the agrarian revolution.[29]

Yeats saw also that the vaunted cosmopolitanism of the eighteenth
century had dwindled, for all Trinity's worldliness, to a pale and

28. "Dublin Scholasticism and Trinity College," *United Ireland*, 30 July
1892.
29. "The Academic Class and the Agrarian Revolution," *Dublin Daily
Express*, 11 March 1899.

vapid provincialism. Irish Ireland, by contrast, he felt to be European. Her ancient lore and tales—the very heart of the literary revival—were common to all Europe.[30] They were the antidote to the provincialism that Yeats discovered behind Trinity's sad lack of imagination and creativity.[31] Little wonder that Yeats countered sharply, while addressing no less an enclave, or confine, than Trinity's College Historical Society, on this very point. The subject was, amazingly enough, "That any attempt to further an Irish Literary Movement would result in Provincialism." Here is part of his charge:

> . . . he hoped the University of Dublin would yet delight to keep watch over all that which was distinctive and racial in this country. He did not believe that a literature rising out of racial characteristics was provincial. A peasant dressed in his national costume was not provincial. The small shopkeeper in the country town dressed in the costume of London or Paris was provincial. Cosmopolitanism had never been a creative power, because cosmopolitanism was a mere mirror in which forms and images reflected themselves. It could not create them, and was the very essence of provincialism. If they went down into any part of England, Ireland, or Scotland, and analysed the things that gave them the impression of provincialism they would find everywhere that they were the cast off fashions, the cast off clothes, the cast off thoughts of some active centre of creative minds. They were, in literature, the opinions which the provincial of Dublin, or of London, or of Edinburgh supposed to be the opinions of London, but which London had cast off many years ago.[32]

Relative to provincialism, Yeats's animus against Trinity during these years often centered, somewhat to his regret, on Professor Dowden, an old family friend. It had been J. B. Yeats's steady belief

---

30. "Feis Ceoil Association. Address by Mr. W. B. Yeats," *Irish Times*, 10 February 1909.
31. "The Irish Literary Theatre," *Freeman's Journal*, 23 February 1900.
32. "Trinity College and the Literary Theatre," *Irish Times*, 1 June 1899.

since his twenties that his old friend was indeed something of an inveterate provincial.[33] His son discovered in Dowden abilities severely reduced by virtually the same decay that had sapped the life of the mind in Trinity in particular and the Anglo-Irish in general. They, like Dowden, feared any attack on British civilization.[34] Influential critic and admirer of Ferguson that he was, Dowden had done nothing, Yeats felt, to enhance Ferguson's reputation.[35] Dowden had, in fact, accused followers of the Irish literary movement of "plastering [themselves] with shamrocks" and "raving of Brian Boru." [36] Yeats countered this slap in the face with the rejoinder that Dowden, the usually accurate and authoritative critic of English literature, was indeed no authority, was more than likely an outright partisan if not a fool, when he came to Irish literature.[37] By thus turning young minds at Trinity away from the exciting new literature outside her gates, Dowden was simple-mindedly helping to perpetuate the creative rot in Protestant Ireland:

> Year after year the graduates and undergraduates of Trinity College compose vacant verses, and how vacant their best are can be seen from a recent anthology; and young ladies from Alexandra College gather in little groups and read Shakespeare, and common-place is the abundant fruit. It is only when some young man or young girl is captured by a despised enthusiasm that the vacancy is peopled and the common made uncommon; and to make such captures and at length overthrow and sack Dublin scholasticism is one half the business of "the Irish Literary Movement." [38]

Yet most such readers, however cultivated they might be, were in Yeats's opinion "only anxious to be academic, and to be servile to

33. *Autobiographies*, pp. 88–89. The whole passage, pp. 85–89, is relevant.
34. "The Poetry of Sir Samuel Ferguson," *Dublin University Review*, November 1886, pp. 924, 941.
35. "Prof. Dowden and Irish Literature," *Dublin Daily Express*, 26 January 1895. See also Dowden's *Irish Universities and the Present Administration* (Dublin, n.d.), *passim*.
36. "Irish National Literature," *Bookman*, October 1895, p. 21.
37. "Irish Literature," *Dublin Daily Express*, 8 March 1895.
38. "Irish National Literature," *Bookman*, October 1895, p. 21.

English notions." [39] In part this was Yeats's fight against a decayed Victorianism, as he wrote his father.[40] We also know that Yeats was especially truculent in this fight in order to assure his nationalist friends that, if need be, he would even attack his own Protestant Irish class to prove his loyalties.

But there was a genuine rancor at work here, one never entirely absent in Yeats's subsequent dealings with Unionists and Anglo-Irish. Peculiarly enough, it often echoes, for all of Yeats's fierce identity with Irish nationalism, the reproaches of another Protestant Irishman —a Tory and Unionist to boot—against his own class. This was Standish James O'Grady, whose many books (like the *History of Ireland*) Yeats read and cited. In his last years, Yeats was prepared to deny O'Grady's attack on the Anglo-Irish aristocracy,[41] but at this time Yeats's tirades against Trinity and his own class were often very close to O'Grady's. O'Grady saw the fall of the Anglo-Irish as both ignoble and farcical. Its certain doom he predicted for reasons much like Yeats's:

> They might have been so much to this afflicted nation; half-ruined as they are, they might be so much to-morrow; but the curse that has fallen on the whole land seems to have fallen on them with double power—the understanding paralysed, the will gone all to water, and for consequence a sure destruction.[42]

Yeats and O'Grady also shared another charge: the Anglo-Irish had put themselves unashamedly into the hands of the vulgar English. Both men had been especially struck by the consequent commonness such support had forced upon the Irish ruling classes. Hence Yeats linked the mediocre and commonplace in the arts at Trinity to a comparable vacuity in the British ruling classes and even in Queen Victoria herself:

39. "The Poetry of Sir Samuel Ferguson," *Dublin University Review*, November 1886, p. 925.

40. *Letters*, p. 603.

41. "The Great Enchantment," *Standish O'Grady: Selected Essays and Passages*, Every Irishman's Library ed. (Dublin and London, n.d.), pp. 174–87.

42. *Ibid.*, p. 181.

14

. . . an aged woman, who is so surrounded by courtiers that we do not know with any certainty, whether she is wise or foolish, bitter or magnanimous, miserly or generous; and who, unlike the great kings and queens of a greater time, has certainly used her example and her influence to cherish mediocrity in music and in painting and in literature. In a few years crowds will gather, in as many thousands, to see a carriage with an elderly man, her son, who has used his example and his influence to make the love of man and woman seem a light and vulgar thing among great numbers in his islands.

It is, then, that although this Royalty, that England sends as her messenger, is vulgar, the loyalty it would have from us is so ennobling, that we should close our eyes and do it reverence? No . . .[43]

Such outbursts were to lose him the support of many of his class like Lecky, who had enthusiastically backed the idea of an Irish national theater until Yeats's jibes at Queen Victoria and her Irish visit came to his ears.[44] But Yeats saw true majesty in the mythological aristocracy of Cuchulain, Deirdre, and the Countess Cathleen, dominant figures in the new Irish drama.[45] They had heroic style. The British stage, demoralized by democracy and vulgarians like Tree, according to Yeats, hated style "because the illogical thinking and insincere feeling we call bad writing makes the mind timid and the heart effeminate."[46]

In short, to thwack the British empire was to thwack her instrument in Ireland, the Protestant ruling classes. Very little in either realm escaped Yeats's accusing eye. The sentimentalities of the British home had degraded her art, and that art was still cherished in most Irish Protestant homes.[47] Edward VII, like George IV, was

43. "Noble and Ignoble Loyalties," *United Irishman*, 21 April 1900. Yeats had had an interview with the Queen. See *Self-Portrait . . . of Charles Ricketts, R.A.*, ed. Cecil Lewis (London, 1939), p. 112.
44. *Our Irish Theatre*, pp. 69–73.
45. "The De-Anglicising of Ireland," *United Ireland*, 17 December 1892.
46. "Is the English Stage Going to the Dogs?" *Playgoer*, 14 April 1904, p. 206. See also " 'Our Age and Its Poetry,' " *Irish Times*, 8 March 1912.
47. "Mrs. Grundy's Domicile," *Evening Standard*, 26 June 1905.

more interested in an Irish dinner than in Irish emancipation or culture.[48] Not even the Poet Laureate escaped.[49] Yeats was reported to have foreseen the prospect that during his own lifetime Gaelic would become the "language of the artistic and intellectual world in Anglo-Saxondom."[50] Meanwhile, he could say,

> Throughout the entire British Empire there were not at the present day ten thousand persons whose opinion was worth anything in any art. . . . That was the result of their modern enlightenment and of their idea of education which says "Reading and writing for the poor man who must earn his bread, but the arts for the wealthy and the happy." The result of that was that not even the wealthy and the happy had the arts. They had the Horse Show. . . .[51]

This slam at the Empire and Protestant Ireland as one seems unmistakable. The Ireland of Yeats's hopes and imagination was Connacht. Dublin was "shabby England."[52]

So far, then, we have seen Yeats baiting Trinity (and Protestant Ireland) for provincialism and vulgarity. His standard was the forgotten culture of Gaelic and Catholic Ireland which was re-entering Irish life in the romantic verse of nineteenth-century national Ireland. Given Yeats's hostility to Trinity's heritage of the Protestant eighteenth century, it is easy to anticipate his hostility to the entire tradition of Unionism in Ireland since 1800. Here he is then, not surprisingly, glancing back over the first hundred years of the Union:

> It has been announced that the Queen will leave Windsor for Ireland on April 2nd. That is a remarkable day, for on that day

48. "The King's Visit," *Freeman's Journal*, 13 July 1903.
49. Marion Witt, "Yeats on the Poet Laureateship," *MLN*, LXVI (June 1951), 385–88.
50. Clipping from the *Dublin Daily Express*, c. 1901, in possession of Mrs. W. B. Yeats.
51. Clipping from the *Freeman's Journal*, c. 1901, in possession of Mrs. W. B. Yeats.
52. "First Principles," *Explorations*, p. 231.

a hundred years ago the Act of Union, having been pushed through the Irish Parliament by bribery, was introduced into the English Parliament.

. . . .

I propose that a great meeting be summoned in the Rotunda on that date to protest against the Union and to dissociate Ireland from any welcome that the Unionist or the time-server may offer to the official head of that Empire in whose name liberty is being suppressed in South Africa, as it was suppressed in Ireland a hundred years ago.[53]

Quite naturally, his hatred of Unionists was much the same as his hatred of Trinity and Protestant Ireland since all three tended to represent the same people. But in using the term Unionist, as in the instance cited, Yeats shrewdly kept to the fore the continued fact of bribery, subtle or otherwise, since the Union:

I had a blue anger against Unionist Ireland. They had opposed to our movement their mere weight and indifference, and had written and spoken as if the finest literature in Ireland . . . was itself provincial or barbarous. They had done this . . . not in the interest of Shakespeare and Milton, but of those third-rate English novelists who were almost their only reading. What was happening in literature . . . was happening through the whole life of the country. An imitation of the habits of thought, the characters, the manners, the opinions, and these never at their best in an alien people, were preventing the native character taking its own natural form, and this imitation was spread by what I called a system of bribery. Appointments, success of all kinds, came only to these, the springs of natural life ran dry.[54]

What's more, the "loyal minority" was a bore. Its point of view was a rigid abstraction with all the appeal of chalk dust to the boy Yeats.[55] To make matters worse, Yeats often found himself identified

53. *Letters*, p. 336.
54. "Autobiography." See also "A Postscript," *Ideals in Ireland*, ed. Lady Gregory (London, 1901), pp. 105–6.
55. "*An Indian Monk*," *Essays and Introductions*, p. 428.

with this class,[56] while its stupidity seemed to him perdurable beyond any of Trinity's wildest hopes; such was the

> . . . class at whose dinner-tables conversation has long perished in the stupor of anecdote and argument, and on whose ears the great names of modern letters fail to awaken no [sic] flutter of understanding, or even of recognition. . . .[57]

Cold of imagination, aping English fashions, Unionists had never taken the populace seriously but had seen Irish life as pure comedy. Perhaps most insidious was not the fact that Unionists were divided from the people, but that their contempt was usually a patronizing pat on the head, their enmity well-bred disdain, their hatred usually better mannered than the love of most nationalists.

But, as he was to express the matter some years later in 1913, what rankled Yeats most was Unionist timidity, its abandonment of the ideal of national service after 1800, its refusal to act as patrons of the arts and intellect of Ireland.[58] Both Unionists and their eighteenth-century ancestors, "had they known the people and the game a little better, might have created an aristocracy in an age that had lost the meaning of the word." [59]

Yeats was later to soften or modify these views. In 1908, looking back to his 1899 speech at the College Historical Society in behalf of Irish studies and culture, he could make light of his previous attacks on Mahaffy and could even admit to his Trinity audience that "he had begun to value hostile intellect better than friendly folly." [60] In later times, what he dubbed as his "Irish propaganda" of these years

56. *Letters to the New Island*, ed. Horace Reynolds (Cambridge, Mass., 1934), p. 140. See also "A Remonstrance with Scotsmen," *Mythologies*, pp. 107–8.

57. "An Irish Patriot," *Bookman*, May 1896, p. 50. See also "The Irish Literary Theatre," *Dublin Daily Express*, 14 January 1899.

58. "Art and Aristocracy," *Irish Times*, 11 January 1913. Though Joseph Hone wrote this editorial, Yeats had suggested the line it should take. See "Some New Letters from W. B. Yeats to Lady Gregory," *REL*, IV (July 1963), 16.

59. "Gods and Fighting Men," *Explorations*, pp. 27–28.

60. "Dublin University Gaelic Society," unidentified clipping, c. 1908, in possession of Mrs. W. B. Yeats.

seemed to be little more than "bitterness." [61] These deliberate, calculated attacks were meant in part to free Yeats to criticize openly national Ireland. Characteristically, however, he came to alienate himself from both Irelands. But at the end of the nineteenth century, given his row with Protestant Ireland, his hatred of the eighteenth century could almost be assured. The Anglo-Irish of the establishment were still more "Anglo than Irish." [62] And they usually had the power.

Or so it seemed. Yet his hatred was not unalloyed. In fact, there was something unavoidably attractive about aristocratic eighteenth-century life that had held Yeats, for all his public disdain, from the beginning. Hence, it is time to turn to a few of Yeats's sharpest castigations of that century, and at the same time glimpse his teasing admiration or sneaking kindness for exceptional members of the Protestant gentry and nobility.

III

First of all, as might be expected from previous discussion, Yeats identified himself with the oppressed native Gael of that century, especially its poets. Singers and wandering ballad makers like "O'Sullivan the Red, O'Sullivan the Gaelic, O'Heffernan the Blind, and many another . . . had made the people, crushed by the disasters of the Boyne and Aughrim, remember their ancient greatness." [63] For Yeats these poets served as a counter to the rationalism of that century and inspired an Irish reaction against the British materialism of the next.[64] His own Red Hanrahan was fashioned after

61. *Autobiographies*, p. 233. In the matter of the Protestant-Catholic conflict in Ireland, Yeats was always a zealous seeker after the truth. For these years, see, for instance, "The Life of Patrick Sarsfield," *Bookman*, November 1895, pp. 59–60, and "Mr. Standish O'Grady's 'Flight of the Eagle' " *Bookman*, August 1897, pp. 123–24.
62. *Irish Fairy and Folk Tales*, Modern Lib. ed., p. 344.
63. Introduction, *A Book of Irish Verse* (London, 1895), p. xii.
64. "The Celtic Element in Literature," *Essays and Introductions*, p. 187.

the example of these eighteenth-century Gaelic poets.[65] They sang the real Ireland, the "hidden Ireland" of Daniel Corkery's book. In black contrast stood the members of the Ascendancy and its offshoot, the Garrison:

> I have just been reading Mr. R. L. Stevenson's *Master of Ballantrae*. We Irish people have a bone to pick with him for his sketch of the blackguard adventurer, Chevalier Burke. I do not feel sure that the Chevalier is not a true type enough, but Mr. Stevenson is certainly wrong in displaying him for a typical Irishman. He is really a broken-down Norman gentleman, a type found only among the gentry who make up what is called "the English garrison." He is from the same source as the Hell Fire Club and all the reckless braggadocio of the eighteenth century in Ireland; one of that class who, feeling the uncertainty of their tenures, as Froude explains it, lived the most devil-may-care existence. One sometimes meets even at this day vulgar, plausible, swaggering "Irishmen," who are its much decayed survivals, and who give Mr. Stevenson his justification. They are bad, but none of our making; English settlers bore them, English laws moulded them. No one who knows the serious, reserved and suspicious Irish peasant ever held them in any way representative of the national type. It is clear that Mr. Stevenson has no first hand knowledge of Ireland. . . .[66]

Yeats's frequent appellation for this class was the standard Irish term of contempt: alien gentry.[67] It was a class in the eighteenth century "ashamed of even the little it had of national circumstance and character," [68] while the remains of the ancient Gaelic aristocracy had hardly the wherewithal to claim either.[69]

Artistically, the young Yeats hated the eighteenth century—if possible—even more. Pope, its greatest practitioner of verse, he never did learn to stomach, either as man or poet. The cadence of

65. *The Library of John Quinn* (New York, 1924), Pt. 5, Item 11460.
66. *Letters to the New Island*, pp. 90–91.
67. *Letters*, p. 147.
68. "William Carleton," *Bookman*, March 1896, p. 188.
69. Mrs. Morgan John O'Connell, *The Last Colonel of the Irish Brigade* (London, 1872), I, 36.

eighteenth-century verse seemed to him mechanical; Blake had taught him to despise its abstractions; he preferred mask and image to its logic.[70] For that despised century had

> taught a school
> Of dolts to smooth, inlay, and clip and fit
> Till, like the certain wands of Jacob's wit,
> Their verses tallied.[71]

Had not Tom Moore "quenched an admirable Celtic lyricism in an artificial glitter learned from the eighteenth century"? [72] Since Irish writers, moreover, could only be those writing on Ireland and influenced by her, Swift, Burke, and Goldsmith struck Yeats as without that title.[73] The works of Sterne, Berkeley, and Ussher were likewise ruled out.[74] Nor could the plays of Sheridan, Congreve, and Goldsmith be taken seriously as Irish literature.[75] In sum,

> English-speaking Ireland had . . . no poetic voice, for Goldsmith had chosen to celebrate English scenery and manners; and Swift was but an Irishman by what Mr. Balfour has called the visitation of God, and sore against his will; and Congreve by education and early association; while Parnell, Denham, and Roscommon were poets but to their own time. Nor did the coming with the new century of the fame of Moore change matters for the better, for his Irish Melodies are to most cultivated ears but excellent drawing-room songs. . . . It was not indeed until Callanan wrote his native and haunting translations from the Gaelic, that anything of an honest style came into use.[76]

The novelists of that century and its traditions fared no better. Maria Edgeworth was limited by the fact that "she was born and bred

---

70. "The Last Gleeman," *Mythologies*, p. 49; *Autobiographies*, pp. 169, 213; *Letters*, p. 773.

71. *Autobiographies*, p. 169.

72. "Irish National Literature," *Bookman*, July 1895, p. 105.

73. "The Best Book from Ireland," *Dublin Daily News*, 11 May 1904.

74. "Irish Literature," *Dublin Daily Express*, 8 March 1895.

75. "Plays by an Irish Poet," *United Ireland*, 11 July 1891. See also *Letters to the New Island*, p. 69.

76. Introduction, *A Book of Irish Verse*, pp. xii–xiii.

among persons who knew nothing of the land where they were born, and she had no generations of historians, Gaelic scholars, and folk-lorists behind her, from whom to draw the symbols of her art." [77] Writers like Lever and Lover used Ireland as a "property shop" and looked to England for their audience.[78]

Still, in condemning that century out of hand, Yeats found it impossible to play down its fire and turbulence in Irish Protestant and Catholic alike. We know, for instance, that in the nineties he worked very hard on a book of reprints of the lives of Irish adventurers and duelists of the eighteenth century. Drawing heavily on John Edward Walsh's anonymous *Sketches of Ireland Sixty Years Ago* (Dublin, 1847), Yeats had planned to include accounts of Fighting Fitzgerald, Tiger Roche, Bryan Maguire, Freney the Robber, and Michael Dwyer among them.[79] The book was to have had an introduction and would probably have taken its place as *The Irish Adventurers* in Fisher Unwin's Adventure Series. The volume was never published, but Yeats's introduction probably became the basis for an essay that is the best evidence available for his double regard.[80] The very title and subtitle—"A Reckless Century. Irish Rakes and Duellists"—suggest the intensity in life that Yeats always glorified.

He begins this essay by focusing on the ruins of the old Hell Fire Club on the top of Mount Pelier—"the whole like a grinning skull, hideous symbol of an age without ideals, without responsibility, without order, without peace." [81] This one would expect. He then continues by describing the dark crimes and sins of this society, and so passes on to the more outrageous feats of dueling, gambling, and drinking by such terrors as Fighting Fitzgerald, Power of Dargle, and Bryan Maguire. The Anglo-Irish aristocracy, oblivious to the warning voice of Swift and as yet unawakened by the Volunteer movement, was otherwise sunk in *carpe diem*. Only the native Irish

77. "William Carleton," *Bookman*, March 1896, p. 188.
78. *Letters to the New Island*, pp. 173–74.
79. *Letters*, p. 227.
80. *Ibid.*, p. 154, n. 1.
81. "A Reckless Century. Irish Rakes and Duellists," *United Ireland*, 12 September 1891.

poor, Yeats continues, had any sense of nationalism. So far the essay sounds in character with the Yeats of these years. But when it comes time to pass judgment on this flamboyant period, Yeats cannot entirely disguise his admiration:

> What judgment are we to pronounce on that eighteenth century? What should it make us expect from the future? I find nothing but fortunate prophecies in that dead century. I see there the Celtic intensity, the Celtic fire, the Celtic daring wasting themselves, it is true, in all kinds of evil, but needing only the responsibility of self-government and the restraint of a trained public opinion to have laboured devotedly for the public weal. The vast energy that filled Ireland with bullies and swashbucklers will someday give us great poets and thinkers. It is better to be violent and irresponsible than full of body-worship and money-grubbing. The duellist Whaley going off for a bet to play ball against the ramparts of Jerusalem is a nobler sight than the railway king putting his millions together. Those eighteenth-century duellists, at any rate, tried to really live, and not merely exist. They took their lives into their hands and went through the world with a song upon their lips; and if a curse was mingled with the song they are none the less better to think of than had they grown rich and much-esteemed, and yet lasted on no more than half alive, toadstools upon the State.[82]

If that class was shallow, Yeats was nevertheless unwilling to deny it dash and energy. As a boy he himself had witnessed what he called the "final degradation" of that turbulent Ireland of a previous century in Castle Dargan, where lived a wild, eccentric squireen, out at the elbows and impulsively given to reckless exploits to kill his boredom.[83] Yet "Castle Dargan's ruin all lit," or the hope of it, never left the mature Yeats.

True enough, it was an aristocracy that had but half-heard the songs of a past age, songs that belonged to the desolate natives, and songs that rang a judgment on the Anglo-Irish more ancient and substantial than they could ever be. Yeats also thought them

82. *Idem.*
83. *Autobiographies*, pp. 53–55.

spendthrift, rash, eloquent, and ephemeral. They had passed away ignominiously. Yet they had had splendor if not always magnanimity.[84] By 1904, we find Yeats relenting even more as he once again attempts to accommodate his mixed feelings:

> I do not think that their own mixed blood or the habit of their time need take all, or nearly all, credit or discredit for the impulse that made our modern gentlemen fight duels over pocket-handkerchiefs, and set out to play ball against the gates of Jerusalem for a wager, and scatter money before the public eye; and at last, after an epoch of such eloquence the world has hardly seen its like, lose their public spirit and their high heart and grow querulous and selfish as men do who have played life out not heartily but with noise and tumult. Had they understood the people and the game a little better, they might have created an aristocracy in an age that has lost the meaning of the word.[85]

As is obvious in the hesitant praise and blame of this passage, Yeats viewed nostalgically the period of Grattan's Parliament as a momentary burst of brilliance that all his love of Celtic Ireland could not dismiss. Hear him, for instance, expounding its glories in a speech given in New York that same year:

> . . . when we think of the whole history of Ireland for the last seven hundred years, there is perhaps only one epoch that we look upon with entire joy and pride—the ten or fifteen years after the declaration of the independence of the Irish Parliament.
>
> During that brief period the manufactures of Ireland awoke; prosperity began to come upon the land. Lord Clare, no friendly witness, said that no country in Europe became so prosperous during so short a period. The Irish gentry suddenly cast off their irresponsibility and became a great class, creating an eloquence whose like has not been in any modern nation. There arose in Dublin a brilliant social life. Many books were published. Many beautiful houses were built—public buildings

84. "A Canonical Book," *Bookman*, May 1903, p. 68.
85. "Gods and Fighting Men," *Explorations*, pp. 27–28.

and great country houses. The nation was growing to greatness and it was precisely because it was so growing that England became afraid and decided to overthrow it.[86]

Finally, despite all his professed hatred of that nefarious century, Yeats found himself politically and ideally committed to two of its most renowned Protestant patriots, Robert Emmet and Wolfe Tone. For instance, in *Cathleen Ni Houlihan* he had written of Ireland and her fight for freedom in the setting of 1798; his play was, he admitted, a "call of country." [87] In writing the play some hundred years later, he was pledging himself, as Tone had, not just to Protestant or Catholic Ireland but, idealistically, to all Ireland. As president of the Wolfe Tone Centennial Association, he had been a leader in the '98 celebrations in London and Dublin. His speech, "The Union of the Gael," delivered in London on April 13, was just as idealistic. In it he identified Emmet and Tone with Ireland's "better self," a self he also equated with Grattan and Burke.[88] Later he was to make a long, detailed speech devoted to the memory of Emmet in New York City, part of which is quoted above. In another part, Yeats confronted his Irish-American audience with the devil of the piece—the opposite of this eighteenth-century Protestant patriot—no less a man than Daniel O'Connell, the so-called Liberator of the nineteenth.[89]

86. "Emmet the Apostle of Irish Liberty," *Gaelic American* (New York), 5 March 1904. See also "Carleton as an Irish Historian," *Nation*, 11 January 1890.

87. "Mr. Yeats's New Play," *United Irishman*, 5 April 1902.

88. "The Union of the Gael," *'98 Centennial Association of Great Britain and France* (Dublin, 1898), p. 8. See also "The '98 Centenary," *United Ireland*, 20 March 1897. Dr. Mark F. Ryan, *Fenian Memories* (Dublin, 1945), pp. 185–86, reports: "A Great Centenary meeting . . . was held in Phoenix Park, Dublin, on the 20th March, 1898. There were four platforms, one for each of the provinces. Speaking from the Connacht platform, Mr. Yeats as President of Great Britain and France said: '. . . we are not celebrating a Cause that is brag and materialism, but a high and holy cause.' "

89. "Emmet the Apostle of Irish Liberty," *Gaelic American*, 5 March 1904. Part of Yeats's difficulty in being true to himself and to the occasion can be seen in a passage from his letter to Lady Gregory on the subject: "I am dreadfully busy over my Emmet lecture, which is a frightful nuisance. It is indeed, as you say, a sword dance and I must give it every moment. I had no idea until I started

IV

Yeats's disparagement of O'Connell brings us full circle. After the death of Synge and the failure of Lane's Gallery scheme, Yeats decided that, whatever his motive—hatred or love—his work in Ireland could not be different.[90] But we see the beginnings of this attitude here. For as he came to suspect during the last decade of his life, the glaring fact of rot in Ireland after the Treaty had resulted from a ruin perpetuated from the nineteenth century—"a century disastrous to the national intellect."[91]

The bête noire was Daniel O'Connell. Yeats's New York audience had not been the first to hear this arraignment. For he had also contrasted O'Connell with Wolfe Tone at the Centennial Banquet. Here and later, Yeats condemned the Liberator's utilitarian attitude that had made for compromise and a political movement of ambitious vulgarians.[92] Committee Room 15 and the subsequent fiasco followed as a matter of course. As Yeats went on to exclaim,

> Can you imagine any Irish leader of our times receiving an English king as O'Connell received George the IV., presenting him with shamrocks and a laurel wreath? O'Connell did it for policy, but for no policy to-day would an Irish leader dare to do the like. Can you imagine Irish crowds of our time welcoming an English king as O'Connell's crowds welcomed George the IV.?[93]

A second contrast was with Emmet:

> I sometimes think that O'Connell was the contrary principle to Emmet. He taught the people to lay aside the pike and the

---

on it how completely I have thought myself out of the whole stream of traditional Irish feeling on such subjects. I am just as strenuous a nationalist as ever, but I have got to express these feelings all differently" (*Letters*, p. 432).

90. "Some New Letters from W. B. Yeats to Lady Gregory," *REL*, IV, 34.

91. *Variorum*, p. 833.

92. *'98 Centennial Association*, p. 8. Yeats doubtless shared this belief with John O'Leary; see *Our Irish Theatre*, pp. 63–68.

93. *'98 Centennial Association*, p. 9.

musket, the song and the story, and to do their work now by wheedling and now by bullying. He won certain necessary laws for Ireland. He gave her a few laws, but he did not give her patriots. He was the successful politician, but it was the unsuccessful Emmet who has given her patriots. O'Connell was a great man, but there is too much of his spirit in the practical politics of Ireland.[94]

A third contrast, made in 1914, was with Davis:

One understands the work Davis set his hand to when one remembers that he began it in the meridian hours of O'Connell. The policy of O'Connell had brought great reforms, but his personal influence had been almost entirely evil. His violent nature, his invective, his unscrupulousness, are the chief cause of our social and political divisions. He was accustomed to defend his manners by saying that such means alone could put spirit into a race dispirited by penal law; everybody knows his saying: "The verdict is the thing," but his exaggeration and his hectoring have corrupted client and jury after the verdict has been given. When at the Clare election, he conquered the patriots of a previous generation by a slanderous rhetoric, he prepared for Committee Room No. 15 and all that followed. In his very genius itself, there was demoralization, the appeal—as of a tumbler at a fair—to the commonest ear, a grin through a horse-collar. We have copied all that, but have not copied his simplicity, his deep affectionate heart.[95]

This was a note to be heard from Yeats again and again in years to come. He is quoted in full here because few are aware of his contempt for O'Connell's public and personal manners. What Yeats took to be his personal viciousness seemed to have infected more and more twentieth-century Irish bourgeois with "the contagion of the throng."

One dire result of this public drift to the expedient, the practical, or the vulgarly ambitious Yeats held to be the trivialization of politics through patriotic dogmas, squabbles, and envies. Irish hatred of

94. "Emmet the Apostle of Liberty," *Gaelic American*, 5 March 1904.
95. *Tribute to Thomas Davis* (Cork, 1947), p. 15. See also "Thomas Davis Centenary," *Irish Times*, 21 November 1914.

disinterested intellect in public life did not preclude "a defiant dogmatism like that of a clever schoolboy." [96] Too often Yeats discovered, as head of the '98 celebrations for instance, that "we tear each other's character in pieces for things that don't matter to anybody." [97] Internecine and deplorable, these party spats stood in shocking contrast to the detached conduct urged by John O'Leary. Reviewing his *Recollections of Fenians and Fenianism*, Yeats held up that contrasting type in a buffoonish figure easily traced to O'Connell:

> . . . the loose-lipped, emotional, sympathetic, impressionable Irishman, who is the only Irishman of whom many Englishmen have ever heard. The very inhumanity of Irish journalism and of Irish politics comes from a tendency to judge men not by one another, not by experience of the degree of excellence one may hope to meet in life and in politics, but by some abstract standard.[98]

By 1910, he had even come to believe that the nationalist movement that went back to the Young Ireland group—the foes of O'Connell—was also helping to destroy the national imagination: ". . . when a group of people are organized about a conception, the result must be commonplace." [99] To this combination of public dogmatism and personal deviousness Yeats may also have attributed "the corrupt influence of the American-Irish in municipal government" in the United States.[100]

Another victim of this malaise was literature. Even before the new century arrived, we witness Yeats taking a hard look at his native literature and reallocating the blame for its failures. For all his trust in "the evangel of folk-lore," the leavening agent in late nineteenth-century Irish literature, it failed to displace entirely the noise and the oratory, the rhetoric and the arguing, the expostulation and the reply

96. Clipping from the *United Irishman*, c. November 1901, in Henderson, Natl. Lib. MS. 1729, p. 89.

97. *Letters*, p. 288.

98. "Mr. John O'Leary," *Bookman*, February 1897, p. 147.

99. Report of Yeats's lecture, "The Theatre and Ireland," in the *Irish Times*, 5 March 1910, p. 5.

100. "Abbey Players in America," *Irish Times*, 16 March 1912.

of previous movements.[101] Even Carleton had not remained untouched by this malady, as his novel *Valentine McClutchy* might testify: "Carleton was a man of genius, but the habit of dividing men into sheep and goats for the purpose of partisan politics made havoc of what might have been a great novel." [102] It was the bane of the practical, the didactic, that Yeats feared for like reasons in Sir Charles Gavan Duffy's editorship of the New Irish Library.[103] Yeats's fears this time were amply borne out.[104] Once again, he felt, patriotic commonplaces insured the impossibility of disinterested research and constricted the imagination.[105] The commodity peddled as literature in the nineteenth century often turned out to be a counterfeit,

> . . . the false coin of a glittering or noisy insincerity which Moore and the rhetoricians had made current in Ireland. Davis, Mangan, D'Arcy Magee, Kickham, Carleton, Banim—almost every story-writer or poet who had taken the popular side in Ireland had ruined a part of his work by didactic writing. . . . they had made themselves, and for the most generous of reasons, a mirror for the passions and the blindness of the multitude.[106]

Years later Yeats was to brand such scribbling "not . . . the handmaid, but the scullerymaid of politics." [107] Ironically, much of this literature, from Moore on, was written to be sold in England, in spite of the shrieking green cover and emblazoned harp on the book, and thus became the literature of the stranger.

Yeats also came to reverse sharply his youthful enthusiasm for the Irish novelists while also reining in his former admiration for the poetry of Davis and the *Nation* group. Not only were they unconsciously full of sentimental English assumptions, not only did a rural

101. "The Evangel of Folklore," *Bookman*, June 1894, p. 86.
102. " 'The Silenced Sister,' " *United Ireland*, 23 December 1893. See also *The Library of John Quinn*, Pt. 5, Item 11604.
103. "The National Publishing Company," *Freeman's Journal*, 6 September 1892.
104. "Some Irish National Books," *Bookman*, August 1894, pp. 151–52.
105. "The Life of Patrick Sarsfield," *Bookman*, November 1895, p. 59.
106. "An Irish Patriot," *Bookman*, May 1896, p. 50.
107. "Irish Literature's Position," *Irish Times*, 9 November 1922.

patriotism enforce a distorted morality play of English landlords and Irish peasants but, when a fresh Irish view did appear, books like Carleton's *Valentine McClutchy*, Kickham's *Knocknagow*, Mitchel's *History of Ireland*, and Davis' poems had thoroughly incapacitated Irish audiences from understanding the countrymen of Synge.[108] What else could result from novelists who employed, whatever their locale, the dialect of the town; who idealized the peasantry; and who tended, for all their solemnity, to make Irish life a farce?

Even Thomas Davis—who once seemed the very paragon of poet and patriot to Yeats—did not depart unscathed for his share in fomenting the rancor and ignorance of the modern Irish audience. After the death of Synge, Yeats was most articulate on the subject:

> Irish national politics dated from the Young Ireland movement, when Thomas Davis and his friends had created by journalism a national ideal which was to take the place of national institutions. The images they had created of the ideal peasant and the charming colleen had spread wherever their race was to be found, creating something like a world-wide national consciousness, in which abstract virtues had taken the place of realities. Out of this consciousness arose the Gaelic movement; but by this time an industrial class had arisen, the first the country had ever seen, and having neither leisure nor a traditional culture, its leaders were banded together only by political hatred and suspicion, so that their journalism was altering for the worse the imagination of the people. Passion in public life without culture was ignoble; the man with no culture could do routine work without doing any harm, but the moment he touched the artist's work of expressing emotion he injured everyone he reached.[109]

From the founding of the *Nation* in 1842 until the Rebellion of 1848, Davis and those around him thought it "possible for any clever man to write a good song, a good history, a good drama, if he only

108. "J. M. Synge and the Ireland of his Time," *Essays and Introductions*, p. 311. See also "First Principles," *Explorations*, pp. 234–35, and *Variorum*, p. 834.

109. "Mr. W. B. Yeats on Irish Literature," *Manchester Guardian*, 15 November 1910.

would." [110] "Ireland, since the Young Irelanders," Yeats pronounced after the death of Synge, "has given itself up to apologetics. Every impression of life or impulse of imagination has been examined to see if it helped or hurt the glory of Ireland or the political claim of Ireland. A sincere impression of life became at last impossible, all was apologetics." [111] For all his admiration of Davis as a man, Yeats acknowledged the deleterious influence of Davis' artificial ideas in his own early work. How inevitable yet ironic Yeats's literary contention with Davis seems when translated into a physical one; the event was *The Countess Cathleen,* shown at the Antient Concert Rooms, May 8, 1899:

> . . . an organized claque of about twenty brainless, beardless, idiotic-looking youths did all they knew to interfere with the progress of the play by their meaningless automatic hissing and senseless comments. . . . "Thomas Davis" seemed to be the particular bee in those misguided youths' bonnets, as they frequently made reference to that poet during their silly display of ill-manners. . . . a comment (made some time ago) of Mr. Yeats on that vigorous poet's work had got Davis's admirers' backs up. . . . [112]

Yeats had come to abhor more than the political and literary heritage of O'Connell's Ireland at the turn of the century. This third element in his hatred was religion, specifically an unlettered, often boorish, fanatical Catholicism that joined cause with extreme nationalism, especially in the gutter journalism that was to fasten itself on the Irish dramatic movement in general and on Synge in particular.

However, Yeats rarely pursued a consciously anticlerical line. He knew that the bigotries of Belfast hindered him as much as those in Dublin. [113] For instance, in looking back on the hostile reception accorded his *Countess Cathleen,* Yeats admitted his mistake in

110. "Young Ireland," *Bookman,* January 1897, p. 120.
111. *Autobiographies,* p. 520.
112. "Dublin Notes," *The Institute and Lecturers' Gazette,* 1 June 1899.
113. "Some New Letters," *REL,* IV, 35.

forgetting that traditional symbols of the theater—like devils, shrines, and sacrilegious peasants—were taken not as symbolic but as actual in Ireland.[114] Still, the lack of charity was certainly on the other side. The religious venom of his political and literary detractors was all too obviously unfair from the nineties on. One may imagine his surprise when he found it necessary to defend his edition of Carleton's stories from an unusually stupid religious misinterpretation of his efforts in Dublin's *Nation*.[115] His subsequent doubts about the literary excellence of the Young Ireland writers also came under heavy scholastic fire.[116] It is but a step perhaps to Yeats's stubborn, fighting reactions, in the pages of *Estrangement* and *The Death of Synge*, to this continued slander. But even more bitter recriminations lie at the heart of the journal from which these pages were taken. The following passage goes directly to the issue:

> The lack of the moral element in Irish public life . . . comes largely from the badness of Catholic education, & the small number of Catholic families with traditions. The sense of form, whether that of Parnell, or Grattan or Davis, of form in active life, has always been protestant in Ireland. O'Connell the one great Catholic figure was formless. The power of self conquest, of elocution has been protestant, & more or less a thing of class— all the tragedians were protestant, O'Connell was a comedian.[117]

The light of a holy candle was somehow joined with the dark ignorance and bombast of literary and political nationalists.[118] Essentially, however, it was the lack of form—in public life, letters, and morality—that Yeats laid at the door of the church. More than once in these years Yeats had hopes that a Catholic university system

114. *Autobiographies*, p. 416.
115. "Carleton as an Irish Historian," *Nation*, 11 January 1890. See also *Letters*, pp. 130–31.
116. "Professor Dowden and Irish Literature," *Dublin Daily Express*, 7 February 1895.
117. Journal begun December 1908.
118. "Some New Letters," *REL*, IV, 34. See also "Statement by Mr. W. B. Yeats," *Irish Times*, 20 January 1912.

would change matters.[119] That too was to prove a chimera. By 1910, then, Yeats could compare the Irish life around him with that of the "early nineteenth century, when national feeling was losing itself in a religious feud over tithes and emancipation."[120] The program of Young Ireland, which had rescued this period, seemed, in retrospect, schoolboyish.[121] Moreover, the rigidity of these persistently immature beliefs, even in the Ireland after Parnell, was in truth a simple-minded seeking after perfection in life that might turn belief into the "world's bane," as Yeats repeated several times in "The Happy Townland." Life demanded form and self-control, not abandonment to pious abstractions and dreams of perfection.

Thus with the advent of the *Playboy* riots, Yeats realized that "a patriotic journalism . . . had for years prepared for this hour."[122] As he watched the rioting, he knew that he was witnessing "the dissolution of a school of patriotism that held sway over my youth."[123] The sentimental Ireland of Tom Moore, Daniel O'Connell, and the Irish novelists no less than the melodramatic Ireland of the Young Irelanders had by then become the possession of an uncomprehending middle class. Yeats's rejection of that century and its worn-out ideals is summed up in his Introduction to *Selections from the Writings of Lord Dunsany*, written in 1912. After praising nineteenth-century Ireland as an age of romance, he continues with this qualification:

> . . . and yet we should not regret too often that it [the nineteenth century] has vanished, and left us poets even more unpopular than are our kind elsewhere in Europe; for now that we are unpopular we escape from crowds, from noises in the street, from voices that sing out of tune, from bad paper made

119. Clipping from *The Leader*, 7 December 1907, in possession of Mrs. W. B. Yeats.

120. *Autobiographies*, p. 494.

121. *Ibid.*

122. "J. M. Synge and the Ireland of his Time," *Essays and Introductions*, p. 311.

123. *Ibid.*, p. 312.

33

one knows not from what refuse, from evil-smelling gum, from covers of emerald green, from that ideal of reliable, invariable men and women, which would forbid saint and connoisseur . . . do what is unaccountable, and forbid life itself. . . .[124]

Yeats then compares the efforts of the Cuala Press at Dundrum with those of the former Library of Ireland:

When our age too has passed . . . students will perhaps open these books, printed by village girls at Dundrum, as curiously as at twenty years I opened the books of history and ballad verse of the old 'Library of Ireland.' They will notice that the new 'Library,' where I have gathered so much that seems to me representative or beautiful, unlike the old, is intended for few people, and written by men and women with that ideal condemned by 'Mary of the Nation,' who wished, as she said, to make no elaborate beauty and to write nothing but what a peasant could understand. If they are philosophic or phantastic, it may even amuse them to find some analogy of the old with O'Connell's hearty eloquence, his winged dart shot always into the midst of the people, his mood of comedy; and of the new with that lonely and haughty person below whose tragic shadow we of modern Ireland began to write.[125]

Parnell, not O'Connell. And Parnell was the heir of Swift. On this note we may pause. For from this time forth Yeats looked at another century when he had hopes for the future of modern Ireland. He saw in the eighteenth century and in his own work and that of his Anglo-Irish compatriots materials for a new Irish image.[126] For, otherwise,

---

124. Introduction, *Selections from the Writings of Lord Dunsany* (Dundrum, 1912), n.p.

125. *Idem.*

126. ". . . the need of a model of the nation, of some moral diagram, is as great as in the early nineteenth century, when national feeling was losing itself in a religious feud over tithes and emancipation. Neither the grammars of the Gaelic League nor the industrialism of the *Leader*, nor the *Sinn Fein* attacks upon the Irish Party, give sensible images to the affections. Yet in the work of Lady Gregory, of Synge, of O'Grady, of Lionel Johnson, in my own work, a school of journalism with simple moral ideas could find right building material to create a

there surrounded him three kinds of ignorance come clamoring from the days of his youth in romantic nineteenth-century Ireland:

> 1st. There is the hatred of ideas of the more ignorant sort of Gaelic propagandist, who would have nothing said or thought that is not in country Gaelic. One knows him without trouble. He writes the worst English, and would have us give up Plato and all the sages for a grammar. 2nd. There is the obscurantism of the more ignorant sort of priest, who, forgetful of the great traditions of his Church, would deny all ideas that might perplex a parish of farmers or artisans or half-educated shop-keepers. 3rd. There is the obscurantism of the politician and not always of the more ignorant sort, who would reject every idea which is not of immediate service to his cause.[127]

An eighteenth-century connection, a haven where his leisure and industry were assured, the sympathy and help of Anglo-Irish compatriots, a traditional bulwark against such upstart ignorance—for all of these Yeats had not far to seek.

---

historical and literary nationalism as powerful as the old and nobler" (*Autobiographies*, p. 494).

127. "The Irish National Theatre and Three Sorts of Ignorance," *United Irishman*, 24 October 1903.

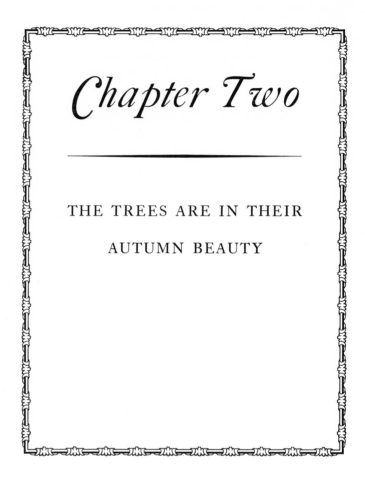

Chapter Two

THE TREES ARE IN THEIR

AUTUMN BEAUTY

I

IN TURNING to Yeats's long friendship with Lady Gregory and her family, I have severely limited my purpose. Since the full account of their artistic partnership remains to be written, I have centered on Yeats's admiration for the Gregory tradition of service to the Irish nation, especially in the careers of Lady Gregory, her son, and her nephews, Sir Hugh Lane and John Shawe-Taylor. In them, day by day, year by year, Yeats discerned continued evidence of the decisive, instinctive, informed, and even authoritative temper that had stamped the family leaders in Georgian Ireland and after. Coole

House, as we shall see, finally came to sum up in its heirlooms, library, history, occupants, and well-wishers most of those virtues of eighteenth-century Protestant Ireland that Yeats would have recalled to the new nation.

Before we look more closely at Yeats's admiration for the Gregorys, a preliminary discussion of the background to Coole is in order. For, according to Lady Gregory herself, the energy of that house in behalf of Ireland's welfare "took hold of people's minds. Perhaps that is why Mrs. Asquith, meeting Yeats for the first time and doubtless finding him full of some enterprise, had told me that she thought she liked him best 'of all your nephews!' " [1] Proud words, yet also a fine measure of Yeats's increasing identity with this house and its tradition of public and artistic service, the devotion of "image-makers," as Lady Gregory saw it.

The image began in the eighteenth century. Galway in that century was, and continued to be, the center of Connacht, the most inaccessible, feudal, and Irish part of a country still only partly subdued by the English after the Battles of the Boyne and Aughrim and the Treaty of Limerick. Connacht—Galway and Sligo in particular—was to Yeats the essential Ireland. [2] Here, where medieval notions of fealty still prevailed, Catholic families might still prosper, while powerful Protestant families like the Gregorys, the Frenches, the Taylors, the Persses, and the Gores often lived in close familiarity with their Catholic tenants. It is also common knowledge that the province and the county abounded in eccentrics, fire-eaters, duelists, and sportsmen like Fighting Fitzgerald, Humanity Dick Martin, and Governor Eyre. [3] This tradition of cruelty, sublime extravagance and derring-do, best seen in the creatures of Jonah Barrington like Mrs. French, did not exclude another tradition exemplified by the "improving" Mr. Gregory. This habit of cultivation and improvement

1. *Hugh Lane*, p. 74.
2. For one of Yeats's many statements to this effect, see "Hypnotised. W. B. Yeats on Commercial Conquest," *Connacht Tribune*, 26 September 1908.
3. See, for example, an article summarizing these matters, J. G. Simms, "Connacht in the Eighteenth Century," *Irish Historical Studies*, XI (September 1958), 116–33.

that the original Robert Gregory brought to Coole in 1768 became
Lady Gregory's proudest heritage:

> . . . through 150 years or more, Coole has been a place of
> peace. . . . a home of culture in more senses than one. Arthur
> Young found Mr. Gregory making a "noble nursery the
> plantations for which would change the face of the district," and
> those woods still remain; my husband added rare trees to them
> and I have added acres and acres of young wood. Richard
> Gregory collected that fine library; William's father died from
> famine-fever brought on through his ministrations to the poor.
> He himself had a highly honoured name in Parliament and in
> Ceylon, loving Coole all the time, all through his lifetime.
> Robert loved it and showed its wild stern beauty in his
> paintings; left it through high-mindedness and died fighting for
> a good cause. I have lived there and loved it these forty years
> and through the guests who have stayed there it counts for
> much in the awakening of the spiritual and intellectual side of
> our country.[4]

Although this passage may seem to jump ahead for the moment, it is
cited to show what Lady Gregory made of Coole's eighteenth-century
tradition. That first Robert Gregory of Coole had been the friend of
Burke, Fox, and Lord Rockingham. He kept Coole resplendent with
a retinue of servants bespangled in gold and black; and it was he who
invited visiting ladies to fish for precious stones in a drawer. His son
Richard, despite an irregular marriage and a mistaken charge of
cowardice against him, filled Coole with the emblems of his fine taste
in books, bronze, paintings, and marble.[5] He was Lady Gregory's
favorite from the past.[6]

She too brought much to augment this rich beginning. If her

4. *Lady Gregory's Journals*, p. 15.
5. *Sir William Gregory, K.C.M.G., An Autobiography*, ed. Lady Gregory
(London, 1894), pp. 4–8. Burke had written Robert Gregory apropos an Indian
matter, "I enter fully into everything you feel. Certainly you must begin with
the natives. This was always your fundamental maxim; and be assured it will be
mine" (*Mr. Gregory's Letter-Box*, ed. Lady Gregory [London, 1898], p.
8).
6. Lady Gregory, *Coole* (Dublin, 1931), pp. 5–6, 39.

family, the Persses, had lacked intellectual distinction in that century, as Yeats once pointed out,[7] they had nevertheless been great sportsmen, soldiers, planters, and members of Grattan's Parliament. Her grandfather had been the friend of Washington.[8] Dean Dudley Persse, who named his mansion house Roxborough in 1703, may not have been a likable man[9]—his daughter was abducted with her own consent and probably at the threat of her father's life[10]—but the name Persse became a famous one in the county. A Robert Parsons Persse of Castleboy had started the famed Galway hunt known as the "Blazers," and for generations after, a Persse had usually been master of the Galway Blazers. In 1902, young Henry Persse headed the list of winning amateur riders in Ireland.[11] To add luster to the name, and another Galway touch, there was the elder Henry Persse, who maintained himself by a distillery rather than by gouging tenants, so that "lying on his death-bed and unable to canvass, he was returned to the new Council by his fellow-townsmen, in spite of his differences from them in both religion and politics." This account includes the telling remark, "Everyone who knows Galway knows the Persses are one of its most ancient families. A Persse is at the head of everything, is everywhere."[12] Colonel William Persse, Lady Gregory's great-grandfather, was a leader of the Galway Volunteers, formed in May 1779, and had been a delegate to the Grand Convention.[13]

After the Union, the fortunes of the Gregorys, like those of most of the Ascendancy, diminished. Yet the habits of the previous century persisted or, in some cases, died hard. William, the youngest son of

7. *Autobiographies*, p. 392. Yeats's summary of his introduction to Coole and its background is found on pp. 388–95.

8. *Our Irish Theatre*, p. 197.

9. Msgr. J[erome] Fahey, *The History and Antiquities of the Diocese of Kilmacduagh* (Dublin, 1893), p. 321.

10. S. F. Maguire, "Loughrea. An Abduction," *The Galway Reader*, III (1950), 117–18.

11. "Pithy Pars," *Tuam Herald*, 14 March 1903.

12. "Brevities," *Tuam Herald*, 25 March 1909.

13. S. F. Maguire, "Galway Scrap Book," *Galway Reader*, II (n.d.), 88–89. See also *Mr. Gregory's Letter-Box*, p. 19.

the "Nabob" who bought Coole, had been High Sheriff of Galway in 1799 and was made Under-Secretary for Ireland in 1812, a position he honored for nineteen years. With his close knowledge of Ireland he was, for some years, the real power behind the Castle government.[14] Though his dismissal in 1830 coincides with the ending of the Protestant Ascendancy, and though he was an inveterate Tory, a hater of Jacobins, and a foe of Catholic emancipation, even Daniel O'Connell had to admit that William Gregory "had some Irish feelings." [15] He was also counted a relentless foe of absenteeism. But his son, Sir William Gregory, Lady Gregory's husband, was the true star of the nineteenth-century Gregorys.

It is hard to believe that there can have been a more ingenuous Victorian autobiography than Sir William's. His folly, his bravery, his kindness, his cruelty, his dissipations, his stupidity, his devotion to art and scholarship, his squandering of his property, and his wisdom as an administrator and governor of Ceylon—all are amazingly present. One also discovers a man who combines two rather noticeable traits of the eighteenth-century Galway tradition—youthful wildness and high talent for public service.

As a young man he attended a famous three-day house party at Carantrila near Tuam, an episode to which he devotes a number of nostalgic pages in his memoir. We hear of the shabby dandies, the extravagant bucks, of Lord Clanrickarde himself, and a bevy of beautiful ladies, all reveling in the drinking, dancing, and dining made prominent in Barrington's *Personal Sketches* as the hallmark of an Ireland that had passed with the Union.[16] Gregory had also been one of the last, if not *the* last, of the noted duelists in Ireland. Reflecting on what might have been a fatal duel with Captain Vaughan in 1851, Gregory—who was a dead shot, had provoked the affair, had Sir Robert Peel for a second, and was determined to kill the captain if he asked for a second shot—had this to say: "I fear that

14. *Sir William Gregory*, pp. 10–11.
15. *Ibid.*, p. 9.
16. *Ibid.*, pp. 40–43.

in too many of us, in spite of culture, education, refinement, something of the tiger lingers in our blood." [17] The cause of the duel was also characteristic: Gregory's heavy devotion to the turf. For six years of his life, as he admits, he was virtually addicted to racing, eschewing public life and society in a prolonged gambling venture that forced him to sell two-thirds of his lands.[18] One sale, that of his holdings at Kinvara, saved his affairs, but the buyer, the notorious Comerford, immediately raised the rents and depleted the tenantry and the town.[19] Finally, no less characteristic of the country gentlemen of his time was Gregory's backing of the South in the American Civil War. He believed the creation of a Southern republic would mean an end to slavery.[20] General P. G. T. Beauregard sent him a piece of the flagstaff from Fort Sumter.[21] Nor had his visit to America before that war done anything to lessen his persistent hatred of political democracy and the extension of suffrage. In parliament he made constant reference to the tyranny of democracy in America in his attempt to check the Reform Bill introduced by Lord Russell in 1852. For Gregory, democracy meant mob tyranny, no matter whether in America, Ireland, or England.[22]

Yet, as a country gentleman in the Augustan mode, he also performed his duties as best he could. He presided at the weekly meetings of the Poor Law Union, appeared at petty sessions, gave dinners to his tenants and lectured them on the evils of land agitation. He put his hopes for peace in Ireland into a plan for the extension of land purchase. He also admired O'Connell. While most of his class maintained the narrowest Protestant bigotry, he constantly declined to be an anti-Catholic. During the height of the land war, his tenants refused to alter their amicable relationship with Gregory, despite a mistaken evil reputation he gained from the

17. *Ibid.,* pp. 153–54.
18. *Ibid.,* p. 148.
19. *Ibid.,* pp. 158–59.
20. *Ibid.,* pp. 214–16.
21. *Lady Gregory's Journals,* p. 331.
22. *Sir William Gregory,* pp. 195–97, 209–10.

misapplication of his plan to help distressed peasants during the Famine.[23] In many ways, both the plight of Coole and its fame in the twentieth century can be traced to the continuation of Maria Edgeworth's double vision of Ireland in Sir Condy, shining so much more resplendently in Sir William Gregory.

The twentieth century saw the ruin of more than one formerly flourishing Protestant family in Galway and Mayo. Castle Taylor was destroyed, Coole was dismantled, Roxborough was burned down, Lough Cutra Castle is now abandoned, Moore Hall is gone. Durus House, former home of Comte de Basterot, was saved at the last moment, and Tulira lives on, reminder of a Catholic glory of past ages that momentarily joined hands with Protestants in the surroundings of Coole. But the point to be made about Galway in the twentieth century is that, at its very beginning, the tides had already begun to run out on an anachronistic landlord class.

Basterot, for instance, who had been a friend of Sir William, was an unflinching aristocrat and an uncompromising believer in the inequality of the races of man. Still, he was a friend of the poor, a man devoted to the culture of France and Galway, and could fondly recall the days when natives raced naked on unsaddled horses along the seashore near Durus.[24] Martyn, whose family had sold land to the eighteenth-century Robert Gregory, also hated democracy in the early nineties.[25] Mention of these two men adds substance to Sir William's undaunted assumption of authority, despite the growing suspicion and hatred that accompanied the renewed land hunger before the death of Parnell. With the portents of ruin all around them, the rather naïve landlords still considered their word law. A Martyn or a Gregory might rebuke a tenant for removing his hat when approaching and beginning his discourse with, "Your Honor, Sir," but such outward behavior still prevailed for all the declared and undeclared open season on landlords. Right into the nineties the

23. *Ibid.*, pp. 72–75, 122, 134–36, 242–44, 359, 368–69.
24. *Our Irish Theatre*, pp. 4–5, and Hone, pp. 129–30. See also Basterot's *Souvenirs d'enfance et de jeunesse* (Paris, 1896), *passim.*
25. See, for instance, Martyn's *Morgante The Lesser: His Notorious Life and Wonderful Deeds* (London, 1890), *passim.*

average peasant still gazed on the Big House with awe and fear. The ferocious among Galway landlords might drive through a closed gate and crowd, horses rearing and coachman slashing, if the way were not cleared immediately, much in the manner of Barrington's half-mounted men, as was done at a race meeting at Knockbarren near Loughrea.[26] Wisely sensing the political demise of his class, Sir William had retired from parliament in 1871, but all around him hatred increased for his more obdurate fellow landlords.[27] How pleasant, then, to read of Gregory even in that day, that "He had a great affection for his tenants, and this love was reciprocated. He was a kindly generous Irish landlord, who always advocated the extension of land purchase. Though he held the estate through the days of the famine, he never evicted a tenant. He was the friend of all, and was beloved by all." [28]

Consequently, in turning to Coole in 1896, Yeats was turning to a still celebrated family out of the eighteenth century that clung to a dwindling house, amid a diminishing class that followed a vanishing religion and looked to a seldom-loved England for its more and more precarious hold on Ireland. Yet we shall hear Yeats exclaim, rightly, that there is no house with such a fine record in Ireland.[29] We shall see him hoping that somehow Coole might be maintained as a protection against the "levelling wind," and as the home of a "sterner conscience" where "passion and precision have been one," where

26. Information from Mr. Eoin Linnane, Ardrahan, formerly Edward Martyn's coachman.

27. "Respect the Priest," *School Manuscripts* (in possession of the Irish Folklore Commission), L, 89, a tale told by an old man named John Hallinan, Ballinamanton, Gort, begins, "There was a man living in Castleboy. His name was Mr. Dudley Persse, he was Lady Gregory's father. He was very cruel to his tenants. There was a priest in Kilchreest and he preached a sermon about Persse, off the altar at mass on Sunday. It is said the priest cursed him, and that soon after he [Persse] died." Another, "The Landlord," *School Manuscripts*, XLVII (25 November 1937–12 January 1939), 292, reads, "Mr. Lattery never interfered with his tenants at Election times. He let them vote as they pleased but Walter Shawe-Taylor adjoining always made his tenants vote for the Protestant M.P., severely punished those who refused. He had two soup-schools in the Kilmacduagh parish and forced the tenants to send their children to these dens."

28. "The Local Landlord," *School Manuscripts*, XLVII, 106.

29. *Lady Gregory's Journals*, p. 17.

"gifts that govern men" have been refined to a "written speech/ Wrought of high laughter, loveliness and ease." We have already seen Yeats's enthusiasm for the life exemplified by Lady Gregory's wild and eccentric brothers—"figures from the eighteenth century. Jonah Barrington might have celebrated their lives." [30] But he was to be moved even more deeply for the rest of his life by a florescence of the ideals of an almost mythical eighteenth century caught in the brief careers of Lady Gregory's impetuous nephews and her son, and then just as magnificently in the last thirty-five years of her own majestic life of service.

II

This discussion of the Gregory connection begins with a name that is all but forgotten in today's Ireland despite the accelerated resurrection of national heroes from Pearse on. Even so recently as 1961, a reviewer in the London *Times Literary Supplement*, a review strangely imperceptive on Irish matters in general and Yeats and Joyce in particular, could simply huddle Yeats's essay on John Shawe-Taylor into a snide reference to his treatment of "Irish worthies." Yet one would be hard pressed to name another man in Ireland during this century who tried to do more to solve the outstanding problems of that country: religious contention, industrial stagnation, unequal division of the land, university education, the drink laws, and the political unity of the entire country.

Born in 1866, Captain John Shawe-Taylor was the son of Lady Gregory's sister Elizabeth and Walter Shawe-Taylor of Castle Taylor, Ardrahan, a land agent, agriculturist, and possessor of some thousand acres. John's early exploits were largely on the hunting field with the Blazers and in the army. He joined the Cheshire Regiment in 1889 and was made a captain ten years later. He served in the Burmese Expedition of 1889 and later in Egypt, and fought at Karee Siding in 1900 during the Boer War. Invalided with enteric fever, he was decorated and retired the following year. Teetotaler,

30. *Autobiographies*, p. 393.

44

nonsmoker, religious evangelical, Shawe-Taylor was an ardent but never fanatical example of temperance and religious good will to the soldiers under him.

He is most famous for his decisive and dramatic appeal in 1902 to landlords and nationalist leaders in Ireland to meet in a convention and settle the land problem. From that time until his death in June 1911, he also managed to curtail the issuing of liquor licenses, promote a conference on the national university question, convene an industrial conference in Galway in 1907, organize a Soldiers Institute in Limerick, and establish a model village near Ardrahan for the promotion of home industries and the cultivation of vegetables on cotters' plots. He identified himself with the All-for-Ireland League and Irish Reform Association, promoted the work of the Gaelic League, stood as a Devolutionist candidate for Galway upon Devlin's retirement in 1906, and very nearly won but for the vilifications of Dillon. His sudden death in London brought notices of shock from Limerick, Cork, Galway, and Dublin, where he was best known; but soon, as we shall see, he was forgotten except in Yeats's pages.[31]

As a man, Captain Shawe-Taylor was first and foremost a gentleman, honor-bred and disinterested in conduct, characteristics which make his life seem even more quixotic and unbelievable since it took its course in the backwash of Irish public life after Parnell's death. He seemed to Yeats to be one of those rounded beings from the Renaissance: inordinately handsome, energetic and decisive, a leader in the modern tradition of Nelson or Garibaldi, who was worshipped by his followers.[32] These traits plus his schoolboy's enthusiasm for Ireland and his selfless motives often made him seem an original. Or so he struck Standish O'Grady; so he was remembered for leading the

31. See *Newspaper Cuttings* (Call Number Ir.92. L24), 82, in the National Library of Ireland. This page is a convenient repository of obituary notices from the *Morning Post*, the *Irish Times*, and the *Freeman's Journal* on 1 July 1911. See also William O'Brien, *An Olive Branch in Ireland* (London, 1910), pp. 140–41; and "Death of Captain Shawe-Taylor," *Tuam Herald*, 8 July 1911. I have relied heavily on the *Tuam Herald*, a weekly paper, for its editor, R. J. Kelly, was an adept antiquary, historian, and recorder of Galway affairs. Throughout these notes I have regularized the spelling of Shawe-Taylor.

32. Hone, p. 232, and information from the late Ernest Walsh.

Cheshire Regiment in the Transvaal on a midnight march through a thunderstorm;[33] and so he appeared when presenting tableaux vivants at the old Castle of Limerick in the midst of the slums: he "went round to the poor women of the neighbourhood begging them to clean their windows and brighten up the places as much as possible. They complied with his request, and he, in return, entertained them at a tea party on a grand scale."[34]

In a family that still insisted as late as 1923 that prayers be said for the King,[35] John Shawe-Taylor came as a shock. On good evidence it is said that he once informed his father in the sanctity of his study that upon receiving the estate he, John Shawe-Taylor, would divide the land, right up to the castle grounds, among his tenants. Walter Shawe-Taylor, infuriated, dipped his pen into the ink and dashed it in John's face.[36] But the young man's impetuosity was usually in the service of peace. In 1905, he was the man asked to settle a land dispute between the United Irish League and Harry Persse. As usual, he saw right on both sides; as usual the Dublin Unionist papers called him a disgrace to his commission; and as usual, he saw the matter in the larger perspective of Ireland, just as he did when he called upon Lord Clanrickarde to return to Loughrea and correct the dilapidation there.[37] Yet he also seems to have had in him, oddly enough, all the near recklessness, without the irresponsibility, of the mythic "Man for Galway," come roaring out of another century:

> To drink a toast,
> A proctor roast,
>   Or Bailiff as the case is;
> To kiss your wife,

33. "Shawe-Taylor, the Man of the Hour. . . ," *All Ireland Review*, III (11 October 1902), 512, and "Pithy Pars," *Tuam Herald*, 19 August 1899.

34. "Who Is Captain Shawe-Taylor?" *Freeman's Journal*, 8 September 1902.

35. *Lady Gregory's Journals*, pp. 29–30.

36. Information from Eoin Linnane, who had the story from a retainer on the Shawe-Taylor estate.

37. "Woodville Farm Dispute. Captain Shawe-Taylor as Peace-Maker," *Tuam Herald*, 18 March 1905.

> To take your life,
>> At ten or fifteen paces.
> To keep game cocks,
> To hunt the fox,
>> To drink in punch the Solway,
> With debts galore,
> But fun far more,
>> Oh, that's the Man for Galway.

For despite the gentle overlay of nineteenth-century idealism, Shawe-Taylor could on occasion show the tiger. When served a mistaken writ in Limerick, he had had the process server locked up by the guard.[38] When the curator of the Kildare Street Museum attempted to dishonor Hugh Lane by suggesting that one of his Corots was in fact by Mezzoly and, with the tacit support of Count Plunkett, hung a photograph of the Mezzoly imitation over the Corot, Shawe-Taylor, armed with but a screwdriver and in the company of a perplexed constable, removed the offending photograph and carted it off. "The family decision once more!" Yeats murmured.[39]

This strength of conviction, coupled with an innate "power of calculation too rapid for the intellect to follow," Yeats discovered in Shawe-Taylor's sudden leap from an ocean liner to the Queenstown tender and then, again, from a train moving out of the Athenry station.[40] Yeats found his handsomeness to be the mirror of his character, so that his whole person seemed his mind. This power of daring and instant decision Yeats marked as the quality behind Shawe-Taylor's famous letter of September 3, 1902, calling for the land conference. This evinced a genius in hidden touch with powerful instincts and wishes in all men. As Yeats went on to write, "Men like him live near this power because of something simple and impersonal within them which is, as I believe, imaged in the fire of their minds,

38. "Captain Shawe-Taylor," *Tuam Herald*, 26 November 1904.
39. *Hugh Lane*, pp. 68–69. For a more rollicking account see "The Ballad of Shawe-Taylor and Hugh Lane" in Susan L. Mitchell's *Aids to the Immortality of Certain Persons in Ireland* (Dublin, 1908), pp. 29–31.
40. *Hugh Lane*, p. 72.

as in the shape of their bodies and their faces." [41] But at the end of his essay, Yeats puts the emphasis where it truly belongs, on Shawe-Taylor's moral genius:

> I do not think I have known another man whose motives were so entirely pure, so entirely unmixed with any personal calculation, whether of ambition, of prudence or of vanity. He caught up into his imagination the public gain as other men their private gain. For much of his life he had seemed, though a good soldier and a good shot, and a good rider to hounds, to care deeply for nothing but religion, and this religion, so curiously lacking in denominational limits, concerned itself alone with the communion of the soul with God. Such men, before some great decision, will sometimes give to the analysis of their own motive the energy that other men give to the examination of the circumstances wherein they act, and it is often those who attain in this way to purity of motive who act most wisely at moments of great crisis. It is as though they sank a well through the soil where our habits have been built, and where our hopes take root or lie uprooted, to the lasting rock and to the living stream. [42]

It is to the examples of this moral genius that we ought to turn for the real sources of Yeats's praise.

The delightful thing about Shawe-Taylor is that his moral quality, like that of such eighteenth-century leaders as Burke, Berkeley, and Grattan, could take so many different courses. In him there still seemed to be alive the authority of the man who was master of all sides of his estate, that is, before nineteenth-century specialization passed him by. And Ireland, morally speaking, was his estate.

In cutting his teeth on the licensing problem, if the figure is possible, he showed both humor and tact. For one thing, the wine was never known to stop flowing from his own decanter for those of his guests who wished it. One is also hard put to say that his facing the drink problem in Ireland may not have been more difficult than his facing the problems of land and religion. On January 20, 1902, as a

41. "John Shawe-Taylor," *Essays and Introductions*, p. 344.
42. *Ibid.*, pp. 344–45.

magistrate he rejected every application for a new spirits license, declaring that there was already one public house for every ninety-five people in Galway.[43] In May of that year, he addressed the magistrates of Ireland in the Round Room at the Mansion House and made an impressive and forceful speech on the same subject.[44] Temperance was one of his lifelong causes. But the quality that Yeats saw in the man is most forthcoming in his insight into the whole problem of temperance. For in another speech, surprisingly full of wit at the expense of the publicans, Shawe-Taylor could say:

"I would be glad . . . to see temperance applied to this country all round—temperance in the field of politics, temperance between rival religious sects, temperance in approaching the thorny and complex educational problems, temperance between landlord and tenant . . . temperance of thought, feeling, and action between the men who are called upon to control and conduct all Irish public affairs."

Then he went to what seemed the real heart of the matter:

"You cannot carry out one reform without its having an effect on others. It seems to me, looking around in Ireland, I see everywhere men building, building." He [Shawe-Taylor] instanced the Gaelic League, building up self-reliance and teaching men how to be self respecting; Sir Horace Plunkett building up an agricultural country; the Literary Societies building up Irish literature and art; the National Theatre bringing forth again the pure Irish drama. Then he pointed to the Industrial Conference, to be held on the 8th February, with the object of trying to restore our manufactures and industries.[45]

In the same manner, Captain Shawe-Taylor's letter dated September 2, 1902, opened by putting the land war in its proper context —the contention between creeds, classes, and sections that ruined trade and commerce. This, moreover, was a war two hundred years old. The story of Shawe-Taylor's success in arranging the conference,

43. "Galway Quarter Sessions," *Tuam Herald*, 25 January 1902.
44. "The All-Ireland Magistrates Meeting," *Tuam Herald*, 17 May 1902.
45. "Captain Shawe-Taylor," *Tuam Herald*, 4 February 1905.

with the aid of Wyndham and Dunraven's conciliation committee, is now a familiar one. In less than a year the unanimous report was embodied in law, and peasant proprietorship was realized at last.[46] Again the real skill in the initial proposal is apparent. He brought together only the leaders on both sides, men, no matter what their individual plans, who knew their backers, were willing to meet with other leaders, formulate large agreements, and then let experts work out the details before meeting again for final approval.[47] This insight into power and the common will among diverse men comes extremely close to justifying Yeats's praise of a public imagination in Shawe-Taylor.

Still, as Yeats suggested, it was truly the man's religion that lay at the heart of him. As Lady Gregory wrote in a letter to Yeats:

> He has dreams which I am afraid will not be realised in his time, but which account for his enthusiasm. He sees a time coming when all who believe in invisible things will unite against unbelief. He thinks Protestants and Catholics will see then, as he sees clearly now, that differences of dogma are nothing, that their belief is practically the same. 'Our doctrine is that by Faith the Saviour enters into us, and lives His life through our body; the Catholic believes that through the Sacraments the Saviour enters into him, and lives His life through his body.' I had never heard theology stated in this way before. Certainly John having that belief, need not be worried by little obstacles.[48]

Thus after his success with the magistrates' conference and the land conference, Shawe-Taylor bravely attempted to settle the University Question, which was largely a matter of Catholic objections to the Queen's Colleges for their dangers to the faith. Looking at Queen's

46. For the pertinent details, see Denis Gwynn, *The Life of John Redmond* (London, 1932), pp. 98–102, and F. S. L. Lyons, *The Irish Parliamentary Party 1890–1910* (London, 1951), pp. 99–100, 238–41.

47. This is a very brief summary of Shawe-Taylor's famous letter to Irish editors. For Shawe-Taylor's further elaborations, see "Irish Land Conference," *Tuam Herald*, 27 September 1902, and "The Land Conference," *Tuam Herald*, 11 October 1902.

48. *Hugh Lane*, p. 71.

College, Galway, with but 118 students where 400 might have been accommodated, he decided to invite representatives of the Orange Society and the Roman Catholic and Protestant churches to a meeting in the Mansion House sometime before December 15, 1903.[49] If nothing came of that meeting, Shawe-Taylor nevertheless spoke out in Galway the next January for a university scheme which would cater to excellence in all Irishmen, Catholic and Protestant, rich and poor. He chided Trinity for being in strict fact Church of Ireland; he praised Trinity for having produced great men. He challenged the complaint that the new scheme was wanted by the Catholic hierarchy and clergy alone by pointing at the meeting itself.[50] His "purity of motive," as Yeats termed it, at moments like this seemed miraculous, too audacious, more than quixotic, as Yeats often thought.[51]

Willing to laugh at the seemingly grandiose nature of his hopes, Shawe-Taylor stuck to his vision. When asked in the spring of 1903 if he intended to take up Home Rule next, he calmly announced that Home Rule was "Number 4 on my list," that religious bigotry was next, and that he planned to lecture Orangemen on the subject.[52] True to form, the subject of his talk in Belfast's Town Hall, while ostensibly the University Question, again settled on the unity of Ireland that all Irishmen wanted, no matter how baffled by differences of creed and politics. Again and again he hammered at the fact that men were men Ireland over: "Irishmen who have been separated politically have learnt that it is possible to be of different political faith and yet be honest men. So too educationally. A difference of creed does not necessarily imply difference of character." [53]

In attempting to settle the University Question by an appeal to the common character and good will of all Irishmen regardless of

49. "Captain Shawe-Taylor and the University Question," *Tuam Herald*, 12 September 1903, and "Pithy Pars," *Tuam Herald*, 19 September 1903, and 7 November 1903.
50. "The Irish University Question," *Tuam Herald*, 9 January 1904.
51. Information from Mrs. W. B. Yeats.
52. "Brevities," *Tuam Herald*, 2 May 1903.
53. "Captain Shawe-Taylor in the North," *Tuam Herald*, 19 September 1903.

religion, Captain Shawe-Taylor foreshadowed his political appeal to all parties to unite in a national policy. And with the uniting of Ireland as with the land question, he looked back to the eighteenth century. Once in appealing for a union between North and South, he could say: "Limerick is the City of the Broken Treaty. To-night I ask you to draft a new treaty—a treaty between peer and peasant, between Protestant and Catholic, between Orange and Green . . . till Ireland has reached her true destination—a nation once again." [54] He wanted a government that would fulfill the hopes of Davis, Mitchel, and Parnell; that would bring together, as had the creation of the department of agriculture, a Unionist like Sir Horace Plunkett and a Nationalist like Redmond; that would see the concerted efforts of a Douglas Hyde in the language movement applauded by the leaders of Sinn Fein.[55]

Although he himself was first a Unionist and then a Devolutionist and leader of the landlords' Reform Association, Shawe-Taylor was ever critical of British shortcomings before the Irish Question.[56] Of course, thanks again to Dillon, Shawe-Taylor was beaten by the Nationalist, Stephen L. Gwynn, by 980 votes in the Galway election of 1906. Gwynn had been backed by the Irish Convention, Shawe-Taylor had stood as the Devolutionist candidate for Galway.[57] But this disappointment aside, when he spoke what must have appeared to be wisdom to both Nationalists and Orangemen, his hearers, though often unconvinced, applauded his courage and usually demonstrated whenever he appeared. There was something infectious about his hopes, though men rejected his political position. Yeats's uncanny sense of the universal touch in Shawe-Taylor, actually cutting deeper than any mere political alliance, seems to be borne out in the inevitable extraordinary enthusiasm of his audiences—whether English, Irish Protestant, or Catholic.[58] In the same sense, even the

54. "Pithy Pars," *Tuam Herald*, 30 December 1905.
55. "Mr. O'Brien and the Party," *Irish Independent*, 12 September 1910.
56. "Captain Shawe-Taylor in America," *Tuam Herald*, 14 February 1903.
57. Announcement in the *Tuam Herald*, 10 November 1906.
58. "Pithy Pars," *Tuam Herald*, 24 December 1904.

landlords disappointed him; for he saw the extreme Unionists as fatefully committed to the belief that "the Irish are incapable of honestly utilising any measure of self-government; that Irish priests and people will leave no stone unturned to exterminate all Protestants, and that it is only out of Ireland that Irishmen can ever hope to attain to success." [59] Yet the shame is that, in politics, as in religion, for all his wisdom and selflessness, Shawe-Taylor lost to the extremists on both sides at a time when others among "the best" lacked all conviction.

The Captain's efforts in behalf of Irish industry were no less indefatigable and no less frustrated. Beyond his usual energy and enthusiasm, the pattern of his efforts—seeing that all men possessed the same hopes for betterment—remained the same: to bring all varieties of Irishmen together to back Irish industry. How habitual seems this portion of his address to an audience in London:

> Years ago in the Ulster Hall in Belfast the Duke of Abercorn roused his audience to a pitch of enthusiasm by his famous utterance, "We will not have Home Rule." To-day he was an ardent supporter of our industries. In Dublin sooner than pay the fine inflicted on him for painting his name in Irish on his carts, Mr W L Cole allowed his goods to be sold by public auction on the streets of that city. He too, was a keen industrialist. Lord Clonbrock, Lord Lieutenant of his country, was able in this matter to stand on the same platform as Alderman Kelly who had torn down the Union Jack from the mast head of the Dublin Corporation steamer. Lord Castletown, a leader of the Pan-Celtic movement; Lord Londonderry; Dr Douglas Hyde, President of the Gaelic League; Mr John Redmond, Chairman of the Nationalist Party; Captain Craig, the Unionist leader; Sir Horace Plunkett and Lord Dunraven could stand shoulder to shoulder in this united effort to promote the industries and welfare of their common country. [60]

59. "Captain Shawe-Taylor on the Irish Reform Association," *Tuam Herald*, 17 September 1904; also "Captain Shawe-Taylor," *Tuam Herald*, 26 November 1904.
60. "Captain Shawe-Taylor," *Tuam Herald*, 28 November 1908.

His efforts to rouse Irish industry also touched on the trade of his own port town, Galway City. He spoke with President Roosevelt in the White House and conferred with the deputy commissioner of commerce of Canada in an effort to make Galway a terminal for Canadian mail packet steamers. He represented Connacht on the Industrial General Committee of Ireland. As chairman of the Galway Industrial Development Association, he traveled to Germany in search of new industrial systems for his own country. He met with the French consul in the hope of opening up direct trade between Galway and France. He strove to bring the railroads and merchants and manufacturers together to settle their difficulties.[61] His efforts were again applauded and recognized. A presentation was made to him and his wife in Galway's Railway Hotel on the occasion of the meeting of the exhibitors at the Galway Exhibition, largely organized by Shawe-Taylor himself.[62] Yet even here disappointments were heavy, as his report reads in the year 1907:

> Poor old Galway! The very fates seem against its progress. This is a record of one year's misfortune as seen at a paper read at a meeting of its Industrial Committee last week by Captain Shawe-Taylor. They have Persse's Distillery closed which once employed 150 persons; Sebastian Nolan once employed 30 men; Cloran's mill stopped that used to employ 30; in the Claddagh there was distress as there was no fish caught, and there were no vessels coming in to employ the dock labourers, and the Granite Co discharged about 40 men a couple of weeks ago. So long, he continued, as there was political unrest in the country, with such disturbances and interference with the rights of property such as the cattle driving, it would keep capital from coming into the country. Captain Shawe-Taylor next referred to the Harbour Board which had bye laws that were out of date

61. See, for instance, "Pithy Pars," *Tuam Herald*, 31 January 1903; "Pithy Pars," *Tuam Herald*, 23 May 1903; *Transit, Trade and Traffic in Ireland* with a Foreword by John Shawe-Taylor (n.d.), p. 1; "Brevities," *Tuam Herald*, 25 November 1905; "Brevities," *Tuam Herald*, 22 September 1906; "Brevities," *Tuam Herald*, 30 June 1906; and "Captain John Shawe-Taylor," *Tuam Herald*, 28 November 1908.

62. "Brevities," *Tuam Herald*, 26 September 1908.

and prevented people from engaging in trade that would employ the dock labourers; also that if the millers and bakers would only use Irish flour it would double the amount of work for the people compared with at present.[63]

Yet his vision never faded: one Ireland, where social, religious, and political differences would be bridged, where men could stand straight, where all would work to push industrial prosperity. Was not "humanity . . . the same all the world over"?[64]

The ceremony and custom surrounding this gifted man, no less attractive than his personality, must also have sharpened Yeats's memory of his disappointments. For all Shawe-Taylor's declaration of landlord enlightenment, there lingered about his life a touch of the feudal sense of master and followers, hierarchy of service, and established country traditions. No less, however, beneath their exterior of fealty and loyalty there doubtless also existed strong suspicion and righteous coldness in the Irish peasants, feelings particularly strong in the West with the renewed hunger for land.

Nevertheless, how very much the sense of home, place, rural Ireland, ancient wild Galway, if that allusion is permitted, surrounds, for instance, the account of Shawe-Taylor's homecoming as an invalid from the Boer War. Both Ardrahan and Castle Taylor were decked out in flags and bunting. Torches, flags, banners of welcome adorned the churches, entrance gate, railway station, and castle. A deputation of all classes and creeds met him; he was mobbed and welcomed by his people with outstretched hands. An employee of nearly thirty years, Mr. William Doherty, made a speech celebrating Shawe-Taylor's kindness, modesty, sympathy, and courtesy. In turn, the Captain replied, praising the Irishmen of all ranks fighting in South Africa, especially the Connaught Rangers, the county regiment. He then concluded:

> We are all fond of home. It is a word that has no counterpart in any other language. I believe it is especially dear to the soldier. As he paces the veldt, keeping watch while his comrades lie

63. "Brevities," *Tuam Herald*, 28 December 1907.
64. "University Philosophical Society," *Irish Times*, 30 October 1903.

asleep all around him, his thoughts turn to those who are at home. In the moment of victory his first thought is, "What will they say at home?" Home is to me the best place I know. But it is home, not because of house or place, but because I believe I have a place and a home in your hearts.[65]

One may choose to call these words sentimental, sad, or naïve; whatever they are called, they came from an age that had passed.

If one turns to an account of the christening of his son in 1907, there gleams the irresistible light of another day, the heritage of a great past in Ireland attempting to join hands with a new and quietly hostile world:

> At the font the child received the names of Walter Michael, after his grandfather and his great great great grandfather, who, in the 18th century, was Mayor of the City of Galway. His christening robe was of white hand-embroidered muslin of delicate design and formed part of the wedding dress of the wife of the late Lieutenant-General Sir John Taylor, K.C.B., who commanded the troops in Connaught in 1798, and which has been used at baptisms in the family ever since. . . . The cake was profusely decorated with shamrocks set in relief, and was surmounted by an Irish flag woven in silk.[66]

He too had his homecoming, after the death of his father, in May 1913. Once again fires were lighted at the Castle and on the road a mile away, while the tenantry and employees lined the route, held torches aloft, discharged rockets and guns, cheered, offered speeches and drank the health of Master Walter. His mother is recorded on the occasion as hoping "her son might live a long and happy life at Castle Taylor, and in some measure come to fill the same place in the hearts of his employees and neighbours that his father had done."[67]

Yet the ironic finale must also be told. It amounts to a recapitula-

65. "Captain John Shawe-Taylor," *Tuam Herald*, 25 August 1900.
66. Announcement in the *Tuam Herald*, 23 February 1907.
67. "Home-Coming of Master Shawe-Taylor," *Tuam Herald*, 10 May 1913.

tion of the unspoken sentiment of the times so far as the Shawe-Taylor name goes—wrong class, wrong religion, wrong politics, wrong family. As early as 1904, the supposedly objective Monsignor Fahey had already impugned the memory of Shawe-Taylor's father, and forefathers before him, in a letter to the *Tuam Herald* on June 14. Shawe-Taylor answered with a pointed denial on the 25th. But the reputation continued, already enshrined in Fahey's *History of . . . Kilmacduagh*.

After the Captain's untimely death, tragedy continued to dog the Taylor name. His brother Frank, an auctioneer and agent of the Marquis of Clanrickarde, had been ambushed and had narrowly missed assassination within a mile of the Castle on December 2, 1905.[68] On March 3, 1920, he was shot dead at Coshla, near Athenry, on his way to the Galway fair. The cause had nothing to do with the war against the British at the time but stemmed from a private land vendetta. Frank had refused to sell his land at the request of a deputation of tenants.[69] His wife, who in 1910 had presented the Galway County Council with eight acres of land, a mansion, Ryehill House, Monivea, and full equipment for a tuberculosis sanatorium, bravely faced the hidden assailants in 1905 and rated them for their cowardice. The day after her husband's killing she went out hunting as usual.[70] But the landlord of Galway thereafter when questioning why he must divide up his land for importunate buyers might be told often enough that it was the "Shawe-Taylor Act," a gentle reminder of this murder and an ironic reflection on the great deed of Frank's brother John.[71] Nor did the Captain's son escape, for Castle Taylor was fired into in July 1929.[72] And now, of course, the Castle is gone and Captain John Shawe-Taylor all but forgotten.

68. Announcement in the *Tuam Herald*, 9 December 1905.
69. "Another Murder in County Galway," *Irish Times*, 4 March 1920. Also, information from Patrick Kennedy, Auctioneer, Galway City.
70. "Mrs. Frank Shawe-Taylor," *Tuam Herald*, 9 December 1905; announcement in the *Tuam Herald*, 24 September 1910; "Galway Shooting Sensation," *Irish Independent*, 5 March 1920.
71. "Land Hunger in the West," *Irish Times*, 3 May 1920.
72. "County Galway Outrage," *Irish Times*, 26 July 1929. See also *Lady Gregory's Journals*, p. 47.

III

Though perhaps too much space has been spent on John Shawe-Taylor because of the paucity of the record, there is not that need in turning to Sir Hugh Lane. Yeats's friendship and admiration for Lane are far better known though more scattered throughout Yeats's prose and poetry. Hence we shall focus not on the disgraceful history of the Gallery affair nor on the later fight for the Lane pictures, but on that side of Lane that Yeats identified with the disinterested service of his fellow "image-maker," John Shawe-Taylor. Yeats, as we have seen, always saw Shawe-Taylor's family resemblance; just so, he relates Lane to John and both to that rich stream of talent associated with the Gregorys since the days of the East India Company. Here is Lady Gregory reporting Yeats on the subject:

> . . . Yeats in talking to me of these two, said: "Hugh said to me once, 'Everybody loves John, he has personality, but I am only an eye and a brain.' Yet his talent was just as much rooted in character as John Shawe-Taylor's. To begin with there was the same audacity. . . . [John's] action came from a power of calculation too rapid for the intellect to follow, like Hugh's in deciding on the authenticity of a picture. I, too, have occasionally had intuitions that surprised me afterwards by their wisdom, but had I been one of your nephews I would have acted upon them.
>
> . . . .
>
> . . . his horoscope shows Mars in opposition to the Planet Neptune, which gives—so far as we can be certain about a newly discovered planet—inexplicable convictions one cannot reason over.
>
> . . . .
>
> . . . unlike John he had a single purpose that filled his life. He began like one of Balzac's heroes . . . apparently all personal ambition, and would, I daresay, have shown himself as

58

brutal . . . and like a Balzac hero put aside his personal ambition and become the providence of others." [73]

Yeats also divined Lane's certainty and sure instinct in artistic matters to be like John's ability to fathom the common desires of men. Lane could catch quality in art long before other men. Or so Yeats could explain in generalizing on Lane's miraculous instinct for a picture:

> No man really knows any taste but his own, and he can seldom explain that to others. A great critic is a man who chooses what numbers come to admire slowly, but profoundly, and not because he has studied their tastes, but because human nature is the same in its foundations. He who lives deeply feels at once what multitudes come to feel after many years. To think of the taste of others is to live upon the surface, and never to go down to the unchanging depth. [74]

As we shall see, Yeats came to see a like trait in Jonathan Swift, namely his attention to the "bent and current" of a people irrespective of any bare majority vote of their representatives.

In embodying an aristocratic ideal of service, Lane also exhibited a patrician's bluntness bordering on arrogance, at its worst a harshness and pettishness that Yeats well knew. Lane was never really satisfied with the results of his visionary hopes for beautifying the world; nor could he easily abide the world's slow pace in meeting his wishes. His exasperation was sempiternal. [75] Moreover, at their first meeting Yeats had disliked him for his seeming worldly ambition, for his dandyism, and for his egotistical self-congratulation. But with Lane's renewed dedication to a gallery for Dublin, though on occasion even more disagreeable, he appeared to Yeats a man transformed:

> . . . he seemed changed not only in mind, but in body. He had returned to his old ambition of a great gallery in Dublin. The great houses where he had visited, the people he had met, were now but means to that end. His face and his bodily movements

73. *Hugh Lane*, pp. 72–74.
74. Unidentified clipping c. 1907 in possession of Mrs. W. B. Yeats.
75. *Hugh Lane*, p. 74.

seemed to have changed, they had a curious precision. He had become exceedingly unworldly, contemptuous even of the old lures and perhaps less anxious to please, less agreeable. From that moment to the last time I saw him he was like a man who knew he had but a few years to live, and who raged against every obstacle to his purpose, saying often what was harsh or unkind where that purpose was involved.[76]

Thus, in response to the Dublin Corporation's folly and irritating delay over the proposed gallery in July 1913, Lane spoke blunt truths which nevertheless bear out Yeats's insight. Not only did he inform the Lord Mayor that he had offered a picture previously purchased as a gift for Dublin to the Edinburgh National Gallery, but he added the fillip that the picture would serve as a monumental reminder to Dublin's lack of taste and communal spirit.[77] Earlier he had been just as honest and, if possible, even more forthright when he informed a newspaper correspondent that the question of a bridge site was a matter for an expert and not for the average man, since the average man's ignorance of such matters would probably oppose him to any original idea.[78]

If one hears the irascible tone of another age here—the tone accompanying a truth as Swift or Burke might deliver it in indignation or violent anger—there were even more endemic sides to Lane's uncompromising character.

For beneath the delicate personal distinction of the man,[79] and underlying his natural refinement of dress and unobtrusive courtesy, were strengths that linked him just as firmly to the tradition that

---

76. *Ibid.*, pp. 32–33.

77. "Sir Hugh Lane and Dublin Corporation," *Irish Times*, 19 July 1913. Gerald Kelly is quoted as saying of Lane to Lady Gregory: "I believe he would have killed his whole family, his grandmother—though perhaps not his aunt—he was very fond of you—but certainly he would have killed me and all his friends for the sake of that Dublin Gallery" (*Hugh Lane*, p. 245). Lane's bluntness of speech and uninhibited behavior before examples of bad art and taste are legion.

78. "Municipal Art Gallery," *Irish Times*, 22 April 1913.

79. E. R. Walsh, "South Frederick Street Memories," *Irish Times*, 20 September 1941.

Shawe-Taylor recalled to Yeats.[80] Lane adored ceremony and grand occasions. His personal courage was extraordinary. He was addicted to hard, even reckless, riding in the best traditions of the old Galway fence-busters. Speed intoxicated him.[81] As the last reported sight of him on the Lusitania sustains, Lane had the patrician's demeanor that J. B. Yeats once described as blending "extreme sensitiveness with absolute intrepidity." [82] He was an inveterate gambler. During the *Playboy* riots he thought nothing of escorting or propelling, with brisk disdain, men far more powerful than himself to the door. He was a man with immense capacities for sweetness, boldness, devotion, and bitterness.

More congenially perhaps, his hopes for Ireland resembled—often consciously—those of the more enlightened of the Anglo-Irish during Grattan's Parliament. In one sense, Lane's even exceeded those of his illustrious predecessors. For by putting in Ireland's possession at least a nucleus of European masterpieces, he meant to start a rejuvenation of Irish art itself.[83] To make modern masterpieces available to young Dublin artists would be to stimulate Irish art.[84] Given that help, Irish painting, Lane once surmised, would bloom as it had in the late eighteenth century and as it had not—for just such lack of master-pieces—in the nineteenth.[85] Thus he could also shrug off any narrow patriotic qualms, as did those earlier Protestant aristocrats, by bringing in Lutyens to design his gallery. As Lane once had the refreshing gall to assert: ". . . the most beautiful and characteristic buildings in Dublin erected in the times of Irish Independence were almost without exception the work of English architects." [86] Fittingly, then, we may look upon the public aesthetic dedication of Sir

80. On Lane's courtesy and grooming, see *Hugh Lane*, pp. 24–25, 163–65.

81. *Ibid.*, pp. 186–87, 250. See also Thomas Bodkin, *Hugh Lane and his Pictures*, 3rd ed. (Dublin, 1956), pp. 4, 24, 72.

82. *Hugh Lane*, p. 217.

83. "Celebrities at Home," *The World*, 28 December 1909, p. 1126.

84. S. C. Harrison, "Sir Hugh Lane [letter to the editor dated 15 April 1921]," *Dublin News Cuttings on the Dublin Art Gallery* in the National Gallery of Ireland.

85. *Hugh Lane*, pp. 52–53.

86. "Sir Hugh Lane's Pictures," *Irish Times*, 10 September 1913.

Hugh Lane as a graceful continuation of the efforts of an eighteenth-century Anglo-Irish aristocracy to beautify what became the second city of the Empire. It was his favorite Irish century.[87]

Where Yeats might look to the ringing oratory of Grattan's Parliament as a forerunner of the new influence of the Abbey, Lane looked to Georgian country houses, to Delville for instance, for part of his inspiration. Early in this century he had exclaimed to an interviewer: "Dublin's going to be one of the fairest cities on the earth instead of one of the world's little back streets. It's coming, coming; if you'd only spent the last few months in Ireland you'd know. But, believe me, it's coming. A new Ireland!" [88] But it did not come for Lane. The opposition of a handful of powerful fanatic nationalists and religious bigots on one hand, and, on the other, the mean spirit of many a wealthy Anglo-Irishman forced Lane's momentary bitterness and hatred against the country he had romanticized from memories of his Galway childhood.[89]

His initial elation and the joy, reminders of eighteenth-century *esprit* and public spirit, were not wasted on Yeats. Lionel Johnson's lines

> Magnificence and Grace,
> Excellent courtesy;
> A brightness on the face,
> Airs of high memory

seemed to Yeats to describe Lane best.[90] But in his own verses recounting the Gallery failure, Yeats holds up a man who had been betrayed in the unlovely Irish tradition of Parnell and even Robert Emmet. Lane like Parnell had been done in by those represented by William Murphy—"an old foul mouth"—and to a lesser extent by his own class. Yeats once described such hideous periods in Irish life at the end of the eighteenth and nineteenth centuries while explaining Norreys O'Connell's play, *The Piper:*

87. *Hugh Lane*, pp. 43, 86, 189.
88. "The Nation That's Going to Be," *Morning Post*, 5 May 1903, p. 4.
89. *Hugh Lane*, p. 133.
90. *Ibid.*, p. 211.

The play, to my mind, meant a satire upon the nine years of the Parnellite split, years of endless talk, endless rhetoric, and futile drifting; years which were taken out of the history of the nation and made nothing. Further, my imagination went back to the Rebellion of Robert Emmet, the folly that surrounded him, the slackness as bad as treachery, which brought that heroic life to nothing. . . .[91]

In poems like "To a Shade," "To a Friend whose Work has come to Nothing," and "To a Wealthy Man . . . ," we see the identification of Lane with Parnell and with the great patrons of the Italian Renaissance.

But it is with "September 1913" that we shall conclude. For Romantic Ireland, dating back from the idealism of O'Leary to that of the Wild Geese, its heyday to be found at the end of the eighteenth century, is the image with which Yeats confronts the pious economies of those who denied Lane his vision. Fitzgerald, Emmet, and Tone, figures with a nearly hallucinatory dash and magnificence about them, alone and in pain, had also been "image-makers" in the midst of slackness and betrayal. They had refused to live by the minimum standards of a "little huckstering nation"—and so had Lane. That refusal Yeats had perpetually urged on him. As early as January 1907, Yeats warned Lane in his fight with the Dublin Corporation:

If you surrender the whole Cause of artistic intellect in Ireland is damaged for a generation, if you give up and scatter the pictures there is no man can blame you, but we in the times to come shall be the poorer for it. You have taken like everybody who works in our damned undisciplined country something of Atlas's job upon your shoulders and all one can say is one gets used to it.[92]

91. Programme, February 20–22, 1908, for *The Piper*. Yeats once called Lane "a passionately patriotic man, whose patriotism never took a political form" ("A Chance for the National Gallery," *The Observer*, 10 December 1916, p. 10).

92. TS. of letter to Lane dated 10 January 1907 in the National Library of Ireland.

This was Lane's ultimate patriotism for Yeats, not the vulgar rhetoric of nineteenth-century politics but the infusion of gentle blood through art into the body politic. He gave himself to the arts in Ireland as other Irishmen gave themselves to religion.[93]

IV

Robert Gregory is the most celebrated of these three men in Yeats's poetry. Yet we know least about him. His glorification is usually attributed to the many-sidedness he offered to Yeats's heroic vision; in truth it is probably as much due to Yeats's admiration for his mother. Yet there is another reason to consider: he too was an "image-maker," possessed of a mind, intuitive and quick in its way, like those of his kinsmen. Yeats had wished to see that mind also at the service of Ireland. When, for instance, we find Yeats in 1915 recommending Robert Gregory to Commissioner Bailey as a candidate for the directorship of Dublin's National Gallery, Yeats's accent on Gregory's mind, family connections, and tradition of service is unmistakable:

> My own opinion is that if we had in Dublin to deal, not with a Committee, but with a single Art patron, a Medici, let us say, he would be very likely to think young Gregory the best of all the candidates. I don't know how the suggestion would be taken at Coole and I feel that I am too notoriously his friend and Lady Gregory's friend, to make it. He is a painter of great distinction and growing reputation here amongst the young men, but there are other painters of distinction and one does not appoint a man because he is a painter. It is more to the point that he seems to me to have a greater knowledge, finer critical insight than any painter of equal power I've ever known. It is precisely this critical insight that has made his development as a painter as slow as it has been. When we begin at any art—verse or painting, no matter what it is, it is necessary to be deceived if we are to develop rapidly. . . . If we are such fine critics that we know we cannot produce a masterpiece for years, our will

93. Holloway, Natl. Lib. MS. 1909 (April–June 1927), opp. p. 654.

grows uncertain and our purpose infirm. This insight which is a defect in a creator, is however, what you want to make a great gallery. In a few years Gregory will have the vast knowledge that Charles Ricketts has to-day alone among painters. To appoint him, however, would be an act of faith, and faith is the gift of the individual soul. A Committee could only acquire it from one enthusiastic member. It would be a fine thing if another of this family which has already given us Shawe-Taylor, Hugh Lane, Lady Gregory herself should have an opportunity for that able, selfless service which is its supreme gift. . . . I know Gregory to be the superior in force of intellect of everyone whose name has been suggested up to this and he is Irish.[94]

This critical ability, seemingly akin to the moral genius of John Shawe-Taylor and the aesthetic genius of Sir Hugh Lane, made Gregory resemble them also in that he possessed a high order of instinctive choice. The finest account of Gregory's elusive career that we possess states that Gregory's many abilities, his many-sidedness, "may have been a doubtful gift" for the living man of this century, while his artistic gift, in Yeats's eyes, might have isolated him.[95] Yet this modern Sidney, given especially his intellectual gift, might have taken his place in the late Renaissance of Georgian Ireland when genius might still be "scholar, soldier, horseman," painter or connoisseur, and governor of men, all at once.[96] His type would be equally at home at Urbino or at eighteenth-century Coole.

However, let us stress this instinctive side of Gregory for the moment, the side represented to Yeats by Gregory's critical intelligence. To the account given by D. J. Gordon and Ian Fletcher, one can add details of his career that make Gregory appear curiously contradictory in personality. As a boy, he is remembered to have been cool, determined, and remarkably silent.[97] On the one hand looms the fabulous rider—stories of his horsemanship are still handed down

94. TS. of letter dated 23 June 1915 in the National Library of Ireland.
95. *W. B. Yeats: Images of a Poet*, eds. D. J. Gordon and Ian Fletcher (Manchester, 1961), pp. 32–33.
96. *Wheels and Butterflies*, p. 13.
97. Information from Eoin Linnane.

from father to son in Co. Galway [98]—full of charity and love of Ireland; [99] on the other appears the typical Oxford product in the Ireland of his time.[100] His selling 2,000 acres to the Congested Districts Board in 1911 [101] is not suggested, but, rather, the anti-Irish sentiment around him,[102] seen most tragically, after his death, in his widow's presence with R.I.C. and English officers at the tennis court massacre at Ballyturin near Lough Cutra.[103] And then, there is the report of his attempt to teach his tenants to play cricket at Kiltartan.[104] Similarly, though Yeats always claimed him as a friend, one senses some vague animosity in Gregory towards Yeats: twitting him on his scholarship, putting the gloves on with him at the Arts Club and then stretching him flat, mysteriously capsizing a boat with Yeats and himself in it.[105] These may be but slight contradictions in the real-life Robert Gregory. Yet they may also seem to be not only conflicts between his art and his society, but even between the Irish and the English in him, the confused background of his critical power.

That power of instinctive choice Yeats caught behind these warring elements he felt to be both a family trait and, perhaps, the very distinctive trait of the Anglo-Irish mind itself. During the years after the Treaty, Yeats often tried to explain this quality, which is summed up in the later lines,

> The people of Burke and of Grattan
> That gave, though free to refuse—
> Pride, like that of the morn,

by comparing the two patriotisms in Ireland, the Protestant and the Catholic. He used his poems, "Red Hanrahan's Song about Ireland"

98. *Idem.*

99. *Lady Gregory's Journals*, p. 43, and *Our Irish Theatre*, pp. 60–61.

100. Information from the late Ernest Walsh.

101. "Pithy Pars," *Tuam Herald*, 11 November 1911.

102. Unpublished letter to Ethel Mannin dated 1 February 1934, in the Sligo public library.

103. Vere R. T. Gregory, *The House of Gregory*, with a Foreword by Thomas Ulick Sadleir (Dublin, 1943), pp. 93–94.

104. J. M. Hone, "Cricket in Ireland," *Irish Statesman*, 23 August 1919, p. 215.

105. "Some New Letters from W. B. Yeats to Lady Gregory," *REL*, IV (July 1963), 37, and information from the late Ernest Walsh.

66

and "An Irish Airman Foresees his Death," respectively, to exemplify this difference. On various public occasions in 1923–24, his point was reported in the Dublin press:

> In "Red Hanrahan's Song about Ireland" he [Yeats] embodied the tragic patriotism of Catholic Ireland—a patriotism different, he said, from the Ireland to which he belonged, that of Anglo-Ireland, which was genuine, too, but not like fate, and not born with one like the colour of one's hair.[106]

And, on another occasion:

> There was another patriotism, the patriotism of Protestant Ireland, with less of certainty than that of Catholic and Gaelic Ireland. Protestant patriotism was a hesitating thing, but had its own nobility, its own heroism. His "Irish Airman Foresees his End" [sic] was written to express that patriotism.[107]

And, finally,

> "There are two kinds of patriotism in Ireland . . . the patriotism of Catholic Ireland, which is inherited, and to which a man holds because he will not change. Then there is the patriotism of those who have grown up in the Church of Ireland, and that has its own special meaning—but in it there is always a choice.[108]

Little more than a year before his death, Yeats returned to considerations of "An Irish Airman" as one of three political poems he had chosen to discuss on a BBC broadcast. Here we get not only the idea of Protestant patriotism as a deliberate and conscious choice, but Yeats's reflections on the ultimate basis of that choice:

> The Irish airman was Robert Gregory—Lady Gregory's son. He was a painter of genius, who, immediately after the start of the Great War, joined the Air Force. Like many Protestant Irishmen he stood between two Nations. He said to me, "I think I am going out of friendship." Meaning, I suppose, that so many of his friends had gone. "The English are not my

---

106. "My Own Poetry," *Irish Independent*, 17 May 1923.
107. "Mr. W. B. Yeats's Secrets," *Irish Times*, 30 June 1923.
108. "A Poet's Memories," *Freeman's Journal*, 26 January 1924.

people. My people are the people of Kiltartan.". . . Presently his mother asked, "Why has Robert joined?" I answered, "I suppose he thought it his duty." She said, "It was his duty to stay here. He joined for the same reason I would have, had I been a young man. He could not keep out of it." She was right. He was a born soldier. He said to Bernard Shaw shortly before his death, that he was never happy until he began to fight.[109]

No conscription law, no religious or family duty, no patriotic orator or mob urged on Gregory. It was his choice, an impulse of delight in single-minded battle, that brought all his skills to bear where there had been confusion or hesitancy.

The genius of that choice was also a solitary one, and the impulse itself was lonely. It is true that Yeats accents the painter in both the Sunday *Observer* appreciation of Gregory and in the later famous elegy. Yet in that essay, and in all the poems written in Gregory's memory, the emphasis is on his *choice* of line and color, on the distinction of his mind, on a traditional learning got from his reading the classics, that made his art intense, grave, and subjective. Even the interpolated stanza of "In Memory of Major Robert Gregory" points to the instinctive speed of his mind: ". . . his mind outran the horses' feet." To maintain his kinship with other men—and we have seen Yeats comment on this process in the actions of Lane and Shawe-Taylor—Gregory sought "through some lesser gift, or through mere excitement, to strengthen that self which unites them [artists] to ordinary men." [110] But the impulse and the choice to fight, Yeats seems to be saying in poem and essay, came from what he would later call an Anglo-Irish choice in solitude, the solitude of a man possessing a multitude of gifts he could not integrate in modern life, and caught between two nations for whom his choices were perpetually new. That kind of transplanted man might well find himself unified, so to speak, in the lesser gift of fighting to death, whereas his choice in the

109. TS. of "My Own Poetry," BBC broadcast read by V. C. Clinton-Baddeley and Margot Ruddock, 3 July 1937, 10:00–10:20 P.M., in possession of Broadcasting House.
110. "Major Robert Gregory," *The Observer*, 17 February 1918, p. 9.

eighteenth century might not have forced him into isolation had he lived as a painter. Moreover, and this is the irony in Yeats's portrait of Gregory, though identified with the speckled bird and the loneliness of the Burren Hills, Robert Gregory's lonely art, like his fighting, might have finally linked him to other men—again the examples of his uncles are similar—for his painting, the image of his moods, was to Yeats "part of the traditional expression of the soul." [111]

To these gifts of critical intelligence, lonely choice, and traditional expression in art that joined Robert Gregory to Ireland can be added the Gregory Galway heritage. In both "Reprisals" and "An Irish Airman" Kiltartan is the center of his allegiance, as it had been for his father and his father before him. Robert Gregory's mind, so instinctively quick and decisive, was also part of his miraculous horsemanship in the West of Ireland where desperate riding was ever enhanced by unmortared stone fences that could release a foot or two of rock upon a horse's slightest touch.[112] That mind might also have advised in the building of a lovely house in Galway or in the buying of pictures for the National Gallery of Ireland, as one might have expected from an exceptional eighteenth-century Connacht gentleman in whom such knowledge, riding, and scholarship were frequently found together.[113]

V

Let us turn now from Robert Gregory to his mother. The resemblance between the two is the resemblance also fixed upon her nephews. They were all "image-makers." The epithet was her own, part of the dedication of her play, *The Image:* "To my nephews Hugh Lane and John Shawe-Taylor, image-makers." In a note at the end of the play she explains her meaning, again with her sisters' sons in mind:

111. *Ibid.*
112. W. H. Maxwell, *Wild Sports of the West,* edited with an Introduction by the Earl of Dunraven (London, Dublin and Belfast, n.d.), pp. 390–91.
113. Thomas U. Sadleir and Page L. Dickinson, *Georgian Mansions in Ireland* (Dublin, 1915), p. 9.

One brought together the Conference that did so much towards the peaceable and friendly changing of land ownership. The other has made Dublin the Orient of all—artists or learners or critics, who value the great modern school of French painting. Yet I fancy it was a dream beyond possible realisation that gave each of them the hard patience needed by those who build, and the courage needed by the "Disturber" who does not often escape some knocks and buffetings. But if the dreamer had never tried to tell the dream that had come across him, even though to "betray his secret to the multitude," must shatter his own perfect vision, the world would grow clogged and dull with the weight of flesh and of clay. And so we must say "God love you" to the Image-makers, for do we not live by the shining of those scattered fragments of their dream? [114]

Her vision was "to restore dignity to Ireland." Her means were complex. One portion was her art, which Yeats justly admired from the beginning. Let there be no doubt about this. As one reporter wrote:

These two were fortified by an intense mutual admiration. I remember my first visit to Mr. Yeats in his little flat in Woburn Buildings. Lady Gregory was there, Mr. Rothenstein, Mr. Masefield, and two others. There came a moment when Mr. Yeats and Lady Gregory were sitting one on each side of the fire —the first speaking eloquently in his beautiful voice and gesticulating with his expressive arms, the other sitting still as a mouse, and talking so quietly. They were praising each other's work, recalling points of surpassing merit in quick succession, carried away. The intoned praises of the one alternating with the quiet but lively praises of the other followed like the strophe and antistrophe of a chorus, advancing and retreating— till Lady Gregory broke the sequence, and turned to one of the party, a young writer, with the words: "I hear you have been criticising us all in the ———." [115]

114. *The Image: A Play in Three Acts* (Dublin, 1910), pp. 100–1.
115. Unidentified clipping on Lady Gregory's death in Holloway, Natl. Lib. MS. 1950 (April–June 1932), opp. p. 891.

Another part Yeats called her personal "magnificence, greatness of soul":

> It was this quality, to which modern books, modern culture had contributed nothing, that gave her historical importance. Ireland was humiliated, Ireland was degraded, political method had been an insincere oratory, an artificial enthusiam, and it had proved useless in a moral crisis.
>
> Lady Gregory was not philosophic, she seldom reflected upon her work, but one phrase she used again and again: "We do our work to restore dignity to Ireland." She remained to the end of her life a connoisseur in nobility in living and in thought.[116]

And last of all, a third instrument to create her image was Coole. That this house was important to Yeats is by now a truism. But it has never been stated more dramatically than in the scene Yeats describes in his unpublished essay, "The Death of Lady Gregory." Yeats had agreed to remain with her coffin at Coole while Margaret and Guy Gough would stay at Lough Cutra. Margaret Gough

> . . . was surprised that I did not mind sleeping in a house with a coffin. I said, "I am not affected by the circumstances of death, but by the parting." Several times we returned to [the] subject and I said, "I said it is not the coffin that wrings my heart but all this," pointing to the books & the pictures. She said, "Yes, it is your home too that is broken up." [117]

He belonged to Connacht and so did Lady Gregory.[118] Coole united them.

It is best to start there. For it is likely that from his first visit, when he marveled at the library filled with fine editions and classics out of the eighteenth century, Coole was virtually an answer to his prayer.

---

116. "Modern Ireland," *Massachusetts Review*, V (Winter 1964), 259.

117. Large white vellum notebook begun 23 November 1930.

118. As Lady Gregory once wrote, ". . . although my husband once represented Dublin in Parliament and I was married in a church in Dublin, where so much of my later work has been, and I sometimes think I should like a grave in Glasnevin—yet I belong to Connacht" ("Americans and the Art Gallery," *Irish Times*, 8 September 1913).

Staying at Tulira some nights before, he remembered fearing solar influence. He had been told to dwell near water. One night he invoked the powers of the moon, his main source of creativity.[119] The results were miraculous:

> My invocations were a form of prayer accompanied by an active desire for a special result, a more conscious exercise perhaps of the human faculties. A few days afterwards a new friend, Lady Gregory, called & invited me to stay at Coole, & even before I arrived began collecting for me, stories of fairy belief. At this moment, I have believed or half believed—we cannot judge the power of those shadows—that she came in reply to these evocations for are not the common people and their wisdom under the moon, & her house is at the edge of [a] lake.[120]

For Yeats, there was from the beginning something sacred about this rather dumpy eighteenth-century country house. In an early short story, "The Cradles of Gold," Yeats had described Lough Gill and its surrounding shore in the following phrases that he later used for Coole lake:

> The wooded islands and the wooded mountainous headlands mirrored in the still waters of the lake, seemed to Peter Hearne full of that mysterious stillness which falls upon the exterior when the interior world is about to open its gates.[121]

At Coole, "where all outward things were the image of an inward life,"[122] all the emblems—busts, pictures, books, statues[123]—suggested the order and repose of the continuous life there.[124] Now, in the

119. "Autobiography."

120. *Idem.*

121. "The Cradles of Gold," *The Senate*, November 1896, p. 407.

122. "Autobiography."

123. *Autobiographies*, pp. 389–91. Also, TS. of "My Own Poetry Again," BBC broadcast, 29 October 1937, 10:45–11:05 P.M.

124. *Autobiographies*, p. 381. In "A Celebrated Galway Woman," *Tuam Herald*, 9 November 1901, we read, "The Gregory family settled in this county early in the 18th century. . . . At no time in the history of Coole has it been made to such an extent the gathering place for all the culture of Ireland, and she is never without someone who has the best of the country at heart visiting her."

twilight or autumn of the Protestant Ascendancy, with this life flaring out in one last efflorescence of intellectual and artistic leadership, a poem like "The Wild Swans at Coole" opens with a like stillness and mystery, in October twilight, against which the swans become eternal emblems of an aristocratic, social, and aesthetic order also visible in house and grounds. Who next would embody forth that interior world? And where?

This is the religion of a courtier.[125] As T. J. Kiernan, who observed Yeats at Coole, has written, the house was in part a cloister for him.[126] And Gogarty, no great friend of Lady Gregory's, puts Yeats's veneration this way:

> The house was magnified by his imagination into an ideal Irish mansion full of the courtliness of a century it may not have seen at all [of course it did]. His imagination endowed it with the traditions of the period he most admired, that century in which the Anglo-Irish mind flowered and "the salt of the earth", as he called them, enunciated opinions, liberal for their period and since unexcelled.[127]

If this is the historical and personal aura that inspired his imagination in Coole House, how did Yeats see its mistress? He saw her as the aristocrat and rebel combined. When one friend tried to sum up her being, he also described the possibility of both these impressions: ". . . hard masculinity and dominance . . . the chatelaine, the woman of gracious old-world manner." [128]

However irritating she might have been personally, Lady Gregory seemed to Yeats a mind built upon social and historical memories, a

125. It is worth noting that Yeats left a marker between those introductory pages of his copy of Hoby's *Book of the Courtier* where Walter Raleigh characterized the discourse of Bembo as the religion of the Renaissance. See Sir Thomas Hoby, *The Book of the Courtier*, with an Introduction by Walter Raleigh (London, 1900), pp. lxviii–lxix.

126. T. J. Kiernan, "Lady Gregory and W. B. Yeats," *Dalhousie Review*, XXXVIII (Autumn 1958), 296. See also the announcement of Yeats's visit in the *Tuam Herald*, 15 January 1898.

127. Oliver St. John Gogarty, *Rolling Down the Lea* (London, 1950), p. 74.

128. T. J. Kiernan, *Dalhousie Review*, XXXVIII, p. 298.

person morally bound to a patrician's code of honor. Without much gift for philosophy, lacking any extensive intellectual curiosity, she was personally humble and impersonally proud. Her great trait was faithfulness; her role, a servant's.[129] To Yeats she was also pre-eminently the aristocrat in the modern world who managed to stay in the vanguard of her time. In part, the fact that she did not own Coole but regarded it as an heirloom to be preserved and handed down had something to do with her alacrity. Though Yeats tended to skirt the family difficulties of her position in his poetry, he clearly saw them in his journals:

> Mrs. Gough when she was Robert Gregory's wife & since had wanted to abandon Coole, & make a home in London, whereas while Robert lived & so long as there seemed any chance that Richard might live in Ireland Lady Gregory would [have] thought it unthinkable that a Gregory should not be Gregory of Coole. She had watched over the house all her life, arranging the treasures, writing its records, she herself had added to its fame.[130]

Otherwise, Yeats chooses to write not so much of the peremptory nature of her nobility as of its control, its infectious nature, and its graciousness. But both sides inspired him.

Hence it is time to speak of the iron quality in her august determinations which had a great influence on Yeats, though at times her firmness may have downright scared him. For one thing, she did not fear to admit her delight that her husband's title, position, and influence made her own efforts for Ireland easier in a later day.[131] Nor did she ever disguise the fact that her early sympathies had lain with the Empire, nor that she retained a regard for those honorable men who had governed Ireland at the beginning of the nineteenth century.[132] Neither did she relinquish her family's absurd prejudice against her sister's marriage to a clergyman, a prejudice she dragged

129. *A Vision* (London, 1956), p. 169–70.
130. "The Death of Lady Gregory," large white vellum notebook begun 23 November 1930.
131. *Lady Gregory's Journals*, p. 245.
132. *Mr. Gregory's Letter-Box*, pp. 2, 289.

74

into the opening pages of her *Life* of Hugh Lane. She was also capable of openly saying to Yeats that she welcomed him at Coole, in this instance during April 1909, because he needed "a few days among normal & simple well-bred people. One always wants that from time to time as a rest to one's mind. They need not be clever. It is one of the reasons why I am going to Lady Laird's." [133] Frank O'Connor, Oliver Gogarty, Thomas Bodkin, Arthur Symons, and Maud Gonne had little good to say of her, as is well known. Even J. B. Yeats seems to have resented her. When Yeats recommended her as a candidate for the Senate in 1925, she was defeated 335 to 36. [134] However you looked at her, she was formidable. The story goes that she retired after lunch to give birth to her son and came down in time to pour tea for her guests. [135] After her death, a correspondent of the *Daily Express* wrote that "as a boy I saw her do a graceful slip jig at a feis while the rain poured down on the open platform." [136] In a predominantly Catholic country, she expressed little interest in the clergy at any time. She also held rigidly to Victorian propriety; for instance, a man might have a wandering eye for other ladies than his own, but a woman for other men—never. [137] As for perseverance, she used to encourage Abbey actors by stating, "Grip is a good dog, but Hold Fast a better." [138] Her courage was almost unbelievable. In his unpublished essay on her death Yeats writes, "I had been at Coole continually for a year, with the exception of brief periods when business called me away. Lady Gregory had never shown any lack of self control, neither moaning nor sighing when in pain, though once or twice when pain was at the worst I have noticed a little moisture on

---

133. Journal begun December 1908.

134. Frank O'Connor, *Leinster, Munster and Connaught* (London, 1950), pp. 237–38; Thomas Bodkin, *Tribute to Sir Hugh Lane* (Cork, 1961), p. 16; J. B. Yeats, *Letters to his son W. B. Yeats and others 1869–1922*, ed. Joseph Hone (London, 1944), pp. 211, 280–81; and *Lady Gregory's Journals*, p. 335.

135. Lennox Robinson, *The Irish Theatre* (London, 1939), p. 58.

136. "Fairy Godmother of the Irish Drama," *Dublin Daily Express*, 31 May 1932.

137. Information from Mrs. W. B. Yeats.

138. T. J. Kiernan, *Dalhousie Review*, XXXVIII, p. 300.

her cheeks," [139] She resolutely refused to take enough morphia, thinking it might blur her mind. Close to death, she had at first also refused to take to her bed, saying "that would be giving in." [140]

These bold instances serve as a prelude to the most obvious expression of her aristocratic will—her dictatorial manner in matters of art and theater. She may have been the charwoman of the Abbey Theatre, by Shaw's word, but she was also a severely authoritative one. This trait is certainly close to those habits of the Gregorys and Persses before her in Irish life and politics, who also had visions from which images grew.

Yeats may have been, at least before the death of Synge, more philosophic than Lady Gregory on middle-class Irish fear and hatred of excellence in the arts. As he wrote in his journal from which *Estrangement* was taken:

> The Irish public, which has been excited into an active state of democratic envy and jealousy, will not accept the pre-eminence of one or two writers—of Lady Gregory let us say—. In the present phase it dislikes, or rather the expressive part of it dislikes, all individual eminence. It lacks generosity. As soon as it has helped to raise any man or woman to a position of importance, it becomes jealous. O'Leary told me of that long ago. The feeling is increased when it recognizes in this individual, the free mind, the mind that plays with life & expresses great things lightly. [141]

One is well enough acquainted with Yeats's firm methods in running the Abbey. But the constant theme of hatred of democratic meddling with the arts runs just as powerfully, if not more powerfully, through *Our Irish Theatre* and the *Life* of Hugh Lane. [142] Lady Gregory easily matches Yeats in her audacity in delivering such opinions to the newspapers or even in scoffing, in the same vein, at the newspapers.

139. "The Death of Lady Gregory."
140. *Idem.*
141. Journal begun December 1908.
142. See, for instance, *Our Irish Theatre*, pp. 104, 113–14, 191–92, and *Hugh Lane*, pp. 62, 132.

Swift could not have done better. Here she is lauding Hugh Lane after the opening of the Municipal Art Gallery:

> This has been brought about by the imperious, uncompromising audacity of the youngest of Directors, Mr. Hugh Lane, whom not even a charge of nepotism can keep me from "the noble pleasure of praising."
> Ireland has no gift for compromise, and suffers often from the lack of it. But now and then she gains when some faculty is enabled to express itself with logical force through a single mind. Parnell did it in our day in politics, and it must surely be done in things of the spirit. "Sinn Fein"—we ourselves—is well enough for the day's bread, but is not "Mise Fein"—I myself—the last word in art? [143]

To set Parnell against Sinn Fein was arrogant enough. But her obstinacy before the public in the matter of the *Playboy*, a play she had no great love for, seems even more gaily grim:

> "We have already declared publicly this winter that, in the opinion of those conducting this theatre, it is the fiddler who chooses the tune. The public are quite at liberty to stay away, but if they come in, they must take what is provided for them. 'The Playboy' will be produced at the Abbey Theatre every night during the week, as originally arranged." [144]

This hardheaded attitude is epitomized in her letter to Arthur Sinclair commenting on his part in a recent play: "I don't know what you mean by a fiasco in Dublin. It got plenty of applause. The Freeman and Independent abused it, the Express and I[rish] Times praised it, but one never gives much heed to Dublin praise or blame." [145] The graciousness and patrician manners we had heard of, but, given this refreshing family arrogance, wherein do we find the nationalist rebel?

143. "Modern Art in Ireland," *Tuam Herald*, 8 February 1908.
144. Clipping from the *Evening Telegraph*, 19 May 1909, in Henderson, III (1909), Natl. Lib. MS. 1732, p. 86.
145. Letter dated 25 April 1915 in Holloway, Natl. Lib. MS. 1821 (April–June 1915), opp. p. 1039.

Again, farfetched as it may seem, the eighteenth century may offer an answer. Here, perhaps, lies the quintessence of her aristocratic heart. One thinks of Grattan and Burke, or earlier Swift, or even Molyneux before them, as on occasion the strongly refractory, aristocratic Protestant type. Perhaps the best example is Lord Edward Fitzgerald, pre-eminently the aristocratic rebel in late eighteenth-century Ireland. As Yeats said of her in 1936, "Lady Gregory never rebelled like other Irish women I have known, who consumed themselves and their friends; in spite of Scripture she put the new wine into the old bottles. Perhaps it was the New Testament that started the bad habit of breaking them." [146] Thus while friends like Lady Ardilaun might lament the passing of the Anglo-Irish importance in Irish life, Lady Gregory tried to maintain the old forms and never faltered in striving to lead and stay abreast of the new Ireland. She was inevitably on the side of the people.[147] Fearless, she nevertheless held to long-term goals and prudent action in fighting for her principles. On this point, Yeats described her to Clement Shorter in 1917:

> Please be careful with the Rebellion poem. Lady Gregory asked me not to send it you until we had finished our dispute with the authorities about the Lane pictures. She was afraid of it getting about & damaging us & she is not timid.[148]

When Yeats first met Lady Gregory she was a Unionist and had written a pamphlet against Gladstone's Home Rule Bill.[149] Nor was Yeats always above criticizing her political friends of those years.[150] Yet she soon changed, due seemingly to her growing love of Celtic Ireland, her concern for Kiltartan's poor, and her translations of ancient heroic Irish myths and tales. She provided some of the imagery and such memorable phrases as the famous "They shall be

---

146. *Letters,* p. 855.
147. *Lady Gregory's Journals,* pp. 41, 221–24.
148. Unpublished letter dated 28 March [1917] in the Berg Collection of the New York Public Library. Reprinted with permission.
149. "Autobiography."
150. *Letters,* p. 684.

remembered for ever" in Yeats's patriotic *Cathleen Ni Houlihan,* as even *An Phoblacht* was later happy to admit.[151] Nor could she help contrasting the commercialism of England's triumphant progress with the spirituality and idealism of the defeated Irish. For a woman of letters the appeal must have been undeniable. In 1900, looking back on the many sacrifices among Ireland's patriots, she wrote:

> In Ireland he [the poet] is in touch with a people whose thoughts have long been dwelling on an idea; whose heroes have been the failures, the men "who went out to battle and who always fell," who went out to a battle that was already lost —men who, whatever may have been their mistakes or faults, had an aim quite apart from personal greed or gain.[152]

If she felt the Rising a mistake, she grieved for the leaders whom she had known at the Abbey.[153] During Black and Tan times, she refused to hug the pavement during an ambush and instead remained standing and shouted "Up the Rebels." During an exchange of gunfire, she climbed her seat on a stopped tram, clapped her hands, and sang rebel songs.[154] In submitting anonymously to the *Nation* parts of her diary during this period, she fixes the reader's eye upon the horrors done among her people by representatives of the British crown—the murder of Mrs. Quinn, the brutal floggings in Gort, and the savage killing of the Loughnane boys.[155] Later in her review of Frank Gallagher's *Days of Fear,* she fell back on her own anguished reactions to the hunger strike in Montjoy in 1920 and called his book

---

151. "The Late Lady Gregory," *An Phoblacht,* 28 May 1932, p. 5.

152. "The Felons of Our Land," *Cornhill Magazine,* LXXXI (May 1900), 634. Throughout this article, Lady Gregory eulogizes "the moving failure of Irish rebels" such as Lord Edward, Emmet, Tone, O'Connell, Kickham, Mitchel, the Manchester Martyrs, and others.

153. Vere Gregory, *The House of Gregory,* p. 89.

154. Robinson, *The Irish Theatre,* pp. 58–59; "Lady Gregory and the Lane Pictures," *Dublin Daily Express,* 22 March 1930.

155. "A Week in Ireland," *Nation,* XXVIII (16 October 1920), 63–64. In the same volume, see also "Another Week in Ireland," 23 October 1920, pp. 123–24; "Murder by the Throat," 13 November 1920, pp. 215–16; "A Third Week in Ireland," 4 December 1920, p. 333; "A Fourth Week in Ireland," 18 December 1920, pp. 413–14; and "A Fifth Week in Ireland," 1 January 1921, pp. 472–73.

"a beautiful, heart-rending book." [156] She understood men who gave themselves selflessly to their country.

But, as Yeats said, she was never the fanatic or the extremist. During the Civil War the Republicans had her sympathy, and she called herself a Republican "without malice" in 1923, though she refrained from voting for them because she had "no surety they will cease doing violence." In 1922 she had remarked on the frequent greed and covetousness behind much Republican idealism. Like Yeats she wanted the Oath removed so that the Republicans could be brought into the government.[157] Yet by 1927 she voted for Cosgrave's government because it seemed the more just cause.[158]

For Yeats, then, she was Lady Gregory of Coole, a completely self-possessed woman who sought the obligations due her position and necessitated by her character through "a choice constantly renewed in solitude." [159] After her death he remembered her more in the social world than in the artist's, since she saw the world as comedy rather than as tragedy.[160] Be that as it may, her vision was close to his: a unified Ireland restored to its ancient dignity in the world. She wanted the best for Ireland.[161] Both saw this in the Lane pictures. Behind their efforts in the Abbey lay the same motive; speaking in Italy in his seventieth year, Yeats made the point clear:

> Lady Gregory, John Synge and I were in some sense typical of an Ireland that was passing away. The Ireland of what the historians call "the Protestant Ascendancy," and it was right that we should give to the new Catholic Ireland that was about to take its place, a parting gift, the Irish National Theatre.[162]

Both she and Yeats freely acknowledged their tradition, that of Protestant Ireland.[163] Yet both hoped to see it as part of a larger

156. "Days of Fear," *Nation and Athenaeum*, XLIV (15 December 1928), 422.

157. *Lady Gregory's Journals*, pp. 23, 26, 179, 188–89.

158. *Coole*, pp. 12–13.

159. *Autobiographies*, p. 395.

160. "The Death of Lady Gregory."

161. "Americans and the Art Gallery," *Irish Times*, 8 September 1913.

162. *The Irish National Theatre* (Rome, 1935), p. 8.

163. *Lady Gregory's Journals*, p. 265.

flourishing unity, one Ireland. That was her penultimate vision as an image-maker.

So, at least, she had seen Lane's Gallery-to-be:

> . . . lately, to Hugh's own memory, and as a symbol of ultimate reconcilement, a friend who had stood by him through all his work for the Gallery has given and put up there portraits of John Redmond and Edward Carson, those stout fighters for South and North.[164]

In 1898 her hopes were set on the reforestation of Ireland. Again, her appeal was aimed at all sides: "I wish that every Nationalist would plant at least one tree in this year of '98, and every Unionist in 1900, and every waverer or indifferent person in the year that separates them."[165] She was quick to show her tenants books and papers that had once belonged to Lord Edward and that showed his attachment to the native Irish.[166] She was just as quick to point out her portrait of another patriot, Daniel O'Connell.[167] In 1913, she saw as one major purpose of the Abbey Theatre the preparation of all Ireland for Home Rule.[168] Her play *The Wrens* reflects on the foolish split that led to the ruinous Union of 1800 as directly relevant to the possible national split over the Treaty with England in 1921–22.[169] Her life was marked by remembered images of her vision:

> [McDonough] was the best of all the wandering pipers, who went about from house to house. When, at my marriage, I moved from the barony of Dunkellin to the neighboring barony of Kiltartan, he came and played at the dance given to the tenants in my honour, and he came and played also at my son's coming of age.[170]

Who can say—even now—that she has failed?

164. *Hugh Lane*, p. 77.
165. Announcement in the *Tuam Herald*, 12 March 1898.
166. "Lady Gregory and the Land Question," *Tuam Herald*, 4 October 1902.
167. *Our Irish Theatre*, p. 198.
168. "Galway Races," *Evening Herald*, 8 April 1913.
169. *The Image and Other Plays* (New York, 1922), p. 253.
170. *New Comedies* (New York, 1913), p. 163.

VI

T. R. Henn has written movingly of the sudden flare-out of Protestant Ireland between the years of 1916 and 1923.[171] If we extend the period slightly, we do so to include the deaths of Synge, John Shawe-Taylor, and Sir Hugh Lane with Robert Gregory's on the one hand, and, on the other, to close the period for Yeats with the death of Lady Gregory and his prophecy of the destruction of Coole. Oddly enough, it was during this period that Yeats loved most the Protestant eighteenth century and tried hardest to rally Ireland to some regard for its importance. After his death, with the wanton destruction of Coole, there came to an end Ireland's finest living memorial to a class, an attitude toward life, and an ideal of service.

Yeats had long seen it coming. He had marked the drift of affairs at Coole as early as 1909:

> I thought of this house slowly perpetuating itself & the life within it, in ever increasing intensity of labour & then of its probably sinking away through courteous incompetence or rather sheer weakness of will for ability has not failed in young Gregory, and I said to myself, "Why is life a perpetual preparation for something that never happens?" Even an Odysseus only seems a preparation to think of ruin or remembrance. Is it not always the tragedy of the great and the strong, that they see before the end the small & the weak, in friendship or in enmity, pushing them from their place, & marring what they have built, & doing one or the other in mere lightness of mind.[172]

As early as 1920 he had begun to ponder the vanishing of great literary houses. Although he wrote to urge the preservation of Keats's house in Hampstead, in this instance, we also hear reference

171. T. R. Henn, *The Lonely Tower* (London, 1950), p. 10.
172. Journal begun December 1908. This passage is dated 6 September [1909].

to his future poems "Coole Park, 1929," and "Coole Park and Ballylee, 1931" in these words to Dr. Williamson:

> Of course I am altogether in favour of your project, and if Keats's house goes a great part of the charm of Hampstead, for many men and women, will go too; and with every passing year the charm grows of a house with an association so imaginative. The house comes to represent not only the great man who lived there, but a form of social life that becomes strange and romantic as it fades into the distance.[173]

Yeats's doubts on the continuation of the house of Gregory also came early. After the war, he had marked down Robert as the lonely, virtually rootless artist in "Shepherd and Goatherd"; he had voiced his doubts about the future of Coole in "Ancestral Houses"; and he had little faith in the later Lough Cutra connection.[174] Lady Gregory was prepared to accept the fact that the days of great estates and landed property had disappeared in Ireland, even though she hoped that a Gregory might preserve Coole.[175] But Yeats saw deeper. He saw the passing of excellence, glory, grandeur, call the quality what you will, in Irish life. He hated that passing. As Gogarty tells us, "Yeats was well aware of this toleration of ruin in the heart of the natives. He knew that they would preserve nothing if left to themselves. He knew that out of their perpetual preoccupation with the past came a desire to make all grandeur portion and parcel of that Past." [176] After Lady Gregory's death, Albert Power wandered from room to room in Coole House, casting his eyes on the Georgian memorials of those the Gregorys had served, and then stopped for a moment before saying to Yeats, "All the nobility of earth." [177] Yeats understood; his aim had been theirs: to extend that nobility to all

---

173. "A Letter from W. B. Yeats," *The John Keats Memorial Volume* (London, 1921), p. 216.
174. Unpublished letter to Ethel Mannin dated 1 February 1934, in the Sligo public library.
175. *Lady Gregory's Journals*, p. 340.
176. *Rolling Down the Lea*, p. 144.
177. *Letters*, pp. 795–96, and "The Death of Lady Gregory."

Ireland. And so it was that he turned full-throated to celebrate that century and class from which the Gregorys sprang. For his comment on Power's words reads: "I felt he did not mean it for that room alone but for lost tradition. How much of my own verse has not been but the repetition of those words." [178]

178. *Letters*, p. 796.

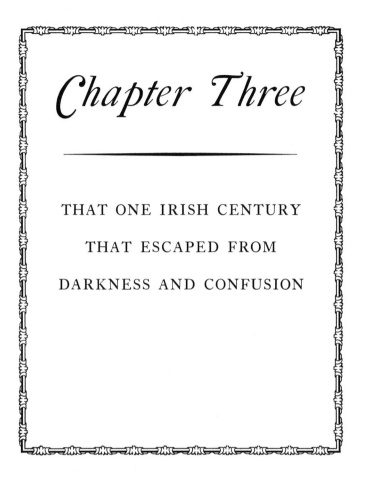

Chapter Three

THAT ONE IRISH CENTURY

THAT ESCAPED FROM

DARKNESS AND CONFUSION

I

WITH THE ESTABLISHMENT of the Free State, Yeats recognized that at long last the artist in Ireland had been freed from his insistent preoccupation with being Irish. At long last he could devote himself entirely to his work.[1] Looking back some ten years, Yeats reviewed how he had then also turned wholeheartedly to the eighteenth century to seek traditions of intellect and government for the new state and, just as importantly, to remind the hesitant twentieth-century Anglo-Irish of the essential

1. "Ireland, 1921–1931," *Spectator*, 30 January 1932, p. 137.

Irish patriotism of Protestant leaders like Swift and Grattan. This turn, its source in his friendship with the Gregorys and Synge, and the new array of authors and ideas he pursued—all these are recorded in the exuberant pages of his essay, "Ireland, 1921–1931." Its central portion is crucial to this argument:

Freedom from obsession brought me a transformation akin to religious conversion. I had thought much of my fellow-workers —Synge, Lady Gregory, Lane—but had seen nothing in Protestant Ireland as a whole but its faults, had carried through my projects in face of its opposition or its indifference, had fed my imagination upon the legends of the Catholic villages or upon Irish mediaeval poetry; but now my affection turned to my own people, to my own ancestors, to the books they had read. It seemed we had a part to play at last that might find us allies everywhere, for we alone had not to assume in public discussion of all great issues that we could find in St. Mark or St. Matthew a shorthand report of the words of Christ attested before a magistrate. . . . Now that Ireland was substituting traditions of government for the rhetoric of agitation our eighteenth century had regained its importance. An Irish Free State soldier, engaged in dangerous service for his Government, said to me that all the philosophy a man needed was in Berkeley. Stirred by those words I began to read *The Dialogues of Hylas and Philonous*. From Berkeley I went to Swift, whose hold on Irish imagination is comparable to that of O'Connell. The Protestant representatives in Dail and Senate were worthy of this past; two or three went in danger of their lives; some had their houses burnt; country gentlemen came from the blackened ruins of their houses to continue without melodrama or complaint some perhaps highly technical debate in the Senate. Month by month their prestige rose. When the censorship of books was proposed certain Protestant Bishops disassociated themselves from it, and had the Government persisted with the Bill in its first form and penalized opinion we might have had a declaration, perhaps from the Episcopacy as a whole, that private judgement implied access to the materials of judgement. Then, just when we seemed a public necessity, our Episcopacy

86

lost its head. Without consulting its representatives in Dail or Senate, without a mandate from anybody, in the teeth of a refusal of support from Trinity College, terrified where none threatened, it appealed, not to the Irish people, but to the Colonial Conference, to keep the Irish Courts in subordination to the Privy Council, thereby seeming to declare that our ancestors made the independence of the legislature and the Courts the foundation of their politics, and of Ireland's from that day, because those Courts and that legislature protected not a nation but a class. When these blind old men turned their backs upon Swift and Grattan, at a moment too when the past actions of the Colonial Conference itself had already decided the issue, they had forgotten, one hopes, or had never learnt, that their predecessors sat in the Irish House of Lords of 1719, when it sent the Irish Court of Exchequer to prison for accepting a decision of that Privy Council.[2]

A question at once arises. Who were the Anglo-Irish, historically speaking, from the Battle of the Boyne down to the founding of the Free State? Until now, a general understanding of the term has been good enough. But now that we are following Yeats's growing concept or myth or fixed idea of the Anglo-Irish—something of all three are involved—it is time to get a glimpse of what he could include or work with. For this purpose, an excellent definition was formulated by Hugh A. Law in 1929:

> . . . whom do we mean by the Anglo-Irish? Note that the name was not chosen by those of whom I speak. *They* have been content, and commonly proud, to call themselves simply "Irish." But that word has of late been so much used as a synonym for "Gaelic" that, for the sake of clearness and convenience, some distinction had to be made in speaking of one particular body of Irish citizens. Very roughly then the term is taken to denote a well-known, though never accurately defined, section of our people, differing from the rest very little in blood (since for centuries past we have been, all of us, of mixed race) —but differing more or less widely in religious belief, or in

2. *Ibid.,* pp. 137–38.

social habits or in political associations, and not infrequently in all three. Endless exceptions must be made; but for our present purpose it may be assumed that the typical Anglo-Irishman is Protestant in faith, has some connection with the land-owning class as it existed here from the end of the 17th to the end of the 19th century, and cherishes family traditions of service to the Crown of these islands.[3]

The first point, then, is that the Anglo-Irish include those who designated themselves the "Irish interest" in Swift's time and who, well into Yeats's own boyhood, identified themselves—even though part of the nineteenth-century Garrison—with Ireland. Swift was being characteristic of his class when he dryly observed the "English colonies" in Ireland to be "much more civilized than many counties in England, and speak better English, and are much better bred."[4] It was no less characteristic that Synge's famous ancestor, the Archbishop of Tuam, should have defended the Catholics in a sermon before the Irish House of Commons in 1725.[5] Nor is Yeats any less himself in remarking of his youth: "Everyone I knew well is Sligo despised the Nationalists and Catholics, but all disliked England with a prejudice that had come down perhaps from the days of the Irish Parliament."[6] And all would have probably agreed that no small part of this disdain for England rested in her supposed vulgarity.[7]

It was in the 1880's, with the rise of the Land League, that the term Anglo-Irish came into generally opprobrious use; so much so that the Irishman of English ancestry frequently fell a sacrificial victim— by virtue of his name or ancestry alone—to the rigors of the new

3. Hugh A. Law, "The Anglo-Irish," *Irish Statesman,* 17 August 1929, p. 467. See also "The Anglo-Irish Tradition," *Irish Statesman,* 15 December 1928, pp. 289–90. Yeats had been from his youth familiar enough with the histories of eighteenth-century Ireland by Froude and Lecky. See *Letters to the New Island,* ed. Horace Reynolds (Cambridge, Mass., 1934), p. 90, and "The Thirty Best Irish Books," *United Ireland,* 16 March 1895.

4. Swift, *Works,* ed. Sheridan (London, 1784), XIV, 195.

5. David H. Greene and Edward M. Stephens, *J. M. Synge 1871–1909* (New York, 1959), p. 1.

6. *Autobiographies,* pp. 33–34.

7. Oliver St. John Gogarty, *Mourning Becomes Mrs. Spendlove* (New York, 1948), pp. 211–24.

nationalism.[8] Captain John Shawe-Taylor, as we have seen, may be counted one severe example. Many a professional peasant or Dubliner, of course, has seen the distinction as but a silly myth of social snobbery.[9] Yet it seems, despite the disclaimers of Denis Ireland,[10] that Shaw put his finger once and for all on the dangers of this nationalistic denial of Protestant Irish worth when he had Larry Boyle rebuke Matthew in the third act of *John Bull's Other Island* thus:

> Do you think, because youre poor and ignorant and half-crazy with toiling and moiling morning noon and night, that youll be any less greedy and oppressive to them that have no land at all than old Nick Lestrange, who was an educated travelled gentleman that could not have been tempted as hard by a hundred pounds as youd be by five shillings? Nick was too high above Patsy Farrell to be jealous of him; but you, that are only one step above him, would die sooner than let him come up that step; and well you know it.

Part of Yeats's insistent iteration that Protestant Ireland's eighteenth century was once again important lay in the fact that the Lestranges had been altogether too acquiescent to the shrill demands of the Gael since the Union, had in fact become too preoccupied with England; yet, for all their separation from public life, still possessed a genius, mournful as that separation made it.[11]

But what attracted Yeats most in eighteenth-century Protestant Ireland was more an attitude or quality of intellect than any necessary class distinction. Whatever the provenance, the mind Yeats celebrated was like that of the Irish airman—capable of selfless, independent choice. Yeats himself, on the evidence of a genealogical-minded cousin, acknowledged his family to have been never more

---

8. David H. Greene, "Synge and the Irish," *Colby Library Bulletin*, Series IV (February 1957), p. 159.

9. See, for instance, *Brendan Behan's Ireland* (New York, 1962), p. 18.

10. Denis Ireland, "Fog in the Irish Sea," *Threshold*, V (Autumn–Winter 1961–62), 65–67.

11. Yeats probably knew well John Eglinton's sympathetic attempt to define that genius in the opening pages of *Anglo-Irish Essays* (Dublin, 1917).

than small gentry at best.[12] Land was not the measure of intellect. Joseph Hone, among his friends, tirelessly reminded the modern Gaelic detractors of the Anglo-Irish that

> The term Anglo-Irish has . . . some value of convenience, but is misleading in many ways, especially as used by political and religious propagandists, who wish to discredit the great figures of Protestant (episcopalian) Ireland by identifying them with the Plantations and so with records of confiscation and oppression. In fact, landlordry, whether Norman, Cromwellian or mixed Irish, can claim credit for comparatively few of Ireland's famous sons. Neither Swift nor Berkeley was born in a great house; Goldsmith came from a country rectory; Burke was the son of a lawyer, Wolfe Tone of a coachmaker; Grattan's father was a Recorder, Thomas Davis's an Army surgeon; Bernard Shaw's ancestor was a lawyer in Kilkenny; and these men were not only born in Ireland but educated there, not at Eton, Oxford and Cambridge, where since the seventeenth century Irish rank and riches have chiefly sent their young.[13]

However boastful Yeats's later reminder to his countrymen that the Anglo-Irish had "created nearly all the literature of modern Ireland and most of its political intelligence" may have sounded, it also tellingly underlined what he chose to single out in "the people of Burke and of Swift . . . of Grattan, of Emmet, of Parnell"[14] for modern contemplation.

Taking off from this considered outburst, which Yeats read aloud in the Irish Senate, I shall investigate in this chapter his deepest familial ties to that eighteenth century and stock, and take a second look at the breadth of spirit and intellect he so much admired in them. Anglo-Ireland also presented itself to Yeats in Georgian memorials in

12. *Wheels and Butterflies*, p. 10, n. 1. This cousin was probably Dr. Francis Butler Yeats of Dunliam, Quebec. See his obituary in the *Irish Independent*, 19 February 1923.

13. J. B. Yeats, *Letters to his son W. B. Yeats and others 1869–1922*, ed. Joseph Hone (London, 1944), p. 23. See also "The Anglo-Irish Strain," *Bell*, II (September 1941), 25, and Hone's "Edmund Burke," *Envoy*, II (April 1950), 26–27.

14. *Senate Speeches*, p. 99.

Dublin and elsewhere. These memorials somehow embodied that spirit and raised his hopes for the resurgence of Protestant genius or ideals in the new, democratic Ireland. Nor must we forget the heavy attacks he came under for such outrageous presumption. Concluding with a calculated anticlimax, I shall try to place the whole subject in final perspective by showing Yeats's continual qualification of his oneness with Protestant Ireland by his relegating her brilliant past to something distinctly second to his absorption in Ireland's peasant lore and tales.

II

In January 1909, Lady Gregory gave Yeats a book designed to aid him in making out a family tree, a task dutifully undertaken by his sister Lily.[15] Yeats's mounting interest in things genealogical soon after brought him to search for the family coat of arms.[16] At a séance in 1912 he was told by a voice from the eighteenth century, "I have been with you from childhood. We want to use your hand and brain. You have the key," or "You are a key mind." [17] He began taking pride in the fact that he had ancestors that had taken a prominent role or flourished in the Dublin of Swift and Grattan. He liked to puzzle over the distant Mary Voisin who might have been a friend of Archbishop King. The name Butler might also link him to one of the great Anglo-Irish families. There had also been a Yeats who won the Bishop Berkeley medal for Greek at Trinity. And there was Uncle Beattie, who, though no blood relative, had been a friend of Goldsmith. The eighteenth-century miniatures of this uncle and of Yeats's great-great-grandfather, Benjamin Yeats, moved him most. For the one urged the boldness and wildness of the century, and the other, the likeness of his distant ancestor, hinted a charm that made his own person seem gauche.[18] Later, Yeats was able to rejoice unblushingly in all these ancestors who served their country well or

15. *Letters*, p. 524.
16. Journal begun December 1908.
17. *Idem.*
18. *Autobiographies*, pp. 22–23. See also Hone, pp. 1–3.

who were linked to power in Ireland—be it the force of Major Sirr or the energy of Robert Emmet.[19]

Perhaps just as powerful a reminder of Yeatsian roots in that century was to be found in his father. So many of J. B. Yeats's predilections smacked of that period. For J. B. Yeats, a gentleman was a man who had "not the doctrine of getting on and the habit of it." He might praise Lamb for accepting life with humor and serenity—"in the manner of the eighteenth century." Then he could add, in the same letter to Ruth Hart, "I had a lot of 18th century relations whom I remember perfectly—and to read Lamb is to be back once more in their company." He urged on his son both the courage and pride—traits long vanished in the arts—of eighteenth-century artists like Fielding, Hogarth, or Gainsborough. No less, he commended to him the "charm and urbanity of the Irish Protestant of the eighteenth century" that he sensed were still alive in the American descendants of Robert Emmet. Customarily, his loyalty to that century and its art burst forth when he berated Sinn Fein for the destruction of the Custom House in 1921: ". . . not loving Ireland they don't mind if they destroy a building like the Custom House, built though it was during those twenty years from 1780 to 1800, when Ireland had her own government and held her own course."[20]

His pride of family entered no less strikingly into his love of the period. J. B. Yeats remembered his grandmother's often speaking of late eighteenth-century Ireland. He gloried in Uncle Beattie and his friendships with Bishop Percy, Johnson, and Goldsmith. But his dearest memories seem to have been of his uncle, Robert Corbet, owner of the eighteenth-century house, Sandymount Castle, unfortunately festooned later on with Walter Scott Gothic effects.[21] The memory and quality of this relative made an indelible impression:

> When I left school I entered Trinity College, and for the next four or five years the man most dominant in my life was my

19. *Autobiographies*, pp. 20–22.
20. J. B. Yeats, *Letters to his son*, pp. 27, 101, 109, 112–13, 145, 183, 276–77, 282.
21. *Ibid.*, pp. 27, 241, 267.

uncle Robert Corbet. I think of my poor uncle as a man of generous impulses who lived up to his creed of being a gentleman, a worldling and a club man, nor did he forget that he was a citizen of Dublin, and of the type that flourished in the eighteenth century. If he suspected his Catholic neighbours, all the same he liked them; and if he had a certain respect for Englishmen, no less he disliked them. Before I was born, he bought or leased . . . Sandymount Castle, and then began creating all around him beautiful gardens. Of business he knew little or nothing, and probably neglected it, but he did not neglect his gardens. . . . He employed four or five gardeners . . . none of these men ever left him and no one ever interfered with them. So treated, they were gentle, pleasant and diligent, and the gardens were lovely.[22]

From his ancestors, his father, and then from Sandymount Castle and the Sligo of his childhood came a voice whose tone and source spoke to Yeats of past Protestant glory in Ireland. He suspected that Lionel Johnson's success in reading his lectures in those days derived from the fact that all "Ireland had still the shape it had received from the eighteenth century, and so felt the dignity, not the artifice, of his elaborate periods." [23] The century breathed all around him as a boy: the "brawling squireen" in Castle Dargan; the "bleak eighteenth-century house" that served as the high school for him in Harcourt Street; his father's studio in York Street with its "beautiful eighteenth-century mantelpiece." [24] The very names Gore-Booth, Wynn, Cooper, and Ormsby whispered of that era. Whatever his early literary biases may have destined for him, the eighteenth century at its worst and otherwise can never be said to have died in Yeats.

III

The Battle of the Boyne overwhelmed a civilization full of religion and myth, and brought in its place intelligible laws

22. John Butler Yeats, *Early Memories* (Dundrum, 1923), pp. 54–55.
23. *Autobiographies*, p. 222.
24. *Ibid.*, pp. 53, 56, 64–65.

planned out upon a great blackboard, a capacity for horizontal lines, for rigid shapes, for buildings, for attitudes of mind that could be multiplied like an expanding bookcase: the modern world, and something that appeared and perished in its dawn, an instinct for Roman rhetoric, Roman elegance. It established a Protestant aristocracy, some of whom neither called themselves English nor looked with contempt or dread upon conquered Ireland.[25]

A greatness of spirit, a capacity for leadership—and an elegance that mirrored both—adorned that civilization, as Yeats goes on to extol it in this essay introducing his play *The Words Upon the Window-pane*. The spirit was marked by that paradox he looked for in his ideal modern reader, one who could appreciate a poem "cold and passionate as the dawn." Just as germane was the mark of the Gregory tradition at Coole, where "passion and precision" were one. These, the strengths of scholar and duelist combined, came out of an Ireland that shamed the Ireland of Synge's time and three generations before where "everything is argued over, everything has to take its trial before the dull sense and the hasty judgment." [26]

This spirit—a power of style or cast of mind, usually so lamentably absent in the Ireland of Synge—included a large element of fantasy which all Irishmen shared: "The duellists at the end of the eighteenth century had it. There was fantasy in the man who made the bet that 'within a year he would play ball against the walls of Jerusalem.' " [27] The gaiety and gallantry that accompanied Irish fantasy Yeats saw come down from that century of duelists to his own in the hair-trigger epigrams, paradoxes, and cleverness of Wilde.[28] He and his family showed how tightly wound learning and imagination might be.[29] Yeats told Gogarty that Wilde had rejected the yacht

---

25. *Wheels and Butterflies*, pp. 10–11.

26. "J. M. Synge and the Ireland of his Time," *Essays and Introductions*, pp. 323–24.

27. Robert Lynd, "The Irish Theatre. An Interview with Mr. W. B. Yeats," *Daily News*, 6 June 1910.

28. "Oscar Wilde's Last Book," *United Ireland*, 26 September 1891.

29. *Autobiographies*, p. 138.

meant for his escape "because he had in him the old duelling spirit of the Bucks of the Eighteenth Century." [30] As a matter of fact, Yeats also put Gogarty in the same tradition, though admitting of himself, "Irish by tradition and many ancestors, I love, though I have nothing to offer but the philosophy they deride, swashbucklers, horsemen, swift indifferent men. . . ." [31]

But the other side of the paradox also had to be present. Yeats appreciated the "old historical passion" of the West of Ireland most when it accompanied a decision and idealism that he praised in Emmet, a quality in a selfless spirit usually wasted on the Irish people, a high style of life and death for which Yeats thought the people unworthy even in 1798.[32] High style made an age.[33] Again, with Emmet in mind, he once declared, "All work which is done without selfishness for something beyond one's self has moral beauty." [34] This selfless idealism and precision of mind he caught in the daring speculation of Rowan Hamilton,[35] and even in what he came to acknowledge as "the free eighteenth century air of Dublin University." [36] This side of the paradox Yeats caught not only in an Emmet, a Wilde, or a Gogarty but also in its embodiment, the Royal Irish Academy, one more intellectual gift from the Protestant nation.[37] Yet the mind had passed that was liberal, expressed itself in

30. "Three Impressions," *The Arrow* (Summer 1939), p. 19.

31. TS. of "Modern Poetry," BBC broadcast, 11 October 1936, 9.05–9.50 P.M.

32. "W. B. Yeats and Robert Emmet," *Evening Herald*, 28 February 1914. The reporter of this speech writes that Yeats "dwelt on the well-known incidents in the movement in which Emmet took such a prominent and heroic part, and said that the failure of Emmet was due to the circumstances of his time—the circumstances were against him, and the people were not worthy of Robert Emmet." Yeats concluded his performance by reading Emmet's speech from the dock.

33. Yeats admired this sentence in Leo Frobenius' *The Voice of Africa*, trans. Rudolf Blind (London, 1913), I, 337–38: "The great ages of universal history are not measured by the duration of their years, but by their style" (Notebook E).

34. "Events," *Samhain*, No. 7 (November 1908), p. 5.

35. "Compulsory Gaelic," *Irish Statesman*, 2 August 1924, p. 650.

36. *Yeats and T. Sturge Moore*, p. 149.

37. "A General Introduction for My Work," *Essays and Introductions*, p. 511.

stately English, and took personal ecstasy in combat, intellectual or physical.[38] Its place had been taken by an opposite attitude from the rank and file of the nineteenth century:

> . . . there was a revulsion not only against the idealism of Grattan's volunteers but also against the easy lavish ways, the liberal speculation, the generous acknowledgment of the right to think otherwise, which had been characteristic. . . . The educated 18th century gentleman was not averse to experiment in politics, religion, morals . . . he was uninfluenced by those two solemn considerations that weighed so heavily on a later age: "What will the neighbours think?" and "What would happen if my tenants got hold of these ideas?"[39]

These gentlemen had performed superbly as magistrates and administrators, if the Sligo Cooper family was any evidence.[40] The occasionally arbitrary side of the best of them probably reflected the times in Europe as a whole before the French Revolution.[41] These Irishmen were usually in the best of spirits during adversity. Gogarty compared them with the best people in Europe, finding a cheerfulness, courage, and refusal to accept defeat that made their administrative brains unmatched.[42] As Richard Lovell Edgeworth put it, people generally "cheated, loved, and despised a mere *easy* landlord."[43] A firm administrator would make no distinction between his tenants on religious grounds; he might raise a corps of troops made up of both Protestants and Catholics; as a Unionist he might also vote against

38. "Lionel Johnson," *A Treasury of Irish Poetry*, eds. Stopford A. Brooke and T. W. Rolleston (London, 1900), p. 467.

39. Hubert Butler, "The Country House—The Life of the Gentry," *Social Life in Ireland 1800–45*, ed. R. B. McDowell (Dublin, 1957), p. 34.

40. *Wheels and Butterflies*, p. 10, n. 1.

41. See, for instance, W. H. Maxwell, *Wild Sports of the West*, ed. the Rt. Hon. Earl of Dunraven (London, Dublin, and Belfast, n.d.), p. 381. When Richard Lovell Edgeworth knocked down a carter who refused to move out of his lady friend's path, he was coolly received for some time by his French friends for not killing the man on the spot. See *Memoirs of . . . Edgeworth* (London, 1820), I, 314–15.

42. Oliver St. John Gogarty, *Rolling Down the Lea* (London, 1950), pp. 100–1.

43. *Memoirs*, II, 31.

the Union, since it did not represent the true will of Ireland. All these Edgeworth did.[44] In towns like Galway, where a system based on the clan or tribe still lingered, a commercial aristocracy reminiscent of the great mercantile families in Italy and Hanseatic Germany held sway. Yet, in this essentially rural Ireland of the West, where the King's writ meant little, where a Protestant gentry was above the law and a Catholic peasantry was without it, there was wildness, barbarity, and brutality.[45] Yet it remains a moot question whether succeeding times were any more moral or happy.[46] In any case, this world of master and man, of devotion on one side and protection on the other—so very abhorrent to us today—Yeats once compared to the American South before the Civil War, a time when wise men could still dispense justice and guide their followers in "a cultivated and leisurely life long passed away." [47]

IV

The monuments to this spirit were the country houses of Georgian Ireland, the gracious streets, the squares, the memorials, the paintings, and the stunning interior decorations, in plaster and wood, of

44. *Ibid.*, II, 148, 212, 246–49, 368–69.
45. Oliver J. Burke, *Anecdotes of the Connaught Circuit* (Dublin, 1885), p. 6. See also Philip H. Bagenal, *Vicissitudes of an Anglo-Irish Family 1530–1800* (London, 1925), p. 149.
46. See, for instance, Stephen Gwynn's account of eighteenth-century Galway in *The Famous Cities of Ireland* (Dublin and London, 1915), pp. 93–95; this praise of Ireland before the Union is perhaps the sole theme of a book dear to Yeats, *Recollections of Jonah Barrington* (Dublin, n.d.). J. J. Hogan, "W. B. Yeats," *Studies*, XXVIII (1939), 38, describes Yeats as "an Anglo-Irish gentleman turned poet, and his verses too keep time with outdoor and active life. Yeats is Sir Lucius O'Trigger and Jack Hinton, and Jonah Barrington, and Buck Whaley, rising at last to poetry, as it were in their swan-song. His code is to praise pride of family, boldness in war and sport, carelessness of cost, the ready meeting of pain and death; and when he adds fine taste and manners, ceremony and the arts, he is still in an eighteenth century tradition." Of course most Irish critics saw this as a renunciation of Ireland. See, for instance, in the same volume of *Studies*, Mary M. Macken, "W. B. Yeats, John O'Leary and the Contemporary Club," pp. 141–42.
47. TS. of "Poems about Women," BBC broadcast, 10 April 1932, 9.05–9.30 P.M.

Georgian Dublin. All formed a silent memento to a past greatness, especially the days of Grattan's Parliament. And even here, Yeats had his favorites. Ely Place, where dwelt Buck Gogarty, delighted him. At one time or another, Yeats had houses or flats in such stylish eighteenth-century squares as St. Stephen's Green, Fitzwilliam Square, and Merrion Square. When walking from 82 Merrion Square to the Senate Chamber, he would pass his favorite Georgian reminder, the little fountain gracefully attached to the Rutland Memorial on the west side of the Square. The Bank of Ireland, formerly the old Parliament House, impressed him mightily. So did the Royal Hospital at Kilmainham and the exquisite ceiling in Adam style of the present Senate Chamber. The Casino at Marino in Clontarf was an especial delight to Yeats as it must be to any viewer. No less the cultured and enlightened Lord Charlemont's memory seems part of the spirit Yeats also imbibed in the free air of the Municipal Gallery and in the red brick repose of the Royal Irish Academy on Dawson Street. Needless to say, in addition to Coole House, Lissadell, and Sandymount Castle, great houses like Carton and Castletown in nearby Kildare were loved by him. Whatever the shortcomings of George II, his equestrian statue in St. Stephen's Green was also a pleasure to Yeats. Yet not only his eye for architecture and his well-known pride in the finely made are involved here. The human histories and associations with Georgian Ireland's spirited mind counted just as much. He treasured the Barry self-portrait given him by Alec Martin, not because it was particularly superb as a piece of portraiture but because it was reminiscent of Burke and his times.[48]

Time and again, these memorials and others like them served Yeats as standards to judge the life around him. He was accustomed to meditate in St. Patrick's; to muse by the pond in St. Stephen's

48. Information from Mrs. W. B. Yeats. See also W. B. Stanford, "Yeats in the Irish Senate," *REL*, IV (July 1963), 72, and *Letters*, p. 888. Descriptions of many of these memorials may be found in the volumes of the Georgian Society *Records of Eighteenth-century Domestic Architecture and Decoration in Ireland* (Dublin, 1909–1913) and in Thomas U. Sadleir and Page L. Dickinson, *Georgian Mansions in Ireland* (Dublin, 1915).

Green. More than once he recalled the heroics of Buck Whaley, who had adorned 86 on the Green. He had hopes, almost invariably disappointed, for Trinity. He admitted great exasperation at the gaudy desecration of the Mansion House. He chose to identify himself with those towering Trinity graduates—Burke, Goldsmith, and Grattan—who form the impressive triangle at her gates. He demanded that the damaged Four Courts be restored as a trust from that dignified past. He expressed great disappointment in Berkeley's portrait in the Trinity Fellows' Room; and equal satisfaction that Tom Moore's statue was located by the public urinal nearby. Just as well known is his public defense of the opening of Merrion Square—space and greenery—so that children might delight in it and remember it. And then there is what seems a pet scheme—his pressing for the Bank of Ireland as a possible site for the new parliament.

As in architecture, so in painting. Both brought to him an age and frame of mind graceful yet purposive in memory. In painting, portraiture attracted him most. Thomas MacGreevy has written of Yeats:

> . . . he would be interested in any eighteenth-century portrait in which the artist was able to convey the impression that the subject, if a man, read his classics as part of his pleasure, and if a woman, took the adventures and misfortunes of life with a noble despair (that did not preclude tenderness or a sense of fair play). But it was the Irish 18th century to which that would apply. . . . He but dreamed of the 18th century people as—at their best—following in the footsteps of Baldassare Castiglione, the Duchess of Urbino, etc.[49]

Clearly, such faces and memorials were not folk art, did not belong to the common people. These were the products of wealth, privilege, and leisure. The tapestries in the Bank of Ireland, originally designed for the Irish House of Lords and representing the Battle of the Boyne and the Siege of Derry, were to Yeats emblems of the

---

49. Letter to the author. In addition to Castiglione's *The Courtier,* Yeats must have read of that Italian Renaissance aristocracy in his own copy of Edmund G. Gardner's *Dukes and Poets in Ferrara* (London, 1904).

intellect and the responsibility celebrated by Irish Augustan art.[50] It may come to this: logical intellect—passionate and cold—best expressed itself by a sense of form in life as well as art. By contrast, native Ireland seemed, except for the verbal arts, formless to Yeats. As he once insisted to Gogarty on viewing Gogarty's newly acquired tower in Kinvara, "The Normans had form, Gogarty, the Normans had form." [51] He would use the idea in the beginning of "Blood and the Moon" to stamp the difference in Irelands on the poem. He could say that eighteenth-century Italian plasterwork in Dublin made classical figures on a wall "look like the first beings slowly shaping in the formless and void darkness." [52] Francini plasterwork, Gandon's Custom House, the new Palladian mode introduced all over Ireland by Richard Castle set the impression of this new spirit on formless Ireland.[53] Yeats's house, built in 1740 on Merrion Square, brought him distinguished Georgian mantelpieces, large, high elegant rooms, a view of the Dublin mountains, and associations with the Duke of Wellington, who first saw the light of day on the Square. Dublin Square or Georgian country house, the deep appeals both made to Yeats are best glimpsed in Elizabeth Bowen's picture of Bowen's Court and like houses:

> These houses . . . are certainly not little. Let us say that their size, like their loneliness, is an effect rather than a reality. Perhaps the wide, private spaces they occupy throw a distending reflection on to their walls. And, they were planned for spacious living—for hospitality above all. . . . they have made no natural growth from the soil—the idea that begot them was a

50. *Variorum*, p. 833.
51. *The Collected Poems of Oliver St. John Gogarty* (London, 1957), pp. xxiv–xxv.
52. "Rosa Alchemica," *Mythologies*, pp. 271–72. Earlier in these pages Yeats also describes this house as "a house my ancestors had made almost famous through their part in the politics of the day and their friendships with the famous men of their generations" and then goes on to speak of the "wide staircase, where Swift had passed joking and railing, and Curran telling stories and quoting Greek, in simpler days. . . ."
53. James Gandon, *The Life of James Gandon* (Dublin, 1846), p. 94. Also see Thomas U. Sadleir, "Richard Castle, Architect," *Journal of the Royal Society of Antiquaries of Ireland*, XLI (1911), 241–45.

purely social one. The functional parts of them—kitchens and offices, farm-buildings, outbuildings—were sunk underground. . . . Yet, in another sense, the most ornate, spacious parts of these buildings *were* the most functional—the steps, the halls, the living-rooms, the fine staircases—it was these that contributed to society, that raised life above the exigencies of mere living to the plane of art, or at least style. There was a true bigness, a sort of impersonality, in the manner in which the houses were conceived. . . . The security that they [the Anglo-Irish] had, by the eighteenth century, however ignobly gained, they did not use quite ignobly. They began to feel, and exert, the European idea—to seek what was humanistic, classic and disciplined.[54]

V

What did this house, class, and spirit have to offer modern Ireland? A great deal, by Yeats's estimate. As we recall, he regarded the earthy drive and purpose of the Renaissance to be a late arrival in Ireland, not having appeared until the Battle of the Boyne. This battle not only settled the fate of Ireland for a century, it also ushered Ireland into the modern world. It was to Yeats the decisive moment in Irish history.[55]

In a series of essays and speeches written in the early thirties, Yeats tried to spell out his theory of the rise of the modern Irish nation and its literature. It goes something like this: There were four periods, with a bell ringing for each at the end of a century. With the Flight of the Earls at the end of the sixteenth century had come the end of Irish feudalism; the conclusion of the seventeenth century had brought the Protestant Ascendancy and the beginning of modern Ireland; the end of the eighteenth century, with the French Revolution, the Union, and the beginning of the Garrison, had brought dreams of peasant freedom. Literature had suffered especially then

54. Elizabeth Bowen, "The Big House," *Collected Impressions* (London, 1950), pp. 196–97. Also see her *Bowen's Court* (London, 1942), pp. 13–22.
55. *Wheels and Butterflies*, p. 7.

from the two false positions of the divided Ireland of agrarian peasant and Garrison Unionist. The fourth bell, the martyrdom of Parnell at Irish hands, had signaled the failure of Irish democracy and brought in a hardheaded and self-critical literature. This general account informs Yeats's essays and speeches. But in all of them, the eighteenth century looms as the most important for the Irish intellect. The three world figures that Yeats usually points to in these pieces are Swift, Burke, and Berkeley. Here, for instance, is a report of such a speech in 1932, given, appropriately, at the Royal Dublin Society in Ballsbridge:

> Summing up the situation which existed before "the striking of the fourth bell" [the death of Parnell], Mr. Yeats said that Ireland had produced three world figures, and possibly a fourth. It had produced George Berkeley, a philosopher—according to Bergson, the creator of modern philosophy. It had produced Jonathan Swift, the first great modern mind to deny the value of life. It had produced Edmund Burke, who rolled back the anarchy of the French Revolution, and perhaps saved Europe.[56]

Shaw seemed to Yeats the possible fourth. But here, and in his *Commentary on "A Parnellite at Parnell's Funeral,"* Yeats offers in the tragic figure of Parnell a symbol of opposition to the nineteenth century, and by suggestion, a man of pride, passion, and cold exterior, who had embodied the services of the ideal eighteenth-century Protestant gentleman. The eighteenth century, then, might yet be a model for an enlightened public opinion in Ireland, recalling as it did models of authority in art and government, after the failure of O'Connell's democratic politics seen in Parnell's death.

Yeats's hopes for an Ireland transformed by the return of such leadership started early. During the Lane Gallery controversy, he had plumped for the bridge site because such a thing of beauty would unite in men's memories with the loveliness of the old Parliament House and Trinity College.[57] Perhaps with conscious irony, Yeats

56. "Modern Irish Literature," *Irish Times*, 18 February 1933.
57. "The Municipal Art Gallery," *Irish Times*, 18 March 1913.

stated that a bridge site for the Gallery would give the area around O'Connell Bridge "the look of being cared for, the look of being valued; it lacks somewhere some touch of ornament, of conscious pleasure and affection." [58] In March 1924, responding to the toast of "The Fine Arts" at the annual dinner of the Royal Institute of Architects at the Shelbourne Hotel, Yeats remarked that "Whether the Government decided to go back to the Old House in College Green or not—he would like to see them back there—it was a magnificent building, worthy of a great country." [59] Such a building might educate a people. [60] In January of the same year, he had warmed to the subject during an interview:

> "We are not too poor to learn to live within our ample income, to care for beautiful things, to employ and, by employing, to create great talent, and make Dublin beautiful. The Parliament of Grattan, and the Parliament before Grattan, planned and built magnificent buildings, and we are proud to-day of what they did. We must not get into any national rut, but study the best that is done in the world to-day, and give the world our best, which can only be given by those men who know our best." [61]

In the arts, part of "knowing our best" was to know the glories of the Augustan age in Ireland. Yeats, like his sister Elizabeth, hoped for a revival of arts that had once flourished in that century. As she said of the Cuala Press: "I desire to revive the art of fine printing, which has not been practiced in Ireland since the eighteenth century." [62]

In his own organization of the new drama, Yeats expended something of the same effort. He had had some early hopes that "the sons and daughters of the landlords and officials" would turn to Irish legends and the new theater that was dramatizing them. [63] With the

58. *Idem.*
59. "The Old House," *Irish Independent*, 5 March 1924.
60. *Idem.*
61. "How to Restore the Arts," *Irish Times*, 26 January 1924.
62. *The Cuala Press September 1911*, with a Foreword by Elizabeth C. Yeats. Relevant also is "The Cuala Industry," *Irish Times*, 26 January 1928.
63. "The Irish Literary Theatre," *Literature*, 6 May 1899, p. 474.

age of oratory gone, Grattan's Parliament past, Yeats, having given up hope for much support from his own class, began to see the National Theatre as something like a great Irish parliament in Grattan's tradition where the perpetual dialogue of Irish life might be clarified. If the oratory before the Union came from but one class, the Abbey would bring all together.[64] Grattan and those who shared his integrity served Yeats as touchstones for "ardent ideas and high attitudes of mind which were the nation itself," [65] ideals indispensable to his theater. Small wonder that he saw the attacks on the Abbey as similar to the attack that finally overpowered Grattan's ideals: the common enemy was a nineteenth-century middle class with no past and no discipline.[66] When the Theatre was handed over to the government Yeats felt that this, like the memory of Grattan's Parliament, was another Protestant gift to the nation.

There was also the matter of dignity in public life—a trait virtually denied Ireland by the English after the Union, and a subject connected w ith his idea of four periods and bells.

The fourth bell, Parnell's funeral, had provided the chance for the cultural rejuvenation of Ireland. As we have seen, Yeats looked to the age of Grattan for some of his inspiration in government and the arts. But the sound of all four bells tolled, for all that might hear, the tragic dignity, the ancient courtesy, that that age might offer to an Ireland without Parnell. If the first bell had seen the crushing defeat at Kinsale, the second had followed the departure of a native aristocracy and ushered in the dominance of the Anglo-Irish. If the third bell had seen the triumph of democracy, the fourth had announced its political failure and brought intellectual transformation. Yeats seems to be saying that the world figures of the second

---

64. *Lady Gregory's Journals*, p. 86, and "Abbey Theatre," *Irish Times*, 10 August 1925.

65. "Poetry and Tradition," *Essays and Introductions*, p. 248.

66. "Mr. W. B. Yeats on Art," *Irish Times*, 11 February 1908. This is a report on part of Yeats's speech apropos a paper by James J. O'Neill, "The Dublin Stage in the 18th Century," given at a meeting of the National Literary Society at 6 St. Stephen's Green.

bell ought still to be heard after the fourth. Conservative and austere as they were to him, Swift, Burke, and Berkeley offered a life that would give dignity to the mind.

At a meeting of one of the transformations he effected, the Irish Academy of Letters, Yeats offered this theory and showed how the last three periods contributed to the forming of modern Ireland.[67] That Academy would insure the writer of dignity in public life and protection against the kind of virulent censorship, public and private, that Yeats had fought after the fourth bell, and Swift, Burke, and Berkeley after the second. As he had prophetically written in 1900, apropos Ireland's cultural future and the waning of British drama, "It should be our business to bring Ireland from under the ruins, appealing to her, as Grattan appealed to her, in his speech on the tithes, by her own example and her own hopes." [68] Just as important, the time of Grattan had seemed to bring something of the best from both Irelands. Standish O'Grady had chided his own class in lofty prose for their lack of public spirit and, for Yeats, had spoken as did Grattan.[69] Dignity included Catholic Ireland's spirit of sacrifice and Protestant Ireland's taste and courtesy. But it precluded the ignorance of the one and the spirit of worldly success of the other if Parnell's funeral was to have meaning.[70]

There was even a theory of history behind these hopes to restore dignity and intellectual authority to Ireland. Its general outline appears in 1937; its particular application to the eighteenth century is apparent much earlier. The outline reads in the pages of *A Vision* thus:

> When I look in history for the conflict or union of *antithetical* and *primary* I seem to discover that conflict or union of races stated by Petrie and Schneider as universal law. A people who have lived apart and so acquired unity of custom and purity of

67. "Irish Academy of Letters," *Irish Times*, 19 September 1932.
68. "Plans and Methods," *Beltaine*, No. 2 (February 1900), p. 6.
69. *Autobiographies*, p. 420.
70. *Ibid.*, pp. 101–2.

breed unite with some other people through migration, immigration or conquest. A race (the new *antithetical*) emerges that is neither the one nor the other, after somewhere about 500 years it produces, or so it seems, its particular culture or civilisation. This culture lives only in certain victorious classes; then comes a period of revolution (Phase 22) terminated by a civilisation of policemen, schoolmasters, manufacturers, philanthropists, a second soon exhausted blossoming of the race. . . . All these cultures, as I am directed to see them, having attained some Achilles in the first blossoming, find pious Aeneas in their second, and that second is preceded by Utopian dreams that come to little because no civilisation can spend what it has not earned.[71]

We may best fill in here from Irish history—the coming of the Normans as conquerors to the culturally unified Ireland of the late twelfth century, then the emergence of the Anglo-Irish at the end of the seventeenth century with a culture neither English nor native Irish. The Utopian schemes of social democracy may be said to have gained their floodtide in late eighteenth-century Ireland under the influence of the French Revolution. Then came the Garrison of nineteenth-century Ireland. It was certainly a civilization Yeats might describe as that of policemen, schoolmasters, and the like. By 1937 he had few illusions and perhaps even fewer hopes about the second foredoomed flowering. He was faced with its weeds by that time, and if Swift can be thought of as the Achilles of the first bloom, more than likely O'Connell was the "pious Aeneas" of the second. But his later doubts had not deterred Yeats in offering this Achilles for Ireland's serious consideration at the beginning of the thirties: "We must, I think, decide among . . . three ideas of national life: that of Swift; that of the great Italian of his day; that of modern England."[72]

According to this theory, then, the descendants of those who sat in

71. *A Vision* (London, 1956), pp. 205–6.
72. *Wheels and Butterflies*, p. 6.

Grattan's Parliament, who served with Charlemont's volunteers, or who were commended by Arthur Young, might still have something to offer Ireland. Hence, when Yeats presided over the assembly at the Tailteann Banquet in the absence of President Cosgrave on August 2, 1924, he could address himself to the new nation as to "a young man just entered upon his property," a man whose descendants would narrow the idea of liberty and reject any belief in progress: ". . . they will set their hearts upon the building of authority, the restoration of discipline, the discovery of a life sufficiently heroic to live without opium dreams." [73] This was part, as we shall see, of the political heritage of Swift and Burke. This Yeats would urge on the nation as later he might urge upon his own son: "I may suggest to him . . . that the thought of Swift, enlarged and enriched by Burke, saddled and bitted reality, and that materialism was hamstrung by Berkeley, and ancient wisdom brought back; that modern Europe has known no men more powerful." [74]

Needless to say, Yeats's credo did not go unchallenged in Ireland. It seemed to many critics and writers during his lifetime and after that not only was he taking a more and more narrow position on Ireland but that he also shared it with his co-workers, most of them of Anglo-Irish stock. One of the most virulent yet representative attacks came from Professor Daniel Corkery in his *Synge and Anglo-Irish Literature*. In Frank O'Connor's answer—O'Connor had been a protégé of Corkery's—one gets a glimpse of the possible programmatic likeness of Yeats and his friends that Corkery objected to:

> The Irishness of Synge and Yeats and Lady Gregory was of a better kind [than that of Corkery]. All three must be considered together, because they shared a common philosophy. They believed that nothing was settled finally; that there was no such thing as progress and that Utopianism was a curse. The

73. "A Victor at Last," *Irish Independent*, 4 August 1924. See also Hone, pp. 364–65.
74. *Pages from a Diary, Explorations*, pp. 297–98.

majority of Irish writers believed that there was such a thing as progress and that Ireland was only a backwater of civilization.

.   .   .   .

They went further than this. They held that acting, philosophy, religion, and language, all needed to be purified from twentieth century materialism—that materialism had spread everywhere, not only in the form of vulgarity, but as opinions, theories, sensibility, humanitarianism, and long novels in literature, and as loud-speakers, wind-machines, properties, cycloramas and lighting sets in the theatre; as pathos, characterization and restlessness in acting. It stood like a barrier between man and the vision of his end; it fussed about the difference between Celt and Saxon, Indian and white, rich and poor, Protestant and Catholic. It was all the time explaining and defining because one abstraction gave birth to another, and when Professor Corkery had explained to them how the Irish mind differed from the English along came somebody else with a completely different set of abstractions.[75]

Now it is true that Protestants like AE, editor of the *Irish Statesman,* Lennox Robinson, author of *Bryan Cooper,* and Joseph Hone, authority on Berkeley and Swift and defender of Protestant Ireland,[76] would seem, along with Synge and Lady Gregory, to have

---

75. "Synge, Yeats and Lady Gregory," *Irish Times,* 10 August 1938. Also pertinent is Lennox Robinson, *The Irish Theatre* (London, 1939), pp. 31–40. For a smattering of Corkery's frenzies on Swift alone, see "Ourselves and Dean Swift," *Studies,* XXIII (June 1934), 203–18, and "Swift Once More," *Ireland To-Day,* II (December 1937), 78–79. The answer to such narrow thinking was given long before O'Connor's remarks in a lecture by John O'Leary in 1886: ". . . you should never be content to take on trust such of our great writers as have spoken to you through the English language. You must give your days and nights to our Swifts, Goldsmiths, Berkeleys, Burkes. . . . To be sure, you will be told by narrow-minded or ignorant people that there is little that is Irish about all or most of them. But if you begin by freeing yourself from narrow-mindedness, you have made a great (perhaps the greatest) step towards freeing yourself also from ignorance" (John O'Leary, *What Irishmen Should Know. How Irishmen Should Feel* [Dublin, n.d.], p. 6).

76. See, for example, "The Anglo-Irish Strain," *Bell,* II (September 1941), 26–27.

come together with Yeats in some vaguely programmatic way. But such is very likely not the case,[77] however much Yeats liked "causes."

Nevertheless, Yeats had to withstand a more or less constant attack on his position both before and after his senatorship. The diatribes of Corkery are representative because they center on the so-called alien position of the Anglo-Irish as regards native Irish religion, nationalism, and soil. If not identified with Catholic, Gaelic, peasant stock, one was not Irish. A good deal of the uproar over the *Playboy* had taken this form of attack, not only on Synge but on his associations with Lady Gregory and Yeats. For Yeats always stoutly refused to consider "literature concerning Ireland written in English" as necessarily un-Irish, a frequent charge of his critics. Despite his support of the language movement, Yeats could also say,

> Side by side with the spread of the Irish language, and with much writing in the Irish language, must go on much expression of Irish emotion and Irish thought, much writing about Irish things and people, in the English language, for no man can write well except in the language he has been born and bred to, and no man, as I think, becomes perfectly cultivated except through the influence of that language. . . .[78]

This early answer to those who would distinguish Anglo-Irish literature from Irish literature was soon to become the basis for Yeats's retort to those who denied the Anglo-Irish themselves any part in Irish Ireland. The appearance of "Leda and the Swan," and such words in his editorial as "we count among atheists bad writers and Bishops of all denominations" in the first issue of *To-morrow*, brought an avalanche of vituperation on Yeats's head. Nor did his speech on behalf of divorce help him in the spring of 1925. As a matter of fact, his association with the early Free State government

77. This is also the considered opinion of such long-time observers of the Dublin scene as A. J. Leventhal, Samuel Beckett, Lennox Robinson, and Ernest Walsh, according to a letter from Walsh to the author.
78. "Mr. W. B. Yeats," *The Leader*, 1 September 1900, p. 13.

was twisted on at least one occasion to evoke a Protestant heritage of cruelty and murder:

> As one of the recent acts of Dr. Yeats was to support capital punishment for those who raise arms for Irish independence, we would suggest that he belongs rather to that other Anglo-Irish minority which gave us Norbury and Fitzgibbon and Major Sirr and all the able gentlemen who—like Dr. Yeats—thought hanging too good for Irish patriots.[79]

The writer then proclaims that Burke, Swift, Emmet, and Grattan would have opposed Yeats.[80] In the next year Yeats and the Abbey came under attack as abysmally Cromwellian.[81] Once again Yeats had little difficulty answering this attack, which criticized the Abbey for not being truly national, by insisting on the essential plurality of Ireland, a nation which continued to think in English.[82] In all these attacks, and many more, such as those by Liam Brophy and James Devane—the animus centered on Yeats's or the Anglo-Irish betrayal of native Irish life.[83]

But the subtlest of all these attacks on Yeats's supposed apostasy came from the Gaelic propagandist and enthusiast, Aodh de Blacam, a Scot often known as Roddy the Rover. He allowed the claim that the Anglo-Irish had been Irish, by blood and persuasion, since the eighteenth century. His accusation was that from Burke to Bryan Cooper they served England. They were essentially rootless in Ireland, de Blacam's account goes, their allegiances were wrong, they ignored and continued to ignore "the immemorial Gaelic tradition . . . and the religion of the masses and the martyrs of the race."[84]

---

79. "The Bergin Trial," *An Phoblacht*, 20 June 1925, p. 3.
80. *Ibid.*
81. "What Is a National Theatre," *Irish Times*, 24 February 1926.
82. *Ibid.* See also Yeats's "A Defense of the Abbey Theatre," *Dublin Magazine*, April–June 1926, pp. 8–12.
83. For Brophy's fantasies see Monk Gibbon, *The Masterpiece and the Man* (New York, 1959), p. 163; for Devane's general attack, see "Four Irish Myths," *Ireland To-Day*, I (June 1936), 14–15.
84. "The Rise and Fall of Anglo-Ireland," *Irish Press*, 3 February 1932.

Later he was to speak quite as falsely of the "autumnal cynicism"—this included Swift and Berkeley!—of Anglo-Ireland, and so condemn the Abbey for having surrendered itself to subjectivity.[85] The interesting thing about de Blacam's attack is the fact that he addressed himself not only to Yeats but to AE, Lennox Robinson, and also Joseph Hone, again as if they were a concerted force in pushing that century. Yeats recognized this when he wrote to Hone,

> An article in to-day's *Irish Press* has put you into my head. De Blacam speaks of the attempt now being made by certain 'Anglo-Irish leaders' to bring back the Irish Eighteenth Century; he names you, me, AE (this I think a mistake) and Lennox Robinson (his *Brian Cooper*). I did not do more than glance at the rest of the article, which is the usual sort of thing—only the Gael or the Catholic is Irish. . . .

. . . .

> De Blacam's passing mention is valuable as it conveys an idea that something is happening, and that may get it [into] some undergraduate's head.[86]

After Yeats's death, de Blacam wrote of him:

> Those of us who have tried to find a synthesis, in which what is best in the Anglo-Irish should be given to the historic nation in its future growth, got no aid from him. In 1932, when Lady Gregory lay dying at Coole, Yeats wrote to me to tell that she was reading my novel, *The Lady of Cromlech*, on her deathbed; and he touched on synthesis only to reject it. "There are two Irelands," he wrote. His Ireland now, on his own admission, had nothing in common with that of Gaels or of Catholics.[87]

85. "Yeats and the Nation," *Irish Times*, 13 June 1935.
86. *Letters*, pp. 790–91.
87. "Yeats as I Knew Him," *Irish Monthly*, LXVII (1939), 209. One laments the absence of the entire letter, which de Blacam's heirs are also unable to discover.

This accusation leads us to what these attacks, early and late,[88] have so obviously missed in Yeats's scheme for the new Ireland.

Yeats's great hope was for one Ireland in which all opinions, classes, and creeds might flourish vigorously while at the same time offering their best to the country as a whole. As Yeats once observed of Nelson's Pillar: ". . . Nelson's Pillar should not be broken up. It represented the feeling of Protestant Ireland for a man who helped to break the power of Napoleon. The life and work of the people who erected it is part of our tradition. I think we should accept the whole past of this nation and not pick and choose."[89] Yeats was interested in Irish realities. At one time he even took the unpopular step of opposing the saying of prayers in Irish at Senate openings. His point was that most of the members did not know the language.[90] He was serious, not merely patriotic, about the unity of Irish life, and also doubtless agreed with Lennox Robinson's conclusion in his sketch of the life of Thomas Parnell:

> It is the tragedy of eighteenth century Ireland that these two cultures, the Gaelic and the Anglo-Irish never met, never seem to have been aware of each other's existence. . . . We think we understand the value of both cultures a little better now. We strain back to them, we fumble in old manuscripts and put fragments of Gaelic verse together, we read again Berkeley, we read Swift, read Burke, and, as a small part of our great Irish heritage, reprint now a few poems of Thomas Parnell.[91]

As Yeats once stated in a speech called "The Child and the State," one ought to feed the young imagination of Ireland on the old legends and Gaelic stories and stir the mature intellect with the works of Burke and Berkeley.[92] Thus both Irelands would form the child. One of

---

88. As late as 1962, Yvor Winters' attack on Yeats was well-received in Dublin if letters to the *Irish Times* are any gauge.

89. "The Pillar," *Evening Telegraph*, 25 August 1923.

90. Stephen Gwynn, "Ireland Week by Week," *The Observer*, 18 November 1923.

91. *Poems by Thomas Parnell*, selected by Lennox Robinson (Dublin, 1927), n.p.

92. *Senate Speeches*, p. 172.

many audacities in a play like *The Dreaming of the Bones* is that Yeats would bring all Irish history to the bar of forgiveness. Later, he could also point out the solid worth of the historical villain Major Sirr.[93] Reading Yeats's copy of Grattan's speeches, we find him penciling passages on Irish rights and Catholic freedom that reflect his agreement with Grattan's devotion to the unity of both Irelands.[94] To what extent Yeats succeeded, in the face of severe criticism and at a time when, as AE once wrote him, the "half-crazy Gaeldom . . . is growing dominant about us," [95] we shall see.

VI

But this chapter must conclude with its promised anticlimax. No one should be surprised at the fact that Yeats, while celebrating the Anglo-Irish eighteenth century, was all his life critical of the Anglo-Irish around him, was aware of the shortcomings of the aristocracy of the Protestant Augustans, and continued to the end of his life to hold the folklore and stories of the Irish peasant as his great literary material. Thus in 1923 he could proclaim in the Senate: ". . . the greater portion of my own writings have been founded upon the old literature of Ireland. I have had to read it in translations, but it has been the chief illumination of my imagination all my life." [96] Moreover, one of his last poems, "Under Ben Bulben," instructs future poets to sing the peasantry first, and only then "hard riding

93. *Variorum*, pp. 836–37.

94. In his copy of Daniel Owen Madden's *The Select Speeches of Henry Grattan* (Dublin, 1845), p. 63, Yeats heavily marked the following passage from the speech "Declaration of Irish Rights," 19 April 1780: "I wish for nothing but to breathe, in this our island, in common with my fellow-subjects, the air of liberty. I have no ambition, unless it be the ambition to break your chain, and contemplate your glory. I never will be satisfied so long as the meanest cottager in Ireland has a link of the British chain clanking to his rags: he may be naked, he shall not be in iron; and I do see the time is at hand, the spirit is gone forth, the declaration is planted; and though great men should apostatize, yet the cause will live. . . ." On p. 440, Yeats also marked the peroration ending Grattan's speech on the "Catholic Question," 3 May 1819.

95. *Letters from AE*, ed. Alan Denson (London, New York, Toronto, 1961), p. 63.

96. *Senate Speeches*, p. 44.

country gentlemen." It was also quite fitting that Yeats should conclude his address to the Irish Race Congress in Paris, 1922, "with a moving recitation of Pearse's 'Wayfarer,' written the night before his execution." [97]

We have seen how Yeats turned his back on "Ireland's dark, insipid period," as he applied Swift's words to the century after the Union. Having read such relatively straight accounts of Penal Ireland as those of Lecky and Arthur Young, Yeats was also familiar with the blacker side of that picture. Moreover, we have seen how in his youth he constantly chided those of his own class, even Dowden, for turning up their noses at all things Irish. In his Preface to Ussher's translation of *The Midnight Court*, Yeats had shown, even in the heyday of his enthusiasm, a proper disdain for the stupidities of the penal laws that could so discourage the native Irish.[98] For another thing, he generally hated most English literature of the eighteenth century during his whole life. We know how he loathed Pope.[99] The poetry of Pope and Gray and the prose of Johnson and Rousseau seemed equally "external, sentimental and logical" [100] to him. In a private notebook he deplored the rigidity of the Roman influence brought into English letters by Milton, and developed by Dryden and Pope; [101] at the end of his life he publicly inveighed against the teaching of Latin.[102] Eighteenth-century English literature until Blake had been part of a sentimental epoch.

If, then, Yeats had to face literary limitations and historical realities in his Augustan preferences, he also doubted the religious vigor of Protestant Ireland. Already we have encountered his suspicion of that spirit of getting-on which seemed so compromising to the Church of Ireland. He also rather cordially disliked the North of Ireland and the crude enterprising nature of what he took to be the

97. "Gaels Gather in Paris," *Irish Independent*, 24 January 1922.
98. "The Midnight Court," *Explorations*, p. 284.
99. Information from Mrs. W. B. Yeats.
100. *A Vision* (1956), p. 296.
101. Manuscript book begun 7 April 1921.
102. *On the Boiler*, p. 28.

typical Ulster man.[103] The opening pages of *If I were Four-and-Twenty* disclose his general unrest not only before the limitations of the Catholic faith but even more amid the tepid religious vulgarity of Protestant Ireland. Speaking apropos of psychical research and phenomena, Yeats in 1919 was reported as admitting that,

> Although brought up in the Church of Ireland, he could point to no authority equal to that of the Roman Ritual [which contained pages on the exorcising of spirits], because in the Church of Ireland they said that the age of miracles was past. They gave no evidence to prove that, but it enabled them not to pay any attention to this subject. He had often wondered if the ordinary man or woman in the Church of Ireland had any institution equally sacred to him or her as that which the Church of Rome had for the Catholic. He had come to the conclusion that the only thing sacred to him or her was Trinity College.[104]

But in thus qualifying Yeats's Anglo-Irish allegiance, his most devastating criticism must be added, namely that modern Anglo-Ireland "lacked hereditary passion." [105] The Queen's visit in 1900 reminded him of the successful bribery that had brought the Union. Moreover, at the turn of the century he had already witnessed this old vacillation and ineffectuality even more shamefully:

> . . . it had seemed for a few months that the old political groupings were about to break up, everywhere people had looked forward, expecting, speculating. A Royal Commission . . . had reported that the over-taxation of Ireland for the last fifty years amounted to some three hundred millions. The Irish Landlord Party, which based its politics upon the conviction that Ireland had gained by the Union, had a revulsion of conscience. Lord Castletown made a famous speech declaring

---

103. See Oliver Edwards' superb article, "W. B. Yeats and Ulster; and a Thought on the Future of the Anglo-Irish Tradition," *Northman*, XIII (Winter 1945), 16–21.
104. "Psychical Phenomena," *Irish Times*, 27 January 1919.
105. *Autobiographies*, p. 419.

that Ireland must imitate the colonists who flung the tea into Boston Harbour. Landlord committees were appointed in every county. Then Lord Salisbury appointed a second Royal Commission to consider the wrongs of landlords, and not one of those committees met again. There was deep disappointment. Protestant Ireland had immense prestige. Burke, Swift, Grattan, Emmet, Fitzgerald, Parnell, almost every name sung in modern song, had been Protestant; Dublin's dignity depended upon the gaunt magnificence of buildings founded under the old Parliament; but wherever it attempted some corporate action, wherein Ireland stood against England, the show, however gallant it seemed, was soon over. It sold its Parliament for solid money, and now it sold this cause for a phantom. Nobody was the better or worse for Lord Salisbury's new Commission. Protestant Ireland could not have done otherwise; it lacked hereditary passion. Parnell, its last great figure, finding that this lack had made the party of my father's old friend Isaac Butt powerless, called in the peasants' tenacity and violence, but for months now the peasants had stood aside and waited, hoping that their old masters might take the leadership again.[106]

Again, at the time of the contention over the Lane Gallery, Yeats laid down the lines for an editorial by Hone in the *Irish Times* chiding Unionists reluctant to help Lane, addressing them as he might have addressed their gallant eighteenth-century ancestors:

Irish Unionism, at least south of the Boyne, derives its main strength from the upper classes. Our upper classes have lost a part of their former reputation for taste in learning and books and a delight in the arts, and who knows but that Unionism has suffered thereby? Without forgetting the modern achievement of Trinity College, which is mainly Unionist, we find it impossible to doubt that Anglo-Irish gentlemen have, in these respects, fallen from the high estate of their ancestors in the eighteenth century. They, as Mr. Yeats has said elsewhere, "had they known the people and the game a little better, might have created an aristocracy in an age that has lost the under-

106. *Ibid.*, pp. 418–19.

standing of the word." What is the fine life but "a part played finely before fine spectators"? They have, one is quite certain, still their chance. Nationalist, or democratic, Ireland has entered upon a period of disillusion. Idealism is gone out of the nationalist politics. Home Rule may come, or it may not; either event will complete the mental reaction. This is not, assuredly, the moment for our upper classes to abandon their Unionism. It is the moment for them to remember their origins and privileges, and, therefore, to "look up in the sun's eye." To change one's mood is not necessarily to change one's politics. It is *apropos* to note the report that the Nationalist Party, with due regard for economy, is content to see an Irish Parliament housed in any brand new building suitable "for all practical purposes." Our upper classes never were content to associate such house-wifely economies with the far different political ideas of their breed. They were proud to exercise their privileges in the past. They still have means of exercising those privileges—by, for instance, protecting the Modern Art Gallery against dissolution. All that is required is another attitude, such an attitude as need not carry with it any denial of principle or of opinion. It will "pay in the end," for the Irish people, who want nourishment for their imagination, will take the best if they are but offered it.[107]

Such a class had also been the enemy of his and Synge's own youthful promise. In many ways the extreme Nationalists and Unionists were much the same, both in their attacks on the new literature and in their indifference.[108] Yeats's opinion never really changed very much from his early indictment of Anglo-Ireland before the new literary world in which he describes the plight of Sir Samuel Ferguson: "He lived in a class which, through a misunderstanding of the necessities of Irish Unionism, hated all Irish things, or felt for them at best a contemptuous and patronising affection. . . ."[109]

Nevertheless, Yeats's reliance on heroic Irish literature in his

107. "Art and Aristocracy," *Irish Times*, 11 January 1913.
108. *Autobiographies*, pp. 234–35, 447–48, 508–10; *Letters*, pp. 350–53; *Hugh Lane*, pp. 59–61.
109. "An Irish Patriot," *Bookman*, May 1896, p. 50.

own work; his faith that the reality of a spiritual world would soon be apparent to all men from psychic research; his hopes for an enlightened nation in which ability and intelligence would rule—all might be quickened by drawing men's attention to the virtues of the Protestant eighteenth century. Moreover, if Yeats identified himself with Giraldus Cambrensis, historiographer and secretary to Henry II, who directed Strongbow's invasion of Ireland, then he not only brooded over the eighteenth century but also over all the fortunes and misfortunes of Ireland during her 700 years of Anglo-Irish trouble. His desire to bring the best from a condemned century to the eye of the new nation follows logically from his imaginative role as Giraldus, pompous, obscure, and brilliant servant to the first detested English in Ireland. Yet they, the Norman-English, had also been the harbingers of a later detested age of elegance; a civilization renowned for its arts, dress, and buildings; a cultivated society for which a grand tour might bring the best of Europe to Ireland; and energetic men who had founded a Royal Dublin Society, Royal Irish Academy, and Independent Parliament.[110] In short, Yeats hoped to perpetuate that late renaissance of which, almost unknown to him, he was the last distinguished member, singer, and eulogist. We catch both the melancholy and the desperation of his hopes as he addresses Anglo-Ireland when his Senate days were over:

> If I were a young man I would start an agitation to show them their task in life. As a beginning I might gather together the descendants of those who had voted with Grattan against the Union that we might ask the British Government to return his body; it lies in Westminster Abbey under a flat plain stone since it was laid there, despite the protests of his followers, less to commemorate his fame than to prevent a shrine and a pilgrimage. Then I would ask the Irish Government to line the streets with soldiers that we might with all befitting pomp open the pavement of St. Patrick's for one last burial.[111]

110. Constantia Maxwell, "Give Me the Eighteenth Century!" *Irish Digest*, VIII (February 1941), 58–60.
111. "Ireland, 1921–1931," *Spectator*, 30 January 1932, p. 137.

Anglo-Ireland had been a worthy partner of Irish Ireland. As he had written in the twenties, "Ireland is not more theirs than ours. We must glory in our difference, be as proud of it as they are of theirs." [112]

112. Hone, p. 371, n. 1.

Chapter Four

IMITATE HIM IF YOU DARE

WHEN T. S. ELIOT'S "familiar compound ghost" speaks of

> . . . the conscious impotence of rage
> At human folly, and the laceration
> Of laughter at what ceases to amuse.
> And last, the rending pain of re-enactment
> Of all that you have done, and been; the shame
> Of motives late revealed, and the awareness
> Of things ill done and done to others' harm

> Which once you took for exercise of virtue.
> Then fools' approval stings, and honour stains,

we sense the presence of the restless ghost of Jonathan Swift. Moreover, we know that Eliot's inspiration at this point was Yeats's Swift in *The Words Upon the Window-pane*.[1] Perhaps this source is fitting. For whether seen in *Little Gidding* or in the latest wearisome explication of Swift's satire, that most substantial ghost is truly given its widest berth, its most turbulent patrol, in the streets of Dublin. Yeats once spoke of Sir Harold Williams as "a scholar in whose imagination Swift has a pre-eminence scarcely possible outside Ireland."[2] This puts the case exactly.

Swift's Irish pre-eminence can probably be sorted into at least three types—the creature of scholars, the persistent folk image, and then the legendary figure of Irish men of letters. Yeats knew them all. He frequently made use of the "Dane" of oral tradition to be found in the manuscripts of the Irish Folklore Commission and, more than likely for Yeats, in Lady Gregory's *Kiltartan History Book*. For she too records the Dean possessed of wily Irish servant, amatory prowess, and roaring sons.[3] As for the Dean of scholars, Yeats had him at his fingertips in his own library.[4] He himself added to the

1. Maurice Johnson, "The Ghost of Swift in 'Four Quartets,'" *MLN*, LXIV (April 1949), 273.

2. *Wheels and Butterflies*, p. 29. Mrs. W. B. Yeats identifies the "scholar" as Sir Harold Williams.

3. Lady Gregory, *The Kiltartan History Book* (London, 1926), pp. 56–58. A full summary of the legends of Swift in Ireland is to be found in Mackie L. Jarrell, " 'Jack and the Dane': Swift Traditions in Ireland," *Journal of American Folklore*, LXXVII (April–June 1964), 99–117.

4. Yeats's library contains the Thomas Sheridan edition of Swift's *Works* (London, 1784), 17 vols.—hereafter *Works*. He may have bought this edition with his Nobel Prize money; the pages are infrequently marked by his hand. His library also contains such books by or about Swift as Sir Harold Williams' edition of *Gulliver's Travels* (London, 1926) and his *Dean Swift's Library* (Cambridge, 1932); F. Elrington Ball, *Swift's Verse* (London, 1929); Stephen Gwynn, *The Life and Friendships of Dean Swift* (London, 1933); Joseph M. Hone and Mario M. Rossi, *Swift, or the Egoist* (London, 1934); and *Swift: Gulliver's Travels and Selected Writings in Prose and Verse*, ed. John Hayward (London, 1934). Random remarks in his Introduction to *The Words Upon the Window-pane* suggest that Yeats may have been familiar with Lord Orrery's *Remarks*,

Dean of Irish belles-lettres the poetic figure who takes his place beside such contemporary wonders as P. S. O'Hegarty's Irish nationalist, Richard Ashe King's "caged beast," D. L. Kelleher's "demon-lover," Joyce's dark, bitter stylist, and Gogarty's man of the people.[5] If few writers of any nation can match the wild distortions offered up as Swift by Frank O'Connor and Sir Shane Leslie,[6] there is this to be said of literary Ireland's Swift: like the Dean of Irish scholar and countryman, he is not the pallid image of a university lecturer so often projected in America and England. Instead, he is an unabashed power lover, a propagandist, an eccentric, a public man of pride, a fractious youth, vigorous churchman, and a rather desperate man with the ladies.

These attributes are pretty much the ones Yeats also claims for Swift.[7] He was also the chief voice speaking to the poet from that One Irish Century just outlined. So, while Yeats may have first fastened on Berkeley in his late love affair with Georgian Ireland, it is clearly Swift who is most important to him among all the Augustans that will be mentioned. Accordingly, we shall start with Swift and explore in this chapter that severe presence from the past which caused Yeats to remark variously: "Swift haunts me"; "Swift

---

Patrick Delany's *Observations*, Samuel Johnson's "Life," Walter Scott's *Memoirs*, and Lecky's account of Swift in *Leaders of Public Opinion in Ireland* (Dublin, 1861). He was also familiar with such background works as the *Grammont Memoirs* and F. S. Oliver, *The Endless Adventure* (Boston and New York, 1931). See also the unpublished dissertation (Temple University, 1950) by T. L. Dume, "William Butler Yeats: A Survey of His Reading," pp. 296–97.

5. P. S. O'Hegarty, "Jonathan Swift: Irishman," *Bell*, X (September 1945), 478–88; Richard Ashe King, *Swift in Ireland* (Dublin, 1895), p. 199 and *passim*; D. L. Kelleher, *The Glamour of Dublin*, 2nd ed. (Dublin, 1920), p. 116; and Oliver St. John Gogarty, *Intimations* (New York, 1950), p. 97.

6. Frank O'Connor, *Leinster, Munster and Connaught* (London, 1950), pp. 14–24, and Sir Shane Leslie, *The Skull of Swift* (London, 1928), *passim*.

7. In addition to the Introduction to *The Words Upon the Window-pane*, one might consult Yeats's remarks on Swift in *Pages from a Diary* and in the Preface to *The Midnight Court and The Adventures of a Luckless Fellow*, trans. Percy Arland Ussher (New York [1926]). Both essays are conveniently located in *Explorations*.

. . . looked upon himself . . . as appointed to guard a position";
and "He/Served human liberty." [8]

II

"Swift haunts me; he is always just round the next corner." This
fitting admission Yeats wrote at Coole and just as appropriately used
to introduce his ghost play on Swift. Swift had always attracted him.
But however great his admiration, Yeats at first identified him as an
English writer in the driest of English centuries. This we have
already noticed, along with Yeats's rejection of Berkeley, Burke, and
Goldsmith on similar romantic and patriotic grounds. But let us
expand for a moment on the always evident attraction. In 1893 Yeats
seconded the historian O'Grady's praise of Swift's "plain and honest
speaking." [9] In an interview in 1910, he could laud the ferocity of
Swift and Tim Healy as Irish satirists. [10] Letters to Lady Gregory in
1913 stress the great importance of Swift to both of them. [11] Yet even
in that year when comparing Strindberg to Swift—"He is as terrible
as Swift"—Yeats could conclude, "but I do not think I underrate
Swift when I say I prefer Sir Thomas Browne." [12] Earlier he had
defended Swift's use of false figures in attacking Wood's halfpence
project on the grounds that "God made certain men mad, & thus it
was those men . . . who possess truths of passion, that were intellectual falsehoods, who created unities." [13] Early or late, however, the
point remains that Swift's intensity as man and writer chiefly won and
finally haunted Yeats. A key statement in 1895, despite its *fin de*

8. Taken respectively from *Wheels and Butterflies*, p. 7, *Pages from a Diary,
Explorations*, p. 334, and Yeats's poem, "Swift's Epitaph."
9. " 'The Silenced Sister,' " *United Ireland*, 30 December 1893.
10. "Irish Drama," *The Sunday Observer*, 19 June 1910.
11. "Some New Letters from W. B. Yeats to Lady Gregory," *REL*, IV (July
1963), 17, 21.
12. "Mr. W. B. Yeats," *Freeman's Journal*, 4 January 1913.
13. "Autobiography."

siècle overtones, attests to Swift's hold on Yeats in his review of Richard Ashe King's *Swift in Ireland:*

> The recognition of the expression of a temperament as an end in itself, and not merely as a means towards a change of opinion, is the first condition of any cultivated life, and there is no better text than Swift for preaching this. He did not become, like the subject of Sir Charles Gavan Duffy's volume [*A Short Life of Thomas Davis*], a great light of his time because of the utility of his projects or of any high standard of honest thinking—for some of his most famous projects were mere expressions of a paradoxical anger, while others he defended with arguments which even he could not have believed—but because he revealed in his writings and in his life a more intense nature, a more living temperament than any of his contemporaries. He was as near a supreme man as that fallen age could produce, and that he did not labour, as Blake says the supreme man should, "to bring again the golden age" by revealing it in his work and his life, but fought, as with battered and smoke-blackened armour in the mouth of the pit, was the discredit of "the century of philosophers": a century that had set chop-logic in the place of the mysterious power . . . that had governed "the century of poets." Some pages of Sir Thomas Browne are, one doubts not, of a greater kind, as pure literature, than any he wrote, but he has given the world an unforgettable parable by building an overpowering genius upon the wreckage of the merely human faculties, of all that the Herr Nordaus of ours and other times have acclaimed and preached; and it is because the most ignorant feel this in some instinctive way that his throne is unassailable.[14]

The grip of Swift's intensity never left Yeats. Later, merely reading Swift could excite him enough to disturb his blood pressure and leave him sleepless.[15] In 1930, he wrote Wyndham Lewis of Swift: ". . . passion enobled by intensity, by endurance, by wisdom.

14. "The New Irish Library," *Bookman*, June 1896, p. 83.
15. *Yeats and T. Sturge Moore*, p. 141.

We had it in one man once. He lies in St. Patrick's now under the greatest epitaph in history." [16] Swift's intensity was also tragic, for his wisdom was prophetic, his hurt human:

Swift beating on his breast in sibylline frenzy blind
Because the heart in his blood-sodden breast had dragged
him down into mankind.[17]

These two channels of Swift's intensity—his prophetic isolation and his powerful devotion to justice—came to haunt Yeats most, probably, because they were foremost traits of his own.

First let's consider the intensity of isolation. On more than one occasion we have noted the Anglo-Irish solitude that Yeats writes of in his 1930 *Diary* and in his essay on Berkeley. The career of Robert Gregory has also summed up the process of choice and the spectacular results derived from an isolated existence between two nations. Swift as heir to this solitude and also as a lover of simplicity, who hated systems, mechanism, and abstractions, this Swift "found in England the opposite that stung [his] thought into expression and made it lucid." [18] But the rub is that he was also a solitary in his own land. Yeats puts himself in the same tradition; for not only did England frequently sting Yeats into violent and highly articulate anathemas, but so did Ireland:

The other day I was asked why a certain man did not live at Boar's Hill, that pleasant neighbourhood where so many writers live, and replied, "We Anglo-Irish hate to surrender the solitude we have inherited," and then began to wonder what I meant. I ran over the lives of my friends, of Swift and Berkeley,

16. *Letters*, p. 776.
17. These lines from "Blood and the Moon" may echo passages from King's *Swift in Ireland*, pp. 11, 146, 195, and 204, where Swift is pictured as a powerless prophet and chest-thumper. A countertype to these lines is Yeats's memorable description of George Eliot: "She is too reasonable. I hate reasonable people, the activity of their brains sucks up all the blood out of their hearts. . . . The only business of the head in the world is to bow a ceaseless obeisance to the heart" (*Letters*, p. 31).
18. "Bishop Berkeley," *Essays and Introductions*, p. 402.

and saw that all, as befits scattered men in an ignorant country, were solitaries.[19]

Austin Clarke has pooh-poohed any such notion of solitude for Yeats himself.[20] Yet even a casual reading of Irish newspapers and periodicals during Yeats's lifetime and after, not to mention a reading of his correspondence, shows the weight of this solitude and the weight of Dr. McCartan's remark that the attack on Yeats had "lasted for fifty years." [21] To some extent also, Yeats may have identified himself with Swift, the historically destined victim in isolation. For, until the end of his life, Yeats probably put altogether too much faith in the future. In 1895 we hear his plaint most clearly to a fellow worker in the vineyards:

> . . . the coming generations in Ireland cannot but value what I have done. I am writing at the end of the day, and when I am tired, this endless war with Irish stupidity gets on my nerves. Either you or I could have had more prosperous lives probably, if we left Ireland alone and went our way on the high seas— certainly we could have had more peaceable lives. However, if the sun shines in the morning I shall be full of delight and of battle and ready to draw my bow against the dragon.[22]

19. Oliver St. John Gogarty, *Wild Apples*, with a Preface by William Butler Yeats (Dublin, 1930), n.p. Where Hone and Rossi saw Swift as an egoist, Yeats saw a solitary (*Letters*, p. 454).

20. See Clarke's review of A. G. Stock's *W. B. Yeats: His Poetry and Thought* (Cambridge, 1961) in the *Irish Times*, 1 July 1961. Cf. St. John Ervine, "The Loneliest Poet: W. B. Yeats," *John O'London's Weekly*, 5 July 1919, p. 375.

21. *Letters*, p. 873. In the same letter, written in December 1936, Yeats adds, "For twenty years I never even sent my books for review in to the Irish newspapers, an ignorant form of Catholicism is my enemy." Nor has it ever ceased to be. Typical of such attacks in the past decade are those by L. F. K. Swords, "How to Read the Poems of William Byrne," *Vexilla Regis* [Maynooth Laymen's Annual] (1956), pp. 104–110, and Basil Payne, " 'Debunking Yeats' " (Letters to the Editor), *Irish Times*, 31 March 1962. The opening of the first is representative: "There is no doubt about the vogue that W. B. Yeats has had in England these fifty years. Nor is there any doubt about the mild bewilderment that this vogue has caused among his people at home in Ireland." It should be added that informed Catholics in Ireland, epitomized by Yeats's friend the late Monsignor Patrick Browne, have always been sympathetic to Yeats.

22. *Letters*, p. 255.

Nearly forty years later, Yeats declared himself on Swift and his age to Mario Rossi:

> When a [man] of Swift's sort is born into . . . dryness, is he not in the Catholic sense of the word its *victim?* A French Catholic priest once told me of certain holy women. One was victim for a whole country, another for such and such a village. Is not Swift the human soul in that dryness, is not that his tragedy and his genius? Perhaps every historical phase may have its victims—its poisoned rat in a hole. . . .[23]

Thus Swift was the lonely man, a reputed enemy of mankind, a sort of witness, and yet a sacrifice to destiny. Swift the solitary, Yeats the solitary—perhaps most alike in the solitude of their common indignations. There is no need to review Swift on the subject, for even Owen Aherne once stated, "Jonathan Swift made a soul for the gentlemen of this city by hating his neighbour as himself."[24] We expect the exaggeration, yet on occasion Yeats shared Swift's joyous indignation to the fullest.[25] Their growing contempt for their surroundings, their marked disdain for "modern times," their lashing out in pamphlet and poem as old men, their common hatred of modern literature—"I must turn from that modern literature Jonathan Swift compared to the web a spider draws out of its bowels; I hated and still hate with an ever growing hatred the literature of the [sic] point of view"[26]—this heritage of indignation floods the mind in reading both men's works.

But this haunting kinship in isolation and hatred will mainly serve to accent the more powerful and tragic intensity of Yeats's love of country, a love he also fixed on Swift. For Yeats, Swift had virtually

23. *Ibid.*, p. 819. For more on the French priest, see *Autobiographies*, pp. 330–31. The "poisoned rat" is of course to be found in Swift's letter to Bolingbroke, March 21, 1729–30. Yeats also admitted, on viewing an Augustus John portrait of himself, that John "had found Anglo-Irish solitude, a solitude I have made for myself, an outlawed solitude" (*Pages from a Diary, Explorations*, p. 308).
24. "The Tables of the Law," *Mythologies*, p. 301.
25. *Letters*, pp. 875–76.
26. "A General Introduction for my Work," *Essays and Introductions*, pp. 510–11.

created "the political nationality of Ireland" in the fourth *Drapier Letter* and had discovered his own nationality in writing all those letters.[27] And Swift, before all men of that century, had the greatest grip on both Irelands. Thus as Yeats went about his task to effect what he hoped would be the fulfillment of Swift's nation, he came to regard Swift as almost a phantom familiar, a ghostly mentor, very nearly an ancestral voice returned to urge his case. Between England and a hostile Ireland, both usually chose for Ireland.

Their bond seems undeniable. Yeats often meditated in St. Patrick's. Burial there was offered him in later life.[28] He often recalled his own father speaking of Swift.[29] He monopolized the conversation on Swift in the company of such eighteenth-century scholars as George Trevelyan and Sir Harold Williams.[30] Whether reminding Sean O'Casey that he stirred Dublin as did Swift,[31] or arranging portraits in his study and recalling Swift at the same chore,[32] Yeats seems to be offering us even more evidence of his personal, almost familial relationship to the Dean. So too in his writing. In the later years, Swift seems all but visibly at his elbow. Yeats told Oliver Edwards in 1934 that he got his "later manner from Swift," and as evidence read the

27. *Wheels and Butterflies*, pp. 10–11. The acceptance of Swift by successive generations of Irish patriots is well known; Grattan's exordium to Molyneux and Swift is famous. See also Thomas Davis, *Essays and Poems with a Centenary Memoir*, with a Foreword by An Taoiseach, Eamon de Valera (Dublin, 1945), p. 73; *Standish O'Grady: Selected Essays and Passages*, Every Irishman's Library ed. (Dublin and London, n.d.), p. 168; and P. S. O'Hegarty, *Bell*, X, 478–88.

28. *Wheels and Butterflies*, p. 8. There is also a letter on the subject of possible burial in St. Patrick's from the Rev. David R. Wilson to Joseph Hone in Natl. Lib. MS. 5919.

29. J. B. Yeats, "Ireland Out of the Dock," *United Irishman*, 10 October 1903, and *Letters to his son W. B. Yeats and others 1869–1922*, ed. Joseph Hone (London, 1944), p. 80. Further information on J. B. Yeats and Swift may be found in his *Early Memories: Some Chapters of Autobiography* (Dundrum, 1923), p. 80, and "J. B. Yeats on James Joyce," *Tri-Quarterly*, III (Fall 1964), 70–76.

30. Sir William Rothenstein, *Since Fifty* (London, 1939), pp. 241–42. In a letter to the author, Sir Harold Williams speaks of Yeats's "continuous monologue" during the afternoon of 21 May 1933 at Riversdale.

31. *Letters*, p. 741.

32. *Ibid.*, p. 664.

third stanza of Swift's "Ode to the Honourable Sir William Temple" from his Sheridan edition.[33] Emulous of Swift's energy and clarity,[34] Yeats spent his life, he tells us, ridding his work of what he called modern subjectivity.[35] Swift haunted Yeats in so many ways:

> Sometimes it is a thought of my great-great-grandmother, a friend of that Archbishop King who sent him to England about the 'First Fruits,' sometimes it is S. Patrick's, where I have gone to wander and meditate, that brings him to mind, sometimes I remember something hard or harsh in O'Leary or in Taylor, or in the public speech of our statesmen, that reminds me by its style of his verse or prose. Did he not speak, perhaps, with just such an intonation? This instinct for what is near and yet hidden is in reality a return to the sources of our power, and therefore a claim made upon the future. Thought seems more true, emotion more deep, spoken by someone who touches my pride, who seems to claim me of his kindred, who seems to make me a part of some national mythology. . . .[36]

No less, Swift's had been a chosen patriotism, no matter how great his solitude, his hatred, and his love.[37] But Yeats knew that of the two patriotisms in Ireland, Catholic Ireland's, which was inherited, could not change. In the years ahead of the Free State, as in the years behind, such rigid nationalism seemed to him dangerous for the intellect of the country. In fact he defined a patriot, in this sense, as

33. Letter to the author from Oliver Edwards. Apparently Yeats thought the stanza was inspired by Swift's opposing poetry to pedantry (Hone and Rossi, *Swift*, p. 77).

34. *Pages from a Diary, Explorations*, p. 293.

35. *Letters*, p. 892, and "A General Introduction for my Work," *Essays and Introductions*, pp. 510–11. However, L. A. G. Strong's claim that "The mind whom Yeats most resembled was Swift's" seems doubtful. See "William Butler Yeats," *Scattering Branches*, ed. Stephen Gwynn (New York, 1940), p. 226.

36. *Wheels and Butterflies*, pp. 7–8.

37. In discovering his patriotism or nationality in writing the *Drapier Letters*, Swift, Yeats seems to be saying, was not only serving human liberty but also exercising the choice confronting all Anglo-Irish in Ireland. Regarding Swift's fame after the publication of *A Tale of a Tub*, Stephen Gwynn had written in his *The Life and Friendships of Dean Swift*, p. 93: "All the glory of such a success was his if he chose to claim it. . . ." Yeats underlined the words "if he chose" in his copy.

"a man who will admit all sorts of faults and ignobilities in himself, but will not admit that there is any flaw whatsoever in his native country." [38] Hence the whole matter of the two patriotisms and Yeats's attempt to bring them together in a modus vivendi is best seen in the question he faced at the end of a lecture at the Rathmines Town Hall on February 24, 1926. Shortly before this he had once again braved another audience of patriotic Gaels when they had howled down O'Casey's *The Plough and the Stars.* As recently as February 19, he had had to defend himself and the Abbey against the strange and wonderful charge of being Cromwellian and of producing drama that could not square with national tradition.[39] Now, less than a week later, the scene was prepared that would allow Yeats to expatiate on the maturing of modern Ireland and to hint the role Swift would play in that drama. Yeats at this point contrasts the two patriotisms—one emotional, the other intellectual; the question comes a little later:

> Whatever they got out of "folk," said Mr. Yeats, went straight to the human heart, because there was no complication of speculation or thought, or any of the things that made us unhappy: it was pure emotion. He thought that the almost overwhelming patriotism of our people and our Gaelic Catholic peasantry had been influenced by thoughts of the other world, and that the thought of Ireland in the folk-mind had got penetrated with emotion that arose originally from what was, perhaps, the paradise of pagan Ireland, and was gradually changing into the paradise of Christian Ireland.
>
> There was another patriotism. He had been told the previous night that he was a Cromwellian, and there was a valuable part of Ireland—the Cromwellian part—which had its own patriotism. It was chosen, and it had great qualities. To illustrate this patriotism he read his recent poem: "The Airman Foresees His End" [sic].
>
> After the lecture a member of the audience asked would Mr.

38. "A Poet's Memories," *Freeman's Journal,* 26 January 1924.
39. "The Abbey," *Irish Times,* 20 February 1926.

Yeats express his opinion on the patriotism that resented the faults of a country being exposed. Were the people of other countries as sensitive as the Irish, if a play showing their faults was put on the stage, and was such a play likely to be hounded down in other countries, or to be considered beneficial, as having the effect of curing their faults?

Mr. Yeats said that he thought that a nation was likely to go through that phase, and it was a very natural phase; but he was quite sure that when it reached intellectual maturity it got over that feeling; but every country that had had in any way the opinion of other nations thrust upon it felt that way for a time. The moment a nation reached intellectual maturity, it became exceedingly proud and ceased to be vain, and when it became exceedingly proud it did not disguise its faults, because it was satisfied to know what were its qualities and powers; but when it was immature it was exceedingly vain, and did not believe in itself, and so long as it did not believe in itself it wanted other people to think well of it, in order that it might get a little reflected confidence. With success came pride, and with pride came indifference as to whether people were shown in a good or a bad light on the stage. As a nation came to intellectual maturity it realised that the only thing that did it any credit was its intellect.[40]

At the end of an unpublished section of his *Pages from a Diary,* Yeats could crack, "I know so much more about Swift than about the saints." Nevertheless, we are meant to be pervaded ourselves, indeed haunted, by something of this same intellectual nationalism in Yeats's play, *The Words Upon the Window-pane.* As Yeats counsels us in *A Vision,* though painful re-enactment be purgatorial it can also be a ghostly instruction to the living. If Yeats knew more of Swift than saint, the teeming life of Ireland, past and present, was no less sacred for his preference. For, though seemingly irrelevant to the questions asked at the séance, Mrs. Henderson's dramatization of Swift points unerringly to that most important question posed above, and posed

40. " 'My Own Poetry,' " *Irish Times,* 20 February 1926. See also "Plays and Poetry," *Irish Independent,* 25 February 1926.

again in the Introduction to the play: which way the intellect of modern Ireland?

III

The question brings us to Yeats's second statement on Swift: "Swift . . . looked upon himself . . . as appointed to guard a position." The context in both Swift and Yeats is religious. But the implications can be extended in another way. For Yeats makes it clear in his 1930 *Diary*, from which the passage is taken, and in the Introduction to his play written in the same year, that Swift and he also defended an older order, that both watched that order slip away, and both hated its replacement—external, sentimental, logical, democratic, and optimistic Whiggery.[41]

By this account—stretching matters a bit—Swift became in Yeats's eyes virtually a deposed prince of intellect. He regarded Swift as one of the last of Renaissance men.[42] Yeats conceived of the epoch closing the seventeenth century as the apogee of intellectual power in our civilization;[43] then "men of intellect reached the height of their power, the greatest position they ever attained in society and the State."[44] Given Yeats's theory of the delayed Renaissance come to Ireland after the Battle of the Boyne, we must see Swift, returned in 1714 to this special, intellectual burgeoning, as one more of Ireland's uncrowned kings, no matter how rusticated, exiled, and reluctant he might feel. Swift's sense of defeat Yeats attributes to the ascendance of the ordinary and conventional in the Whig administration. Yeats can even explain that sense of defeat by a misreading of Lord Orrery's *Remarks*. Orrery had it that Swift's bitterness rose from King

41. See also Swift, "Thoughts on Religion," *Works*, X, 187.
42. Yeats found "in Bolingbroke the last pose and in Swift the last passion of the Renaissance" (*Letters*, p. 773). In Bentley, Yeats saw the beginning depredations of the specialist on Renaissance Unity of Being (*On the Boiler*, p. 24).
43. *A Vision* (London, 1956), p. 255.
44. *Wheels and Butterflies*, pp. 8–9.

132

William's broken promise that he should have the first prebendary vacant at Westminster or Canterbury.[45] Now Yeats:

> I think it was Lord Orrery who said that if the Jacobites succeeded Swift was to be Archbishop of Canterbury. If he had cherished such an ambition, his later sense of defeat is intelligible. I see in the defeat of Swift, Bolingbroke, Ormond the defeat of a European phase by an incoming phase which was successful because mechanical, commonplace & normal:—the iron was cooling.[46]

Furthermore, as a Tory—if not Castiglione's—prince of intellect, Swift, according to Yeats, left a permanent distaste for Whiggery in Ireland:

> I still read Swift, and have tried on Mrs. MacNeill the theory, that we dislike the present Royalty because of the impression Swift made on the nation, when his enemies the Whigs brought their ancestors from Germany. Ever since we have been "The Boys of Queen Anne." I think the idea may be useful in London. I heard young Cecil at Oxford explain that, though the Whigs brought them in, they considered them socially impossible.[47]

The enemy in both cases was Whiggery:

> A levelling, rancorous, rational sort of mind
> That never looked out of the eye of a saint
> Or out of a drunkard's eye.

The eye that glared out from the metaphysical dabbler in politics and from the religious fanatic threatened both Yeats and Swift, as shall be pointed out more fully later.

Not so obvious is Yeats's recognition that Swift conducted his defense as an ethical rigorist. Civilizations inevitably rose and fell, but Swift believed they might be temporarily prolonged by practicing

45. John, Earl of Orrery, *Remarks on the Life and Writings of Dr. Jonathan Swift* (Dublin, 1752), p. 29.

46. Unpublished letter to Joseph Hone, 2 September 1932, Natl. Lib. MS. 5918.

47. Unpublished letter to Lady Gregory, December 1928.

the virtues and avoiding the vices that all men understood.[48] So, at least, Yeats interpreted his favorite essay by Swift, *A Discourse of the Contests and Dissentions between the Nobles and the Commons in Athens and Rome* (1701).[49] This ethical rigorism is a major theme of *The Words Upon the Window-pane*. We know the purpose of Yeats's Introduction: to persuade modern Ireland of Swift's vision of national life, an ideal distinct from that of Vico (precursor of Fascism, according to Yeats) or modern England and, less obviously, from Catholicism and Marxism. We are regaled in this Introduction and elsewhere with Swift's battles against various destroyers of national cultural unity—the Bentleys, the theorists of the third book of *Gulliver*, the selfish private interests of the many that would oppress men of public spirit, in short, "all that whiggish world Swift stared on till he became a raging man."[50] By strong implication, Ireland of the 1930's might well heed these dangers.[51] But the play itself in its butterfly way goes to the heart of these warnings.

David R. Clark and a number of other critics have informed us of levels of meaning in the play, have invoked the magic words "irony," "tensions," and "ambiguity," and have generally demonstrated how eighteenth-century Dublin mocks its survivals in the modern day, how Swift's passionate re-enactment contrasts with our apathetic lives.[52] So far so good. But they have explained neither the significance of the title nor those themes of the play embraced by ethical rigorism and a hatred of Whiggery. The words upon the pane are

48. *Wheels and Butterflies*, p. 19. However, in *Pages from a Diary*, Yeats had qualified this thought by writing "civilization is driven to its final phase not by the jealousy and egotism of the many, as Swift's too simple statement implies, but by 'pure thought', 'reason', what my System calls 'spirit' and 'celestial body', by that which makes all places and persons alike" (*Explorations*, p. 316). In any case, Yeats goes on to admit that Swift also abhorred pure thought. Otherwise, the statement about Swift's ethical rigorism remained unqualified.

49. *Wheels and Butterflies*, p. 19.

50. *On the Boiler*, p. 26.

51. All the introductions, or wheels, in *Wheels and Butterflies* were meant to comprise "a scheme of intellectual nationalism" (*Letters*, p. 779).

52. See, for example, David R. Clark, "Yeats and the Modern Theatre," *Threshold*, IV (Autumn–Winter 1960), 36–56, and *Plays of Changing Ireland*, ed. Curtis Canfield (New York, 1936), pp. 5–7.

actually Stella's. Like those words cut with a diamond on a pane of Fairfield, the house where Yeats lived during 1910, they are a cryptic reminder from the eighteenth century.[53] In their way, then, Stella's words pay the tribute to Swift that Yeats pays him for his hopes to prolong the epoch of that civilization:

> You taught how I might youth prolong
> By knowing what is right and wrong;
> How from my heart to bring supplies
> Of lustre to my fading eyes.[54]

These are the only words from Stella's birthday poem of 1721 actually to appear on the window pane. But later in the play, Swift repeats them and adds a few more lines:

> How soon a beauteous mind repairs
> The loss of chang'd or falling hairs;
> How wit and virtue from within
> Can spread a smoothness o'er the skin!

and finally utters the conclusion to the poem:

> Late dying, may you cast a shred
> Of that rich mantel o'er my head;
> To bear with dignity my sorrow,
> One day alone, then die to-morrow.

These first four lines and their elaboration may establish the point. Swift might teach modern Ireland, as he had taught Stella and had not taught eighteenth-century Ireland, how to prolong its youth by knowing right from wrong and listening to the promptings of the heart.[55] Swift as a moral agent in modern Ireland was a figure dear to

53. *Letters*, p. 891, n.1. The words on the pane at Fairfield were

> Mary Kilpatrick—very young
> Ugly face and pleasant tongue

as this letter to Gogarty makes clear.

54. "Stella to Dr. Swift," *Works*, VII, 237–38.

55. Interestingly enough, one of Yeats's few place-markers in his edition of Swift is found between two pages which end in the following reflection on the fall of the Duke of Marlborough:

Yeats in these years, as the following unpublished passage shows:

> . . . if I communicate with the living mind of Shakespeare when I read of Coriolanus among the servants of Aufidius, do I not communicate with the living mind of Swift still in that almost equal moment when discovering that his life or liberty depended upon an unsatisfactory servant, he dismissed him that he might not through fear endure any man's negligence or insolence, & restored him & honoured him when all danger had passed. As the difference between these two acts is that Shakespeare had for object the creation of a mental image, while Swift had for object an effect upon our life within defined limits; it would be more easy therefore to believe if we had only ties to cause it, his eternal moment, to become—through the universal mind—a conscious moral agent in our own lives.[56]

Beyond showing Swift as a moral agent, the passage goes a long way toward suggesting why Yeats chose to dramatize Swift.[57] Swift's idea

---

> There has not perhaps in the present age, been a clearer instance, to show the instability of greatness, which is not founded upon virtue. . . . This lord, who was beyond all comparison the greatest subject in Christendom, found his power, credit, and influence, crumble away on a sudden; and except a few friends or followers by inclination, the rest dropt off in course. From directing in some manner the affairs of Europe, he descended to be a member of a faction, and with little distinction even there: that virtue of subduing his resentments . . . having now wholly forsaken him, when he stood most in need of its assistance; and, upon trial, was found unable to bear a reverse of fortune, giving way to rage, impatience, envy, and discontent (*History of the Last Four Years of the Queen, Works,* IV, 49).

56. Unpublished section of *Pages from a Diary.* In another unpublished section, Yeats explains Swift's supposed failure to see the final tyranny of pure thought as "fated" by the fact that he was a "reformer."

57. Part of the drama was also natural to a medium and her summoned spirit. On this score, Yeats heavily marked the following passage in his copy of G. N. M. Tyrrell's *Science and Psychical Phenomena* (London, 1938), p. 216, confirming a long-held belief: "I think we can argue, with a minimum of fantasy, the existence of an impulse to dramatize on the part of the medium (a natural and respectable impulse when the mediumship is of high grade), combined in greater or less degree with an impulse to co-operate with and assist the dramatization on the part of the discarnate person."

for forming a nation—"a self-imposed discipline, a deliberate limit" [58] —expressed the same truth to Yeats. He seldom forgot the import of Swift's warning in the *Contests and Dissensions:*

> The fate of empire is grown a common-place: that all forms of government having been instituted by men, must be mortal like their authors, and have their periods of duration limited as well as those of private persons. . . . there are few, who turn their thoughts to examine, how those diseases in a state are bred, that hasten its end; which would however be a very useful enquiry. For, though we cannot prolong the period of a commonwealth beyond the decree of heaven, or the date of its nature, any more than human life beyond the strength of the seminal virtue; yet we may manage a sickly constitution, and preserve a strong one; we may watch and prevent accidents . . . and by these, and other such methods, render a state longlived, though not immortal. [59]

What better words for a precarious new state—the Irish Free State— come to birth at the end of a great cycle of Western civilization?

Vanessa's character, by its contrast with Stella's, may best explain the ruin that Swift foresaw and, by implication, the enemy that Yeats and Swift fought. We know that Yeats theorized about the characters of the two women, and that he was for the most part bored by Vanessa's correspondence with Swift. [60] In fact, he liked her character not at all, [61] and probably agreed with Lord Orrery's unflattering description of her. [62] In any case, the play shows her to be as intractable as the new age Yeats faced and as dangerous as the future

---

58. TS. of Introduction to *Fighting the Waves*, Natl. Lib. MS. 8774(1).

59. *Works*, II, 411–12. Yeats was emphatic on this means of preserving the best of the old in the new Ireland: "Indeed the *Discourse* with its law of history might be for us what Vico is to the Italians [under Mussolini], had we a thinking nation" (*Pages from a Diary, Explorations*, p. 293). In the same year, 1930–31, Yeats likened his own efforts in *A Vision* to Swift's above when he wrote Olivia Shakespeare: "I think I have done one good deed in clearing out of the state from death to birth all the infinities and eternities, and picturing a state as 'phenomenal' as that from birth to death" (*Letters*, p. 781).

60. Rothenstein, *Since Fifty*, p. 241, and *Wheels and Butterflies*, p. 27.

61. Information from Mrs. W. B. Yeats.

62. *Remarks* (Dublin, 1752), pp. 107–8.

he thought Swift quailed before. Yeats reminds us that much more than Swift's ministerial friends was soon to disappear, for already the age of Rousseau and Marat rose on the eighteenth-century horizon. The play insists that Swift's rejection of Vanessa depends on this vision. Yeats makes this crux clear in his Introduction:

> . . . the intellect of Swift's age, persuaded that the mechanicians mocked by Gulliver would prevail, that its moment of freedom could not last, so dreaded the historic process that it became in the half-mad mind of Swift a dread of parentage: "Am I to add another to the healthy rascaldom and knavery of the world?" [63]

Both Swift and the intellect of his age react in revulsion—on grounds of blood and excellence—to Vanessa's visions of maternity.

Thus to the opposite of Stella's words upon the windowpane. That opposite is summed up in Vanessa's phrase to describe herself, "common ivory dice," also the opposite of Swift whom she calls "dice loaded by the intellect." By her "common ivory dice" Yeats shows us that, eugenically speaking, chance and choice are not one here. Swift has not succeeded in building Rome in her mind nor is she really any more than the ignorant girl he claims she was at their first meeting. Even she admits that his intellect separates them. How very closely she must also resemble the new Ireland that Yeats would educate. And how attractive the beastly wench was to both men. But Swift, passionate man that the play insists he is, finding himself locked in with her beats on the door and sinks to the floor—certainly in character with the Swift whom elsewhere Yeats pictures as "dragged . . . down into mankind." If the conclusion remains ambiguous, Yeats's contrast in ladies and intellects does not. Moreover, in the presentation of Swift and Vanessa, we get a scene very close to Yeats's interpretation of Gulliver's last voyage. For when Swift resists the chance of hurling Vanessa into maternity, and thus spares an increasingly hopeless age yet one more brat, is he not recoiling as did Gulliver at the end of Book IV when gathered into the joyous arms

63. *Wheels and Butterflies*, p. 30.

of his wife? Gulliver swoons, having seen, for a time at least, a superior order of mind. Swift, branding Vanessa his enemy, prays that he may grant only his intellect to posterity. This is the horror in *Gulliver* of which Yeats often spoke.[64] He also never forgot that Swift had termed the Houyhnhnms "the perfection of nature." In an early draft, Yeats defines this as "nature bred, trained and disciplined, nature made perfect by intellect." In the play Stella comes as close as any to deserving the same sobriquet.

Yet the price of Swift's chaste attachment to Stella must not go unnoticed in the play. His fear of solitude and dread of what life held in store for him she will mitigate for but a few more years. We know she must soon die. No doubt his guilt for the sorrows of both women is evident in his purgatorial return. Both his humanity and lack of humanity—the price of his intellect—before Vanessa and Stella urge his purgation. But the seductive danger to the intellect, however pious or patriotic the ensuing rascaldom might be, had the example of Stella, no matter how tragic her lot, as its antidote in Ireland.[65]

If we cannot forget Swift's last words in the play—"Perish the day on which I was born!"—that hearty phrase from Job reserved during Swfit's lifetime for his birthday, we may be struck by the closeness of that birthday to the first performance of the play in November 1930. For Swift's voice was truly the only one possible, given its vigor and command, to represent the wisdom of that much maligned, partially guilty, and just as human Protestant eighteenth century. The play, however, is much more than a simple lecture to modern Ireland. Its final impress is one of tragic wisdom and harsh sweetness, not the thin subjectivity of most "spiritual" drama. Thus Yeats's unpublished comment on Swift's impact in this play must be quoted:

64. *A Vision* (1956), p. 28.
65. In a Diary of Thought begun 23 September 1928, Yeats wrote, "Mediums have a few fixed types of controls. . . . Perhaps the national mind at each epoch is limited also to a few types. The medium types are apparently those which can be dramatized most easily by voice alone. The dramatizations of the national mind are more numerous because the various means are greater but those capable of vigorous expression must be few." Stella is never heard in the play, but her verses on Swift, and Swift's admiration for them and her, are its central matter.

In Ireland political wrongs may have created the unconscious dialectic she needed . . . though Swift had said all when he wrote the fable of the bee and the spider in Sir William Temple's library; ancient thought had nothing but the hum and its wings—it sought everywhere wax and honey, sweetness, light; like those wise horses in Gulliver it was "the perfection of nature"; but the modern literature "spat it all out the guts," cared not how foul the substance so that it built its mathematical structure. When I was a young man trying to revive Irish self-confidence by talk about the concrete beauty of the old poems and stories, I boasted that in the Gaelic language "it was almost impossible to speak an artificial thought" and now I say that the Protestant memory which seemed to me so unIrish expressed in the intellectual forms of the modern world a like vision; that they were indeed the chief modern voice of empirical speculative genius: "To garret or cellar a wheel I send." [66]

For concrete models of that genius, Yeats's play joins *Gulliver's Travels* and *The Battle of the Books*. Only Swift's epitaph seemed greater to Yeats.[67]

IV

Perhaps nothing written by Swift so moved Yeats as did that epitaph in St. Patrick's Cathedral. It could, as Yeats wrote, make him question his very sanity.[68] If hatred and love were the warring elements that tugged at his reason in reading these lines, it was essentially Swift's "passion" for an undefined liberty—"something not himself that Swift served"—that most excited Yeats.[69]

66. Large white vellum notebook begun 23 November 1930.
67. *Yeats and T. Sturge Moore*, p. 141.
68. "A General Introduction for my Work," *Essays and Introductions*, p. 519. As early as 1909 Yeats had written: "And is not that epitaph Swift made in Latin for his own tomb more immortal than his pamphlets, perhaps than his great allegory?" ("Preface to the First Edition of John M. Synge's *Poems and Translations*," *Essays and Introductions*, p. 308).
69. *Letters*, p. 791.

> Swift has sailed into his rest;
> Savage indignation there
> Cannot lacerate his breast.
> Imitate him if you dare,
> World-besotted traveller; he
> Served human liberty.

Of course there is poetic license here—where did the "World-besotted traveller" come from? Yet in the presence of at least three drafts and as many more published versions of the poem,[70] we must recognize it for what it is: a distinctly Yeatsian poetic formulation of Swift on liberty. "World-besotted traveller" suggests a Swift who was not infatuated with the world. He coincides with that Swift Yeats called a solitary, a defender of a religious position, a lover of perfect nature, and hater of men en masse. Recalling that epitaph, Yeats once declared that the liberty Swift "served was that of intellect, not liberty for the masses but for those who could make it visible." [71] This is obviously not the interpretation that most Swift scholars offer. Still Yeats had in mind a special sort of intellectual liberty, fiercely aristocratic and narrowly Augustan—part of the great Irish song against Whiggery. Yeats's fullest elaboration of the idea is to be found in his interpretation of the *Discourse of the Contests and Dissensions . . . in Athens and Rome,* his favorite tract by Swift:

> What was this liberty . . . served through all his life with so much eloquence? "I should think," he wrote in the *Discourse,* "that the saying, *vox populi, vox dei* ought to be understood of the universal bent and current of a people, not of the bare majority of a few representatives, which is often procured by little arts, and great industry and application; wherein those who engage in the pursuits of malice and revenge are much more sedulous than such as would prevent them." That *vox populi* or "bent and current," or what we even more vaguely call national spirit, was the sole theme of his *Drapier Letters;*

70. Rapallo Notebook II; *Lady Gregory's Journals,* p. 266; and *Variorum,* p. 493.

71. *Pages from a Diary, Explorations,* p. 315.

its right to express itself as it would through such men as had won or inherited general consent. I doubt if a mind so contemptuous of average men thought . . . that it found expression also through all individual lives, or asked more for those lives than protection from the most obvious evils.[72]

Such a concept of liberty is barely recognizable to us. The drift is toward the few, toward imperious intellect, authority, mystical nationalism—some have even said toward fascism. Yet it cannot be repeated too often that the Ireland of Yeats's old age and the England of Swift's pamphlet had just survived revolution and civil war, acute religious contention, assassinations, and threats of foreign invasion, not to mention the spread of new leveling and democratic forces—sectaries and republicans before the reign of Queen Anne, a left-wing IRA and a militant Christian Front before the end of the thirties in Ireland. Moreover, the Ireland that finally rid herself of British despotism possessed a peasantry, as Swift had predicted, ready to inflict the even more despotic rule of a zealously Gaelic and Catholic majority. After 1927, this spirit more and more informed Fianna Fail attacks on such ex-Unionists as Bryan Cooper and on an Irish Senate that had been as distinguished as any second house in Europe. Consequently, there is a fine eighteenth-century ring in Yeats's subsequent hatred of those he termed "Jacobin and Jacobite." [73]

The Jacobites—fanatical political Catholics—seemed to Yeats a sharp threat to the freedom of the intellect. And Irish intellectual and artistic freedom to Yeats was often a matter of civil liberty. Thus it became part of his task as a celebrant at Swift's tomb to fight such "Whiggery," as he once intoned in the poem "The Seven Sages," as would oppress the human mind.

Part of the problem lay in the courageous but still immature patriotism, so sensitive to any imagined slight to Ireland, that remained after 1923 and that Yeats described so ably in 1926 as a product of insecure vanity rather than of confident pride.[74] But there

72. *Wheels and Butterflies*, pp. 22–23.
73. "Louis Lambert," *Essays and Introductions*, p. 447.
74. "My Own Poetry," *Irish Times*, 25 February 1926.

is an even more unfortunate side to the story. From the days of *The Countess Cathleen,* he had been more and more the target of an ignorant, lower-middle-class Catholic press. Nor had Yeats ever been very politic in the face of such attacks—why should he have been? After the establishment of the Free State, magazines like the *Catholic Bulletin* and the *Catholic Mind,* to name but two, had little more than vituperation for Yeats. Both employed the usual catcalls of paganism, Ascendancy, filthy literature, and the nonsense Yeats well knew.[75] But these ignoble exceptions to Holy Church did not stop at name-calling. Like Swift, returned to Ireland amid the jeers and vulgar threats of the Whigs, Yeats in the twenties and thirties lived more and more under the explicit threat of Catholic action, always a bracer to him.[76] Now Yeats knew as well as any man the folly of either clericalism or anticlericalism, as the following comment, with its Swiftian echo, assumes at the end of his Senate career:

"We have created a native literature—a vigorous intellectual life in Dublin, but the blundering of a censorship may drive much Irish intellect into exile once more, and turn what remains into a bitter polemical energy.

"We have created something at once daring and beautiful and gracious, and I may see my life's work and that of my friends, Synge, 'AE,' and Lady Gregory, sinking down into a mire of clericalism and anti-clericalism.

"I am glad . . . to be out of politics. I'd like to spend my old age as a bee and not as a wasp." [77]

75. See, for example, *Catholic Mind,* III (November 1932), 247, and (December 1932), 276–77, and then the sinister, unsigned editorials allegedly written by Father Timothy Corcoran, S.J., in *Catholic Bulletin* during, for instance, 1924–25. *Catholic Mind* is typical of such publications in its unrelieved anti-Semitism, bigotry, and inquisitorial listing of Free Masons. Yeats liked to remind these magazines of Catholic Austria's record in illegitimacy before World War I. See "Civilization," *Irish Times,* 12 November 1925. During March and April 1939, *Catholic Bulletin* printed articles showing at great length that Yeats had never been what it chose to call an Irish poet.

76. *Letters,* pp. 746–47.

77. " 'As a Bee—Not as a Wasp.' Senator Yeats in his Old Age," *Irish Independent,* 22 October 1928.

But the increasing threat of mob action against his and his friends' work was something new. For to be told by Mrs. Kevin O'Higgins in 1928 that she had been instructed at a retreat never to even recognize Yeats or Lennox Robinson was merely to be offered a presage for the attack within ten years on all supposedly unorthodox art.[78]

The quarrel was a long one. How tragic and yet very nearly comic its bare recital is. But the major point is that intellectual oppression in Ireland invariably, whether by mob, cleric, or ruler, took the form of a curtailment, often legal curtailment, of civil liberties. Both Swift and Yeats recognized this. And Yeats's defense of civil liberties, like Swift's, is legendary in Ireland. Yeats's indignation was equally savage on the point.

But, before continuing to describe Yeats's fight against pious tyranny, it is best to remember that like Swift, he cut his teeth on English injustice in Ireland. His objections to the Queen's visit and his rows with Trinity College are well known. Yet it is usually forgotten that, for instance, in 1900 he could attack Lord Cadogan for his secret suppression of the *United Irishman,* beginning his accusation with the words, "It should be a principle of political life that all acts which involve public liberties should be done publicly."[79] In 1909, in defying the British by putting on *The Showing Up of Blanco Posnet,* Yeats could comment, "We want in Ireland . . . neither indirect censorship from the Lord Chamberlain through the Lord Lieutenant nor directly under the English Censor."[80] He also had hopes of showing Connolly's *Green Pastures,* censored in England, because he felt his countrymen would applaud its religious

78. *Letters,* pp. 747, 871, 885. There is a valuable comprehensive survey of this subject by Marion Witt, " 'Great Art Beaten Down,' " *College English,* XIII (February 1952), 248–58.

79. "The Freedom of the Press in Ireland," *The Speaker,* 7 July 1900, pp. 386–87.

80. "Blanco Posnet," *Daily Express,* 26 August 1909. See also the formal statement by Yeats and Lady Gregory in the *Evening Telegraph,* 23 August 1909. Characteristically and rather ominously for future times, the *Irish Catholic* retorted in an editorial on 4 September, "in the name of the decency of the drama and to safeguard the stage, we most heartily . . . protest against the theory advanced by Mr. Yeats and Lady Gregory that Ireland needs no Censor. In our opinion no country in the world needs one more."

THE TOWER

"Blessed be this place,
More blessed still this tower . . ."

SANDYMOUNT CASTLE AND FAMILY GROUP

"Sandymount Castle. . . . I vividly recall those photographs . . . of a great door
suggesting not Abbotsford but Strawberry Hill—the door that my dream recalled."

ENTRANCE TO YEATS'S FLAT AT 42 FITZWILLIAM SQUARE
"George has made our flat at 42 Fitzwilliam Square charming. . . ."

GEORGE BERKELEY D.D.
Fellow 1707, Bishop of Cloyne 1733

JAMES LATHAM'S PORTRAIT OF BERKELEY
"I hate what I remember of his portrait in the Fellows' Room at Trinity College."

COURTESY OF THE GREEN STUDIO

FOLEY'S STATUE OF BURKE
IN FRONT OF TRINITY COLLEGE,
DUBLIN
"And haughtier-headed Burke that
proved the State a tree . . ."

COURTESY OF BORD FAILTE

FOLEY'S STATUE OF GOLDSMITH
IN FRONT OF TRINITY COLLEGE,
DUBLIN
"Oliver Goldsmith sang what he had
seen . . ."

BUST OF DEAN SWIFT,
ST. PATRICK'S CATHEDRAL, DUBLIN
"Swift haunts me; he is always just
round the next corner."

THE STATUE OF GRATTAN
IN COLLEGE GREEN, DUBLIN
"Protestant Ireland should ask permis-
sion to bring back the body of Grattan
from Westminster Abbey to Saint
Patrick's."

OLD SOLDIERS HOSPITAL,
KILMAINHAM, DUBLIN

From James Malton's *Picturesque and Descriptive View of the City of Dublin*
(1792–99)

"It is a masterpiece of architecture. It is not only the work of a great architect, but the work of a great architect of a great period."

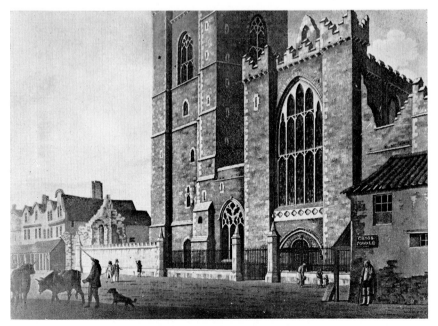

ST. PATRICK'S CATHEDRAL

From James Malton's *Picturesque and Descriptive View of the City of Dublin*
(1792–99)

"S. Patrick's, where I have gone to wander and meditate. . . ."

THE FOUNTAIN OF THE RUTLAND MEMORIAL IN MERRION SQUARE

From the aquatint by J. G. Stadler, after an engraving by J. J. Barralet, in The National Gallery of Ireland

—One of Yeats's favorite Georgian memorials

THE FOUR COURTS, DUBLIN

"We have there a building of great importance and great dignity, which we ought to have looked upon as a trust received from the past."

THE CEILING OF THE SENATE CHAMBER IN LEINSTER HOUSE, DUBLIN
"May I ask if precautions have been taken not to interfere in any way with the dignity and beauty of the ceiling of that remarkable room."

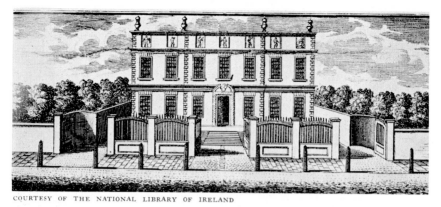

THE LORD MAYOR'S HOUSE
From Brooking's *Map of Dublin*, 1728

THE MANSION HOUSE, DUBLIN
". . . get the Mansion House into its eighteenth century state."

THE ROYAL IRISH ACADEMY

". . . the Royal Irish Academy had begun the study of ancient Irish literature. That study . . . was a gift from the Protestant aristocracy. . . ."

CONSTANCE AND EVA GORE-BOOTH
"Two girls in silk kimonos, both
Beautiful, one a gazelle . . ."

LISSADELL HOUSE
"The light of evening, Lissadell,
Great windows open to the south . . ."

W. B. YEATS'S PASTEL OF THE LIBRARY AT COOLE
"Beloved books that famous hands have bound,
Old marble heads, old pictures everywhere . . ."

ROBERT GREGORY

"Soldier, scholar, horseman, he . . ."

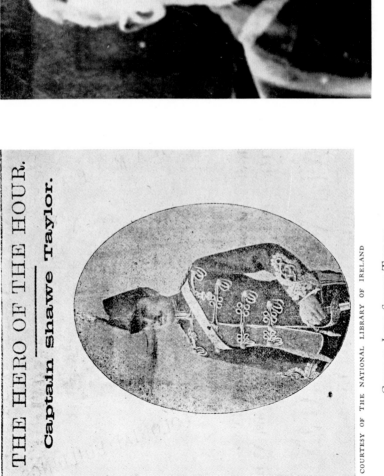

CAPTAIN JOHN SHAWE-TAYLOR

"Impetuous men, Shawe-Taylor and Hugh Lane . . ."

At the Convention—Left to right—Comdt. Cronin, Mr. Ernest Blythe, Gen. O'Duffy, Col. J. Ryan and Dr. T. F. O'Higgins, T.D.

BLUE SHIRT LEADERS, JULY 1933
From the *Irish Independent*, 21 July 1933
"Soldiers take pride in saluting their Captain,
Where are the captains that govern mankind?
What happens a tree that has nothing within it?"

THE SIEGE OF DERRY AND THE BATTLE OF THE BOYNE
From tapestries hanging in the Bank of Ireland
"The Irish House of Lords . . . when it ordered the Huguenot tapestries, probably
accepted the weavers argument that the Battle of the Boyne was to Ireland what the
defeat of the Armada had been to England."

beauty rather than reject it as blasphemy.[81] In 1913, Yeats could even take issue with the Liverpool police, not with the transplanted Irish patriots, for their presumption in threatening to halt the production of the *Playboy* without due process of law.[82] As late as February 1921, during a debate at the Oxford Union Society on the question, "That this House would welcome complete Self-Government in Ireland and condemns reprisals," Yeats angrily reminded the audience "that not law, only English law, has broken down in Ireland. Sinn Fein brought real justice into his part of Ireland for the first time for centuries. The only complaint was that they protected property perhaps a little too vigorously." [83] Where civil liberties were concerned, no official was safe from Yeats's wrath. During the Dublin strike of 1913, he could take on Nationalists, Unionists, Dublin police, Holy Church, and the Castle government itself. His rage here is very much like Swift's before the shame of Irish misery:

> They [directors of the police and editors of newspapers] are supposed to watch over our civil liberties, and I charge the Dublin Nationalist newspapers with deliberately arousing religious passion to break up the organization of the workingman, with appealing to mob law day after day, with publishing the names of workingmen and their wives for purposes of intimidation. And I charge the Unionist Press of Dublin and those who directed the police with conniving at this conspiracy. I want to know by what right the police have refused to accept charges against rioters; I want to know who has ordered the abrogation of the most elementary rights of the citizens, and why authorities who are bound to protect every man in doing that which he has a legal right to do—even though they have to call upon all the forces of the Crown—have permitted the Ancient Order of

81. Dr. Patrick McCartan, "William Butler Yeats—The Fenian," *Irish-American Review*, I (n.d.), 417.

82. " 'The Playboy,' " *The Times*, 1 December 1913, p. 66, and " 'The Playboy' at Liverpool," *The Times*, 4 December 1913, p. 12.

83. Report in the *Freeman's Journal*, 19 February 1921. For a fuller and slightly different account, see Norman Jeffares, *W. B. Yeats: Man and Poet*, 2nd ed. (London, 1962), pp. 227, 328.

Hibernians to besiege Dublin, taking possession of the railway stations like a foreign army. Prime Ministers have fallen, and Ministers of State have been impeached for less than this. I demand that the coming Police Inquiry shall be so widened that we may get to the bottom of a conspiracy, whose like has not been seen in any English-speaking town during living memory.[84]

And so with Jacobites in Ireland after the Treaty. For Yeats's concept of liberty was clearly one inspired not only by Swift but by the practice of English-speaking countries throughout the world.[85] Thus in his later fight with a section of the Catholic Church, it was not only Swift's concern for Irish liberty but also a world-wide, though highly aristocratic, standard of intellectual freedom that Yeats defended. How else interpret his part in defending Parnell, *The Countess Cathleen*, the *Playboy*, Hugh Lane's proposals for a new gallery, the coinage designs, a divorce law, the publication of *Tomorrow*, the production of *The Plough and the Stars*, the organization of an Irish Academy of Letters, the need for copyright laws, or resistance to the proposed Censorship Act? [86] A brief discussion of two

84. "Dublin Fanaticism," *Irish Worker*, 1 November 1913.

85. In commenting on his Roger Casement ballads, Yeats reminded Dorothy Wellesley that "I am fighting in those ballads for what I have been fighting all my life, it is our Irish fight though it has nothing to do with this or that country." He then added, "We remember our age-old quarrel against gold braid and ermine, and that our ancestor Swift has gone where 'fierce indignation can lacerate his heart no more,' and we go stark, staring mad" (*Letters*, p. 876). At the turn of the century, Yeats had been especially shocked by the attentions paid Edward VII and his horse Ambrose II by Maynooth. See *The World* (New York), 22 November 1903, p. M3.

86. Perhaps Yeats's remark on the attack on Synge sums up this point: "The truth is that the objection to Synge is not mainly that he makes the country people unpleasant or immoral, but that he has got a standard of morals and intellect. . . . they shrink from Synge's harsh, independent, heroical, clean, wind-swept view of things. They want their clerical conservatory where the air is warm and damp. . . . Nothing is ever persecuted but the intellect, though it is never persecuted under its own name" (*Letters*, p. 495). The Irish Academy of Letters, as Yeats once explained, "was intended to protect Irish literature against those who insist that it must be exclusively medieval, Gaelic, and Catholic" (unidentified newspaper clipping, Holloway, Natl. Lib. MS. 1953 [October–December 1932], opp. p. 783). The expected hysterical rejoinder to the

146

of these actions—his defense of divorce and his attack on censorship
—may make his reverence for Swift's services to liberty even
clearer.

Reading Yeats's divorce speech, one can only be amused by the
imperceptive comments of a Monk Gibbon or L. A. G. Strong.[87] Nor
can one take much more seriously the vicious attack on Yeats by
Donal O'Sullivan, whose factually accurate—so far as the facts go that
he chooses to present—*The Irish Free State and Its Senate* is equally
marred by his unrelenting attack on De Valera, his praise of the Blue
Shirts, and his castigation of Yeats's divorce speech.[88] O'Sullivan
seems never to face the problem Yeats raised: that the rights to
separation and divorce accorded Irishmen under the British government should continue to be made available in Ireland, to include
divorce *a vinculo matrimonii* hitherto made possible for Irishmen
through the submission of private bills in Parliament. Nor, of course,
was the freedom Yeats demanded to be necessarily that of any one
class. Moreover, the charge of being "divisive," in the divorce
speech, recently leveled against him simply puts the cart before the
horse.[89] The very essence of his speech was that the proposed
legislation would permanently divide the whole of Ireland—just as
today compulsory Gaelic and the Censorship Act have added to the
difficulty of ever bringing in the North. Doubtless Yeats was
somewhat excited and tactless, as he admitted in the course of his
speech. But three things must be remembered: that Yeats was not
interested in divorce per se; that he did not expect to influence one vote

---

founding of the Academy came this time from the Rev. P. J. Gannon, S.J., in a
lecture at the Theatre Royal entitled "The Irish Academy of Letters—
Unwelcomed and Unauthorized" ("The New Irish Academy," *Irish Times*, 14
November 1932). See also *Variorum*, pp. 818–20, 832–37.

87. Monk Gibbon, *The Masterpiece and the Man* (New York, 1959), pp.
111–13, and L. A. G. Strong, *The Minstrel Boy* (New York, 1937), p. 206.
Equally imperceptive is Michael Tierney, *Daniel O'Connell* (Dublin, 1949),
pp. 275–76.

88. *The Irish Free State and Its Senate* (London, 1940). Chapter X is
devoted especially to the attack on Yeats's divorce speech.

89. "Letters to the Editor," *New Statesman*, LXIII (19 January 1962),
85.

in what he took to be a hopeless situation; and that the purpose of his speech, like that of much of Swift's satire, was the education of the nation as a whole. He also feared a trend toward theological legislation, against the very dictates of a constitution which guaranteed equal religious rights in the Free State. For all Yeats knew, this was the beginning of the suppression of all nonconformist liberties.

Did he ironically recall John O'Leary, his former mentor, who had once assured Protestants "we are all Irish" in 1886 in his essay, "Some Guarantees for the Protestant Unionist Minority in Ireland"? [90] In any case, he must have recalled his own brave words at a meeting of Irish Protestants at the Antient Concert Rooms on January 24, 1913. The meeting had been called to allow public-minded Protestants to oppose the attempt to inject religious contention into the Home Rule controversy. To appreciate Yeats's feelings of betrayal in his divorce speech, one ought to ponder these earlier hopes for a Protestant minority in a unified Ireland:

> Mr. W. B. Yeats . . . said that that that was the first time he had ever spoken to Irish Protestants. He was a Protestant— of a sort. (Laughter.) He had done all his work amongst Irish Catholics. If there was intolerance in Ireland, he knew it; if there was tolerance in Ireland, he knew it. He believed on that subject they should speak with entire sincerity, without any thought of political expediency. There was intolerance, and because there was intolerance he had asked to have committed to him the third resolution, which stated—

> That this meeting subscribes to the view that the clear verdict of the history of civilized nations in modern times is that the responsibilities of self-government and the growth of political freedom are the most powerful solvents for sectarian animosities.

90. John O'Leary, "Some Guarantees for the Protestant Unionist Minority in Ireland," *University Review*, December 1886, pp. 959–65. Yeats had also once signed an open letter to John Redmond stating that the signatories, as Protestants in Southern Ireland, did not "live in fear of their Catholic neighbours" in the likely prospect that Home Rule would come ("Dublin Protestants and Mr. Redmond," *Irish Times*, 11 April 1912).

He was an Irish Nationalist, because he believed since he first gave thought to these things that no country could prosper unless the greater portion of its intellect was occupied with itself. Every vigorous country would send away intellectual men to work in other lands, but it would not prosper unless the majority of those it produced were occupied in making the land fruitful materially or intellectually. In no country were the best minds intolerant. It was the mediocre minds that were intolerant. (Applause.) They were asking nothing but an arena in which the best might come out, and the best might rule. (Applause.) The intolerance which he dreaded was the intolerance that existed amongst Catholics and Protestants, against ideas, against books, against European culture, and he saw nothing that would put down that intolerance but the obtaining of that arena that would teach them how to sift out the best men. (Applause.) In North-East Ulster they did not know it, they believed quite honestly that they would be persecuted. There would be no persecutions. (Applause.) Bring the various elements together in a Legislature, set them to do business, and then the common interests would come. (Applause.) Ten years of common business and common interests would destroy what had mostly been sterile party contests. (Hear, hear.) [91]

To be faced within three years of the Treaty with a legislature quite willing to curtail not only religious freedom but also ideas, books, and European culture through censorship must have been a bitter pill indeed. Little wonder that Yeats felt that Catholic Ireland was making the same mistake in 1925 as did the ancient Jews in demanding legality.[92] His consequent bluntness or outspokenness not only recalls Swift's onslaughts against theological legislation in "The Legion Club," it also smacks of Swift's frequent isolation and violence of method. Yeats alone—even Gogarty walked out of the Senate chamber during the speech, rumors were started that Yeats himself wanted a divorce, and a typist wept rather than record his

91. "Home Rule and Religion," *Irish Times*, 25 January 1913.
92. *Lady Gregory's Journals*, p. 91; *Pages from a Diary, Explorations*, p. 338.

speech [93]—Yeats alone was nevertheless the equal of Swift alone, both of them courageous, bristling, and combative.

The other central fact is that Yeats saw the proposed legislation as an encroachment on the intellect that possessed liberty of choice. Some three months before his Senate speech, he had printed an undelivered speech on divorce in the *Irish Statesman* in which he declared the proposed bill an aggressive act.[94] It was an aggression by a majority of the Irish people not only against those outside the Catholic Church, but also an aggression that would help perpetuate the unexamined life in Ireland. Here it is Yeats's abiding preoccupation with the freedom of the human mind of proven and historical genius that is so consistent with his interpretation of Swift's epitaph. When allowed to speak on June 11, 1925, he defended "the living, changing, advancing human mind" [95]—a most un-Swiftian description; yet he meant the mind that refused to be bound by ignorance or by the legislation of the mass of men. At that moment he saw that heritage of intellectual choice as an eighteenth-century gift from the Anglo-Irish, precisely the operation of the intellect that a religious attack had tried to remove from the nation. Not snobbery but pride, not two nations but possibly one in a future that would see the defeat of bigotry, not rudeness but a high inspired appeal in the midst of despair for a coming intellectual transformation—these were Yeats's lonely intentions. If his arguments were not always those of Swift— Swift tended to resent *state* interference in religions—his indignation, isolation, and racial memory were inspired by that stern intellectual ancestor. Yeats was one of the "people of Swift." [96]

So far as Swift, Yeats, and liberty go, the Censorship of Publications Bill was almost a foregone conclusion after the divorce legislation. Yet, on September 22, 1928, Yeats stepped forward once more, sensibly and prophetically, to denounce what he took to be but one more attack on the free intellect in Ireland. After showing the

93. *Letters*, p. 709, and information from Mrs. W. B. Yeats.
94. "Divorce: An Undelivered Speech," *Irish Statesman*, 14 March 1925, pp. 8–10, reprinted in *Senate Speeches*, pp. 156–60.
95. *Senate Speeches*, p. 96.
96. *Ibid.*, p. 99.

ridiculous definition of the term "indecent" in the Bill, Yeats concluded his *Irish Statesman* essay with this sane plea: "If you think it necessary to exclude certain books and pictures, leave it to men learned in arts and letters, if they will serve you, and, if they will not, to average educated men. Choose what men you may, they will make blunders, but you need not compel them to with a definition." [97] On the same day, Yeats spoke even more freely and candidly in the *Manchester Guardian*. Here he saw Irish religious fanatics in much the same way that Swift pictures Jack in *A Tale of a Tub*. Once again it was the mind of Ireland that was threatened. Smelling hypocrisy and medievalism in the religious pressure put upon the legislators, Yeats focused again, as Swift had, on the historical forces behind the rise of the fanatic in Ireland:

> The zealots have been wise in their generation; they have struck at the moment when the country is unprepared to resist. The old regime left Ireland perhaps the worst educated country in Northern Europe. . . . We were helots, and where you have the helot there the zealot reigns unchallenged. And our zealots' idea of establishing the Kingdom of God upon earth is to make Ireland an island of moral cowards. [98]

A week later, the *Spectator* carried an elaboration of these remarks on the proposed censorship. The crux here, as Yeats saw it, lay in the difference between the intentions of the proposers and the very letter of the law as it might affect some future generation. [99] Always the victim would be "the solitary man of imagination or intellect," the enemy "those reasonable committee-men." Once again, like Swift, Yeats feared those modern utopians, in modern Ireland those perfectionists of patriotism, whom he had once identified with believers in the Tir-na-nOge, who would find in censorship but another instrument to simplify life and lend it the rigid trappings of perfection.

97. "The Censorship and St. Thomas Aquinas," *Irish Statesman*, 22 September 1928, pp. 47–48.

98. "Censorship in Ireland," *Manchester Guardian*, 22 September 1928, p. 8.

99. "The Irish Censorship," reprinted in *Senate Speeches*, p. 177.

In 1932, three years after the bill had become law, Yeats admitted that his hatred of censorship remained unabated, though he was grateful that the worst aspects of the original bill had been cut out or toned down, and that the Censorship Board itself had been as sensible as might be expected. But Yeats's first public challenge of an action by the Board was the real purpose of this *Manchester Guardian* interview:

> The prohibition of Mr. O'Flaherty's "The Puritan" is the prohibition of a novel which may grow into the importance of Maria Edgeworth's "Absentee" . . . I think it is probable that if the censors were to examine their consciences they would discover that those consciences were biased by the fact that "The Puritan" in its external superficial aspect is a satire on a movement which has produced the Censorship Board itself.[100]

With this now familiar concern for Irish intellect and eighteenth-century Ireland goes an even more important hope for the future Ireland:

> I make this protest in part that I may assure him that he has the sympathy of every Irish writer and that if he will go on ignoring the attack he will have our gratitude as well. He is a great novelist, and no opposition can prevent him from doing much to mould the next two generations.[101]

The untrammeled maturing of the Irish mind at the hand of the artist rather than the polemicist, in short the education of the nation— Yeats had also used this phrase in the divorce speech—had the censorship as its enemy. That other patriotism of Anglo-Ireland—the one that could exercise choice—must be a part of that educating and molding. And so thought Lady Gregory:

> Yeats and George here. He is greatly combative over the Censorship Bill. I tell him we should proclaim it as a triumph for Protestants—we, keeping our intellectual freedom, can claim the Bill as a new guarantee of Protestant ascendancy—only we

100. "Irish Ban on 'The Puritan,'" undated clipping from the *Manchester Guardian*, Holloway, Natl. Lib. MS. 1948, II (January–March 1932), n.p.
101. *Idem.*

and the Censor will possess the knowledge of good and evil—
the courage to taste or test forbidden fruit.[102]

Yeats saw the conflict as one between "ignorance organized under
its priests, and unorganized and largely terrified intelligence looking
on helpless and angry." [103] But the bucking up of the intelligent was
one thing, and the persuasion of politicians to sweet reason was quite
another. The consequent hopelessness Yeats felt when addressing the
Senate for the last time in the summer of 1928 is echoed in his
impatience to get to Rapallo that fall. Clearly his fight had failed.
He had done all he could.[104] He had also passed like the Dean of St.
Patrick's from audacious middle age to an even more audacious old
age. He knew that the Irish intellect must continue the fight that
Swift had led in Ireland against those perpetuations of seventeenth-
century materialism—optimism, faith in utopian schemes, trust in
democracy—that lay behind the new pious legislation and hedged
about modern life.[105] Outside of Ireland he had been accustomed to
the extreme opinions of youth, often outrageous and contrary to his
own. But not in Ireland. Therefore Yeats felt mightily obliged to be
the Swift of his day and to outrage youth itself.[106] If in the thirties he
never wavered in this quest, still the misinterpretations of his greater
and deeper intent, the freeing of Irish intellect, were nettling.
Rereading Swift for days on end in 1930, he could write of himself,
after Augustus John had done his portrait at Coole,

John painted this portrait from studies made at Coole in 1907.
One portrait which I have never seen was recommended to the
Cork Municipal Gallery by their advisor, & was almost pur-

102. *Lady Gregory's Journals*, p. 319.
103. *Letters*, p. 747. In the matter of an O'Casey story Yeats once had to
battle the organized ignorance of printers. See "Sean O'Casey's Story," *Time and
Tide*, 27 May 1933, p. 640.
104. *Yeats and T. Sturge Moore*, p. 137. A good account of the Censorship
Act and the decline of Irish literature since Yeats is to be found in Sean
O'Faolain, "Ireland After Yeats," *Books Abroad*, XXVI (Autumn 1952),
325–33.
105. "The Need for Audacity of Thought," *Dial*, LXXX (February 1926),
116–18.
106. "The Sphere of Women," *Irish Times*, 17 November 1925.

chased when public [opinion] intervened—I was an immoral person & had defended divorce & attacked the Censorship bill. The Gallery bought a portrait of the Prince Regent by Barry instead.[107]

Yeats's fight for a liberty representing the "bent and current" of the Irish people had other enemies also—in Ireland the extreme Republicans and in Europe socialism and communism. This struggle, especially, involves us in a deep paradox. For in Yeats's search for individual liberty, he was clearly ready to curtail drastically political liberty, which he believed left individual conscience and sensibility at the mercy of party, power blocks, and a frequently misinformed majority.[108] Thus in taking up Yeats's path from the eighteenth century of Swift to the period of General O'Duffy and his marching Blue Shirts, one must not forget his earlier aristocratic bias long before his senatorship, nor his subsequent increased admiration for Italian fascism in the twenties and thirties. But after the disappointment of those Senate battles in the twenties, Yeats's mind continued to labor at the problem of intellectual conviction in Ireland. Hence in a 1930 notebook he can chide a writer for indiscriminately labeling the modern age as without such conviction:

> He did not notice there are spots where the very opposite is true, where men not only possess will, conviction, but are increasing it in themselves and others. There is Hitler in Germany, Stalin in Russia, Mussolini in Italy, & now we have Ireland passing into a similar [stage] in its intensity, in fanaticism. I have tried to explore, for the sake of my own peace of mind, the origin of what seems to me most unique & strong in our Irish existence. That I may describe it, I must go back two hundred years. The modern Irish nation began when at the end of the 17th century the victorious Protestant governing class quarrelled with England about the wool trade. In 1705 or 6

107. Canceled section of *Pages from a Diary* MS.
108. Information from Captain D. A. MacManus.

Irish intellect declared its separate identity . . . Swift was their De Valera. . . .[109]

Yet by January 1933, when De Valera had been returned for the second time, the extreme elements of the IRA still seemed to roam at will; and an eighteenth-century tradition of government and independent thought, seemingly without a Swift or a Mussolini, appeared doomed to extinction before it was reborn. Consequently, though he was charmed by the personal "simplicity and honesty" of the man when he first met De Valera in the thirties, Yeats could agree with him then no more than ever.[110] He could not forget the Republican insincerity in rejecting the Treaty in 1922, an irresponsibility, he felt, that could make possible a new civil war by extreme nonjuring Republicans after 1932.[111] Nor, like Swift before him, did Yeats approve of the leveling fellow travelers—in this case left-wing haters of capitalistic England and Ireland—associated with the IRA.[112] So, with the second return of De Valera, Yeats wrote that he was "about to be involved in a four years' conflict with the ignorant. . . . If I were a young man I would welcome four years of conflict, for it creates unity among the educated classes, and force De Valera's Ministers, in all probability, to repudiate the ignorance that has in part put them into power." [113] De Valera was forced, to be sure, to repudiate finally those Republicans who continued to regard Ireland as a nation at war. But long before that time there arose a militant nonparliamentary opposition that identified itself with the three dead architects of the Free State—Griffith, Collins, and O'Higgins—that demanded a restoration of public order, and that called itself the Blue Shirts, though its official titles were of necessity ever changing.

---

109. Large white vellum notebook begun 23 November 1930. See also "Modern Ireland," *Massachusetts Review*, V (Winter 1964), 256.

110. *Letters*, p. 806.

111. Large white vellum notebook begun 23 November 1930.

112. Mary C. Bromage, *De Valera and the March of a Nation* (New York, 1956), p. 233; Frank O'Connor, "The Old Age of a Poet," *Bell*, I (February 1941), 16.

113. *Letters*, p. 805.

Who were the Blue Shirts? Briefly, they rose from a fairly harmless organization known as the Army Comrades Association or "White Army." Ex-fighters against the British, and then against the Republicans, they had been organized after the murder of Superintendent Curtin in Tipperary in the fall of 1931. Like the American or British Legion, the Association was started as a benevolent society of former army men led by Colonel Ryan and Commandant Cronin. And like such organizations, it quickly set its sights on the dangers of communism and decided to become a national bulwark.[114] With the beginning of Fianna Fail attacks on free speech, the Blue Shirts became a self-appointed civil guard designed to protect those rights. In April 1933, the uniform of the blue shirt was adopted; in Dublin on July 20 the title "National Guard" was proclaimed; and Dr. Thomas O'Higgins, Kevin's brother, relinquished the headship to General Eoin O'Duffy, who had been dismissed as Commissioner of the Civic Guard the previous February by De Valera.

O'Duffy, a Monaghan man, had been foremost in Volunteer service and in the G.A.A. He had also led a Northern division during the Troubles. He had been a TD, at one time Chief of Staff, and had been asked by the mortally wounded Kevin O'Higgins to carry on the good work of the Cosgrave government.[115] O'Duffy had been a good chief of police, and was usually a jovial man, a competent organizer, something of a fanatic Catholic, a bachelor unburdened with intellect, and a man who drank too much at the end of his life. His emphasis on physical drill, disciplined service, and stark slogans about national honor often proved irresistible to the youth of rural Ireland, and the Blue Shirt ranks swelled. Although Blue Shirt leaders were disarmed

114. "The ACA No More?" *United Irishman*, 15 July 1933, p. 4. Most of my information on the Blue Shirts is taken from this newspaper, from the *Blueshirt*, and from Captain MacManus, who brought General O'Duffy to Yeats and who himself was a leader in the movement. Other helpful sources are Terence de Vere White, *A Fretful Midge* (London, 1957), pp. 93–99, and *The Irish Free State and Its Senate*, pp. 329–39, 342–435. This last, while offering the fullest printed account of the movement, is also demonstrably sympathetic to it.

115. See "O'Duffy's Life of Battles," *Blueshirt*, 22 and 29 December 1934. Also "An Irishman's Diary," *Irish Times*, 20 February and 9 October 1928.

by Civic Guards at the end of July 1933, O'Duffy continued with his plans for a huge Blue Shirt march-by in Dublin on Sunday, August 13, thereby hoping to revive the Leinster Lawn ceremony and celebrate the memory of Griffith, Collins, and O'Higgins—perhaps even to embarrass the government. De Valera put the country under martial law on the midnight of the 12th and ordered armored cars into the streets. At the last minute, to avoid an armed clash, O'Duffy called off the parade. But his star continued on the ascendance. On September 8, the Blue Shirts under a new name, the Young Ireland Association, became the right wing of a coalition opposition party called the United Ireland Party that also included Cumann na nGaedheal and the National Centre Party. O'Duffy became the leader of this coalition, although he held no seat in parliament. During the ensuing fall and winter, the conflict between the party in power, Fianna Fail, and the opposition, the United Ireland Party, and especially between their extremists, the Blue Shirts and the IRA, became murderous. Following another official banning, the Blue Shirts changed their name once again to the League of Youth, fought pitched battles at election rallies, while O'Duffy narrowly escaped death from a Mills bomb in Tralee, at the same time having his hair improperly creased by a hammer.

Disillusion with O'Duffy set in early. Tendered the crown originally for publicity reasons, O'Duffy more and more attracted Fascist hotheads to his side, more and more fulminated for the communal delights of the corporate state, and more and more assumed or allowed the salutes and pugnacity, the bigotry and racism of his European counterparts to color the movement. When the Blue Shirts began actively helping farmers to resist paying their land annuities, they had clearly gone too far. By late September 1934, it was announced that O'Duffy had resigned as head of the United Ireland Party, and by June 1935, those Blue Shirts who had followed him were renamed the National Corporate Party. Soon after, they were off with the buffoonish Irish Christian Front headed by Patrick Belton to save Christendom in Spain. Their bloody disorganized farce is innocently recorded by O'Duffy in his book, *Crusade in Spain.*

157

O'Duffy had planned to season and harden his followers on Spanish battlefields and return in glory to all the possibilities of a coup d'état in Ireland.[116] But the return six months later was rather ignominious, and O'Duffy disappeared from national politics.

116. Information from Ernest Blythe, former minister for finance under Cosgrave and a leader in the early Blue Shirt movement. A glance at this movement, the usual rightist reaction after any modern revolution, reveals two curiously universal facts. On the one hand, there is the innocence protested, even today, of any Fascist intentions on the part of two-thirds of the Blue Shirts. As Frank MacDermott said in 1961, only a handful of the leaders could in any way be called Fascists. Yet a systematic reading of the *United Irishman* and the *Blueshirt* from autumn 1932 until August 1933 shows how insidiously totalitarian ideas could be sweetened and dribbled out to that rank and file. The *United Irishman*, for instance, featured anti-Semitic verse; a recommendation that the government be run by "sages" (written by Yeats's friend, Desmond Fitzgerald, a Cosgrave minister and TD); praise of Mussolini for his restrictions of suffrage and attacks on the parliamentary system; further praise of the Italian system, along with abuse of proportional representation and political parties; and recommendations that the Blue Shirts arm themselves with truncheons and that the "alien voice" no longer be heard in Ireland, even if blows from the Blue Shirts were required. All these innocent propositions were raised before the designed march by Leinster Lawn on 13 August 1933. Is it any wonder that the government put troops in the streets?

On the other hand, like so many other right-wing organizations, past and present, the Blue Shirts constantly raised the bogey of communism, while at the same time taking a high moral line themselves and extolling each other as exemplary Christians. Thus, while the *United Irishman* could thunder with some reason against IRA interference with free speech—after De Valera took control of the government, the police were momentarily uncertain about how to handle the IRA—Blue Shirt jeremiads against communism did just as much to quell free speech. Hence in a strike-bound town, two "Communist agents" were ordered by sixty ACA members to be out of town in a half hour. Actually, De Valera was able to show from reports of O'Duffy himself, while Commissioner of the Gardai Siochana, that there was little if any Communist activity in Ireland. However, from our memories of the pious ejaculations of other right-wing groups, we might expect, and in fact get, the obvious: a strong line against strikes and "disastrous labour disputes"; the whipping up of a youth organization of 12- to 17-year-olds, properly provided with an adolescent martyr, one Hugh O'Reilly; escorts for girls coming home from late dances; the terror of the provocative Blue Shirt and marching men; the emblazoned banners with the red cross of St. Patrick, the black berets, the militant girls armed with hatpins ready for use "in the most effective place." See "Talking to Frank MacDermott," *Irish Times*, 8 April 1961. Also the *United Irishman* for 10 and 17 September, 26 November, and 10 and 17 December 1932; then 22 April, 3 and 17 June, 8 and 15 July 1933. Of special interest are items like "For All Ranks: No Guarding Communists," *United Irishman*, 1 April 1933; General Eoin O'Duffy, *Why I*

This then was the organization looking back to early Sinn Fein policy, to the Volunteers of 1916, to the great leaders of the twenties, that offered itself unwittingly to Yeats as a possible restorer of public order and intellectual liberty when virtual anarchy reigned in Ireland after the downfall of the Cosgrave government in 1932. But Yeats was in truth no Fascist, though Fascist thought interested him. He was an aristocrat who looked to an eighteenth-century aristocratic Ireland, shortsighted as it might have been, that had a code of honor and a regard for intellect. That age was heralded, he felt, by Swift's early pamphlet, the *Discourse,* which could be a warning to modern Ireland against the incursions of the "many" in politics, the weakening of the landed "few," and the development of a tyranny from the resultant anarchy.[117] Consequently, Yeats ultimately could not, would not, bridge the compromising gap between those ideals, however remote, of the Anglo-Irish eighteenth century (with its own illustrious Volunteers and United Irishmen) and the rather grubby, thick-witted pomposities of over 100,000 marching farmers, firebrands, backwater attorneys, auctioneers, and disgruntled merchants, who looked to an uninspiring megalomaniac for their leadership.

Yet there is also something of that fierce, sometimes theatrical and antic, disposition—he called it anarchistic—that Yeats hurled into his brief flirtation with the Blue Shirts. One detects high-flown persiflage in his letters from April to September 1933. When Yeats tells us, then, in these letters of his excitement in working out "a social theory that can be used against Communism in Ireland—what looks like emerging is Fascism modified by religion"; and then that "politics are growing heroic" or that "a Fascist opposition is forming behind the scenes" (note that Yeats spots it as Fascist from the beginning), we can only expect the full boastful tale: his "constantly urging the

---

Resigned from Fine Gael (Dublin, 1934), p. 21, and his *The Labour Policy of Fine Gael* (Dublin, 1934), p. 11, and *An Outline of the Political, Social, and Economic Policy of Fine Gael* (Dublin, 1934), pp. 24–25, 157. See also Colonel P. J. Coughlan, *The Truth: the Story of the Blueshirts* (Skibbereen, 1935), p. 63, and M. J. MacManus, *Eamon De Valera* (Dublin, 1934), pp. 302–3.

117. *Wheels and Butterflies,* pp. 14–17.

despotic rule of the educated classes as the only end to our troubles";
his admission that it was probably his suggestion that made the Blue
Shirt flag "a red St. Patrick's cross on a blue background"; and his
spluttered trumpeting over the Blue Shirt convention, its new leader
O'Duffy, the salute, his meeting with O'Duffy and hopes for him, his
realization that he will hate the new regime but that he also hates
"Irish democracy," and finally the account of O'Duffy's subsequent
triumph in leading the opposition against De Valera.[118] Well, how
can one not agree with Auden and patronize Yeats as being silly like
the rest of us?

The answer lies in the fact that both Yeats and Swift thought that
willful disruption of public order was indeed virtually as great a crime
before God as before man. For Swift, public spirit was a matter for
prayer: "I pray God protect his most gracious majesty, and this
kingdom long under his government; and defend us from all ruinous
projectors, deceivers, suborners, perjurers, false accusers, and oppres-
sors; from the violence of party and faction."[119] The rule by the
landed "few" in balance with the "one" and the "many" might
accomplish this defense.[120] Yeats never tired of pointing to this
warning by Swift. After his loss of interest in the Blue Shirts, he
explained his motives in somewhat the same way:

> In politics I have but one passion and one thought, rancour
> against all who, except under the most dire necessity, disturb
> public order, a conviction that public order cannot long persist
> without the rule of educated and able men. . . . Some months

118. *Letters*, pp. 808–15.
119. "Doing Good," *Works*, X, 169, 178.
120. "Drapier Letter VII," *Works*, IX, 190, and "Letter to Pope," *Works*,
XIV, 26. In addition to this emphasis on the need for a propertied class, Swift
also shared Yeats's fear of a puritanical religion linked to a republican political
scheme: "About the middle of Queen Elizabeth's reign, I take the power
between the nobles and the commons to have been in more equal balance, than it
was ever before or since. But then, or soon after, arose a faction in England, which
under the name of puritan began to grow popular by molding up their new
schemes of religion with republican principles in government . . . did at last
overthrow the constitution, and, according to the usual course of such revolutions,
did introduce a tyranny, first of the people, and then of a single person" (*A
Discourse of the Contests and Dissentions . . . , Works*, II, 414).

ago that passion laid hold upon me with the violence which unfits the poet for all politics but his own.[121]

This seems to be the counterpart to Yeats's serious attempt to sound out the Blue Shirts, or so it appears from his description of that famous Monday the 24th of July, 1933, meeting with O'Duffy, arranged by Captain D. A. MacManus, Yeats's old friend, leader of the Blue Shirts, and marshal for the prohibited grand parade of Blue Shirts on August 13:

> On Monday, MacManus brought O'Duffy to see me. O'Duffy is the head of the A.C.A. MacManus brought him that I might talk about the situation. If the I.R.A. attempts to seize power (& MacManus believes they will but I do not) or if the economic war brings chaos, then democratic politics will be discredited in this country & a substitute will have to be found. Talk went in the usual line: the organized party directed from above. Each district dominated through its ablest men. My own principle is that every government is a tyranny that is not a government by the educated classes and that the state must be hierarchical throughout. De Valera has described himself to somebody as an autocrat expressing the feeling of the masses. If we must have an autocrat let him express what Swift called "the bent & current" of a people not a momentary majority. I urged the getting of a recent 3 volume description of the Italian system (Fitzgerald talks of it) & putting some Italian scholars to make a condensation of it. I urged also that unless a revolutionary crisis rose they must make no intervention. They should prepare themselves by study to act without hesitation should the crisis arise. Then, & then only, their full program. I talked the "historical dialectic," spoke of it as proving itself by events as the curvature of space was proved (after mathematicians had worked it out) by observation during an eclipse. O'Duffy probably brought here that I might talk of it.[122]

Suffice it to say that O'Duffy departed intellectually unscathed from this encounter; the interview might just as well have been in a

121. *Variorum*, p. 543.
122. Private journal beginning "On examining Michael's school reports. . . ."

foreign language.[123] If this journal entry begins to show the impossible distance Yeats would have to travel if he might practically effect his Swiftian notion of intellectual freedom, there is also another journal entry, this time canceled, which can only be cited as possible further evidence. It may well have been Yeats's contribution to that "social theory to be used against Communism in Ireland." It is entitled "Political Organization" and makes similar fantastic demands upon the ideal Blue Shirt. Here is part of it:

> An organization to be lasting & powerful must resemble a group of families or else a single family. It must be aristocratic or royal. It must found its morality on the phrase "We do not do those things." [124]

The emphatic point is the aristocratic code that Yeats holds up. For it was just such a code that he found wanting in Mussolini during his cheap thrust after empire in Libya and Abyssinia. A Hitler and a Mussolini had not the background, Yeats came to feel, nor the self-control, to say, "We do not do those things." They were upstarts, not members of a traditional aristocracy.[125]

Nor, finally, had the Blue Shirts much time for the kind of Anglo-Irish aristocratic feeling that Yeats would have inculcated in them. His cancellations of early versions of his Blue Shirt songs—echoing so many of his eighteenth-century heroes—show that. And so does a comment in the *United Irishman* reflecting on Yeats's lecture in September 1932, "The Creation of Modern Ireland." As the anonymous reviewer put it:

> Mr. Yeats' main theme seems . . . to be the glorification of Ascendancy in modern Ireland to the exclusion of everything else. He gave a list of four Irishmen who became "world-figures." They are Berkeley, Burke, Swift and Shaw—all of them Protestant, and only one of them Irish in any real sense at all. He made mention of Parnell, but none of O'Connell, who after all was a bigger world-figure than any of them. Mr. Yeats

123. Information from Captain MacManus.
124. Large white vellum notebook begun 23 November 1930.
125. Information from Captain MacManus.

declares that "the first declaration of the independence of the Irish intellect was made by Berkeley." This is just grotesque Protestantmania. . . . In recent years Mr. Yeats seems to have become more and more addicted to trailing a somewhat unbecoming Protestant coat.[126]

Given Yeats's loathing of O'Connell, this was more than blunt contradiction. How telltale then in their bald insistence are those early versions of Yeats's proposed marching songs, based on his memory of the ribald songs sung by Caesar's soldiers,[127] yet in their own way also looking at a golden age in another classic century. Here the role of Swift with that of other members of a renowned century is stressed again and again as a heritage for Ireland's new builders:

> Ring after ring goes the growth of the oak trees
> Ring after ring in the way of their kind
> But slow grows nature and slow grows the great
>   oak tree
> While he builds fast that can build in the mind
> Molyneux and Swift began, Grattan toiled at the
>   plan
> These fanatics etc.

> A hollow heart hides in a withered oak tree
> Strength to the heart is the song that I sing
> Wisdom to the heart & the whole state
>   enlightened
> Beauty to the heart, then to ring after ring
> Swift, Grattan, Burke
> Began—finish the work.
> These fanatics etc.[128]

In other words, the sublime task to which Swift had set himself, at least according to Yeats, was the building of one Irish nation of mature heart and mind, sentiment and intellect. This was the duty

126. "The New Reading," *United Irishman*, 24 September 1932.
127. Passage dated 18 March 1934 in private journal beginning "On examining. . . ."
128. *Idem.*

Yeats would pass on to blue-shirted marching men. The thought is staggering. And so it must have seemed to Yeats when he canceled this version and others. Already cited has been his great fear of public disorder expressed in a note dated February 1934. That April, he again explained the original purport of his marching songs in terms of the intellectual liberty that we have been reviewing:

> . . . our upper class cares nothing for Ireland except as a place for sport . . . the rest of the population is drowned in religious and political fanaticism. . . . Sometimes as the representative of the Abbey Theatre I have called upon some member of Mr. Cosgrave's or Mr. de Valera's government to explain some fanatical attack . . . once as a member of the Irish Academy to complain of the illegal suppression of a book, and upon each occasion I came away with the conviction that the Minister felt exactly as I felt but was helpless: the mob reigned. . . . our men of letters live like outlaws in their own country.[129]

Yeats had concluded this passage by asking for a government or party that would grant such freedom and unify the descendants of those ancient Irish disparates—Ascendancy and Wild Geese—into one audience before one great historical drama. To such a government or party he offered these songs. Yet his postscript to this passage, dated August 1934, only demonstrates the gay hopelessness of his plan. The Blue Shirts he admits could not or would not accomplish this aim, and thus he wrenched his songs so "that no party might sing them." [130]

This aftermath to Yeats's hopes for a mature nation would read tragically were it not for the rough humor of these commentaries and the flashes of common sense he reveals. For that matter, Swift does have the last word, the last laugh, as Yeats contemplated what he took to be venal governments and simoniacs, and accepted the fact that the mob that had impugned intellectual liberty might indeed be the very Church and State themselves.[131] Otherwise, the fitting

129. *Variorum*, p. 836.
130. *Ibid.*, p. 837.
131. The poem "Church and State," published in November 1934.

benediction to this tragicomic interlude of a wise, foolish, passionate poet is one of his own poems graced by the wisdom of Jonathan Swift, especially in its conclusion:

> Had de Valera eaten Parnell's heart
> No loose-lipped demagogue had won the day,
> No civil rancour torn the land apart.
>
> Had Cosgrave eaten Parnell's heart, the land's
> Imagination had been satisfied,
> Or lacking that, government in such hands,
> O'Higgins its sole statesman had not died.
>
> Had even O'Duffy—but I name no more—
> Their school a crowd, his master solitude;
> Through Jonathan Swift's dark grove he
>   passed, and there
> Plucked bitter wisdom that enriched his blood.[132]

V

Perhaps these lines best sum up the burden of this chapter—Swift's haunting blood-presence from the past, his bitter wisdom that informed the position that Yeats defended, and that dark grove of the mind that Yeats tried to keep free for those proud enough and solitary enough to follow him there. Nor is this variant on the Irish myth of Swift inappropriate as a conclusion. For when we think of the Irish political roils and assassinations of the twenties and thirties, it is clear that it was Swift's distrust of the mass mind, "the Natural Man," as Arland Ussher once put it,[133] that Yeats shared most. He refused as Swift refused to take part in what Ussher has called "the racket," [134] that is, the sliding, compromising, trimming acceptance of the mindless world of mass communications. Such communicants or anarchs both men hated, for both Swift and Yeats served human liberty.

132. From "Parnell's Funeral."
133. Arland Ussher, *The Face and Mind of Ireland* (New York, 1950), p. 130.
134. *Ibid.*, p. 131.

To be sure, on his seventieth birthday, Yeats received his Swiftian due from the *Irish Times:* "From the national point of view W. B. Yeats occupies an almost unique position in Irish life; for he is virtually the first man since Swift who has been able to bring the Anglo-Irish tradition into line with positive Nationalism." [135] How Yeats must have cherished that phrase "positive Nationalism." Even now, however, one wishes the sentiment well. Yet after more than thirty years of a censorship that has virtually emasculated Irish literature, one may have the temerity to seriously doubt this charming hope. One would also like to believe in Yeats's attempts to educate or stir up with his enthusiasms for Georgian Ireland one or two of those vague undergraduates he often mentioned. And to recall Yeats writing in one of his journals that "A child's mind is mythical" [136] is also to think of his equally high hopes for the divine, historical, and literary figure of Swift, which he held up to those phantom undergraduates, those Young Irelanders. But then doubt descends again. No, the real importance of Swift to Yeats appears to have been that of a bracer, an astringent, the acid cleanser of a poet's own mind and work.

Hence in recalling how Swift haunted Yeats, how both in a sense defended a hopeless position, and how both held to a liberty that has angered many men and is beyond the strength of most, one cannot help reading the conclusion of an interview between Yeats and an Indian professor with some impatience. At this interview in June 1937, Yeats had closed the proceedings by brandishing a Japanese sword and exclaiming, "Conflict, more conflict!" Thereafter, the Indian remarked to his Irish university colleague:

"Sad. Very sad. That a lifetime's devotion to poetry should lead in the end to so little joy. He is a prophet. It is as a sort of St. John the Baptist that he calls on my people to repent and

135. Hone, p. 442. The link with Swift offered Yeats by the same paper at his death wasn't much better: "In common with Swift, he [Yeats] had the burning patriotism which aroused a people to higher dignity, which spurred a community to action, and which left to his country the abiding inspiration of his poetry" ("Yeats," *Irish Times,* 30 January 1939).
136. Private journal beginning "On examining. . . ."

166

change their outlook. There was none of the idealism of John the Baptist yet it is clear that he lives in the wilderness and feeds on honey and locusts." [137]

Had not that good Indian ever heard of Swift?

137. Natl. Lib. MS. 5919.

Chapter Five

BURKE'S GREAT MELODY

I

IF YEATS could write in his 1930 *Diary* that Burke was "only tolerable in his impassioned moments,"[1] he nevertheless seems to have had reason enough in the previous ten years to recall a number of these moments. He could, in fact, impress them into the fabric of his own impassioned speech. Speaking in February 1921 before the Oxford Union Society, he had defended the guerrilla campaign of his Irish countrymen against the Black and

1. *Pages from a Diary, Explorations,* p. 293.

168

Tans, and clinched his point by adding, "As Burke says, you cannot indict a nation."[2] Nor, speaking in the Irish Senate, had Yeats forgotten that dramatic moment when Burke threw down a scalping knife in Parliament to protest the shipment of such knives to the American Indians. Yeats called Burke's violent reaction "a fact which has been burning in my imagination" and saw in it another Anglo-Irish exposure of perfidious Albion.[3]

As we have come to see, Burke once seemed to Yeats as alien to Ireland as Swift and Goldsmith had been—men who appeared hardly "to have come out of Ireland at all."[4] Yet by 1918 Yeats, living in Oxford, was seriously reading Burke. In the 1920's he purchased a set of Burke, probably with part of his Nobel Prize money.[5] He vigorously marked passages in this set during his Senate days, confirming, it would seem, many of his already strongly held aristocratic biases. In fact, his most thoroughly marked text, *An Appeal from the New to the Old Whigs*, might very well be called, according to Mrs. Yeats, his political bible. Like Burke in this tract, Yeats would also frequently try to recall his fellow Senators to an earlier period—the Ireland of Grattan's Parliament. And like Burke, Yeats thought his own parliamentary speeches extremely important and insured their stylistic felicity by revising them before the final printing.[6]

Yeats's markings in his copy of *An Appeal* stress that prudential, aristocratic, and conservative plea which looks to the past rather than

2. Reported in the *Freeman's Journal*, 19 February 1921.
3. *Senate Speeches*, p. 88.
4. "The Best Book from Ireland," *Daily News*, 11 May 1904. See also *Plays and Controversies* (London, 1923), p. 110, and *Wheels and Butterflies*, p. 7.
5. Information from Mrs. W. B. Yeats. Yeats's set of Burke includes James Prior's *Life of the Right Honourable Edmund Burke* (London, 1824)—hereafter Prior's *Life*; *The Works of the Right Honourable Edmund Burke* (London, 1883)—hereafter *Works*; and *The Speeches of the Right Honourable Edmund Burke on the Impeachment of Warren Hastings*, Vol. I (London, 1881) and Vol. II (London, 1882). These last two uncut volumes comprise volumes VII and VIII of the *Works*.
6. Information from Mrs. W. B. Yeats. Relevant information may also be found in *Senate Speeches*, pp. 5–6, and W. B. Stanford, "Yeats in the Irish Senate," *REL*, IV (July 1963), 73–74.

the future. For the *Appeal* is directed to the dead spirits of an older order continued by the Whigs of 1688 and then rejected by the Whigs and Jacobins of Burke's day. The emphasis is on the pull of circumstance in political transfer of power, or on the relative nature of political change, the fact that all revolutions contain some evil, the fear of the unbridled will behind the acts of the few or the many, but especially behind the ambitions of the multitude. No less does Burke, here as elsewhere, offer man's divine placement in society as a counter to the itch for revolution and upheaval in the masses. The radical enthusiasms of the ignorant are condemned as madness, just as Swift had condemned them. To be called a people, men had to exist in a round of social discipline where the wise, the expert, and the landed few were guides. To be blessed with fortune, breeding, rank, and culture was indeed a matter of first importance.

Yeats's markings show him in substantial agreement with this drift, not only here but elsewhere in his edition of Burke. Given Yeats's interpretation of Swift on liberty, we might anticipate his noting Burke's insistence on orderly rather than on extravagant freedom for a citizen.[7] Other passages which had a special ring for Yeats are those where Burke denies that politics may be reduced to morality, to the realm of the true or false, or to hazy goals in the future. We also find marked passages that scorned the absolutes of patriotic idealists, absolutes very like the abstractions rigidly held by the Republicans in the Irish Dail.[8] Equally persuasive to Yeats were passages celebrating the need to have in government intelligent and able men, who comprised, as Burke supposed, the collective genius behind the British constitution.[9] Passages eulogizing the propertied

7. Yeats marked the following passage in Prior's *Life*, p. 349: "Permit me then to continue our conversation, and to tell you what the freedom is that I love. It is not solitary, unconnected, individual, selfish liberty. It is social freedom." On p. 371 of the same volume, Yeats marked a shorter statement by Burke on the same subject: "*But the liberty, the only liberty I mean, is a liberty connected with order.*"

8. *An Appeal from the New to the Old Whigs, Works*, III, 16, 81.

9. *Ibid.*, p. 113.

nobility, that might perpetuate the order of a society, seem to have been just as compelling to Yeats.[10] He also appreciated Burke's belief in reform by degrees rather than by outright innovation, his concern with present as well as future welfare, his insistence on restraint as the goal of government in preserving the historic nation.[11]

Now Burke was by no means a new hero on the Irish horizon.[12] Nor have Yeats's similarities to Burke passed entirely unnoticed.[13] But the excitement Burke at his great moments could fire in Yeats seems to be based on a large analogy. Yeats remembered him for the crises he faced in India, America, France, and Ireland—but especially for his attack on the French Revolution. The dangerous aftercourses that modern revolution had brought to Ireland after 1916 struck Yeats as swirling back to those of 1789 and gaining new momentum from the Russian Revolution of 1917. Small wonder then that Yeats chose, in his warnings to the new peasant democracy, to emulate the Burke who asked that England be governed by able men; who saw the slow growth of his country symbolized in the British oak; and who questioned the abstractions, manners, and morals of the revolutionary government in France. These were the chief themes in Burke's great melody against Whiggery.

10. *Reflections* . . . , *Works*, II, 324.

11. *An Appeal, Works*, III, 78, 111.

12. See, for instance, Prior's *Life*, p. 1. For William O'Brien, *Edmund Burke as an Irishman*, 2nd ed. (Dublin, 1926), p. ix, Burke was "the greatest name in the history of civilization"; for Sir Shane Leslie, *The Irish Tangle for English Readers* (London, 1946), pp. 90–91, he was "the greatest Irishman," "the supreme instance of what can come of the Anglo-Irish stock." John Eglinton, *Anglo-Irish Essays*, pp. 120–21, offered the same praise without the exaggerations.

13. Austin Clarke, "Poet and Artist," *The Arrow* (Summer 1939), p. 9, made this imaginative comparison: "Yeats regarded his work as the close of an epoch and the least of his later lyrics brings the sense of a great occasion. English critics have tried to claim him for their tradition but, heard closely, his later music has that tremulous lyrical undertone which can be found in the Anglo-Irish eloquence of the eighteenth century. So might we listen to Edmund Burke telling of his first glimpse of Marie Antoinette, or Henry Grattan speaking for the last time in the old Irish Parliament before the Act of Union."

II

Long after his Senate days, Yeats, as we have seen, added a note to his "Three Songs to the Same Tune" that begins characteristically: "In politics I have . . . a conviction that public order cannot long persist without the rule of educated and able men." [14] Without such men at the helm, he went on to say, a government became a tyranny. He and Burke agreed on this point, and each had a sharp eye for educated ability.

Part of Burke's veneration of nobility may be explained by his friendship with members of the Whig aristocracy in the Rockingham connection. There is a striking parallel in Yeats's own career in the Irish Senate from 1922 to 1928. He aligned himself early with the Southern Unionist group. In fact, according to the late Joseph Hone, Yeats "wished to insinuate into the ex-Ascendancy Senators a nationalism conceived imaginatively as their heritage from the magnanimity of Swift, Burke and Grattan." [15] Whatever their previous sympathies, whatever their popularity, Yeats saw in these Senators, appointed by President Cosgrave, ability founded on education, intellect, and experience. Yeats regarded himself as a failure in the Senate—at the end shooting pains coursed through his back and head whenever he spoke.[16] Moreover, he was not roundly admired. But he was appreciated by this group.[17] According to its later secretary, Mrs. H. Wilson, Yeats was a member of a small band of those Southern Unionist Senators who called themselves the Independents and met at 102 Grafton Street (above the present West and Son jewelry shop) to formulate policy. The leaders were such men of ability as Sir Andrew Jameson, S. L. Brown, and James Douglas, and included such ornaments of the then most distinguished second house in

14. *Variorum,* p. 543.
15. "Yeats as Political Philosopher," *London Mercury,* XXXIX (March 1939), 494.
16. Information from Mrs. W. B. Yeats. See also *On the Boiler,* p. 27, and "Homage to Dr. Yeats," *Irish Times,* 28 June 1935.
17. Even Lord Glenavy, Chairman of the Senate, acknowledged in his son's presence Yeats's uncanny influence over the Senate (Hone, p. 398).

Europe as Sir John Keane, Henry Guinness, and the Earl of Granard.[18] For the rest of his life Yeats thought a government not controlled by these or other educated and able men to be a tyranny. Public order would break down without them.[19] We know that Yeats's memories of great houses like Hazelwood, Markree, Lissadell, and Coole combined with his later revulsion at the Parnell, *Playboy*, and Lane Gallery squabbles to help fix this aristocratic allegiance. Yet so did Burke.

Here then we may emphasize the implications of but one long passage, heavily marked by Yeats, in the closing pages of *An Appeal from the New to the Old Whigs*, that lays stress on Burke's passion for wisdom and intellect in public men:

> . . . none, except those who are profoundly studied, can comprehend the elaborate contrivance of a fabric fitted to unite private and public liberty, with public force, with order, with peace, with justice, and, above all, with the institutions formed for bestowing permanence and stability, through ages, upon this invaluable whole.
>
> Place, for instance, before your eyes, such a man as Montesquieu. Think of a genius not born in every country, or every time; a man gifted by nature with a penetrating, aquiline eye; with a judgment prepared with the most extensive erudition; with an herculean robustness of mind, and nerves not to be broken with labour; a man who could spend twenty years in one pursuit. Think of a man, like the universal patriarch in Milton . . . a man capable of placing in review, after having brought together from the east, the west, the north, and the south, from the coarseness of the rudest barbarism to the most refined and subtle civilization, all the schemes of government

18. Information from Mrs. H. Wilson. Hone, p. 352, also saw this association as important.

19. *Variorum*, p. 543. In Burke's *Thoughts on the Cause of the Present Discontents*, *Works*, I, 372, Yeats had marked this sentence: "When bad men combine, the good must associate; else they will fall, one by one, an unpitied sacrifice in a contemptible struggle." In the "Speech on American Taxation," *Works*, I, 406, Yeats marked the passage celebrating Grenville's combination of wide experience, generosity, knowledge, and nobility.

which had ever prevailed amongst mankind, weighing, measuring, collating, and comparing them all, joining fact with theory, and calling into council, upon all this infinite assemblage of things, all the speculations which have fatigued the understandings of profound reasoners in all times!—Let us then consider, that all these were but so many preparatory steps to qualify a man, and such a man, tinctured with no national prejudice, with no domestic affection, to admire, and to hold out to the admiration of mankind, the constitution of England! And shall we Englishmen revoke to such a suit? Shall we, when so much more than he has produced remains still to be understood and admired, instead of keeping ourselves in the schools of real science, choose for our teachers men incapable of being taught, whose only claim to know is, that they have never doubted; from whom we can learn nothing but their own indocility; who would teach us to scorn what in the silence of our hearts we ought to adore? [20]

Alluding to the fact that men of intellect reached the summit of their public influence in the eighteenth century, Yeats once took as one of his texts "a famous passage in the *Appeal from the New to the Old Whigs* commending the old Whig aristocracy for their intellect and power and because their doors stood open to like-minded men." [21] It may well have been the passage just cited, although equally pertinent ones occur elsewhere. In any case, the matter was gospel for Yeats before and after his Senate career. Able men were to be the life-bearers of the new nation. It was his constant theme in Senate speeches. Speaking on December 12, 1922, about selecting a chairman for the new Senate, Yeats urged that his colleagues "consider nothing whatever but whether the man we are going to choose will have the necessary legal and necessary political knowledge to steer this Seanad." [22] Six years later, his last year in the Senate, he voiced the same belief: "I think that we should not lose sight of the simple fact that it is more desirable and more important to have able men in this

20. *Works*, III, 113.
21. *Wheels and Butterflies*, p. 9.
22. *Senate Speeches*, p. 30.

House than to get representative men into this House." [23] What Irishmen, we may ask, could fulfill such hopes?

The first name to come to mind ought to be that of Kevin O'Higgins, Vice-President of the Executive Council and Minister for Justice after the deaths of Arthur Griffith and Michael Collins in August 1922. But before turning to O'Higgins, we might first consider a less notable man, an Anglo-Irishman whose Ascendancy background and cultured life in Sligo had nevertheless made a deep impression on Yeats. He was Bryan Cooper. For the boy Yeats, the Coopers of Markree Castle were the very mirror of county style and society.[24] Commander E. F. P. Cooper, the statesman's son, has stated that his father and Yeats certainly knew each other well in later years —earlier, Irish notions of class would have kept them apart—and that Yeats not only was a frequent visitor to Cooper's Dublin residence, Khyber Pass in Dalkey, but also stayed at Markree in 1929. After this visit, he could write Mrs. Cooper, "I have realized the ambition of my life by staying with you, as we have always looked on the Coopers and Markree Castle as greater than the Royal Family and Buckingham Palace." [25]

Yet as an Independent member of the Dail from 1923 to 1927, Major Cooper must have seemed, at first, a rather unlikely choice as an Irish leader. An extreme Unionist and an M.P. before the war, he had for a time afterwards been press censor in Ireland, before resigning because of unfair British suppression of news in a Sinn Fein newspaper.[26] Bryan Ricco Cooper came to feel, nevertheless, that he and his class were important for the new Ireland. As the descendant of a man who had served in Grattan's Parliament, Cooper saw in the events of 1919 his class's second great opportunity. Thus he could suggest in his unpublished "Ireland Under Sinn Fein" that

> . . . though the Southern Unionists are comparatively few in numbers they can give Sinn Fein leaders two things it badly

23. *Ibid.*, pp. 151–52. See also pp. 33, 53–54, 58, 76–77, 85, and 114.
24. *Wheels and Butterflies*, p. 10, n.1.
25. Information in letters to the author from Commander E. F. P. Cooper and from Mrs. Bryan Cooper.
26. "Election Speeches," *Irish Times*, 6 September 1927.

needs. The Sinn Fein leaders to-day are for the most part young men who possess education and enthusiasm but have neither a stake in the country nor the tradition of dealing with affairs. The tradition behind the Southern Unionists, on the other hand, is enormous . . . though during the last generation they have been excluded from public life. . . . If Sinn Fein could win the Southern Unionists it would gain both confidence and leadership and it knows it. . . . Then indeed would England have cause to fear Sinn Fein.[27]

In August 1923, when Cooper offered himself as an Independent candidate for South Dublin County, Yeats must have held somewhat the same opinion. Here is a report of his speech in Rathmines in behalf of Cooper:

> Senator W. B. Yeats said that he came there to recommend the electors in the Rathmines area to return Major Bryan Cooper to the Dail. When he was a child in Sligo Major Bryan Cooper's grandfather was the most prominent man in the county, respected by everybody for his integrity and ability. Sligo was full of the traditions of his family, and it was in 1770, he thought, that an ancestor of Major Bryan Cooper's, Joshua Cooper, was elected to what afterwards became Grattan's Parliament. He sat in that Parliament until the Act of Union. He could not be bribed; he refused a peerage, and he voted against the Union. It gave him great pleasure now to support Major Bryan Cooper for the sake of his family and its traditions, as well as for his own sake. He had a good deal of administrative experience, and he (Senator Yeats) regarded him as just the sort of man who would be exceedingly useful to the country in the immediate future.

27. Cited by Lennox Robinson, *Bryan Cooper* (London, 1931), pp. 126–27. I am thoroughly indebted to this book for general information on Cooper. One of Cooper's ancestors, Governor Verelst, who succeeded Clive as governor of India, was praised by Burke as "one of the honestest men that ever served the East India Company" (Rev. T. O'Rorke, *History . . . of Ballysadare and Kilvarnet* [Dublin, n.d.], p. 168). Cooper was justifiably proud of his family's service to the Empire and Ireland. See the end of his article, "Literature and Life," *Irish Statesman*, 22 September 1928, p. 52; also "Death of Major Bryan Cooper," *Irish Independent*, 7 July 1930.

The old Ireland was dead—an Ireland that had its own idealism, its own principles, its own sentiments, which produced some good oratory and much self-sacrifice. He knew the virtues of that Ireland, and its faults, and he was glad that it had passed away. A new Ireland was beginning, with a new idealism—an idealism of power, patience, and economy.[28]

28. "Major Cooper's Candidature," *Irish Times*, 25 August 1923. The report of the rest of Yeats's speech is remarkable for the light it throws on his ability to speak concretely on government matters:

They who were on that platform could speak more frankly of the financial situation of the country than the Government. The Government had a great responsibility; if they spoke out plainly they might, perhaps, injure the national credit. Major Bryan Cooper had told them of the heavy deficit of something like £20,000,000, £10,000,000 of which was, he thought, spent on the Army. Every country had at one time or other to meet exceptional expenditure and every country met that burden by borrowing, and it was right that they should. £10,000,000 of the deficit would largely be paid in respect of compensation for destruction.

What was far more serious was recurring expenditure. The Army would always cost £2,000,000 or £3,000,000. That was what the Army of Canada cost, and he thought that it would be quite enough for this country. The Civic Guard cost nearly twice as much per man as the old police force, and the Post Office was more than £1,000,000 short. He believed that future generations would be engaged in a fight, just as one had been waged by generations that were gone. But the struggle of future generations would not be to win political independence, but to win financial independence. A man might have all the political independence that he ever dreamt of and yet have no freedom if he had an immense overdraft at the bank. (Applause.) They would have to teach their young men to labour, to be patient, and to be economical if they were to reduce expenditure and to increase income. They had to make the nation overflowing with activity, to make it rich and successful, and its burdens light. They had to restore credit, to advance it beyond where it was, and he believed that would be accomplished. He was perfectly satisfied that it would be done when he looked back on Ireland's past, when he thought of the innumerable number of leaders of men Ireland had produced. (Applause.) It had produced agile minds and strong wills, and he believed that it would grasp the opportunity of patience and sacrifice—the ideal of the new Ireland. (Applause.)

If they would devote themselves to those ideals, then their troubles would soon pass away. Ulstermen would then be very glad to unite themselves with the rest of Ireland. They would need no eloquent persuasions, and certainly no threats. They would draw Ulster to them, because they would have the necessary magnet to attract it. When the nation was prosperous and the population 9,000,000, it would be honoured and courted, and could obtain any liberty or any powers that it considered necessary to its existence. (Applause.)

If we shall come to expect such optimism from Yeats in the early days of the Free State, it is nonetheless pleasant to hear Cooper's reply at this time that from boyhood on Yeats's work had strongly influenced him "and helped to make me the good Irishman I hope I am."[29]

In rereading the *Dail Reports,* one discovers this ex-officer in the British Army, former Carsonite, and Protestant landlord to be supremely "the invisible mender" that his biographer terms him. Moderation and sensitivity to public opinion had been a mark of the leaders in his family.[30] Moreover, Cooper's literary skill—he was an avid reader, actor, and promoter of Shakespeare in addition to being a playwright and short story writer—plus his mastery of detail and easy familiarity with world literature and historical documents served him well on more than one occasion.[31] Like Burke, he could cope with the many technical and routine hobgoblins that beset the larger issues for the new government. Year by year he immersed himself in the business of grants for demobilized officers, stenographers for the

---

Senator Andrew Jameson, who spoke after Yeats and Captain Stephen Gwynn, was reported as saying of Yeats's speech: "He did not think—and he had a good deal of experience in financial affairs—that he had ever heard a clearer statement of the present financial condition of affairs in Ireland, and the means to remedy them, than Senator Yeats had given them."

29. *Idem* and *Bryan Cooper,* p. 48. Major Cooper once defined the good Irishman as "the man who lives in Ireland, spends his money in Ireland, employs Irish labour, pays his rates and taxes, and does his best to promote the prosperity of Ireland" ("Election Speeches," *Irish Times,* 8 September 1927).

30. Rev. T. O'Rorke, *History of Sligo: Town and County* (Dublin [1889]), II, 350. Cooper's play, *The Chief Secretary,* shows him to be sensitive to both the Unionist and the Republican traditions of eighteenth-century Protestant Ireland. However, the leading character, Arthur Wellesley, the Chief Secretary and later 1st Duke of Wellington, doubtless speaks for Cooper when exclaiming, "I think aristocracy means being governed by the best man. I certainly believe in that, and I believe that the best man is likely to be one who has been brought up from his childhood to feel responsibility and to exercise power, who has position enough not to seek rank for its own sake, and wealth enough to make the acquiring of a fortune a minor matter. That is my creed." See Cooper's *The Collar of Gold and other Fantasies* (London, 1920), pp. 103–4.

31. See, for instance, his articles "The Estimates" and "Further Thoughts on the Estimates" in the *Irish Statesman,* 20 March 1926, pp. 35–36, and 10 April 1926, pp. 119–20.

Courts of Justice, postal facilities, luggage examination at the Customs, Post Office weighing machines, yes, even dog licenses. His famed defense of the Cosgrave government in August 1927 is proof of his ability to keep a sharp eye on the great issues in a most concrete fashion:

> What is it that the average man wants? A man driving his cattle to the fair wants to know that there will be a fair, that a bridge has not broken down so that he cannot get his cattle to the fair. He wants to know if he gets his cattle to the fair whether there is likely to be any interruption of the railway service, or whether there will be men at the fair to give him a price for his cattle. When he gets a price he wants to know that the dealer can go into the bank and get cash, and that the bank manager was not held up on the way and the money taken.
>
> Whatever have been the failings and the faults in the present Government, they have made it possible, at any rate, for the plain man in the country to take his cattle to the fair and to get a price for his cattle. (*Dail Reports*, XX, 1705–06.) [32]

Once the nonjuring Republicans entered the Dail in 1927, Bryan Cooper pledged his services to the Cosgrave government and led the Co. Dublin poll in September. Little wonder that Yeats could say of this man after his death in 1930, "Had he lived he would have become one of the most prominent and important men of his time. His qualities of clarity and good sense and integrity and power of speech would have drawn men to him more and more." [33]

In August 1927 Yeats wrote the poem "Blood and the Moon" in revulsion at the assassination of Kevin O'Higgins. The verses mock modern Ireland with the memory of Swift, Berkeley, Burke, and Goldsmith, men whose wisdom might have excited the national

32. From the very first, Cooper saw Cosgrave's quiet strength, writing of him on one occasion that "he has had to face ruin and devastation, personal danger and personal loss, and he bears traces of the experience. But his virtues are those that Ireland needed and still needs: determination, fearlessness, the courage that chooses a hard course and pursues it to the end" ("Our Rulers," *Irish Times*, 26 January 1924).

33. *Bryan Cooper*, p. 187.

imagination in politics, philosophy, and song, and left no stain of blood. Yet the murder of O'Higgins, Yeats declared, proved imaginative wisdom impossible in life.

O'Higgins had seemed to Yeats the next best thing to Burke reborn.[34] A strong conservative realist in politics, an accomplished speaker and man of inflexible will, O'Higgins was also a ceremonious and principled statesman. A decorous man—he tipped servants in true eighteenth-century fashion [35]—he was capable of practical jokes and horseplay in private,[36] and had in fact led a mildly dissipated youth. He could be extremely witty, once saying of a group urging censorship that he had never seen twelve men with such obscene faces.[37] Unlike Burke, he dedicated himself to building a new Ireland based on the rule of a democratic majority. Like Burke, however, he found his political principles in "conformity with the Law of God." [38] He dreamed of a truly united Ireland where "Irish-speaking Orangemen will be boasting about Henry Joy McCracken in a Dublin Parliament." [39] And like Burke he dreaded the monstrous forces set free by civil disruption and revolution.[40] He never feared to term terrorists among the Republicans "mugs" rather than "patriots." In fact he seemed to have no fear. Mrs. O'Higgins told Yeats that just

34. Bryan Cooper also saw the Augustan resemblance. He once wrote of O'Higgins, "He sits in the *Dail* with his head resting on one hand, as though the burden of his thoughts were greater than he could bear, and he seldom is seen to smile. His face recalls some half-forgotten memory. There is a touch of Mussolini, though without Mussolini's pose. Mr. O'Higgins does not pose: it is not worth while. At last I realised where that sad, almost scornful, look was to be found. It is on Swift's bust in St. Patrick's Cathedral, and it betokens a spiritual kinship between the two men" ("Our Rulers," *Irish Times*, 2 February 1924).

35. Information from Mrs. W. B. Yeats.

36. Information from Ernest Blythe.

37. Information from Mrs. W. B. Yeats. O'Higgins also refused to prosecute the paper *To-morrow* (*Lady Gregory's Journals*, p. 280).

38. Terence de Vere White, *Kevin O'Higgins* (London, 1948), p. 96. Most of my general information on O'Higgins comes from this important book.

39. Nichevo, "Kevin O'Higgins. A Personal Memoir," *Irish Times*, 11 July 1927.

40. "An Internal Loan," *Irish Times*, 30 October 1923. Also relevant here is O'Higgins' *Three Years Hard Labour. An Address Delivered to the Irish Society of Oxford University on the 31st October, 1924*, with a Foreword by Eoin MacNeill (Dublin, n.d.), p. 7.

before her husband died he said, "My dear, I did try to save myself, I could not help it." Yeats recognized this supreme combination of courage and courtesy by commenting in his diary: "He must have felt that he was deserting her & that he had to excuse himself." [41] Apparently, his last words were, "Poor country . . . poor country . . ." and, "Tell them to be brave and to carry on!" [42]

Minister for Home Affairs and Vice-President of the Executive Council at the age of thirty, O'Higgins insisted in his iron way—as Yeats never lets us forget—that the life of the state was worth any single life, in fact any number of individual lives. Yeats saw Grattan's Parliament and Cosgrave's government as equally weak for failing to gain the respect from Protestant and Catholic alike on this point. [43] O'Higgins' Dail and Senate speeches leave one with the chilling impression of a man who indeed knew death to the very bone, as Yeats had intoned in the poem "Death," with its magnificent pun, "supersession of breath." For in those treacherous years after the Treaty, death confronted O'Higgins at every turn. His best friend Michael Collins was gunned down in the Civil War; his father fell at the hands of Irregulars soon afterward. Out of principle O'Higgins agreed to the execution of Rory O'Connor, who had been best man at his wedding. He himself was mortally wounded in Booterstown on Sunday, July 10, 1927, more than likely by I.R.B. assassins. Asking forgiveness for them before he died, he yet remained, one would think, as Yeats once described him: "A soul incapable of remorse or rest."

Perhaps this wraith of death gives the memorable, incisive ring to his speeches. But it is also his magisterial sense of style, so much like Burke's, derived from his lifelong devotion to books and languages, that tempers his pronouncements on life-and-death issues into permanent eloquence. [44] If Bryan Cooper recalls the Burke of army

41. Diary of Thought begun 23 September 1928.
42. Simone Tery, "As Others See Us," *Irish Statesman*, 13 October 1928, p. 110.
43. *Pages from a Diary, Explorations*, p. 338.
44. According to Terence de Vere White, "It was his style, 'in the direct line of Burke,' that attracted Yeats to him in after-years" (*Kevin O'Higgins*, p. 4).

estimates and Indian finances, O'Higgins, though equally proficient, reminded Yeats of that Burke whom he most admired, a man writing or speaking to assembled men at some great moment that could rouse all his fire.[45] Such a moment had occurred when O'Higgins was called upon to justify the execution of four young men—James Fisher, Peter Cassidy, Richard Twohig, and John Gaffney—taken with loaded weapons on November 17, 1922. His peroration resembles some of Burke's appeals to the established and organic state:

> The life of the Irish Nation as a Nation, the life of the Irish Nation as a democratic organism, is at stake. The whole question as to whether it is to be a Nation in the future governed by constitutional principles, or whether it is to be a mob dictated to by an armed minority was at stake. . . . Well, this Nation must live. . . . We are the Provisional Transitional Government set up pending the formal coming into existence of Saorstat Eireann. We speak the authentic voice of the people of Ireland. . . . And if we, in grave consultation and in grave Council, have decided that it is necessary to take the lives of many individuals then the lives of many individuals will be taken. (*Dial Reports*, I, 2268–69.)

O'Higgins castigated the armed few just as much as he did the irresponsible mob.[46]

The murder of Deputy Hales on December 7 of the same year brought the executions of four more men—Rory O'Connor, Liam Mellows, Joseph McKelvey, and Richard Barrett, each an IRA leader from a different province, all taken at the Four Courts. Just as Burke had denied the analogy of the Revolution of 1688, or for that matter the American Revolution, to that in France, so O'Higgins

---

Ernest Blythe has spoken to the author of O'Higgins' ability to write out a speech and then repeat it verbatim. According to Patrick Hogan, Cosgrave's Minister for Agriculture, O'Higgins was the grandson of the poet T. D. Sullivan (Tery, "As Others See Us," *Irish Statesman*, 27 November 1928, pp. 148–49). An example of his literary ability is to be found in his eulogy of Michael Collins, "The Quenching of Our Shining Light," *Arthur Griffith. Michael Collins* (Dublin, n.d.), pp. 42–43.

45. *Pages from a Diary, Explorations*, p. 294.
46. *Civil War and the Events Which Led to It* (Dublin, 1923), p. 3.

refused the analogy of the recent British executions. He made it clear that while the Irish people had in 1918 abjured constitutional means for dealing with the British, the same could not be said in dealing with the present Republicans. They did not represent the consensus of Irish feeling. Yet on that morning of December 8, 1922, the chamber bristled with anger at the killing of men who had so recently fought the British oppressor. Here was another impassioned moment. Interrupted several times—once by a deputy who interjected "The weasel must spit"—O'Higgins confronted the government's accusers with these bitter words:

> We have no talisman except force. Ultimately all government is based on force. If human nature were other than what it is, no doubt one could devise some other method. . . . Fate, or the will of the people, call it what you wish, has placed us in this position that we are the custodians of the life of the nation . . . there was not an act done that was inspired by any other motive than the securing of the welfare and the safety and the freedom of the Irish people. . . . Personal spite, great heavens! Vindictiveness! One of these men was a friend of mine. (*Dail Reports*, II, 71–73.)

Thus for Yeats spoke the ablest minister of them all. Here was one of those "terrible decisions" that the ex-Senator could evoke a year before his death, along with tributes to Burke and the other great Anglo-Irishmen, as a measure of the national spirit.[47] And there in all his pride and "distracted gentleness" stood "the one strong intellect in Irish public life."[48] The death of such a man and such a personal friend was another of those deaths that took Yeats's heart for speech. Writing to Mrs. O'Higgins, he said:

> What can one say? I think of these words in an old Irish poem: "The sorrowful are dumb for her." What one can say is that the country has lost the man it most needed, its great builder of a nation. When obscure men die in battle we say "their country will never forget them," and it forgets them before daybreak;

47. *On the Boiler*, p. 12.
48. *Letters*, p. 727.

but a martyred intellect is the most powerful of all things. One remembers that when men write the history of this generation they will tell his life and know that all is told; one tries to find consolation in that thought, and then one remembers all that he had still to do.

I have during these last four and twenty hours tried again and again to find something less inadequate to say, but before certain events one feels most of all the helplessness of human life.[49]

The case of the Countess Markievicz is more complicated. Her greatness seemed the wrong kind to the poet-Senator. As the former Constance Gore-Booth, daughter of one of the powerful Anglo-Irish Sligo families, she had early traded the life of county belle and London debutante for that of art student in London and Paris, Dublin actress, and wife of a Polish count. But her greatest days were passed amid the rigors of Sinn Fein, command in the Easter Rising, agitation for Jim Larkin, the labor leader, and the role of Minister for Labour in the Provisional Government. And all this in spite of the ravages of prison and a later life "on the run" as first Queen of the Irish Republic, pursued by British and Free State agents. Ability enough! we might say. Yet according to Yeats, this delirium of drive and energy was a sacrifice of innocence and beauty which might well go unappreciated.

From his early letters and *Autobiographies* we know the welcome that Yeats received at Lissadell House in Sligo. The record speaks of his skating with Con and her sister Eva, interesting them in Irish folklore, watching the intrepid Con ride to hounds, and encouraging Eva with her verse. Yeats was early struck by a combination in the family of impetuosity and strong will, but no less by their "instinct for excellence." [50] Already the stories and anecdotes from both sides have become legion: Yeats during one stay at Lissadell getting up in the middle of the night to announce, "I have just seen a ghost I have

49. "Sympathy with Mrs. O'Higgins," *Irish Times*, 14 July 1927.
50. *Letters*, p. 254.

not seen for seven years"; [51] the tale by Sarah Purser of Con's attempt, with a friend from the Slade School, to make Yeats fight a duel with a man named Brown—who they imagined had insulted them—but unsuccessfully; [52] the fact that one of his paintings so much delighted Sir Henry that Yeats was granted shooting rights on the Gore-Booth estates; [53] Yeats's later statement that prison might not do Constance any harm; [54] her presentation of *The Land of Heart's Desire* at the Theatre Royal, "as played at Kilmainham Jail by women prisoners." [55] But in later life it was the memory of her former beauty and extravagant behavior that lodged closest in him: her riding down an old shopkeeper who deliberately blocked her path during a hunt; her beauty that caused a newspaper editor to write a sonnet on a tablecloth, cut it out, pass it to her, and leave Yeats to face the proprietor with the promise of a new cloth. [56]

Part of the unpublished draft of Yeats's *Autobiographies*, however, throws even more light on his regard for both girls, later expressed in the nostalgic melancholy of his famous elegy "In Memory of Eva Gore-Booth and Con Markiewicz":

> In my childhood I had seen on clear days from the hill above my grandmother's house or from the carriage if our drive was towards Ben Bulben . . . the grey stone walls of Lissadell among the trees; we were merchant people of the town. No matter how rich we grew, no matter how many thousands a year our mills or our ships brought in, we could never be county, nor indeed had we any desire to be so. We would meet on grand juries, those people in the great houses—Lissadell among its woods, Hazelwood House by the lake's edge, & Markree Castle encircled by wood after wood, & we would speak in malicious gossip & knew ourselves suspected in turn, but the long-settled habit of Irish life had set up a wall. One man, a merchant at the

51. Information from Miss Gabrielle Gore-Booth.
52. Information from Mr. S. Dunin-Markievicz.
53. "Where W. B. Yeats Will Lie," *Irish Times*, 6 February 1939.
54. Hone, p. 353.
55. "Charity Entertainment," *Irish Independent*, 11 February 1924.
56. TS. of "Poems about Women," BBC broadcast, 10 April 1932, 9.05–9.30.

other end of the town, did indeed sometimes drift a little into such society but we despised him for it. . . . But my going to the Gore-Booths was different—I had written books & it was my business to write books, & it was natural to wish to talk to those whose books you liked, & besides I was no longer of my grandfather's house. I could no longer say "we do so and so or we think so and so."

I have no memory of when I first met the Gore-Booth girls, or how I came to be asked. Con Gore-Booth all through my late boyhood had been romantic to me & more than once as I looked over to the green wall & roof I would repeat to myself Milton's lines

> Bosomed deep in tufted trees
> Where some lofty beauty lies
> The cynosure of neighbouring eyes.

She had often passed me on horseback going or coming from some hunt, and was acknowledged beauty of the county. I heard now and then some Con boyish feat or of her reckless riding, but the general impression was always that she was respected & admired. To the country people she was always Miss Gore for they never spoke the name Booth which had brought with it English merchant blood I believe, & it was a Gore whom their fathers had served and obeyed. She surprised me now at our first meeting by some small physical resemblance to Maud Gonne—though so much shorter and smaller—& by a more exact resemblance in voice. In later years her voice became shrill & light, but at the time I went up it was low & soft. I was perhaps the first to give her any detailed account of one in imitation of whom perhaps, she was to earn the life sentence she is now serving. I was at once in closer sympathy to her sister Eva whose delicate gazelle-like beauty reflected a mind far more subtle and distinguished. Eva was for a couple of happy weeks my close friend, & I told her all of my unhappiness in love. Indeed so close it was that I nearly said to her, as William Blake said to Catherine Blake, "You pity me, then I love you." But now I thought "This house would not accept so penniless a suitor" & besides I was still decidedly in love with that other. . . .[57]

I linger over this language of affection and friendship to suggest the roots of the disappointment and reproof that Yeats later directed against himself and both girls. His objection is Burke's objection to Jacobins at the end of the long passage from *An Appeal* marked by Yeats. In their addiction to common abstract political slogans, held with breathless enthusiasm and voiced with unqualified assurance, they and he had forfeited their birthright of natural beauty and traditional wisdom for mere golden dreams.[58] Or so Yeats could also ask of Con in such a poem as "On a Political Prisoner":

> Did she in touching that lone wing
> Recall the years before her mind
> Became a bitter, an abstract thing,
> Her thought some popular enmity:
> Blind and leader of the blind
> Drinking the foul ditch where they lie?

And earlier make the same comparison in "Easter 1916":

> That woman's days were spent
> In ignorant good-will,
> Her nights in argument
> Until her voice grew shrill.
> What voice more sweet than hers
> When, young and beautiful,
> She rode to harriers? [59]

57. "Autobiography." Joseph Hone used part of this passage in his life of Yeats; see p. 115. The Gore-Booths believe Yeats met the family while he was staying with his Aunt Jackson in Sligo and was then invited to Lissadell.

58. Two of the many accounts of the sisters' legendary impatience are to be found in AE, *The Living Torch*, ed. Monk Gibbon (New York, 1938), pp. 162–64, and Sean O'Casey, *Drums Under the Window* (London, 1945), pp. 249–51.

59. In the Countess' Notebook No. 347 in the National Museum of Ireland there is a pen drawing of three sea gulls. Another unnumbered Notebook contains a characteristic drawing of a spirit liberated from prison and returning with fire and hatchet. For more on her beauty and wildness, see *Seventy Years Young, Memories of Elizabeth, Countess of Fingall,* told to Pamela Hinkson (London, November 1937), p. 191.

In these poems, and in the later "In Memory of Eva Gore-Booth and Con Markiewicz," written after the death of Con in July 1927, Yeats quarreled not so much with her courageous part in two rebellions as he did with the kind of politics she espoused. Once he summed up this point by saying, "We had never been on the same side at the same time." [60] Hence, after recalling the beauty of Lissadell and the two girls,

> The light of evening, Lissadell,
> Great windows open to the south,
> Two girls in silk kimonos, both
> Beautiful, one a gazelle.

Yeats points to the results of their politics with Burke's disdain for a Utopia—Eva had written a vague poem with that very title—and with Burke's refusal to separate aesthetics and politics:

> The older is condemned to death,
> Pardoned, drags out lonely years
> Conspiring among the ignorant.
> I know not what the younger dreams—
> Some vague Utopia—and she seems,
> When withered old and skeleton-gaunt,
> An image of such politics.

And then, addressing himself to the now dead girls, he turns the accusing finger on himself as well:

> Dear shadows, now you know it all,
> All the folly of a fight
> With a common wrong or right.
> The innocent and the beautiful
> Have no enemy but time;
> Arise and bid me strike a match
> And strike another till time catch;
> Should the conflagration climb,
> Run till all the sages know.
> We the great gazebo built,

60. TS. of "Poems about Women."

> They convicted us of guilt;
> Bid me strike a match and blow.

Con's savage attacks on her own Southern Unionist class—denouncing them as anti-Irish and capitalistic—not to mention her screaming tirades on the corrupt life of the aristocracy during the Dail debates on the Treaty, could only have offered Yeats further evidence.[61] So probably could statements like the following, upholding communism and advocating terror as a political weapon:

> I haven't given up the Bolshies yet: I believe that they will greatly improve conditions for the world. Of course, I agree with you in disliking the autocracy of any class, but surely if they have the sense to organise education, they can abolish class. While they are menaced by the moneyed classes of the whole world their only hope lies in the success of a strong central government: a tyranny in fact, but once the pressure is relieved, Lenin survives, and he has not lost his original ideals, we may hope. Of course, they may go mad with the idea of Empire, and go out with their armies to force the world to come under their ideas and do awful things in the name of freedom, small nationalities, etc., but even so, they have done something. The French Revolution gave France new life, though all their fine ideas ended in horrors and bloodshed and wars. The world, too, gained. Nothing else would have given courage to the underdog and put fear into the heart of the oppressor in the way it did.
>
> I believe all the reforms at the beginning of the nineteenth century have their roots in the Terror.[62]

61. *Dail Eireann Debates on the Treaty between Great Britain and Ireland*, 14th December 1921–10th January 1922 (Dublin, n.d.), pp. 184–85.

62. *Prison Letters of Countess Markievicz*, ed. Esther Roper with a Preface by President de Valera (London, 1934), pp. 255–56. Aside from the evidence of these letters, the Countess' continued sympathy for the Russian Revolution can be found in her *Women, Ideals and the Nation* (Dublin, 1909), p. 1; *A Call to the Women of Ireland* (Dublin, 1918), *passim; James Connolly's Policy and Catholic Doctrine* (Dublin, n.d.), *passim;* and "Wolfe Tone's Ideals of Democracy," *An Phoblacht,* 26 June 1925. At a debate, "The Truth about Russia," at the Abbey on 11 May 1919 she clearly identified herself with the Soviet sympathizer and English suffragette, Miss Sylvia Pankhurst ("What Is Happening in Russia," *Freeman's Journal,* 12 May 1919). The Countess was

How Burke would have loved that! Yet the beauty of the poem is that, unlike Sean O'Faolain with his patronizing attitude in *Constance Markievicz* (London, 1928), Yeats can see his own dereliction in these Jacobin abstractions, possibly his own direct influence in bringing the legend of Maud Gonne—"the detailed account of one in imitation of whom perhaps, she was to earn the life sentence"—to Lissadell. How telling then is the statement from Con in Aylesbury Prison to Eva after the heroism of 1916: "That play of W. B.'s was a sort of gospel to me. 'If any man would help me, he must give me himself, give me all.' " [63] Or her description of a morning camp-out with the Fianna, her beloved boy scouts, before the more exciting days of Howth gun-running and embattled College of Surgeons: "Early as we were, the boys were still earlier, and one was already improving his mind with W. B. Yeats's poems." [64] If such a career was talent wasted, Yeats's haunting memorial implicates himself, implicates modern Ireland, comes very close to implicating time itself, which only sage or miracle may confute.

III

We have seen that Yeats and Burke would have agreed that able men in government need not be representative of constituencies. They would have agreed also that such men should fervently devote

also denied permission to speak in Glasgow because of her IRA and Communist sympathies (reported in the *Irish Independent*, 27 July 1923). See also the articles on her by Hanna Sheehy-Skeffington in *An Phoblacht* for 12 April and 5, 12, and 19 May 1928.

63. *Prison Letters*, p. 155. Indeed, Yeats's account may have been of Cathleen Ni Houlihan herself.

64. The Christmas Number of the *Fianna Journal*, December 1914, p. 3, kindly made available to me by Mr. S. Dunin-Markievicz, the Countess' stepson. After defending Yeats and Lady Gregory against Ernest A. Boyd's criticism in a letter to the editor of the *Irish Times*, the Countess had written "All honour to Mr. Yeats and Lady Gregory and their little band of pioneer authors and actors" ("Letters to the Editor," *Irish Times*, 1 January 1913). Her unofficial title, "first Queen of the Irish Republic," and the story that a Republican and a Unionist doctor quarreled over her on her death bed sustain the theme of the divided lady that Yeats hints at. See Maud Wynn, *An Irishman and His Family* (London, 1937), p. 270, and *Seventy Years Young*, p. 193.

themselves to the persistent issues of the historic nation.[65] In fact the figure that Yeats hit upon was Burke's memorable analogy of the British oak.[66] If we have reason to doubt that Burke was thinking of organic development, or, as Yeats also supposed, that he was the first to term the state a tree,[67] there is no doubt about what Yeats intended: "A State is organic and has its childhood and maturity and, as Swift saw and Burke did not, its decline. We owe allegiance to the government of our day in so far as it embodies that historical being." [68] The symbol of the tree also allowed Yeats to attribute historic continuity to the state. It allowed him, further, to conceive of the state as at once peasant-based and aristocratic. Ultimately this symbol allowed him to envision the state as ideally shaped by art and religion together. Throughout his use of this figure, Yeats's accent is on the growing, developing mind of man. For, like Burke, he believed man made for the state, not the state for man.[69]

The first thing to mark then is the deep attraction that Burke's symbol had for Yeats. It is well known that, during his Senate years and after, Yeats never tired of iterating "Burke [proved] that the State was a tree, no mechanism to be pulled in pieces and put up again, but an oak tree that had grown through centuries." [70] Without that slow growth a state was likely to become a tyranny.[71] The lines

> And haughtier-headed Burke that proved the State a tree
> That this unconquerable labyrinth of the birds, century
>   after century
> Cast but dead leaves to mathematical equality

are an even more elaborate and suggestive version of the same thought. Yet, since Yeats's enthusiasm for Burke was as much a case

65. *Senate Speeches*, p. 33; *An Appeal, Works*, III, 2.
66. *Reflections, Works*, II, 357.
67. *Lady Gregory's Journals*, p. 265.
68. *Pages from a Diary, Explorations*, p. 318.
69. In his copy of *Biographia Literaria* (London, 1876), p. 360, Yeats marked a passage that included the following words: ". . . men (i.e., the aggregate of the inhabitants of a country at any one time) are made for the state, not the state for the men."
70. *Senate Speeches*, p. 172.
71. "Bishop Berkeley," *Essays and Introductions*, p. 402.

of reaffirmation as it was agreement, further light on this symbol can also come from portions of two speeches during Yeats's earlier days.

The first appears in a speech given May 19, 1893, to the National Literary Society at a meeting in Molesworth Hall in Dublin. It presents the tree as an analogy for the growth of a country's literature. The process is peculiarly akin to the one Yeats was to describe in the twenties in urging the growth of a mature and responsible Irish nationalism:

> Is there any object which we can isolate and watch going through its growth and decay, and thereby perhaps discover a law of development which is common alike to it and to literature. Any tree or plant is just such an object. It grows from a simple seed, and having sent up a little green sprout of no great complexity, though much more complex than its seed, it develops a complex trunk and last of all innumerable and intricate leaves, and flowers, and fruits. Its growth is from unity to multiplicity, from simplicity to complexity, and if we examine the method of this growth, we find that it takes place through a constant sub-division of the constituent cells. I hope to show you that a literature develops in an analogous way, and that this development takes place by a constant sub-division of moods and emotions, corresponding to the sub-division of the cells in the tree. In its youth it is simple, and in its mid-period it grows in complexity, as does the tree when it puts forth many branches, and in its mature age it is covered by an innumerable variety of fruits and flowers and leaves of thought and experience.[72]

At a later point in the same article, Yeats asserts that the same analogy of a tree's growth might be applied to human society, civilization, and life itself.

The second is part of a lecture given in New York City ten years later:

> A nation is like a great tree, and if it is to grow strongly and abundantly it must lift its boughs towards the light not only of

72. "Nationality and Literature," *United Ireland*, 27 May 1893.

the warm sun that is love for all things that are comely and of good repute, but towards that cold moon of noble hate, of hate for all things that are oppressive and all things that are evil. Only when that double light shines upon it can it grow great enough to shelter the birds of Heaven among its leaves and the children of Earth under its boughs.[73]

A mature nationalism, its hates and loves intelligently guided, aware of the increased complexity of its history—rather than simplifying it through abstract or pious obsessions—was Yeats's hope after the Treaty. By then, he had come around to urging a reading of the old Gaelic tales for the young imagination, but a more thorough study of Berkeley and Burke to sharpen the more intricate, mature, choice-making Irish mind.[74] Thoughts like these must lie behind the verve of his letter to Olivia Shakespeare from Merrion Square in June 1923: "Here one works at the slow exciting work of creating the institutions of a new nation—all coral insects but with some design in our heads of the ultimate island." [75]

Historic continuity meant much to Yeats in those days. His markings in the pages of *An Appeal from the New to the Old Whigs* reflect this importance as well as many another marked passage in his edition of Burke. Here is one that will give the substance of what I mean:

> . . . a nation is not an idea only of local extent, and individual momentary aggregation; but it is an idea of continuity, which extends in time as well as in numbers and in space. And this is a choice not of one day, or one set of people, not a tumultuary and giddy choice; it is a deliberate election of ages and of genera-tions; it is a constitution made by what is ten thousand times better than choice, it is made by the peculiar circumstances, occasions, tempers, dispositions, and moral, civil, and social habitudes of the people, which disclose themselves only in a long space of time.[76]

73. TS. of a speech given in New York, 1903–4.
74. *Senate Speeches*, p. 172.
75. *Letters*, pp. 698–99.
76. "Reform of Representation in the House of Commons," *Works*, VI,

A like concept of historic Ireland was often on Yeats's lips in the Senate, especially in addressing those who thought of Ireland as merely Gaelic and Catholic. Great buildings, for instance, like the Four Courts and the Bank of Ireland, were trusts from the past; hasty legislation, he warned, might live on as a precedent; typically he hoped the public memory might be maintained by any war memorial erected in Merrion Square.[77] Burke and Arthur Griffith both drew his praise for refusing to separate a sense of history from politics.[78] Very shrewdly Yeats saw the new state as one with few if any indigenous legislative precedents to consider,[79] and for that reason as a country that would have to discover its true rather than its imagined past. In the same way it would have to be mindful of the future. At important moments in the present, say during the struggle for the Lane Gallery or during the establishment of the Free State, Ireland lived "more or less in the eyes of an unborn public . . . playing our part before . . . a great audience of the unborn." [80]

Yet in keeping before a people's eyes a view of the historic nation past and future, one could not abandon the present. Yeats noted in his 1930 *Diary* that "a love for others must . . . include their lives, their lives which are as yet unknown and unlived. We re-make the world for the sake of those lives. Karl Marx puts too much emphasis upon this re-made world and not enough upon the living; only when we contemplate those living can we re-make the world." [81] In the light of Ireland's tragic Civil War, this was especially apt. How relevant here seems one of Yeats's many characteristic marked passages from Burke on the idealism of revolutionists who envisioned a golden future:

146–47. Yeats had not only marked this passage but also made reference to it in the flyleaf of the volume by writing "Nation—not only the people living at one time 146."

77. *Senate Speeches*, pp. 66, 67, 135.
78. *Ibid.*, pp. 35, 172.
79. P. L. Dickinson, *The Dublin of Yesterday* (London, 1929), p. 126.
80. "Municipal Art Gallery," *Irish Times*, 10 May 1913.
81. *Pages from a Diary, Explorations*, p. 326.

The burthen of proof lies heavily on those who tear to pieces the whole frame and contexture of their country, that they could find no other way of settling a government fit to obtain its rational ends, except that which they have pursued by means unfavourable to all the present happiness of millions of people, and to the utter ruin of several hundreds of thousands. In their political arrangements, men have no right to put the well-being of the present generation wholly out of the question. Perhaps the only moral trust with any certainty in our hands, is the care of our own time. With regard to futurity, we are to treat it like a ward.[82]

Land, family, and religion were paramount in the historic Irish nation. Yeats therefore rejoiced in 1922 over what he took to be Ireland's turn to conservative politics, when so many other nations were veering to the left.[83] As a young man he had welcomed Kropotkin's condemnation of the French Revolution for destroying old customs, institutions, and traditions.[84] He himself said of its modern recrudescence, socialism,

. . . an eighteenth century fanaticism, born, when philosophy was lost, and science not yet discovered would to-day (all the greater problems visible but unsolved) change the design of the world. Those who would so change it are like some fourth-rate artist who imposes upon his work a symmetry, not born out of his subject, or his own mind, but anonymous and superficial, because he has not patience in discovery, nor the courage to look confusion in the face without flinching.[85]

In the matter of the organic state Yeats could not forget Burke's dictum: *"to innovate is not to reform."* [86]

82. *An Appeal, Works*, III, 15.
83. *Letters*, p. 693.
84. Hone, p. 65.
85. Unpublished fragment beginning "and what has Ireland to do with internationalism . . ."
86. Yeats marked this passage in "A Letter to a Noble Lord," *Works*, V, 120.

This last was more than ever true in an agricultural country. Yeats feared a Dublin proletariat that might brush aside the peasant base of Ireland.[87] He agreed with Burke's phrase—"the first creditor is the plow." [88] Yeats's dream was of the ancient ideal, a land of the soil not the factory, the very antithesis of the garish, neon-splattered O'Connell Street of his old age. He hated that sight.[89] More than any other type, the landed interest—whom he had met among the Gregorys and at the Kildare Street Club—were the class to think most surely of the historic nation, past and future.[90] His conviction was that "We owe allegiance to the government of our day in so far as it embodies that historical being." [91]

Such an Ireland would have a ruling, leisured, propertied class. These ruling families, the heart of the tree, had to predominate in Ireland. He had hopes that the Post Office of 1916 would be looked upon as the *Mayflower* for the ruling families of the future.[92] Perhaps Yeats never made the point more clearly than when he declared to his Senate colleagues on the subject of the Damage to Property Bill, "This Country will not always be an uncomfortable place for a country gentleman to live in, and it is most important that we should keep in this country a certain leisured class. I am afraid that Labour disagrees with me in that. On this matter I am a crusted Tory. I am of the opinion of the ancient Jewish book which says

87. *Letters*, p. 915.

88. He also marked this passage in "Speech on the Nabob of Arcot's Debts," *Works*, III, 164.

89. "A General Introduction for my Work," *Essays and Introductions*, p. 526.

90. Yeats once wrote "Swift's 'few' not less 'the Landed Interest' " on p. 21 after the following passage in his copy of *Biographia Literaria:* ". . . it is no less an essential mark of true genius, that its sensibility is excited by any other cause more powerfully than by its own personal interests; for this plain reason, that the man of genius lives most in the ideal world, in which the present is still constituted by the future or the past; and because his feelings have been habitually associated with thoughts and images, to the number, clearness, and vivacity of which, the sensation of self is always in an inverse proportion." The last thirteen words of this sentence are to be found on p. 22.

91. *Pages from a Diary, Explorations*, p. 318.

92. *On the Boiler*, p. 12.

'there is no wisdom without leisure.'"[93] And around the same time Yeats just as clearly marked a like sentiment in Burke's pages:

> . . . he felt, that no great commonwealth, could by any possibility long subsist, without a body of some kind or other of nobility, decorated with honour, and fortified by privilege. This nobility forms the chain that connects the ages of a nation, which otherwise (with Mr. Paine) would soon be taught that no one generation can bind another. He felt that no political fabric could be well made without some such order of things as might, through a series of time, afford a rational hope of securing unity, coherence, consistency, and stability to the state. He felt that nothing else can protect it against the levity of courts, and the greater levity of the multitude.[94]

A landed aristocracy—inequality inhered in landed property[95]—would identify itself with the existence of the state. The vision was of a golden age before the French Revolution, an Ireland accustomed to "the long-settled rule of powerful men, no great dogmatic structure, few great crowded streets, scattered unprogressive communities, much handiwork, wisdom wound into the roots of the grass."[96] Leaders from these communities would not be like the drab, unimaginative Saxons who had been losing the Empire—as he and

93. *Senate Speeches*, pp. 38–39.
94. "A Letter to a Noble Lord," *Works*, V, 148. Yeats also praised this bias in Balzac ("Louis Lambert," *Essays and Introductions*, p. 444).
95. *Pages from a Diary, Explorations*, p. 313. Yeats also turned down p. 324 in his copy of Burke's *Reflections on the Revolution in France, Works*, II, a page containing the central statement that property must "be, out of all proportion, predominant in the representation. It must be represented too in great masses of accumulation, or it is not rightly protected. The characteristic essence of property . . . is to be *unequal*." A related idea on the same page was probably also important to Yeats: "The power of perpetuating our property in our families is one of the most valuable and interesting circumstances belonging to it, and that which tends the most to the perpetuation of society itself. It makes our weakness subservient to our virtue; it grafts benevolence even upon avarice. The possessors of family wealth, and of the distinction which attends hereditary possession . . . are the natural securities for this transmission."
96. *Wheels and Butterflies*, p. 26.

Burke both argued [97]—but, as he hoped, like the Swedish royal family whom he praises in *The Bounty of Sweden*. Individualism had had a revolutionary success evident in the able leaders of the new Irish government; the future lay in the strengthening and nurturing of landed families.[98] And by landed families Yeats probably meant much more than we usually credit him with:

> I understand by 'soil' all the matter in which the soul works, the walls of our houses, the serving-up of our meals, and the chairs and tables of our rooms, and the instincts of our bodies; and by 'family' all institutions, classes, orders, nations, that arise out of the family and are held together, not by a logical process, but by historical association, and possess a personality for whose lack men are 'sheep without a shepherd when the snow shuts out the sun.' [99]

It is no great step to acknowledging that Yeats like Burke also saw the state in a religious light. True, Yeats no longer believed in the traditional emblems and ceremonials of orthodox religions. But he did believe in God, freedom, and immortality. He could, moreover, say in their behalf, "An idea of the State which is not a preparation for those three convictions, a State founded on economics alone, would be a prison house. A State must be made like a Chartres Cathedral for the glory of God and the Soul." [100] A mechanical, geometrically planned state did not allow that vaulting glory. It began in families and passed on through locales and habitual associations.[101] This in fact was the mode Yeats recommended in teaching and expanding the child's awareness, a process that would be crowned with a return of Irish children from the anarchy of the Civil War to a sense of civic duty: "The proper remedy is to teach religion,

---

97. See Monk Gibbon, *The Masterpiece and the Man* (New York, 1959), pp. 103–4. The likely source of Yeats's slur on the schoolboy mind running the British Empire—if a turned-down page is any indication—was Burke's "Speech on Mr. Fox's East-India Bill," *Works*, II, 195.
98. Information from Mrs. W. B. Yeats.
99. "If I were Four-and-Twenty," *Explorations*, pp. 273–74.
100. *Pages from a Diary, Explorations*, p. 335.
101. *Reflections, Works*, II, 467.

civic duty and history as all but inseparable." [102] The aftermath of this troubled Ireland seemed to Yeats a time when men no longer hated their own sins but hated the sins of their neighbors.[103] This was to turn one's neighbors into objects and society into a mechanism. Yeats made this not surprisingly religious point most pertinently during his first year in office when, in welcoming Hilaire Belloc to Ireland, he was described as saying

> . . . that in the present position of Ireland Mr. Belloc's visit was very important. He thought of Mr. Belloc and his friend, Mr. G. K. Chesterton, as trying to check the depravity of a revolutionary epoch by bringing them back to the cultural, religious, and social traditions of Europe.
>
> They were saying: "Stop, you must not allow either mechanical wealth or revolution to change the world into a mechanism."
>
> Ireland was now entering a period in which those great social problems would be constantly present before their minds, and they should seek the guidance of Catholic countries who had solved those problems.[104]

Finally, then, it became the artist's duty—almost his religious duty —to urge the living tree of the nation into natural symmetry and beauty. This Yeats took very seriously. If men would judge their neighbors and not themselves, then they needed an objective and just picture of those neighbors—party, class, or section. This was the job for the Abbey, "because it could do a great deal to soften the terrible bitterness that would remain over—to explain party to party and section to section." [105] Earlier during one of his gloomy, prescient

---

102. *Senate Speeches*, p. 173.

103. "The Abbey Theatre," *Irish Times*, 6 May 1921.

104. "Mr. Hilaire Belloc Honoured," *Irish Independent*, 21 June 1923.

105. "The Abbey Theatre," *Irish Times*, 6 May 1921. In his Introduction to *Essays and Introductions*, p. viii, Yeats spoke of an inherited subject matter to which the artist is bound and which he passes on: "This subject-matter is something I have received from the generations, part of that compact with my fellow men made in my name before I was born. I cannot break from it without breaking from some part of my own nature. . . ."

moments he had seen the Easter Rising as a threat to his hopes for national unity. He wrote Lady Gregory that "at the moment I feel that all the work of years has been overturned, all the bringing together of classes, all the freeing of Irish literature and criticism from politics." [106] His fears were often to be reaffirmed. They were not allayed in 1928 when Yeats was told that a high government official had asserted, "I doubt if we should put any more of those stale pictures into the Gallery. I think that it is all British propaganda. Gaelic Ireland has no affinities with those Mediterranean nations." [107]

Yet between 1916 and 1928 his hopes had been high. Dublin after the Civil War presented the ingredients for a new social order. In the absence of great wealth and the aristocratic hostesses of the past, Yeats pinned his hopes on his drawing-room dramas: "I want to begin arranging performances. The psychological moment has come, for Dublin is reviving after the Civil War, and self-government is creating a little stir of excitement. People are trying to found a new society. Politicians want to be artistic, and artistic people to meet politicians, and so on." [108] The authoritative guide would be the artist. He would bring a noble voice, "the imagination and speech of the country," to the ears of townsmen. Had not Lady Gregory, Synge, and he already partially educated "the young Ministers and party politicians of the Free State"? [109] This is the religion of art that Yeats has been accused of with a vengeance. It is not by chance that "Among School Children," which meditates the ideal becoming or education that merges art and religion, should have as its resplendent symbol of unity in historic time a great rooted blossomer. It was the ideal living form for the nation that Yeats had already helped adorn with a new coinage, judges' robes, designs for lace and stained glass industries, and later with an Irish Academy of Letters.

106. *Letters*, p. 613.
107. Diary of Thought begun 23 September 1928.
108. *Letters*, p. 702.
109. *Autobiographies*, pp. 570–71.

IV

The Burke who restored European order excited Yeats with the same pride that he discovered in reading Swift's epitaph.[110] Like his interpretation of Swift on liberty, Yeats's pairing of Burke and European order needs some elucidation. For in restoring that order, Burke, in Yeats's conception, rolled back European anarchy.[111] In other words, Yeats had in mind not only the ceremony and custom associated with Coole, but that force which would destroy it or Europe—Whiggery. Whiggery was a quality of mind—"A levelling, rancorous, rational sort of mind"—benighted with abstractions, ill-mannered, and finally murderous. Burke had fought this spectre at its birth, and Yeats fought it at its demise, his head full of Burke, his eye on his new country:

> Everything seems to show that the centrifugal movement which began with the Encyclopaedists and produced the French Revolution, and the democratic views of men like Mill, has worked itself out to the end.

> . . . .

> Movements that had for their aim the setting free of the individual were found to produce anarchy in the end.

> . . . .

> When the democratic movement was in its beginning Burke opposed it in speeches and in essays, and what he did vainly when the movement was in its sunrise, Peguy and Claudel have done in poems and plays in its sunset.

> Authoritative government is certainly coming, if for no other reason than that the modern State is so complex that it must find some kind of expert government—a government firm enough, tyrannical enough, if you will, to spend years in carrying out its

110. *Pages from a Diary, Explorations*, p. 337.
111. "Modern Irish Literature," *Irish Times*, 18 February 1933.

plans. The Marxian Socialist wants to re-create the world according to a scientific theory, while men like Peguy, Claudel and Maurras—whom one can admire as a thinker without admiring his practical politics—see the nation as something like a growing child or an old man, as the case may be, and not an automaton, as Socialists would make it.

I see the same tendency here in Ireland towards authoritative government. What else can chaos produce, even though our chaos has been a very small thing compared with the chaos in Central Europe? . . . [It will be] a steady movement towards the creation of a nation controlled by highly trained intellects.

. . . .

I shall be a very old man if I live to see it [the new movement] capable of taking up the tasks for which I care and of which I dream. . . . One of them certainly is to make a Dublin as worthy of our new Parliament as the great buildings, like the Bank of Ireland, were worthy of the old one.[112]

All the ingredients are here, although Yeats's mention of Mussolini and Teddy Roosevelt has been omitted. Burke, the French Revolution, socialism, the memorials of Georgian Ireland, all recall the comparable associations derived from Swift on liberty in the last chapter. In fact, Yeats marked just such a passage in his copy of Prior's *Life of Burke* defining what Burke meant by social freedom:

It is that state of things in which the liberty of no man, and no body of men, is in a condition to trespass on the liberty of any person, or any description of persons, in society.[113]

Yeats had sensed such liberty and order during his visit to the Swedish royal court and royal family. Nature had mocked by her device of the exceptional family new ideas of equality. Moreover, the able and brilliant men of the realm had gathered around that royalty. This display at court had also proved just as exciting to another spectator, a man, according to Yeats, possessed by "a Jacobin frenzy"

112. "From Democracy to Authority," *Irish Times*, 16 February 1924.
113. Prior's *Life*, p. 349.

at witnessing what he took to be a ridiculous and anachronistic ceremony. He was a product of English democracy.[114] This scene and the preceding long quotation by Yeats will best introduce us to his fears of what might scotch Burke's idea of order in the modern day: an abstract, autonomous state that would refuse the intellect of unique men; a revolution in manners that would deny public and private magnificence; a loosing of murderous forces that inevitably followed upon any revolution in the name of abstract liberty.

The subject of political abstractions finds Burke and Yeats with many hates in common. We know of Yeats's sympathy and admiration for those who sacrificed themselves in 1916. But self-sacrifice for a mere abstraction only rarely seemed a virtue to him. One hardly examines a year of his life without finding Yeats condemning the barren intellect that mouthed the trite slogans of Irish history:

> A zealous Irishman, especially if he lives much out of Ireland, spends his time in a never-ending argument about Oliver Cromwell, the Danes, the penal laws, the Rebellion of 1798, the famine, the Irish peasant, and ends by substituting a traditional casuistry for a country; and if he be a Catholic, yet another casuistry. . . .[115]

Similarly, the attack on what Yeats called "mathematical democracy" seemed Burke's distinguishing Anglo-Irish trait. Burke's onslaught against the French dogma centered on the rule of the majority. To recall Yeats's sneer at the new breed of elected Senators—vague, restive, heated, bothered—is to be reminded of Burke's derision for the "warm, hot-headed, zealous atheist" spouting slogans of the equality and power of the people.[116] Burke had described this mind as ambitious, one that would substitute logic for prudence, confuse morality with mathematics, seek true or false in politics rather than good and evil.[117] Yeats marked all these passages in Burke, as if to bear out an equal hatred of the amateur casuist in politics.

114. *Autobiographies*, pp. 548–49.
115. "J. M. Synge and the Ireland of his Time," *Essays and Introductions*, p. 314.
116. "Thoughts on French Affairs," *Works*, III, 352.
117. *An Appeal, Works*, III, 16, 78, 81.

This abstract mind seemed virtually without tradition in Ireland except for the slogans it threw up. It was a mind that "had been without influence in the generation of Grattan, and almost without it in that of Davis." [118] Its mode of operation was fairly predictable, as Yeats saw it: ". . . you must find 'a lever' as it was called, some practical grievance; and I do not think I am fantastic in believing that this faith in 'levers,' universal among revolutionaries, is but a result of that mechanical philosophy of the eighteenth century." [119] This delusion in Ireland made for great talkers and popular orators rigidly given to principle; so much so, that no compromise was possible and little achieved. Minds so possessed refused the Lane Gallery for Lutyens was but half Irish. Yeats's comment on hearing this had been, "Ireland like an hysterical woman is principle mad." [120] Rights, not duties; hatred, not love; fear, not affirmation characterized this mind. It usually had lower middle-class origins; a prime example of it was to be found in J. F. Taylor: "He has the pedantry of Irish Catholic education, inspired by an almost mad energy, which made his mind like some noisy & powerful machine. This pedantry comes from intellectual timidity, from the dread of leaving the mind alone among impressions which all seem historical, & from the habit of political and religious apologetics." [121] If Burke despised the writings of Rousseau and Voltaire for making one with the common mind by their agreeable simplicities and abstractions, Yeats too rallied that perverse talent: "Perhaps a great popular thinker, a Rousseau, a Voltaire, a Wesley is a misfortune. He is too clever, too logical, too definite. He enables the little to believe their minds great, to believe they understand, till they muddy all the fountains of truth." [122] The intelligent possessors of this mind, like Pound and Maud Gonne, Yeats thought of as "revolutionary simpletons." They had become "reactive." Hating success, hating tradition, hugging noble failure,

---

118. "Poetry and Tradition," *Essays and Introductions,* p. 250.
119. *Autobiographies,* p. 358.
120. "New Letters," *REL,* IV, 40.
121. Journal begun December 1908.
122. *Idem.*

they had been ruined by "reactiveness." [123] That mind could also take a sentimental course. Again Rousseau seemed its personification in his "constant resolution to dwell upon good only" and his equal distrust of conflict in a flowing, changing world.[124] And who more sentimental than the professional Irish patriot?

The Republicans' attempt after the Treaty to force their will on the majority through terrorism drew this remark from Yeats: "Perhaps there is nothing so dangerous to a modern state, when politics take the place of theology, as a bunch of martyrs. A bunch of martyrs (1916) were the bomb and we are living in the explosion." [125] The Republicans failed. Nevertheless, especially after 1927, they appealed instead to mass instinct and democratic representation which Yeats condemned for delivering Ireland to "the incompetent." [126] The seeming contradiction in first violently denying the majority and then wooing it came as no surprise to Yeats. For the modern fanatic, in sacrificing himself, approximated rather than opposed the ideals of the crowd.[127] That kind of idealism soon left the mob to its own vulgar devices, once hostilities had ceased. In Sweden, harboring these fears, Yeats at a ceremonial banquet exclaimed, "Think what the people have made of the political thought of the eighteenth century, and now we must offer them a new fanaticism." [128]

Now it is customary to call Yeats a political fool for these beliefs. The accusation has been so frequent that it is hardly worth citing all the distinguished names who have made it. Yet compared to the mind that has been described—one that has bedeviled Irish politics since O'Connell—Yeats often seems to have shown a positive genius for practical politics, whatever his theories might have been.

Like Burke, his instincts were conservative but reasonable. He

---

123. Norman Jeffares, *W. B. Yeats: Man and Poet,* 2nd ed. (London, 1962), p. 268.
124. "If I were Four-and-Twenty," *Explorations,* p. 275.
125. *Letters,* p. 690.
126. *On the Boiler,* pp. 11, 31.
127. *Wheels and Butterflies,* p. 75.
128. *Autobiographies,* p. 542.

disliked, as an Irish nationalist should, the British Empire; yet he also saw the value of a commonwealth or "voluntary Federation of Free Nations." [129] He had had a rather clever—he called it grandiose —plan for turning a Dublin patriotic council into, for all practical purposes, an Irish parliament at the turn of the century.[130] Similarly, he was also shrewd enough to recognize that the absence of the personal note in Redmond's speeches, and the presence of the professional manner of the advocate about his business, was not a weakness at all:

> "Now I am beginning to think that the seeming defect is perhaps the secret of his power. He is able to take a larger view, a wider outlook, to see further ahead than most of our Parliamentary leaders, because he is less interested in the argument of the moment." [131]

In exactly the same objective way, he could see that England had pushed Ireland into no other recourse but revolution by 1920. So far as the solution of the Irish problem went, he, as he told an American reporter, was an Irish nationalist

> "desiring only as much self-government as is compatible with the circumstances," and he would leave it to politicians "how much this ought to be." English party spirit had engendered the present state of things, so that the Irish majority "have lost all belief in the political honesty of English parties, and have fallen back on first principles." The country, in Mr. Yeats's opinion, "has been worked into a state of ecstatic passion," and until this subsides he sees no immediate hope for solution. "Ireland," he adds, "is content for the present to live by faith." [132]

As a patriot Yeats is subtly able to suggest the weaknesses on both sides while not for a moment siding with the British.

His attitude toward the Oath was no less practical and, to use a word his critics deny him, realistic. In 1923, when it appeared that

129. *Ibid.*, p. 536.
130. "Autobiography."
131. "Mr. William Butler Yeats," *Echo*, 25 April 1902.
132. "Mr. Yeats on an Irish Solution," *Irish Independent*, 6 April 1920.

the Civil War might be interminable, Yeats on his own initiative spoke to influential Englishmen on the possibility of removing the Oath, so as to get the contending forces together in the Dail and bring the fighting to a halt. On the boat to England, he had met Cosgrave, who told Yeats that the removal of the Oath was government policy. Later, probably after consultation with O'Higgins and Hogan, Cosgrave apparently denied that there was such a policy. Dr. McCartan brought up the whole matter in 1926 but received official and probably necessarily evasive denials from both Cosgrave and Yeats. But there is a letter extant from Yeats to his wife that mentions his efforts and their refusal.[133] The possibility that he might

133. Information from Mrs. W. B. Yeats. Dr. McCartan had made his statement on Yeats's mission during a political rally at Dundrum on Sunday, 7 February 1926 ("Lively Exchanges," *Irish Times*, 8 February 1926). Formal denials from President Cosgrave's secretary and from Yeats appeared in the *Irish Times* on Tuesday the 9th under the heading "An Alleged Mission." Both letters though formal were necessarily ambiguous. Dr. McCartan then wrote a letter published in the *Irish Independent* on the 11th in which he challenged these denials, pointed to their ambiguity, and disclosed further details:

President Cosgrave's secretary says the statement made by me in Dundrum on Sunday is "untrue," and Senator Yeats writes: "I did not see any member of the British Government on the subject, nor did I make any such report to the Irish Government." Senator Yeats will not state a lie. Will he, therefore, deny that he saw prominent Englishmen on the subject, and that he reported the result to President Cosgrave? I challenge both the President and Senator Yeats to make such a denial.

To make a suggestion much less a statement on such a subject without foundation would be vile on my part. Therefore I shall now give my authority. When Madame McBride [sic], Miss McSwiney, Miss Costello, and Miss Ryan were on hunger strike I called on Senator Douglas to request him to take certain action in the Senate to save the lives of these women. In the course of conversation we discussed the possibilities of peace, and were agreed that the Oath was the great obstacle.

Senator Douglas said it would be possible to have the Oath modified. He had approached Senator Jameson to see if he, Senator Jameson, would go to London for that purpose. Senator Jameson replied: "Why go to London? If it brings peace let us do it ourselves. The English can protest, if they wish."

Senator Douglas also informed me in the presence of Denis McCullough that Senator Yeats had interviewed prominent English statesmen on the subject, and that he, Senator Yeats, had reported to President Cosgrave in London; that President Cosgrave was delighted, and advised him to see a few others whose names had been mentioned by Senator Yeats.

have succeeded—and it seems to have been a good one—may cause
Irish superpatriots a moment of thought. In any case, he was out
after the Oath once more after De Valera's second success in capturing
the government. This time Yeats was just as practical, though more
wily in treating the vexing abstraction of the Oath which had earlier
taken Ireland to Civil War. In fact, the Oath still rankled since it left
De Valera's extremists outside his government where, as we have
seen, they roved with great heat and abandon and threatened another
civil war:

> W. B. Yeats . . . yesterday stated to a Press reporter in
> London that he would like to see the Oath of Allegiance either

---

In telling the story to Senator Douglas later, Senator Yeats said:
"President Cosgrave did not seem so enthusiastic after he had spoken to
Mr. O'Higgins and Mr. Hogan."

At a later date Senator Douglas told me that he himself had interviewed
a number of prominent Englishmen on the same subject, and that none of
them objected to a modification of the Oath.

President Cosgrave in his own office told me that Premier MacDonald
had sounded him indirectly on the question of modifying the Oath in
exchange for Article 12 of the Treaty. "We would be accepting a shadow
for a substance," said the President, but the substance is now gone, and we
should look for the shadow ("Abolition of Oath," *Irish Independent*, 11
February 1926).

Yeats remained silent, but Cosgrave's secretary wrote a second letter ("Abolition
of the Oath") that appeared in the *Irish Independent* on the 12th. His secretary
stated that Cosgrave saw no purpose to be served by engaging in a controversy
with Dr. McCartan and denied any recollection of MacDonald's proposals. Dr.
McCartan went on to make MacDonald's stipulations explicit in April 1926:
"He made the following proposals, which fell on deaf ears in Ireland:—(1) The
Boundary to remain as it was under the British Act of 1920; (2) A Council of
State on which the six and twenty-six counties should be equally represented was
to take over the Reserved Services in the North; (3) The Oath was to be
removed on condition that M. De Valera and his party went into the Dail"
("Clann Eireann and the Oath," *Honesty*, n.s., III [April 17, 1926], 9). For
more information on Cosgrave's second denial, Yeats's subsequent silence, and
Dr. McCartan's reply to Senator Douglas' letter implying a breach of faith, see
"Events of the Week," *An Phoblacht*, 19 February 1926, and "Dr. McCartan on
the Oath," *An Phoblacht*, 26 February 1926. In a letter, dated "Emmet's
Birthday" (March 4 [1926]), to a correspondent, W. J. M. Maloney, Dr.
McCartan throws more light on his disclosures and admits that he probably had
not been playing according to the rules (P. McCartan Papers, Maloney
Collection, Manuscript Division of the New York Public Library). When
interviewed by the author in Dublin during 1962, neither Dr. McCartan nor ex-
President Cosgrave had any memory of the affair.

abolished or modified, to make it acceptable to Ireland and Great Britain.

"So far as I can judge by legal statements I have seen," he said, "the Oath is not an integral part of the Treaty. True, it is mentioned in the Treaty, but there is an omission to state that any person must take it. The Treaty was an ambiguous document which brought peace when a perfectly defined document might not have brought peace. I, certainly, do not want Ireland to attempt to set up any independent Republic. Ireland will not be a pennyworth more loyal because Ireland has taken the Oath. The London County Council takes no Oath, and it governs far more millions than the Free State Parliament. It is no question of disloyalty, this objection to the Oath. A considerable part of our population objects to it, and it is very difficult for us to keep the peace in Ireland until everybody feels that he can safely enter the Dail and agitate there for his rights. As long as we have the Oath we shall have little revolutionary bodies disturbing the peace. It is as much, therefore, in the interests of Great Britain as of Ireland that we be rid of the Oath, or modify it." [134]

If Burke had restored European order, in part by his onslaught against the metaphysics of the French Revolution, Yeats similarly had kept his eye early and late on Irish order by practical thinking on problems that seemed to baffle the idealistic abstractions—a Republic, the Oath, Government Policy—of Irish revolutionary bodies large and small.

From these bodies appeared another threat to national order. In his day Burke called it a revolution in manners and gave us the famous passage on the death of chivalry seen in the insulting treatment offered Marie Antoinette. Yeats would have seconded Burke's equally famous epigram on this matter: "To make us love our country, our country must be lovely." Order included elegance. With De Valera's walk-out during the Treaty debates and Griffith's setting up a provisional government, Yeats knew that he and Lady Gregory

---

134. Unidentified clipping in Holloway, Natl. Lib. MS. 1948 (January–March 1932), II, n.p.

had "to be 'that old man eloquent' to the new governing generation. If we write our best, the spiritual part of the new Ireland will be in our books and the Free State's struggle with the impossibilists may even make some of our unpopular struggles shine with patriotic fire."[135]

Both Burke and Yeats despised the Revolutionary France of the late eighteenth century, and both were attracted by the cultured civilization it had displaced. On November 11, 1925, Yeats had endured attacks on that elegant culture from both sides while presiding at a debate in the Trinity College Historical Society. The subject of debate, if this can be believed, was "That civilization has progressed since this Society first met." No wonder that Yeats finally turned with some exasperation to the "statements made regarding the degeneration of France":

> He would ask them to give up this nonsense of talking about France as an immoral country. She began it in the 13th century, he added, and had been at it ever since. Let them not judge any nation by what they knew of its morality. France excelled in beauty, in virtue, in fine art, and in works, and had created a great and gracious life. Let them take intellect into consideration when they considered morality. If there was progress it was, he thought, very slow: it was a gradual enriching and enlarging of the human soul.[136]

Yeats was accustomed to praise the inherent graciousness of ancient Gaelic life, whether in hut or castle, a life particularly happy in its courtesies. The absence of grace in the new Ireland he blamed on the departure of the Wild Geese, "who might have grown to be leaders in manners and taste," and who had abandoned native Ireland thereafter to political leaders only.[137] Thus, for instance, both the Russian sympathies and the artistic crudities of *An Phoblacht* during

135. Hone, p. 344.
136. "Civilization," *Irish Times*, 12 November 1925.
137. "A People's Theatre," *Explorations*, p. 257.

the late twenties and early thirties must have seemed all too typical to Yeats.[138]

He was always extremely sensitive to the traditional refinements and demeanor that identified a lady, no matter what substitutes his intellectual contemporaries might name in their stead. One such substitute the age held up was a narrowly artistic one: the modern woman might produce a masterpiece. Yeats thought not. So far as providing masterpieces went, women

> never did, never would, and would never want to. The reason was that women between the ages of 15 and 35, decently good-looking, got greater honour than was ever conferred on any-body, be he the greatest statesman or a man victorious in war. Why, then, should she toil for many years to produce a masterpiece? Looking into her glass, she saw a greater master-piece than had ever been created in art or in sculpture. Why should she toil? He hoped women would never take the trouble and spoil their lives trying to produce a great masterpiece.[139]

In the same manner he had earlier condemned a mind like George Eliot's, termed higher education for women "pure delusiveness," and warned, "If we do not see daily beautiful life . . . we become theorists—thinkers as it is called,—or else give ourselves to strained emotions." [140]

As with women, so with literature. After the French Revolution

138. The Red Scare of these years may indeed have been a fabrication, as *An Phoblacht's* intermittent editor in those times has written (Peadar O'Donnell, *There will be Another Day* [Dublin, 1963], p. 126 and *passim*), but part of that fabrication seems to have been the work of *An Phoblacht* itself. See, for instance, "A Bolshevic Ireland?" *An Phoblacht*, 28 August 1925, and "Russia 'On the Up Grade,' " *An Phoblacht*, 6 November 1925. Yeats himself was virtually anathema to *An Phoblacht*. See, for example, "Who Stands for Ireland a Nation?" 26 June 1925; "Our Open Columns," 28 August 1925; "Abbey Theatre Subsidy," 4 September 1925; "Huge Republican Meeting in the Rotunda," 18 September 1925; "What I Saw at the Abbey," 19 February 1926; "Thanks, Mr. Yeats," 30 July 1926; "To Certain Anglo-Irish Writers," 18 March 1927; "Na Bac Leis," 12 November 1927; " 'An Phoblacht' at the Abbey," 6 October 1928; "Mrs. C. Despard's Letter," 24 January 1931; and "Plea for 'Bad Popular Poetry,' " 14 July 1934.
139. "The Sphere of Women," *Irish Times*, 17 November 1925.
140. *Letters*, p. 123, and *Autobiographies*, p. 474.

and the proliferation of democratic ideas, ill breeding in taste and literature was the threat:

> Sometime in the middle of the eighteenth century there came into the faces of women, as painted by the great painters, an exquisite subtlety which they called a mark of high breeding. They got it in Gainsborough and one or two painters before him, and they got it in the first volume of "Sir Charles Grandison." Then he found the same thing in the novels of Jane Austen. These novels were simply a description, an elaboration, of the pursuit of good breeding—that was to say, a quality which only a few happily nurtured people ever found. Then he did not find that pursuit again until they got to the writings of Henry James.
>
> He discovered, about five years ago, the particular devil that spoiled that celebrated quality in literature. "Pickwick" was the devil. In "Pickwick" the qualities celebrated were qualities any man could possess: good humour, a certain amount of openness of heart, kindness—qualities which everyman might hope to possess; they were democratic qualities. It gave them the kind of sculpture they saw in Dublin, like Tom Moore and the statue in Leinster Lawn. That smile of vacuous benevolence came out of "Pickwick." [141]

Yeats himself, of course, exemplified this ideal of breeding and manners, and has still the thanks for it, in Ireland, of being excoriated as a poseur. His courtesy got him into no end of trouble. In matters of politics and courtesy, for instance, he tried to follow the decision of Parnell to pay no official honor to English rule in Ireland. But at a Corinthian Club dinner in 1907, he chose to stand when "God Save the King" was played, and later defended himself in *The Leader* against insinuations from D. P. Moran by writing that he had elected "to follow those old rules of courtesy in which, as Balzac has said, we are all Conservatives." [142] Manners, urbanity, lack of self-consciousness may have seemed like singular demands for perfection

141. "The Modern Novel," *Irish Times*, 9 November 1923. See also *Lady Gregory's Journals*, p. 262, and *A Vision* (1925), pp. 208–9.
142. Letter to *The Leader*, 30 November 1907, p. 226.

to the mass of men preoccupied with getting on in life and hating England. But in the artist and his patron these were model traits, Yeats felt, for a nation's leaders.[143]

Graciousness was not a trait of most revolutionists. Even worse, as the poem "Easter 1916" illustrates in Countess Markievicz, graciousness might well be lost in the revolutionary career. As Burke had concluded in his passage on Marie Antoinette, revolutionaries often lacked natural feelings in matters of life and death, a lack first seen in their unmannerly selves. This may indeed be snobbery. But in all fairness to Yeats, and Burke, one must add that both took decorum seriously. This fact lies behind such a remark to Gogarty as "This country has been ruined by transcendentalism. It has been ruined by dreams—vague, objectless, unrealizable dreams." [144] As O'Leary had told him, and Yeats never forgot, "No gentleman can be a socialist though he might be an anarchist." [145] In the new Ireland Yeats found a decided lack of generosity and tolerance—the ill-breeding of the democratized peasant. In the left wing, he discovered intellectual ill-breeding, an imitation of the manners of the mob. One could multiply these examples of Yeats's concurrence with Burke that culture, traditional culture, was "the sanctity of the intellect." [146] For here manners and morals joined hands in the traditional word "form." It came down to a rather unpleasant distinction, hinted at in all these pronouncements, never forgiven in Ireland, and, in part, certainly wrong. This inflammatory distinction was between Protestant and Catholic. Catholics lacked form.[147] What then must Yeats have thought when Fianna Fail entered the Dail only to smear Major Bryan Cooper, to have young Frank Aiken suspended for insulting

143. Ninette de Valois, *Come Dance with Me* (London, 1957), pp. 94–95. Yeats did not believe in the necessary poverty of the artist or that great merchants might not continue to be patrons of the arts ("Yeats's 'Hello to Everybody!' " *The Northern Whig and Belfast Post*, 9 September 1931).

144. Gogarty, *Going Native* (London, 1941), p. 10. See also *Letters*, pp. 735–36.

145. *Letters*, p. 869. More and more Yeats was struck by the personal and public ill-breeding of left-wing revolutionaries (pp. 875–76).

146. *Autobiographies*, p. 489.

147. Journal begun December 1912.

213

the Speaker, and to allow Sean MacEntee to deride Trinity, the *Playboy,* and so on.[148] He might have said with Burke—in a passage Yeats marked—"when men in that rank lose decorum they lose everything." [149] He did, in fact, say to O'Casey close to this time, apropos communism, "Would you set the rabble in power against the finer and fuller things common to great and gracious people?" [150]

By now our direction must be obvious. To Yeats and Burke, it was but a step from the revolutionary's lack of manners to his condoning murder. Behind both behaviors lay the abstract mind. As we know, Burke conceived of no more cold-blooded murderer than the metaphysician.[151] Likewise, an early draft of "The Second Coming," a poem which took off from Yeats's apprehensions about the socialist revolutions in Germany, Russia, and Italy during and after World War I,[152] locates the original anarchs in the French Revolution. But even more relevant are the connections Yeats makes between the insult to Marie Antoinette and revolutionary massacre, and between Marxism and the threat to modern innocents. His eyes are Burke's:

> Fair that
> Marie Antoinette's train
> More brute birds, &
> Burke has answered
> With his voice to Pitt
> Arraigns revolution. Sings to seems
> But common men— [153]

Nor are manners and murder separated in the continuation of that revolution:

> The Germany of Marx has led to Russian Com
> There every day some innocent has died
> [?Recalls] the mob from other lands

148. "Scene in the Dail," *Irish Times,* 29 June 1928.
149. "A Letter to a Noble Lord," *Works,* V, 147.
150. *Rose and Crown* (London, 1952), p. 142.
151. "A Letter to a Noble Lord," *Works,* V, 141.
152. Information from Mrs. W. B. Yeats.
153. My reading of the MS. differs from that of Jon Stallworthy, *Between the Lines* (Oxford, 1963), p. 17.

Of course all this was to be generalized. One is also persuaded that the beast of pitiless eye in the next section of the printed poem parallels closely the kind of monster images that abound in the feverish pages of Burke's *Letters on a Regicide Peace*. There is, for instance, this portent of the future Burke sees in the new French Republic:

> Here we have, formed, a new, unlooked-for, monstrous, hetero-geneous alliance; a double-natured monster; republic above, and monarchy below. There is no centaur of fiction, no poetic satyr of the woods, nothing short of the hieroglyphic monsters of Egypt, dog in head and man in body, that can give an idea of it. None of these things can subsist in nature (so at least it is thought): but the moral world admits monsters which the physical rejects.[154]

With its origins in Burke and the French Revolution, "The Second Coming" seems even more grim than we had thought. Its spelling out the iron connection between manners and massacre, anarchy and tyranny, abstract rationalism and immorality, the breakdown of an age and the coming of totalitarianism betokens a recrudescence we had not imagined. The sheer terrifying energy—unrestrained by man or God, as Burke might say [155]—and the "passionate intensity" of evil escaped neither man:

> We had fed the heart on fantasies,
> The heart's grown brutal from the fare;
> More substance in our enmities
> Than in our love. . . .

I quote these lines as a reminder that brutality, torture, massacre, and regicide most affrighted Yeats in his very real fear of the new revolutionary socialism. Yeats honestly felt, after the murder of Czar Nicholas II and his family, not only that George V of England should have resigned but that England should have declared war on

---

154. *Works*, V, 410. Yeats describes this "brazen winged beast" in his Introduction to *The Resurrection* as an imagined figure (*Wheels and Butterflies*, p. 103).

155. *The Policy of the Allies*, *Works*, III, 437.

her former ally.[156] Yeats, close to the event, his thoughts riveted on the spread of socialism in both Europe and Ireland, had this to say at a time very near to his beginning "The Second Coming":

> Mr. W. B. Yeats . . . said that Russia had, in the name of progress and in the name of human freedom, revived tyranny and torture of the worst description—had, in fact, resorted to such a mediaeval crime as burning men for their opinions. Mr. Yeats recalled that in his young days he was a friend of William Morris, the great Socialist. He was one of the best of men. At the same time he knew George Bernard Shaw, who at that time, too, was a Socialist. He recently heard Mr. Shaw speak, and he found that his views on the question had not undergone any change. He still pleaded for State Socialism; he believed it possible to have a perfect bureaucracy. He (Mr. Yeats) did not think it needed any great knowledge of economics to refute such a claim. Two years ago, while in Paris, he came across a Russian revolutionary, who, in the course of conversation, predicted many things, some of which had come true. He said that England would become the centre of a group of capitalist nations fighting against revolutions. He said that there would be trouble in the future, and he (Mr. Yeats) thought the signs of the times could not be mistaken. I know we have reached a very serious moment in Ireland, Mr. Yeats proceeded, because we have a revolutionary party in power (which has much sympathy from me on the national question) that may seek revolutionary allies. If they seek these allies, and endeavour to create a dictatorship of Labour, as in Russia, they will split this nation into two, and destroy it, because it is a nation of peasant proprietors and capitalists, who would not accept such a dictatorship. I have come here to ask Mr. Johnson [of the Irish Trades Congress] a question. I do not ask it through any lack of sympathy with the workers of Dublin. I know [sic] Dublin for years, and the conditions under which the people have to live. I

156. *Letters on Poetry from W. B. Yeats to Dorothy Wellesley* (London, 1940), p. 188.

ask Mr. Johnson whether Labour, which is now going into alliance with Irish Nationalism, is seeking a dictatorship of Labour by a minority of the country, or aiming at bringing about a reform by process of law, whether in an English or Irish Parliament? [157]

The French Revolution had been the triumph of naked, unrestrained speculation. Burke had foreseen the rise of Napoleon, having already deduced from Cromwell's example, Yeats felt, the rise of military tyrannies out of violent revolutions.[158] Moreover, to the philosophical materialists, economics became the reality, while law was reduced to appearance. Aside from this likelihood of tyranny from chaos, Yeats also concluded that Ireland's following Lenin's economics would "not help one to express the character of the nation through varied intellect." [159] Thus from pure thought might come the denial of natural law, a narrowing of intellect, and, in the subsequent vacuum, the rule of force. Perhaps the only difference between Hegel and Rousseau as political philosophers was that the

157. "College Historical Society," *Irish Times*, 30 January 1919. Mrs. W. B. Yeats informs the author that Yeats was unaware that the Russian government had tortured political prisoners long before the revolution. In 1901, Yeats had written of John Eglinton, "I believe him right in thinking that the great movement of our time is a movement to destroy modern civilization, but I cannot but believe him wrong in thinking that it will be ended by 'liberated individuals' who separate themselves from the great passions, from the great popular interests, from religion, from patriotism, from humanitarianism" ("John Eglinton," *United Irishman*, 9 November 1901). In 1915, Yeats, in solemn and perhaps witty reply to Julia Ellsworth Ford's question if he were in sympathy with the Labour Government in England, answered, "I am a Tory" (Francis H. Bangs, "Julia Ellsworth Ford: An Appreciation," *Yale University Library Gazette*, XXVI [April 1952], 167).

158. *Pages from a Diary, Explorations*, pp. 315–16. At the bottom of page 315, substitute "Burke" for "Berkeley" in "lacks the lucidity of Berkeley and Swift." In the margin of his copy of Bertrand Russell's *An Outline of Philosophy* (London, 1927), p. 86, Yeats also made this claim for Burke.

159. "If I were Four-and-Twenty," *Explorations*, p. 268. Part of a passage marked by Yeats in his copy of Croce's *Historical Materialism and the Economics of Karl Marx*, trans. C. M. Meredith (London, 1922), p. 31, reads: ". . . historical materialism must consist in asserting that economics is the true *reality* and that law is a fallacious *appearance*."

first was responsible for more bloodshed than the second.[160] And, since dialectical materialism was personified in Lenin and his efforts, Yeats could say, "I consider the Marxian criterion of values as in this age the spear-head of materialism and leading to inevitable murder."[161]

There had been murder, arson, and wanton destruction in Ireland. She had been especially susceptible to these. For all his sympathy with Ireland in her war with England, Yeats never evaded that knowledge:

> A trumpery dispute about an acre of land can rouse our people to monstrous savagery, and if in their war with the British Auxiliary Police they were shown no mercy, they showed none; murder answered murder.[162]

In the Civil War he found the bitterness on both sides overwhelming, and especially its effect on children.[163] At one point in 1921 Yeats was so appalled that he planned to take his family to some far country to escape Irish vindictiveness and the likelihood of strident defensiveness should they move to England.[164] For all of Peadar O'Donnell's recent pooh-poohing any Red scare in Ireland,[165] Yeats continued to be wary of the tinder that Republican Ireland presented the sparks from revolutionary Russia. This is not to say that Yeats was incapable of seeing the ability of left-wing leaders like Sean MacBride and O'Donnell, the clever propagandist. In fact, for a brief moment in early 1932, Yeats may even have hoped for some important role for

160. "The Holy Mountain," *Essays and Introductions*, pp. 468–69.

161. *Letters*, p. 656. Further evidence that Yeats was disturbed by the possible introduction of communism to Ireland in 1919 is this passage written in that year: "Now our young men sing *The Red Flag*, for any bloody catastrophe seems welcome that promises an Irish Republic. They condemned Morris's doctrine without examination. Now for the most part they applaud it without examination; but that will change, for the execution of Connolly has given him many readers. I have already noticed Karl Marx's *Kapital* in the same window with Mitchel's *Jail Journal* and with *Speeches from the Dock* . . ." ("If I were Four-and-Twenty," *Explorations*, p. 268).

162. *Autobiographies*, p. 561. Also see " 'The Bounty of Sweden,' " *The Sunday Times*, 9 August 1925, p. 6.

163. *Senate Speeches*, p. 172.

164. *Letters*, p. 675.

165. *There will be Another Day*, pp. 117–32.

O'Donnell in the troubled Ireland of that year.[166] But what Yeats had predicted in 1919 of Ireland and Europe seemed to him at the end of his life pretty much what had come true. Musing on the cruelty and victims of governments all about him, he wrote Ethel Mannin then, "If you have my poems by you, look up a poem called *The Second Coming*. It was written some sixteen or seventeen years ago and foretold what is happening. I have written of the same thing again and again since. This will seem little to you with your strong practical sense, for it takes fifty years for a poet's weapons to influence the issue." [167] Perhaps one can say the same of Burke. At any rate part of the truth of Yeats's prediction seems in no small way one shared with him, going as it does back to the French Revolution, which, in spirit, Ireland had just joined.

V

Once free of the Senate, Yeats's hatred of Irish democracy and his concomitant hope for the rule of able men grew more and more insistent, sometimes even desperate. He continued to focus on the golden age of the eighteenth century as a model for the present, but he could equally well cite the tragedy of that period as an omen for his own age. Often he seemed to look through the eyes of Burke: "The influence of the French Revolution woke the peasantry from the medieval sleep, gave them ideas of social justice and equality, but prepared for a century disastrous to the national intellect." [168] Yeats's flirtation with Irish fascism in the thirties we know well enough. Yet, as we have also seen, he soon rejected General O'Duffy's stump-orator's mind and Captain McManus' demands for immediate action, even while his own hope for public intellect in modern swordsmen

166. Large white vellum notebook begun 23 November 1930. Yeats once mentioned his liking for the affable O'Donnell—"he is the head of the most extreme of all Irish organizations and of course my bitter opponent politically"—and went on to describe him as "by temperament vague and gentle and so always sees himself as a terrible gunman" (*Letters*, p. 793).

167. *Letters*, p. 851.

168. *Variorum*, p. 833.

and ladies gay soared to an outrageous hope beyond any brand of national politics. Thus shortly before his death he warned:

> I was six years in the Irish Senate; I am not ignorant of politics elsewhere, and on other grounds I have some right to speak. I say to those that shall rule here: If ever Ireland again seems molten wax, reverse the process of revolution. Do not try to pour Ireland into any political system. Think first how many able men with public minds the country has, how many it can hope to have in the near future, and mould your system upon those men. It does not matter how you get them, but get them. Republics, Kingdoms, Soviets, Corporate States, Parliaments, are trash, as Hugo said of something else "not worth one blade of grass that God gives for the nest of the linnet." These men, whether six or six thousand, are the core of Ireland, are Ireland itself.[169]

This stirring, impossible piece of rhetoric, part of the slashing prose of *On the Boiler,* leads to our conclusion. For if we recall the content of this pamphlet, which Yeats once called his *Fors Clavigera,* we recall its demand for able men got somehow, whether through eugenics, education, or the exigencies of violence. Interspersed in this prose, moreover, are savage bits of verse lamenting the absence of such men. One thinks especially of the poems later entitled "Why should not Old Men be Mad?" and "The Statesman's Holiday" that curse the Irish blight on youthful promise, diminished blood and rank, and the ascendance of demagogue and crowd-appeasing man. But the short, highly symbolic play, *Purgatory,* which ends the pamphlet, is the most damning bit of all.

The drama is a cruel one. An old pedlar, the Old Man, and his bastard son, the Boy, return to the Old Man's mother's ruined ancestral house. She had married—in a Catholic church, according to the manuscript scenario—a groom who later burned down the mansion in a drunken debauch. Their son, the pedlar, had killed his father, left his body in the flames, and fled. The Old Man had got the loutish Boy on a tinker's daughter in a ditch. Watching his ghostly

169. *On the Boiler,* p. 13.

father and mother, returned in a purgatorial vision, re-enact their wedding night in the ruined house, the Old Man stabs his son with the same knife that had killed the Boy's grandfather, the drunken groom. By this second killing the Old Man had hoped to stop the pollution of his family line and alleviate "the misery of the living and the remorse of the dead." Yet he fails.

But Yeats did not fail. For *Purgatory* dramatically exorcises the curse of that late eighteenth century which he felt had spawned the vulgarity of the present Irish democracy. Accordingly, there is a moment at the play's end which ought to give us special pause. After the Old Man kills the Boy, the stage darkens, and the bare tree beside the ruined house is bathed in light. The Old Man remembered it full and flourishing. Now he addresses his tormented mother—and what was in 1938 a mystified Dublin audience—with the words:

> Study that tree.
> It stands there like a purified soul,
> All cold, sweet, glistening light.

Yet at the end he must pray for the purification which his murders failed to accomplish. If we remember Yeats's most famous lines on Burke, we may also come to see the play as itself a kind of prayer— for a nation after the French Revolution, after the Act of Union, after 1922, and after Yeats's own public career, denied or denying its destined generation of men; a nation like a tree, casting not only dead leaves to mathematical equality but surviving only to glare under the cold light of hate; and, finally, a nation which no amount of burning, philandering, buffoonery, or murder can restore to its lost Augustan splendor.

Chapter Six

GOD-APPOINTED BERKELEY

I

IN 1932, Yeats dramatically recounted his turning to the pages of Berkeley by exclaiming, "An Irish Free State soldier, engaged in dangerous service for his Government, said to me that all the philosophy a man needed was in Berkeley. Stirred by these words I began to read *The Dialogues of Hylas and Philonous*. From Berkeley I went to Swift. . . ."[1] However, as I

1. "Ireland, 1921–1931," *Spectator*, 30 January 1932, p. 137. See also *A Vision* (London, 1956), p. 19. The "Free State soldier" was the Rev. Jephson Byrne O'Connell. A Catholic priest, he fought, even though a chaplain, in the Great War. Because of this experience, he was readily accepted in the Irish

have stressed, Swift was very nearly a lifelong preoccupation with Yeats, whereas his most important reflections on Berkeley were not to be heard until the end of the twenties and the early thirties. Yet, during Yeats's last few years, Berkeley's thought was just as crucial as Swift's ghostly presence.

Why Yeats should have found Berkeley so congenial is not hard to understand. Aside from the tremendous pull that Berkeley as an eighteenth-century Anglo-Irishman had on Yeats—he regarded him almost as a philosophical father [2]—Berkeley's immaterialism also had its appeal. To have the world and the spirit too had been Yeats's wish even before his serious study of Blake. Even in his youth Yeats had fought to prove the existence of all things perceived, illusions and spirits included. This hope persistently expressed in one form or another all his life shows how easily Berkeley might seem to lend him the assurance of an established philosopher. Thus Yeats could write of Blake in 1896:

> William Blake expounds the history of inspiration by a very curious and obscure symbol. A lark, he says, mounts upward into the heart of the heavens, and there is met by another and descending lark, which touches its wings to its wings; and he would have us understand . . . that man attains spiritual influence in like fashion. He must go on perfecting earthly power and perception until they are so subtilised that divine power and divine perception descend to meet them, and the song of earth and the song of heaven mingle together.[3]

Then again, the following year, how very much like Yeats's later interpretation of Berkeley this sounds:

> We are in the midst of a great revolution of thought, which is touching speculation and literature alike; an insurrection against everything which assumes that the external and material are the only fixed things, the only standards of reality. There have

revolutionary forces. Despite his passion for Aquinas, he recommended Berkeley to Yeats during a visit at 82 Merrion Square. Later Father O'Connell wrote a book on finance, *The Administration of Saorstat Eireann* (Dublin, 1934).

2. Information from Mrs. W. B. Yeats.

3. "William Carleton," *Bookman*, March 1896, p. 188.

indeed been always plenty of men to write and to say that "thought is the only reality," but since the rise of the scientific philosophers they have said it with a merely academic conviction, and all their criticisms of life and of literature have assumed that the world and nature were alone realities.[4]

And, finally, a seemingly more distant, less relevant passage yet, as I hope to show, one reflecting an important side of Berkeley for Yeats:

> Medieval mystics represented . . . ultimate paradise as a round mirror, and Jacob Boehme, who gathered into himself the dying mysticism of the Middle Ages, made it almost a fourth person of the Trinity. It was almost certainly a familiar symbol in ancient Ireland, for two years ago an old man on the north island of Aran told me of it. Nobody, he said, might look into it but God and this vexed Satan, who was then an angel, and Satan looked in "and Hell was made in a minute." Jacob Boehme describes God the Father as seeing Himself in it as God the Son, and meditating about what He saw, and so making God the Holy Spirit. Blake called it "the looking-glass of Enitharmon," his name for the mother of all, and "the imagination of God," and many names besides.[5]

This mention of an all-embracing perception, the oft-iterated hatred of materialism, the reference to a wedding of earthly and divine power, and then the mirror-resembling creation of spirits by God, all will ultimately find their way into Yeats's interpretation of Berkeley. There may also have been a number of other predisposing factors leading Yeats to Berkeley. His own aristocratic bias certainly inclined him to the clarity and ease of Berkeley's style. Berkeley's Irish background also provided the proper number of historical connections to insure Yeats's passionate pursuit of his logic. As he once wrote during the height of his interest in Berkeley, "I cannot discover truth by logic unless that logic serve passion."[6] He was doubtless also

4. "The Treasure of the Humble," *Bookman*, July 1897, p. 94.
5. "High Crosses of Ireland," *Daily Express*, 28 January 1899.
6. *Pages from a Diary, Explorations,* p. 301.

familiar with the frequent praise of Berkeley in Ireland, perhaps even with Standish O'Grady's words: "It is now about two hundred years since our great Bishop Berkeley astonished the world by declaring and proving that there was no such thing as matter, that everything was mind, and in this modern science seems to be supporting him." [7] Something might also be said of Yeats's hankering after metaphysics, even his habit of lecturing his friends "in a metaphysical way." [8] So far as Berkeley went, then, the bent and disposition were ready.

Once he did turn to Berkeley, Yeats read him in full. His basic reading was probably from the two-volume edition that Lennox Robinson bought for him on the Dublin quays.[9] Otherwise, Yeats seems to have been familiar with the Everyman Berkeley (*A New Theory of Vision and Other Select Philosophical Writings by George Berkeley, Bishop of Cloyne*), with Mary W. Calkin's edition of Berkeley's selected works, and probably with Collyns Simon's edition of *The Principles of Human Knowledge*.[10] In addition to the Hone and Rossi *Bishop Berkeley*, Yeats had a number of other secondary works on Berkeley in his library.[11] Yet the text that attracted Yeats most was one of Berkeley's earliest works, not published until 1871, the *Commonplace Book*. For Yeats this document was Ireland's declaration of intellectual independence. He repeated this belief again and again in his work and apparently also in his conversation. John Sparrow recalled him speaking of Berkeley at Oxford during 1931: "He talked of his interest in Berkeley and the *Commonplace*

7. "Labour Problems," *Irish Times*, 22 February 1912.
8. P. L. Dickinson, *The Dublin of Yesterday* (London, 1929), p. 55.
9. *A Vision* (1956), p. 17. The edition was *The Works of George Berkeley* (Dublin, 1784), 2 vols.—hereafter *Works*.
10. Norman Jeffares, *W. B. Yeats: Man and Poet*, 2nd ed. (London, 1962), p. 267. See also T. L. Dume, "William Butler Yeats: A Survey of His Reading," unpublished dissertation (Temple University, 1950), p. 196.
11. There is, for instance, G. A. Johnston's *The Development of Berkeley's Philosophy* (London, 1923) heavily marked and containing the clipping "The Dublin of Berkeley (1703–1710)," *Irish Statesman*, 7 September 1929, pp. 8–9. There are also two copies of Johnston's edition of *Berkeley's Commonplace Book* (London, 1930), and a copy of A. A. Luce's *Berkeley and Malebranche* (London, 1934).

Books [sic] especially the passage where he thought Berkeley distinguished Irish thought from that of other nations, an event as important as the Battle of the Boyne. He was trying to inspire the youth of Ireland with the national ideals to be found in Berkeley and Swift." [12] The Berkeley who turned the arguments of British materialism was an Irish patriot.

II

Yeats's Introduction to the Hone and Rossi volume was part of his campaign to influence young Ireland. This essay contains an element that comes very close to being evangelical in Yeats's identification with Protestant Ireland. He wrote T. Sturge Moore in this regard, "It is in part Irish polemics aimed at fools and bigots at home." [13] AE wrote mockingly to Hone after the book's publication, "I am glad that you and your collaborator are not complete enthusiasts. If you were I fancy Yeats would have tried to make all his friends Berkeleian and have conceived of Ireland as the Vatican tendency of that Pope of the spirit." [14] Yeats himself also admitted that his essay on Berkeley was obscure.[15] And on first glance it certainly is. But there are other more characteristic Yeatsian traits. For it is not just Berkeley's philosophical system that attracts Yeats; it is Berkeley's personality, his inner biography, or the man hidden behind the benevolent mask that Yeats also seeks out.[16] He especially wants to catch Berkeley in the world of eighteenth-century Ireland. Hence the essay represents

12. Jeffares, p. 267.

13. *Yeats and T. Sturge Moore*, p. 170.

14. *Letters from AE*, ed. Alan Denson (London, New York, Toronto, 1961), p. 195.

15. *Letters*, p. 786.

16. Yeats marked the following passage in his copy of Unamuno's *The Tragic Sense of Life*, trans. J. E. Crawford Flitch with an Introductory Essay by Salvador de Madariaga (London, 1921), p. 2: "In most of the histories of philosophy that I know, philosophic systems are presented to us as if growing out of one another spontaneously, and their authors, the philosophers, appear only as mere pretexts. The inner biography of the philosophers, of the men who philosophized, occupies a secondary place. And yet it is precisely this inner biography that explains for us most things."

what is fairly close to a concerted and programmatic effort. Hone himself had been publishing bits of his section of the book—the biographical and historical parts—for some time before final publication.[17] Hone has written since then, "I finished a book on Berkeley which Lady Gregory liked and then Yeats suggested I should get some professional philosopher to look over it. In the end Rossi put in the philosophical commentary." [18] In the same letter Hone adds, "My article ["Bishop Berkeley in Ireland"] in the *Dublin Magazine* 1926 interested Yeats as a contribution to his then desire to emphasize the contribution of Irish Protestants to the national life." [19] Hone also remarks that Yeats's final views on Berkeley were, as might be expected, strictly his own. This fact in no way dims his great respect for Mario Rossi nor does it lessen the fact that after their meeting in August 1931 Yeats apparently took a number of philosophic views from him.[20]

But to the essay. Fragmentation is the first exasperating impression one gets. "Bishop Berkeley" is broken into fourteen sections, thirteen of them numbered and dated July 1931, and the last designated a postscript. However, the real structure of the piece is far more simple. For Yeats first chooses to reveal the real Berkeley, the thinker born into Anglo-Irish solitude. Only then does he go on to hold up to us the man who exploded English abstractions, the most important being Locke's belief in the primary qualities. Yeats then

17. "Bishop Berkeley in Ireland," *Dublin Magazine*, January–March 1926, pp. 15–26; "Berkeley in Italy," *New Statesman*, 2 October 1926, pp. 703–4; "Berkeley at Cloyne," *London Mercury*, April 1929, pp. 593–602; and "Swift and Berkeley," *New Statesman*, 8 February 1930. I also suspect that Hone wrote "The Dublin of Berkeley," *Irish Statesman*, 7 September 1929, pp. 8–9.

18. Letter to the author. Yeats realized that Lady Gregory would not be interested in Berkeley's philosophy but in the quality of his mind. On this point he wrote Hone that she was pleased with the book (*Letters*, p. 779). Earlier, she had commented in her journals: "Some good sentences in the *Irish Statesman* by 'AE.' 'We want the quality of mind we find in Bishop Berkeley, in Bernard Shaw and in many others who had that aristocracy of mind which probes truth for itself' " (*Lady Gregory's Journals*, p. 84).

19. Letter to the author.

20. In a letter to the author, Rossi states, "I am, just now, correcting the proofs of my last book on Berkeley, in which I maintain again the views Yeats accepted from me."

offers a most compelling theory of literature based largely on Berkeley's immaterialism. He concludes with his eye on Europe and Ireland, calling for a return to a philosophy and belief that contemplate God, freedom, and immortality, and drawing the attention of his readers to Berkeley as one important example. These four divisions are worth tracing for the moment, since they also sum up Yeats's strongest use of Berkeley in poetry and criticism.

Yeats begins by locating the greatest period of philosophy in that time bounded by the works of Spinoza and Hegel. Berkeley is placed not only at the center of this period but also at the beginning of what Yeats calls modern Ireland. With little more ado, Yeats plunges into the recesses of the hidden Berkeley, particularly into the mind of "that fierce young man" who wrote the *Commonplace Book:*

> What he then was, solitary, talkative, ecstatic, destructive, he showed through all his later years though but in glimpses or as something divined or inferred. It is not the fault of his biographer but of the inanimate record, or of his own inanimate pose, that he is not there in all his blood and state.[21]

Yeats continues his search for the real Berkeley right into the third section of his essay. Here he rejects the Berkeley of Latham's portrait in the Fellows' Room at Trinity. This dignified, benign, or sentimental Berkeley, also depicted in his correspondence, was

> . . . the sage as imagined by gentlemen of fortune—a rôle accepted by Berkeley that he might not be left to starve in some garret by a generation terrified by religious scepticism and political anarchy, and loved because it hid from himself and others his own anarchy and scepticism.[22]

This passage also gives the gist of Yeats's slanted interpretation. But there is more. Yeats can even ask if Berkeley did not in fact try to animate his benign mask by his Bermuda scheme, and, by his pain-allaying tar water, achieve the peace of the Augustans after civil war, religious rancor, and metaphysical verse were at last in abeyance.

---

21. "Bishop Berkeley," *Essays and Introductions*, p. 397.
22. *Ibid.*, p. 398.

Yeats may be very wrong about Berkeley, but right or wrong, we are reading still one more of his general insights into the art, history, and thought of an age—his Shelley essays also come to mind—seen as a total. I dwell overlong on this third section—still introductory— because Yeats is all this time also establishing Berkeley as one of those Anglo-Irishmen born into Irish solitude, caught between two nations, noteworthy for

> . . . their curiosity, their rich discourse, their explosive passion, their sense of mystery as they grew old, their readiness to dress up at the suggestion of others though never quite certain what dress they wore, their occasional childish worldliness.[23]

In the fourth section Yeats takes up Berkeley's attack on British empiricism, especially Locke's distinction between primary and secondary qualities. The resultant convenient abstraction, absolute extension or external substance, had been a useful one but had also led to the mechanization of human life. The industrial revolution is Yeats's evidence. By contrast, the pursuit of eternal truth—"truth that is always moth-like and fluttering and yet can terrify"—is the task Yeats consigns to solitaries like Berkeley. The next three sections allow him to salute those solitary men of genius, as he calls them, Swift, Burke, Berkeley, and Goldsmith, who fought the English abstractions of their day, Berkeley in particular "with his belief in perception, that abstract ideas are mere words." The hint is also obtruded that Berkeley was not only influential, though his disciples were widely spaced in time and place, but that one vessel of his inspiration might indeed be Yeats himself. Beyond heritage or solitude, Yeats finds Berkeley persuasive also by reason of his style, a shimmer of eternity and life's mystery caught in a trim, easy language allowing him to insinuate the solid world about us into the realm of spirit.

At this point, with our entry into sections eight and nine, Yeats turns to his most difficult, because so highly imaginative, speculation. The subject is the connection between philosophy and literature. At

23. *Ibid.*, p. 400.

the core of Yeats's argument lies his view of Berkeley as realist and idealist alike:

> The romantic movement seems related to the idealist philosophy; the naturalistic movement, Stendhal's mirror dawdling down a lane, to Locke's mechanical philosophy, as simultaneous correspondential dreams are related. . . . When I speak of idealist philosophy I think more of Kant than of Berkeley, who was idealist and realist alike, more of Hegel and his successors than of Kant, and when I speak of the romantic movement I think more of Manfred, more of Shelley's Prometheus, more of Jean Valjean, than of those traditional figures, Browning's Pope, the fakir-like pedlar in *The Excursion*.[24]

Yeats goes on to contend that, with romanticism past, the literary naturalism of Joyce, Pound, and Proust had behind it the new realism in philosophy "which thinks that the secondary and primary qualities alike are independent of consciousness."[25] This was a literature unconcerned with active consciousness and willing to leave man's mind at the mercy of the contradictory objects that swam into its ken. Yeats rejects this objective literature just as his forefathers had rejected its opposite, the chaotic romanticism of the previous century. As we shall see, Berkeley becomes the philosopher of his kind of traditional writing, neither, strictly speaking, romanticism nor realism.

The three sections following are almost as abstruse. Here Yeats peers behind Berkeley's reputed mask of benevolence. He gazes at the only trustworthy Berkeley, the writer of the *Commonplace Book*. He finds in this young and unwary Berkeley a leaning toward the belief "that Man in so far as he is himself, in so far as he is a personality, reflects the whole act of God."[26] However, this is really Yeats's belief, not Berkeley's. He admits that Berkeley in his

24. *Ibid.*, pp. 404–5. For a thorough botching of these distinctions and others to follow, see Donald Davie, "Yeats, Berkeley, and Romanticism," *Irish Writing*, No. 31 (1955), pp. 36–41.
25. "Bishop Berkeley," *Essays and Introductions*, pp. 405–6.
26. *Ibid.*, p. 408, n. 1.

published work never went that far. But the hope that he had privately done so remained with Yeats. In *A Vision* (1956), reconsidering *Siris*, he asks, "Did he [Berkeley] in his private thoughts come to regard Light as a creative act of a universal self dwelling in all selves?" [27] However, instead of identifying God with individual spirits, Berkeley, as Yeats elaborates in these sections, ". . . thought of God as a pure indivisible act, personal because at once will and understanding, which . . . creates passive 'ideas'—sensations—thrusts them as it were outside itself; and in this act all beings . . . share in the measure of their worth: not the God of Protestant theology but a God that leaves room for human pride." [28] Where we as human beings share the speed, activity, pure election, and unity of God our lives become joyous. Otherwise we sink into modern subjectivity. Our contemplation must also include the philosophy, myths, and literature associated with the words "God," "Freedom," and "Immortality." The essay is rounded out with Yeats's return to what he calls Berkeley's first position on this matter of God and individual selves: "Berkeley in his youth described the *summum bonum* and the reality of Heaven as physical pleasure, and thought this conception made both more intelligible to simple men." [29]

Yeats then concludes by recommending study of the eighteenth century to intellectual Ireland now that Ireland's traditional political goals have been accomplished. His postscript is anticlimactic. It acknowledges his reading Rossi's additions to the book only after finishing his own essay. Thus, given Hone's biographical contribution, Yeats's polemics are understandably based on his wish to celebrate a forgotten intellectual ethos sorely needed in his day.

III

Pure thought seemed to Yeats mistakenly applied to politics and more properly devoted to philosophy and religion.[30] Berkeley's was

27. *A Vision* (1956), p. 191, n. 2.
28. "Bishop Berkeley," *Explorations*, p. 408.
29. *Ibid.*, p. 410.
30. *Pages from a Diary, Explorations*, p. 314.

the right application. If no more need be said on Yeats's brooding over Anglo-Irish solitude, we might profitably open discussion of Yeats's interpretation of Berkeley at its very core, i.e., his being idealist and realist alike. Pure thought was able to conceive of the real world as spiritual and unified because the world was sensuous, concrete, and perceived. Yeats attached great importance to this idea of substantial spirituality: "When Berkeley declared that all existence is only known or perceived, it became possible to . . . show not only our history but nature herself as the creation of the 'elemental forms' of the human mind." [31] Anything less than this unity was abstraction. In his argumentative youth Yeats felt that he had taken into his "flesh the poison of the abstract." [32] Moreover, abstraction could take many forms. The foe of national unity was any abstraction that fixed not on "the distinction but the isolation of occupation, or class or faculty." [33] In the world of abstract thinkers all things became alike. Just before his death Yeats wrote, still with an air of urgency, ". . . I say, 'Man can embody truth but he cannot know it.' I must embody it in the completion of my life. The abstract is not life and everywhere draws out its contradictions." [34]

Yeats's naming Berkeley idealist and realist together also assured the divinity of the world. Berkeley the bishop he rates. But the Berkeley who argued for the reality of appearances in the *Commonplace Book* might command any Irishman's attention:

> Preserve that which is living and help the two Irelands, Gaelic Ireland and Anglo-Ireland, so to unite that neither shall shed its pride. Study the great problems of the world, as they have been lived in our scenery, the re-birth of European spirituality in the mind of Berkeley, the restoration of human order in the mind of Burke.[35]

31. Large white vellum notebook begun 23 November 1930.
32. "Autobiography."
33. *Autobiographies*, p. 190.
34. *Letters*, p. 922.
35. *Pages from a Diary, Explorations*, p. 337.

In his copy of Luce's edition of *Berkeley and Malebranche,* Yeats turned down a page containing this central statement which he himself liked to repeat in various forms: ". . . Berkeley declares, in lofty language, that God is the substance of all the choir of heaven and of the furniture of earth, and that this truth is 'near and obvious to the mind.' That passage states with restraint and in untechnical terms Berkeley's primary vision of all things in God." [36]

Now it is common knowledge that Yeats had held to the existence of disincarnate beings on religious and philosophic grounds long before he read Berkeley.[37] He had never seriously doubted, for all his questioning, the existence of spirits. In fact, he had even imagined an ultimate spiritual world that had, like the young Berkeley's *summum bonum,* shadowy physical properties:

> There was a state beyond dreams in which persons recovered again their personality, only more transcendent and in a more intensely living state, in which physical expression intensified life. . . . This was that state of intense light of reality in which one recovered one's personality. . . .[38]

Berkeley's guarantee of the divinity of the world became for Yeats philosophic authority for his belief in spirits. Hence we must not be surprised to find Yeats arguing both from spiritualism and from his study of Berkeley, as though they both agreed, for the existence of spirits. He feared a coming disbelief, a denial not only of God but also a revolt against spirituality, even in Ireland. That is why in 1919 he could go so far as to defend a belief in evil spirits against the opinion of the Catholic Church in Ireland. Speaking to an audience at the Abbey, he reminded them that

> They were on the edge, as he believed, of a complete revolution. They were now in a position similar to that which men were in at the end of the fourteenth century. An age of belief was passing, and an age of unbelief was coming. He suggested to

36. Luce, *Berkeley and Malebranche,* p. 113.
37. " 'A New Theory of Apparitions,' " *Irish Times,* 13 January 1912.
38. "Ghosts and Dreams," *Irish Times,* 1 November 1913.

Ireland that it was well to come to the issue with the age that was coming. Why should Ireland throw away her advantages of belief and put on cheap scepticism? Why should the Irish bishop, as he was told he did in the country, discourage exorcism? Why should he be ashamed to be called superstitious? Superstition was about to become science. It was about to have evidence. Incredulity was about to become superstition.[39]

By making perception, ultimately God's eye, the proof of reality, Berkeley would offer Yeats a logical argument, the next best thing to evidence, for such belief in a Catholic country. Spirits made the physical world real and permanent. And spirits were created by God.[40]

In the third place, after Yeats's hatred of abstraction and his equal insistence on spirituality, still another of his beliefs derived from Berkeley's combined idealism and realism. It is embodied in the sentence, "Berkeley has brought back to us the world that only exists because it shines and sounds." [41] The probable source of this idea in Yeats's copy of *The Logic of Hegel* is highly illuminating:

The Essence must appear or shine forth. Its shining or reflection in it is the suspension and translation of it to immediacy, which, whilst as reflection-on-self it is matter or subsistence, is also form, reflection-on-something-else, a subsistence which sets itself aside. To show or shine is the characteristic by which essence is distinguished from being,—by which it is essence; and it is this show which, when it is developed, shows itself, and is Appearance. Essence accordingly is not something beyond or behind appearance, but just because it is the essence which exists—the existence is *Appearance* (Forth-shining).[42]

39. "Psychical Phenomena," *Irish Times*, 27 January 1919.

40. In his copy of G. A. Johnston's *The Development of Berkeley's Philosophy*, Yeats turned down p. 193 where appear the chapter division "The Existence of Spirits" and a relevant discussion following.

41. *Pages from a Diary, Explorations*, p. 325.

42. William Wallace, *The Logic of Hegel*, 2nd rev. ed. (Oxford, 1892), p. 239. Yeats marked this passage.

Bergson had accused Berkeley "of making it [matter] one with our own minds." [43] Yeats carefully corrected him at the bottom of the page by writing: "B. denies that he does this. It is 'in' mind but not itself mind." [44] Beautiful appearances were real because they were perceived. But Yeats stresses the sounding and shining, sensuous qualities, so that there may be no doubt about the reality or the divinity of appearance. [45] Yet, as we shall see, he was quite prepared to turn about, brand all things appearance, the whole world a dream, if the general man insisted on the world's being a fact external to the mind.

With this proviso in mind a reader may want to take another look at lines hitherto usually misinterpreted:

> And God-appointed Berkeley that proved all things a
>   dream,
> That this pragmatical, preposterous pig of a world, its
>   farrow that so solid seem,
> Must vanish on the instant if the mind but change its
>   theme . . .

In a generally sympathetic yet mildly reprimanding comment, A. A. Luce has had this to say of Yeats's lines:

> The Berkeley of those lines is not the true Berkeley, not the Berkeley Yeats really loved; for the "Berkeley that proved all things a dream" filled no notebooks, published no philosophy, never existed in the flesh. He exists only in the mind of critics and scoffers, and of those who never read the *Principles* but glean their scraps of knowledge about it from criticisms and witticisms. [46]

43. Henri Bergson, *Matter and Memory*, trans. Nancy Margaret Paul and W. Scott Palmer (London, 1912), p. ix.
44. *Ibid.*
45. Yeats marked the following passage in his copy of Coleridge's *Biographia Literaria* (London, 1876), p. 345: "In religion there is no abstraction. To the unity and infinity of the Divine Nature, of which it is the partaker, it adds the fulness, and to the fulness the grace and the creative overflowing. That which intuitively it at once beholds and adores, praying always and rejoicing always— that doth it tend to become."
46. A. A. Luce, *Berkeley's Immaterialism* (London, 1945), p. ix.

Luce may indeed be right; but if he is, his reading of the lines is also extremely literal. For it is possible to read them more imaginatively and just as consistently and remain even closer to the context of the poem. Thus "God-appointed Berkeley" may be read as a pun on Berkeley the bishop and divine who also showed the world—in his use of God—to be spiritual. Proving "all things a dream" might also be thought of as Berkeley's calling things ideas. On the other hand, it may well refer to his refusing substantiality to absolute extension. Although Yeats preferred the *Commonplace Book* to *Siris*, he was probably familiar with the frequent references in the latter to the mechanist's concept of "substances and causes" as shadowy and fleeting: [47]

> Sense at first besets and overbears the mind. The sensible appearances are all in all: our reasonings are employed about them: our desires terminate in them: we look no farther for realities or causes; till intellect begins to dawn, and cast a ray on this shadowy scene. We then perceive the true principle of unity, identity, and existence. Those things that before seemed to constitute the whole of being, upon taking an intellectual view of things, prove to be but fleeting phantoms. [48]

To call all things a dream also agrees with Yeats's linking dream life to the existence of spirits. We know that, strictly speaking, Berkeley has Philonous distinguish between ideas and dreams per se in the Third Dialogue. But in these lines Yeats is more interested in turning the argument of the neorealists, who see the world as solid, independent substance, by showing that, even by their account, that world has more substance considered as dream.

The last lines of the passage may make this interpretation even more convincing. For it is the pig of the world and its progeny who hold and exemplify the materialist's view of the world: "Descartes, Locke, and Newton took away the world and gave us its excrement instead." [49] The piggish world may well be this impossible plaything

47. *Siris, Works*, II, 597.
48. *Ibid.*, p. 596.
49. *Pages from a Diary, Explorations*, p. 325.

of practical men. However, this useful but repulsive British construct might vanish, philosophically speaking, if the mind would but change its concept of itself or its epistemology. Yeats acknowledged the belief in a physical substance without secondary qualities to be a useful construct that had heralded the world of the Industrial Revolution.[50] Thus the pig metaphor probably also refers to the swinish multitude that grew out of that revolution, and also to Yeats's conclusion that a belief in physical substance was "the grosser half of . . . dialectical materialism." [51]

IV

A second major thrust of the essay on Berkeley was what Yeats took to be Berkeley's Irish quality, personally a mischievous, explosive and childlike irreverence hidden behind a mask of benevolence, and philosophically an abiding hatred of abstractions. Both came together for Yeats in Berkeley's *Commonplace Book*. On October 17 he wrote in his 1930 *Diary*:

> Before Berkeley's account of his exploration of certain Kilkenny laws which speak of the "natives" came that intellectual crisis which led up [to] the sentence in "The Commonplace Book" "We Irish do not think so." That was the birth of the national intellect, & [from] it arose the defeat in Berkeley's philosophical secret society of English materialism, the Irish Salamis.[52]

The relevant passage in his essay on Berkeley reads:

> I delight in that fierce young man . . . who established . . . a secret society to examine the philosophy of a 'neighbouring nation'; who defined that philosophy, the philosophy of Newton and Locke, in three sentences, wrote after each

50. "Bishop Berkeley," *Essays and Introductions*, p. 401.
51. *Ibid.*
52. Although Yeats may have written "Between" instead of "Before" to start this passage, I suspect that in either case he meant the latter. Cf. *Pages from a Diary, Explorations*, pp. 333–34.

that Irishmen thought otherwise, and on the next page that he must publish to find if men elsewhere agreed with Irishmen. What he then was, solitary, talkative, ecstatic, destructive, he showed through all his later years though but in glimpses or as something divined or inferred.[53]

These four swordstrokes were recorded in 1925 by Yeats with what seem to be his own brief comments in a footnote to his essay "The Child and the State." The footnote reads:

The passage in the *Commonplace Book* is as follows:—"There are men who say there are invisible extensions. There are others who say that the wall is not white, the fire is not hot." (Meaning that there is a substratum differing from the appearance and outside mind.) "We Irishmen cannot attain to these truths. The mathematicians think there are insensible lines. About these they harangue: these cut at a point in all angles: these are divisible *ad infinitum*. We Irishmen can conceive no such lines. The mathematicians talk of what they call a point. This they say is not altogether nothing, nor is it downright something. Now we Irishmen are apt to think something" (meaning the mathematicians' "something" which is an abstraction) "and nothing are near neighbours. . . . I publish this . . . to know whether other men have the same ideas as Irishmen."[54]

Berkeley's intellectual nationalism, Yeats would have us believe, was an embattled one. It rose from his Irish trait of concreteness and was stirred by its opposite in English philosophy. Thus Berkeley

---

53. "Bishop Berkeley," *Essays and Introductions*, pp. 396–97. Hone, sharing Yeats's belief in Berkeley's Irishry, later pointed out that this national identification came after his family had been but one generation in Ireland ("The Anglo-Irish Strain," *Bell*, II [September 1941], 24). A. A. Luce has cast doubt upon any nationalistic interpretation of these entries. See George Berkeley, *Philosophical Commentaries*, ed. A. A. Luce (London, Edinburgh, Paris, Melbourne, Toronto, and New York, 1944), p. 395, and *Philosophical Commentaries, The Works of George Berkeley Bishop of Cloyne*, ed. A. A. Luce and T. E. Jessop (London, Edinburgh, Paris, Melbourne, Toronto, and New York, 1948), I, 124.

54. "The Child and the State [Part I]," *Irish Statesman*, 5 December 1925, p. 394 n.

closed the division of primary and secondary qualities, cast doubt on Hobbes's stream of particles, and restored innate ideas. In *Siris,* according to Yeats, Berkeley substituted for Newton's substance invisible ether, fire, or light—Yeats called it intellectual fire. His Irish followers would surely comprehend Berkeley's meaning: ". . . that this light, this intellectual Fire, is that continuity which holds together 'the perceptions,' that it is a substitute for the old symbol God." [55]

Yeats's sense of Ireland versus England almost turns a philosophic difference into a personal vendetta. Yet this is what grips Yeats— Berkeley's intensity in winning the Irish Salamis against great odds and reputations. One discovers him turning down or marking page after page in his copy of G. A. Johnston's *The Development of Berkeley's Philosophy* where Berkeley seemingly attacks some mathematical, epistemological, or ethical abstraction he attributes to Locke or Newton.[56] Yeats even appears to have found some evidence in Johnston's text for his claiming Berkeley as an Irish maverick and prankster. For instance, there is this marked passage: "It is, indeed, characteristic of Berkeley always to have opponents in view; and if he is not criticising somebody, he is thinking of the criticisms that others will bring against him." [57] Berkeley's concreteness and willfulness are of course as much, if not more, a part of Yeats himself. The Irish intellectual rebelliousness he attributed to Berkeley in the *Commonplace Book* is as much a part of his own philosophic intransigence in *A Vision.* He once described himself in that book as having

> . . . done one good deed in clearing out of the state from birth to death all the infinities and eternities, and picturing a state as 'phenomenal' as that from birth to death. I have constructed a myth, but then one can believe in a myth—one only assents to philosophy.[58]

55. *Pages from a Diary, Explorations,* p. 325.
56. Johnston, pp. 228, 266–67, 292–93, 298.
57. *Ibid.,* p. 299.
58. *Letters,* p. 781.

Berkeley's use of God to cap his own system compels something of the same belief. For both men—and for all Irishmen by Yeats's guess —belief in spirits and a skepticism before scientific abstraction were indigenous traits.[59] Berkeley's *Commonplace Book* had been the first modern, systematic demonstration of Irish intellect.

Though the term "Irish intellect" may sound pompous, Yeats truly believed in the distinction and could even say of the Abbey Players that "they had been true ambassadors of Irish intellect."[60] The incompetence of British officers in the opening months of the Great War brought this comment from him: "England is paying the price for having despised intellect."[61] The word intellect could mean many things to Yeats. Sometimes it meant mother-wit. It often meant an idealism that included the virtues commended by Berkeley and Swift in their Irish tracts—economy, planning, coordination rather than the old wildness and extravagance.[62] But philosophically and artistically speaking, Yeats could speak of Irish intellect as making British philosophy appear childish. For in its quarrels over idealism and realism it had forgotten, as the Irish mind had not, "the ancient hierarchy of being from man up to the One. What I do not see but may see or have seen, is perceived by another being. . . . I remember what he forgets, he remembers what I forget."[63] No democrat in matters of intellect,[64] Yeats tended to glorify historic institutions that embodied or perpetuated Irish intelligence. Again and again in his

59. "Psychical Research," *Irish Times*, 3 February 1919.
60. Unidentified clipping in Holloway, Natl. Lib. MS. 1949 (April–June 1932), I, n.p. On the subject of drama and national intellect, Yeats once stated, "As a nation came to intellectual maturity it realised that the only thing that did it any credit was its intellect. If a dramatist had a great intellect the nation began to realise that that great intellect was a glory to the nation far greater than any good it might get from having its people shown on the stage in a particularly charming way" ("Plays and Poetry," *Irish Times*, 25 February 1926). And with the exceptions of Berkeley and Duns Scotus, Yeats thought the Irish intellect an essentially irreligious one ("The Need for Audacity of Thought," *Dial*, LXXX [February 1926], 118).
61. *Letters*, p. 588.
62. *Senate Speeches*, p. 45.
63. *Letters*, p. 728.
64. "Greek Folk Poetry," *Bookman*, October 1896, p. 17.

Senate speeches one hears reference to the Royal Irish Academy, the Royal Dublin Academy, the National University, Trinity College, the National Museum and Art Gallery, the Municipal Gallery, the National Library, many of them dating from the eighteenth century, and some, the Royal Irish Academy and the Royal Dublin Society, associated with Berkeley or his friends.[65]

Berkeley's Irish immaterialism, then, took its proper place alongside Burke's defense of European order and Swift's service to intellectual liberty. Theirs was a conflagration of the intellect Yeats hoped could still illuminate the future of modern Ireland. In his essays "Prometheus Unbound" and "Louis Lambert," written close to his Berkeley essay, Yeats reveals his preoccupation with what he thought to be Berkeley's major problem—the fact that perception seemed intermittent.[66] Yeats also faced that problem himself in writing *A Vision*. His answer was light, as he thought Berkeley's had also been.[67] Though he was not happy with what he felt to be Berkeley's Platonism in *Siris*, he marked in the margin of his own copy certain sections which made light or intellectual fire assume the same role as Newton's ether.[68] Yeats's key quotation on that fire appears, however, in "Louis Lambert." It derives from the first half of Section 211 in *Siris*. He begins by considering Berkeley's use of fire in general and then quotes the passage:

'In the *Timaeus* of Plato,' writes Berkeley, 'there is something like a net of fire, and rays of fire in the human body. Doth this not seem to mean the animal spirit flowing, or rather darting, through the nerves?' This fire is certainly that energy which in *Séraphita* is distinguished from will, and it is doubtless through its agency that will can rise above the human lot, or act beyond the range of the normal senses. 'If we believe Diogenes Laertius,' writes Berkeley, 'the Pythagorean philosophers thought there was a certain pure heat or fire which had

65. TS. of a "Congratulatory Address from the RSL to the RDS on the occasion of the BCC."

66. *Pages from a Diary, Explorations*, p. 331.

67. *Ibid.*, pp. 331–32.

68. *Siris, Works*, II, Sections 166, 226, 229.

something divine in it, by the participation whereof man becomes allied to the Gods. And according to the Platonists, Heaven is not defined so much by its local situation as by its purity. The purest and most excellent fire, that is Heaven, saith Facinus.' [69]

Accordingly, this passage may also explain why the first part of "Blood and the Moon" ends with the line "Everything that is not God consumed with intellectual fire." To have regarded the purity of Berkeley's thought, to have heeded the light and sweetness advocated by Burke, Swift, and Goldsmith might have made Ireland a heaven for the wise. T. R. Henn is most relevant when he draws our attention to the passage in *Per Amica Silentia Lunae* that distinguishes between the terrestrial condition and the condition of fire.[70] But the passage Yeats quotes from *Siris* also coincides with that Irish belief that finds divinity and spirituality, even heaven itself, in natural things. This may also be why Yeats frequently places the Irish natural world against the world conceived, as it seemed to him, by English materialism. Rural Ireland, not cut off from the flow of tree, leaf, and rock by any rigid urban geometry, adhered to the total world, not its slim, abstract remnant conceived by mechanical philosophers:

> Move upon Newton's town,
> The town of Hobbes and of Locke,
> Pine, spruce, come down
> Cliff, ravine, rock:
> What can disturb the corn?
> What makes it shudder and bend?
> The rose brings her thorn,
> The Absolute walks behind.[71]

69. "Louis Lambert," *Essays and Introductions*, pp. 440–41. Cf. *Siris, Works*, II, 557–58.

70. T. R. Henn, *The Lonely Tower* (London, 1950), pp. 44–45.

71. *Wheels and Butterflies*, p. 77. In a TS. of this Introduction to *Fighting the Waves*, Yeats wrote, ". . . teach Berkeley side by side with more modern philosophy, or side by side with Aquinas, as though he were Gaelic and Kant or Aquinas Greek . . ." (Natl. Lib. MS. 8774[2]). Yeats once marked the

V

These lines, despite their occult implications, also hint the role Berkeley plays in Yeats's theory of literature, ideally heroic literature. Swift's liberty, Burke's order, and Goldsmith's poetic observations had about them a severity or singleness of purpose in Yeats's conception that was as much a matter of his conservatism as of their neoclassicism or Irish Protestant background. Similarly, Yeats employed Berkeley to substantiate a literature that was not only heroic, but might also, in Yeats's day, compel new, disciplined, total states. This last suggestion is extreme and comes to the surface momentarily, so to speak, in the pages surrounding the above lines in Yeats's Introduction to *Fighting the Waves*. I mention this drift in order to show the striking likeness in Yeats's use of all these men to bind together his far-flung conservative preoccupations.

In his essay on Berkeley, Yeats had related a subjective romanticism to philosophic idealism, and literary naturalism, old and new, to Locke's philosophy or its modern continuation, neorealism. But the literary mind Yeats admired shared God's creativity, did not sink into itself or direct the reader to consider his own passivity and personal misery in the helpless reflections of the author. The traditional literature that Yeats approved, whether outlined in Swift's parable of the spider and the bee or expressed in Wordsworth's *Excursion*, combined realism and idealism. These were also found in Irish heroic literature in a way Berkeley might also have approved:

> Though I am not confident that Berkeley's secret society of seven Trinity undergraduates knew anything of Irish folk, it seems important that Irish folklore runs back to a time when body & soul, mind & matter were not separated—an error dear

following passage in his copy of *Biographia Literaria* (London, 1876), p. 347, where Coleridge berates the philosophers of the French Revolution: "Man of understanding, canst thou command the stone to lie, canst thou bid the flower bloom, where thou hast placed it in thy classification? Canst thou persuade the living or the inanimate to stand separate even as thou hast separated them?"

to poets. I explore the past that I may re-create; I bring together things long disassociated. . . .[72]

In Balzac, Blake, Keats, and Blunt, Yeats thought he found the proper accord between body and mind, intellect and flesh otherwise so seldom bound together since the death of Cowley. The rhythms of these poets seemed "to combine the bull and the nightingale." [73]

Yeats's remarks on the transition from a traditional literature where man was most himself to a naturalism or realism where he was inconsequential are well worth reading:

The mischief began at the end of the seventeenth century when man became passive before a mechanised nature; that lasted to our own day with the exception of a brief period between Smart's "Song of David" and the death of Byron, wherein imprisoned man beat upon the door. Or I may dismiss all the ancient history and say it began when Stendhal described a masterpiece as a "mirror dawdling down a lane." There are only two long poems in Victorian literature that caught public attention, "The Ring and the Book" where great intellect analyses the suffering of one passive soul, weighs the persecutor's guilt, and "The Idylls of the King" where a poetry in itself an exquisite passivity is built upon an allegory where man's soul is a vague characterless King. I read few modern novels but I think I am right in saying that in every novel that has created an intellectual fashion from Huysmans' "La Cathédrale" to Ernest Hemingway's "Farewell to Arms," the chief character is a mirror.[74]

72. Large white vellum notebook begun 23 November 1930.
73. "Louis Lambert," *Essays and Introductions*, p. 446.
74. TS. of "Modern Poetry," BBC broadcast, 11 October 1936. Yeats had also placed a marker, on which he wrote "plating behind a looking-glass," between pp. 56 and 57 of his copy of *Biographia Literaria*. The relevant passage begins on p. 57, where Coleridge criticizes the Hartleian theory of the self and soul: "Thus the whole universe co-operates to produce the minutest stroke of every letter, save only that I myself, and I alone, have nothing to do with it, but merely the causeless and effectless beholding of it when it is done. Yet scarcely can it be called a beholding; for it is neither an act nor an effect; but an impossible creation of a *something-nothing* out of its very contrary! It is the mere quicksilver plating behind a looking-glass; and in this alone consists the poor worthless I!"

Because this passage and theory have generally gone unheeded—
apart from the interesting light thrown on

> . . . that William Blake
> Who beat upon the wall
> Till Truth obeyed his call

—they are worth repeating in another form if only for inclusion of
more of Yeats's modern reading:

> When Stendhal described a masterpiece as a 'mirror dawdling
> down a lane' he expressed the mechanical philosophy of the
> French eighteenth century. Gradually literature conformed to
> his ideal; Balzac became old-fashioned; romanticism grew
> theatrical in its strain to hold the public; till, by the end of the
> nineteenth century, the principal characters in the most famous
> books were the passive analysts of events, or had been brutalised
> into the likeness of mechanical objects. . . . Certain typical
> books—*Ulysses*, Mrs. Virginia Woolf's *Waves*, Mr. Ezra
> Pound's *Draft of XXX Cantos*—suggest a philosophy like that
> of the *Samkara* school of ancient India, mental and physical
> objects alike material, a deluge of experience breaking over us
> and within us, melting limits whether of line or tint; man no
> hard bright mirror dawdling by the dry sticks of a hedge, but a
> swimmer, or rather the waves themselves. In this new litera-
> ture . . . man in himself is nothing.[75]

This whole process of change and narrowing in literature is also
caught in the lines

> Shakespearean fish swam the sea, far away from land;
> Romantic fish swam in nets coming to the hand;
> What are all those fish that lie gasping on the strand?

The poem has been related to Yeats's diary note on diminished
passion in literature. But the cause of this diminution would seem to
be the considerable thinning out of man's experience, and then the
final reduction of known experience to a kind of impassive wriggling
before the changing sea of an external reality. Likewise, it might

---

75. *Wheels and Butterflies*, pp. 72–73.

appear that the poem "The Nineteenth Century and After" characterizes the new literature and its reliance on the new realism in philosophy. Here Yeats as elsewhere recognizes the merit and genius of writers like Pound and Joyce. Still, man in this literature seems nothing or merely something tossed by the waves or the very waves themselves. Nor can we forget the echoes of "Dover Beach":

> Though the great song return no more
> There's keen delight in what we have:
> The rattle of pebbles on the shore
> Under the receding wave.[76]

The poem that comes between these two is "Statistics." It may derive from Yeats's observation on W. J. Turner's poetry in an early version of "Modern Poetry,"

> I know him for the first man to read a mathematical equation, a musical score, a book of verse, with an equal understanding, and think of him as riding in an observation balloon, blue above, earth beneath in abstract pattern.
>
> All we know are abstract generalisations, mathematical equations, yet though much havoc has been wrought by newspaper articles, and government statistics, two abstractions may sit down to lunch.[77]

Thus the lines

> 'Those Platonists are a curse,' he said,
> 'God's fire upon the wane,
> A diagram hung there instead,
> More women born than men'

make the contrast between "God's fire" or intellectual fire, which may be thought of as perception or Berkeley's substitute for Newton's ether, and the diagram or chart of the statistician. God's fire is equally spiritual and substantial, male and female; the abstract interpretation would be a statistical survey of decline or imbalance. On

---

76. Yeats of course recognized that "James Joyce differs from Arnold Bennett and Galsworthy, let us say, because he can isolate the human mind and its vices as if in eternity" (*Pages from a Diary, Explorations,* p. 333).

77. TS. of "Modern Poetry."

the other hand, the poem "Symbols" coming before these three offers literature traditional and heroic symbols that are real, supernatural, and luminous of God, freedom, and immortality:

> A storm-beaten old watch-tower,
> A blind hermit rings the hour.
>
> All-destroying sword-blade still
> Carried by the wandering fool.
>
> Gold-sewn silk on the sword-blade,
> Beauty and fool together laid.[78]

An opposite danger to literature lay in those who daintily pursued or quested after spirituality alone. They usually missed the brutality of life and flesh which made literature heroic, forceful, and tragic, not just the waves but also a fighting against the waves. Since, aside from Berkeley, psychical research had so much to do with his theory of literature, Yeats's words in the flyleaf of his copy of Tyrrell's *Science and Psychical Phenomena* are apt:

Description of the SPR People

They all belong to the English upper middle class, they all admire Gilbert Murray, they all have run on stepping stones of their dead selves to higher things, they are all scholars. 'What would they say, Did their Catullus walk that way.'[79]

As he once wrote to Laura Riding of the poets around her, ". . . her school was too thoughtful, reasonable and truthful, . . . poets were good liars who never forgot that the Muses were women who liked the embrace of gay warty lads."[80]

More frequently, however, the enemy of traditional literature was what Yeats used to call "organized thought," and by this he usually meant journalism. The beginning of success in literature was a distrust of journalism. Journalism dealt perforce in those useful

78. On all four of these poems, cf. John Unterecker, *A Reader's Guide to William Butler Yeats* (New York, 1959), pp. 208–9.

79. G. N. M. Tyrrell, *Science and Psychical Phenomena* (London, 1938).

80. *Letters*, p. 857. See also "Yeats and Reeves," *New Statesman*, 30 October 1964, p. 651.

abstractions—Locke's "conception of a physical world without colour, sound, taste, tangibility" was the most successful one [81]—that made daily communal life possible. Yeats had listed some of the familiar Irish abstractions in his Berkeley essay:

> I spoke in the Irish Senate on the Catholic refusal of divorce and assumed that all lovers who ignored priest or registrar were immoral; upon education, and assumed that everybody who could not read the newspaper was a poor degraded creature; and had I been sent there by some religious organization must have assumed that a child captured by a rival faith lost its soul; and had my country been at war—but who does not serve these abstractions? Without them corporate life would be impossible.[82]

The danger was that these daily constructs might also infect literature. Hence Yeats could claim O'Casey's *The Silver Tassie* was rejected on Berkeley's theoretic grounds:

> We were biased, we are biased, by the Irish Salamis. The war, as O'Casey has conceived it, is an equivalent for those primary qualities brought down by Berkeley's secret society, it stands outside the characters, it is not part of their expression. . . . The English critics feel differently, to them a theme that 'bulks largely in the news' gives dignity to human nature, even raises it to international importance. We on the other hand are certain that nothing can give dignity to human nature but the character and energy of its expression.[83]

The pure, active, joyous expression of the spirit that illuminates and gives imperishable volume in literature shares a divinity with all created things. This belief we have already heard in Yeats's likening literary creation to divine creation after Berkeley's analogy of individual spirits and God. Thus subject matter had first importance in literature, "something" as Yeats explained, "I have received

81. "Bishop Berkeley," *Essays and Introductions*, p. 401. This distrust of journalism was, of course, an old theme with Yeats. See, for instance, "Lecture on Irish Theatre," *Irish Independent*, 4 March 1910.

82. "Bishop Berkeley," *Essays and Introductions*, p. 400.

83. *Pages from a Diary, Explorations*, p. 339.

from the generations, part of that compact with my fellow men made in my name before I was born." [84] That subject matter displayed the active spirit. Once again the natural and supernatural are one.[85] Tabloids, movies, best sellers offered instead an abstraction in the form of a problem or answer for middle-class aspirations. One abstraction frequently voiced was the life of the rich, a standard portrayal that seemed to justify revolution and make the prospect of murder one of the satisfactions of reading or viewing.[86] On this account, one can understand why Yeats hated the Marxian view of literature, given especially his Berkeleian devotion to the expression of "personality and the flowering of the spirit." [87]

The artist as creator—"The world knows nothing because it has made nothing, we know everything because we have made everything" [88]—abjured the useful or dogmatic abstractions of journalist or Marxist. The total creative act had all of man's world for its material:

> Locke took away the living world and gave instead its excrement, Berkeley gave back the living world but the newspapers talk as if it were still an excrement. All emotion seeks the unconditioned, the pure act of Berkeley and Aquinas, what else do our Gaelic poets seek in their journeys over sea or into the hearts of mountains? Such thoughts come from the waste places and the begging bowl and are our sole protection from that doctrine imagined in towns separated by rigidity from torrent and foliage, which benumbed daring and made art photographic.[89]

84. Introduction, *Essays and Introductions*, p. viii.
85. "A General Introduction for my Work," *Essays and Introductions*, p. 518.
86. "A People's Theatre," *Explorations*, pp. 244–46.
87. Jeffares, p. 267.
88. "A General Introduction for my Work," *Essays and Introductions*, p. 510.
89. TS. of Introduction to *Fighting the Waves* in Natl. Lib. MS. 8774(2). It is pleasant to note that A. A. Luce, *Berkeley's Immaterialism*, pp. 158–59, agrees that Berkeley assured Yeats of the reality of the world's beauty. However, Luce is incorrect in saying Yeats was uninterested in "the dry metaphysics of the question."

Moreover, literary art—the Word—encompassed figure and substance, form and matter, intellect and percept. Yeats once feared that Coleridge might have read *Siris* to mean that through concrete details we arrive at the realm of God's ideas. To do this was to arrive at abstractions.[90] Yeats preferred to confer reality on a flood of images, spirits, or beings unrestricted by time or space, determining and determined by each other.[91] However, he did mark in Coleridge a passage on the literary symbol that more or less coincides with Berkeley's world as Yeats chose to interpret it: ". . . by a symbol I mean, not a metaphor or allegory or any other figure of speech or form of fancy, but an actual and essential part of that, the whole of which it represents." [92] The emphasis here, as in his poem "Symbols," is on the living actuality of the symbol. And, in the third place, immortality, the basis of tragedy, went hand in hand with the immateriality of the world: "The power to create great character or possess it cannot long survive the certainty that the world is less solid than it looks and the soul much solider—'a spiritual substance' in some sense or other." [93] Thus, in spite of journalist, Marxist, or playwright with a message, characters like spirits determined themselves and each other, were ends in themselves. For this reason Yeats praised Sara Allgood's acting. It was not determined by history, but itself determined history: ". . . she made whole masses of emotion possible which otherwise would have lain latent in the mind of the author. Like other great actresses, and great artists of every kind, she possessed the power to 'mould history.' " [94]

Perhaps Yeats never summed up quite so boldly, possibly because so anonymously, his belief in literature divinely real and ideal as in the editorial "To All Artists and Writers," which he wrote, but let Stuart and Salkeld sign, for the first issue of *To-morrow*. Apart from the bow-wow tone of the old-man-young, the piece contains much of what has been outlined as a theory of literature based upon Berkeley's

90. *Pages from a Diary, Explorations*, p. 304.
91. *Ibid.*, p. 305.
92. *Biographia Literaria*, p. 348.
93. *Senate Speeches*, p. 180.
94. "Abbey Theatre Ceremony," *Irish Times*, 1 October 1932.

philosophy. Not the least important theme is the insistence that literature, or, better, the intellect itself is divine:

> "The Holy Spirit is an intellectual fountain," and did the Bishops believe that Holy Spirit would show itself in decoration and architecture, in daily manners and written style. . . . We condemn the art and literature of modern Europe. No man can create, as did Shakespeare, Homer, Sophocles, who does not believe, with all his blood and nerve, that man's soul is immortal, for the evidence lies plain to all men that where that belief has declined, men have turned from creation to photography. We condemn, though not without sympathy, those who would escape from banal mechanism through technical investigation and experiment. We proclaim that these bring no escape, for new form comes from new subject matter, and new subject matter must flow from the human soul restored to all its courage, to all its audacity. We . . . call back the soul to its ancient sovereignty, and declare it can do whatever it please, being made, as antiquity affirmed, from the imperishable substance of the stars.[95]

VI

Yet the Berkeley who fought Whiggery was probably even more important to Yeats than the philosopher of literature. Yeats had a way of laying all manner of evil at the feet of those—Locke, Newton, Marx, Bertrand Russell—who seemed to him to declare the absolute reality of an external world. Part of his study of philosophy was a seeking after arguments with which to confute them. Berkeley plays an important role here but certainly not the only one nor even the major one. Yet the lines

A voice
Soft as the rustle of a reed from Cloyne
That gathers volume; now a thunder-clap

95. "To All Artists and Writers," *To-morrow*, I (August 1924), 4. Although several critics have quoted or cited this passage, none seems to have taken it seriously.

are meant to suggest the power of Berkeley's philosophy and growing influence in combating modern Whiggery. Philosophically speaking, Whiggery was neorealism, its leader none other than, according to Yeats, that plebeian, that ill-bred man, that seeker after popularity, Bertrand Russell.

Foremost among those Yeats chose as allies against neorealism were the Italian idealist philosophers, Gentile and Croce. Although they exerted considerable influence on Yeats, the fact that he called them disciples of Berkeley is what interests us here. As Yeats wrote in his copy of Croce's *Logic as the Science of Pure Concept*, ". . . much of this book is Berkeley clarified." [96] He had already read and praised Gentile for his comprehensive and concrete theories of education. Both in his Senate speeches and, as has been shown, in his poem "Among School Children," Yeats held up the concrete development of the spirit, the ideal education as a constant becoming, a process combining the forces of religion, art, and philosophy. [97] Though Croce declared that Berkeley logically led to Hume, the Italian philosopher added that philosophically ". . . he laid the foundations of a spiritualist and voluntarist conception of reality, which in our opinion should be preserved and adopted by modern thought." [98] No less appealing to Yeats seems to have been Croce's passage

> When we speak, for instance, of *matter* or of *nature* as not existing, we mean to refer to the puppet of the naturalists, which the naturalists themselves and the philosophers of naturalism, forgetting its genesis, take for a real if not a living being. That matter (said Berkeley) is an abstraction; it is (say we) an empirical concept, and whoever knows what empirical concepts

96. *Logic as the Science of Pure Concept*, trans. Douglas Ainslie (London, 1917), p. 42.

97. See the author's " 'Among School Children' and the Education of the Irish Spirit," *Excited Reverie*, eds. A. N. Jeffares and K. G. W. Cross (London, 1965), pp. 123–50.

98. *Logic as the Science of Pure Concept*, p. 531. Yeats marked this passage in his copy.

are will not pretend that matter or nature exists, simply because it is spoken about.[99]

In the left margin Yeats wrote "Berkeley's 'nonexistence of matter.'" If we keep in mind Yeats's abhorrence of abstractions and his identifying Berkeley's patriotism with his attack on Locke and Newton, this heavily marked passage may sum up the importance of what he took to be the modern Italian heritage of Berkeley:

> If it is proved of a concept that it is inapplicable to reality, and therefore is not concrete, it is thereby confuted as a true and proper concept. It is said to be an *abstraction*, it is not reality; it does not possess *concreteness*. In this way, for example, has been confuted the concept of spirit as different from nature (abstract spiritualism); or of the good, as a model placed above the real world; or of atoms, as the components of reality; or of the dimensions of space, or of various quantities of pleasure and pain, and the like. All these are things not found in any part of the real, since there is neither a reality that is merely natural and external to spirit, nor an ideal world outside the real world; nor a space of one or two dimensions; nor a pleasure or pain that is homogeneous with another, and therefore greater or less than another; and for this reason all these things do not result from concrete thinking and are not concepts.[100]

Berkeley's Italian heritage stressed not only the blend of matter and spirit but seemed to assure human uniqueness also. Thus, while Yeats opposed variously naturalism, mechanism, or what he felt to be the descendant of historic British empiricism in his time, neorealism, his real thrust was against their political concomitants, socialism and Marxism. At least this was the association he drew at the end of his life between Whiggery, Locke, and modern revolutionary massacre:

> No educated man to-day accepts the objective matter and space of popular science, and yet deductions made by those who believed in both dominate the world, make possible the stimula-

99. *Ibid.*, p. 344.
100. *Ibid.*, pp. 43–44.

tion and condonation of revolutionary massacre and the multiplication of murderous weapons by substituting for the old humanity with its unique irreplaceable individuals something that can be chopped and measured like a piece of cheese; compel denial of the immortality of the soul by hiding from the mass of the people that the grave diggers have no place to bury us but in the human mind.[101]

This trend had gained headway at the end of the seventeenth century:

> Locke sank into a swoon;
> The Garden died;
> God took the spinning-jenny
> Out of his side.

The spinning-jenny becomes a symbol of absolute substance, the result, as Yeats thought, of Locke's separating the primary and secondary qualities.[102] As he explains in a passage prefacing this poem: "I can see in a sort of nightmare vision the 'primary qualities' torn from the side of Locke, Johnson's ponderous body bent above the letter to Chesterfield, some obscure person somewhere inventing the spinning-jenny. . . ."[103] This symbol, almost like Eve, tempted man to worship the unholy abstraction of absolute matter, and the Garden, Unity of Being, died. A concomitant was the breakdown in literary patronage and belief in traditional literature—perhaps more reasons why the Garden died. Other abstractions followed. For Yeats believed that pure reason applied to human affairs sought for universals, made "all places and persons alike."[104] Thus the time of Locke seemed responsible for a philosophic materialism that became the basis of revolutionary Marxism and merciless capitalism. Free thought stripped human life of traditions, prejudices, and superstitions that might have protected the peasantry. Even a passage Yeats canceled in his 1930 notebook may help explain the connection he tried to make

101. *On the Boiler*, p. 26.
102. "Bishop Berkeley," *Essays and Introductions*, p. 401.
103. *Wheels and Butterflies*, pp. 24–25.
104. *Pages from a Diary, Explorations*, p. 316.

between Locke and economic or political oppression: "The last quarter of the seventeenth century gave birth through a series of complex discoveries to 'liberal individualism' & made possible 'inhuman capitalism.' "[105] Otherwise, the concept of absolute matter became "the grosser half of that dialectical materialism the Socialist Prince Mirsky calls 'the firm foundation-rock of European Socialism,' and works all the mischief Berkeley foretold."[106] Berkeley's great political service had been to cut the line that connected the offending abstraction, matter, to supposed reality.

This was partly Yeats's motive in trying to hamstring neorealism. It was not real enough. The full impact of this charge can be seen in a notebook entry Yeats made in 1932 when he had in mind an enlargement of his introduction to *Fighting the Waves:*

> Speak of our failure as resulting from our being too Greek, & not realistic. Might speak of uniting philosophy to our early eighteenth century—Berkeley mainly—as Greek should be with Gaelic.[107]

This statement may seem to be at odds with his urging Gaelic folk literature on the young, and the works of Burke and Berkeley on the more mature intellect in Irish education.[108] Yet a second look at what Yeats thought to be Berkeley's service to Irish intellect—"Berkeley proved that the world was a vision"[109]—again finds Irish concreteness pitted against English abstraction: "The modern Irish intellect was born more than two hundred years ago when Berkeley defined in three or four sentences the mechanical philosophy of Newton, Locke and Hobbes, the philosophy of England in his day, and I think of England up to our day. . . ."[110] In arguing against neorealism, then, Yeats by insisting that the world was a concrete vision or a dream was doing the same thing that he had attributed to Berkeley. Hence the great importance of his long correspondence with T.

105. Large white vellum notebook begun 23 November 1930.
106. "Bishop Berkeley," *Essays and Introductions*, p. 401.
107. Large white vellum notebook begun 23 November 1930.
108. *Senate Speeches*, p. 172.
109. *Ibid.*
110. *Ibid.*

Sturge Moore that fixed on the existence of a phantom cat that Ruskin was said to have tossed out of a window. For in plumping for the reality of the phantom cat, Yeats was attacking the abstractions of neorealism, the philosophic progeny of the period of Hobbes, Newton, and Locke responsible for the unreal concept, matter, the basis of modern massacre.

We shall not trace this polite but heated controversy step by step. Virginia Moore has already done this in her book *The Unicorn*.[111] However, from the very beginning of the argument, Yeats's method was in part Berkeley's—using empiricism to prove ultimate immaterialism. Thus he begins by ironically taking G. E. Moore's and Russell's philosophy as warrant for opposite views from those they intended: that dreams, visions, or even hallucinations were real. Yeats's contention is based on his causing a friend to behold a vision, specifically to turn the pages of a missal invisible to Yeats. His sly conclusion is that since neorealism calls sense data evidence of an object outside the mind, then it must be said that his friend's vision had real existence.[112] Maintaining this ironic discourse, Yeats then produces Chapter IV (an attack on Berkeley) in Russell's *The Problems of Philosophy* as evidence that both Russell and G. E. Moore would agree that the vision and missal were real. Paraphrasing Russell he writes: "If we have 'an act of apprehension,' a 'sensation,' we must not infer as Berkeley did that the object apprehended is in the mind. This error has, Russell says, entirely made idealism 'of no validity whatever.'"[113] Yeats then draws his own conclusion:

> *If an act of apprehension, a sensation (say) of colour or of weight, could be proved to exist without an object it would obviously refute Russell's argument. I am therefore right in finding in this Chapter IV proof that my friend's dream missal really exists.*[114]

111. Virginia Moore, *The Unicorn* (New York, 1954), Chapter X, *passim*.
112. *Yeats and T. Sturge Moore*, p. 59.
113. *Ibid.*, pp. 60–61.
114. *Ibid.*, p. 61.

Thus the foundation of Yeats's side of the argument. Enter Ruskin's cat.

Here as before Yeats claims that neither Russell nor G. E. Moore has the means of distinguishing between Ruskin's cat and any other cat. Speaking as Berkeley might have spoken had he shared Yeats's hopes in spiritualism and the occult, Yeats concludes, "Ruskin's cat is a 'sense-datum'—it has weight, colour, shape." [115] Moore's rejoinder is to accuse Yeats of trying to make private reality and common experience the same. However, Yeats's next major objection—and I am skipping some of his reasoning—is that the neorealist puts so much of what is the working of the imagination "outside the mind that it turns that mind . . . into the quicksilver at the back of a mirror." [116] By contrast, Berkeley had kept sensations in the mind and maintained, with Yeats, "that we know nothing but spirits and their relations." [117] He then asks and answers his own question:

> Why should nature create that useless quicksilver? My own belief is that we know nothing but 'spirits and their relations,' but if I could escape from the useless quicksilver [I] would see nothing I care for involved if I had to consider the stream of images ('sense-data,' Ruskin's cat and the house cat), which since Berkeley have seemed part of the mind, as separate from it.[118]

Yeats is certainly beyond Berkeley now, especially Berkeley the philosopher who distinguished between ideas and dreams or reality and chimeras in the Third Dialogue between Hylas and Philonous. But, given his interpretation of Berkeley—the *true* Berkeley behind the mask who wrote the *Commonplace Book*—we should expect, and indeed find, Yeats in his next letter embracing the second of three beliefs on the make-up of the *external world* (italics mine) that had seemed possible to a *Times Literary Supplement* reviewer. This version of the world had seemed to say: "Nothing can exist that is not

115. *Ibid.*, p. 64.
116. *Ibid.*, p. 67.
117. *Ibid.*, p. 66.
118. *Ibid.*, p. 67.

in the mind as 'an element of experience.'" And Yeats then added in parentheses, "Neither Ruskin's cat nor the house cat is real." [119] The root of his statement lies in the words "external world," and in the supposition of those who would declare it to have absolute existence apart from the mind. This second of the three propositions makes everything unreal to such eyes, but real enough in Berkeley's, Yeats's, or God's eye. Here, then, is another turn on Yeats's lines beginning "And God-appointed Berkeley that proved all things a dream," a dream being by Yeats's choice of external realities the ultimate truth of independently real *things*. The third formulation, that of the neo-realists as T. Sturge Moore admitted,[120] assumed the physical substratum that Yeats hated: "There is a physical world which is independent of our minds—'real'—but we can only know it through 'representations' that are part of our mind and quite unlike it." [121]

We shall not pursue the rest of the argument except to say that while Yeats's reliance on Berkeley is definite it is by no means unalloyed. Blake, for instance, is also important; Yeats writes to Moore:

> My Berkeley is the Berkeley of the *Commonplace Book*, and it is this Berkeley who has influenced the Italians. The essential sentence is of course 'things only exist in being perceived,' and I can only call that perception God's when I add Blake's 'God only acts or is in existing beings or men.' [122]

Moreover, a good deal of Yeats's argument is based on what he would call the empirical evidence of psychical research. Dreams,

119. *Ibid.*, p. 68. In this review of William Pepperell Montague's *The Ways of Knowing* (London, 1925), the reviewer's actual words on the three positions had been: "The first theory, 'objectivism,' says that everything I perceive, including so-called illusions, exists in the physical world. . . . The second theory, 'subjectivism,' says that, because everything which I perceive is in relation to my mind, it cannot exist except as an element in experience. . . . Next comes the dualist, who holds both that the physical world exists independently of us and that we can only know it indirectly by means of our representations" ("Ways of Knowing," *TLS*, 4 February 1926, p. 72).
120. *Yeats and T. Sturge Moore*, p. 70.
121. *Ibid.*, p. 68.
122. *Ibid.*, p. 80.

visions, and phantoms were not part of a private untested reality but were in the public domain, were shared by other men, and were frequently collective. Nevertheless, in accusing Russell of appealing to "'the physical stratum' people," Yeats was again arraigning the philosophical tradition he had traced from Locke:

> In the seventeenth century people said [that] our senses are responsible for colour, scent and sound, and that colour, scent and sound are 'appearances' but that mass and movement really exist. In the eighteenth century one or two men pointed out that mass and movement are just as much 'appearances,' because the invention of our senses, as colour, scent and sound.[123]

As befits a man who could retort to the neorealists, "I think that my own position is more realist than idealist," and then add, "I do not however see any final contradiction," [124] Yeats's majestic answer to those who believed that we may know sense-data only was the charge of blind faith and English provincialism. Of these he writes T. Sturge Moore:

> Part of the trouble is that your brother, like the ecclesiastics, does not examine evidence because he is satisfied with faith or thinks evidence is impossible, and another part is that your brother has that English University habit which made it possible for the editors of *The Cambridge Ancient History* to ignore India and China. . . . This is English provincialism.[125]

This unexamined faith was pronounced in Bertrand Russell. Consulting his *An Outline of Philosophy*, Yeats finds him very close to Berkeley in his concept of events but seemingly afraid to describe them in any terms but those taken from the terminology of materialism. As Yeats wrote in the flyleaf of his own copy of the book:

> The vice of this book & all books of this school is that though they say events are neutral between mind & matter they

123. *Ibid.*, p. 92.
124. *Ibid.*, p. 99.
125. *Ibid.*, p. 104.

think in terms of matter—event, radiation, stuff are now
material terms. In substituting "mental stuff" for the union of
subject and object they are therefore by implication materialists.[126]

And at the bottom of page 166,

> In the first part of this chapter he seems to assume that
> whatever is common to individual "percepts" is outside mind.
> He should take Berkeley's step & assume there is a mind
> common to all minds or within all minds: "outward" may be
> inward.
>
> Russell's position—if logical—would be that of the "Com-
> monplace Book." To go further we must accept "concepts."
> Berkeley's affirmation of the mind of God was an act of faith
> because he had then not.[127]

Russell, Yeats wrote on another page, "was pining for 'the primary
qualities' of 17th century materialism."[128] Yeats had spattered the
pages of this volume and many another with objections based on his
reading of Berkeley. In his correspondence with T. Sturge Moore, he
caps his remarks on this reverence for an unnamed absolute in
Russell's thought by jibing, "He like all of his sort is afraid that if he
used any other language he might have to go to Church. He has got
the Archbishop of Canterbury in his belly."[129]
Part of Yeats's dislike of Russell was doubtless political. The
liberal implications of his position were obvious. Just as objectionable
were what Yeats thought the incessant polemics of Russell's discourse. In marked contrast was the aristocratic mind of Alfred North
Whitehead—"His packed logic, his way of saying just enough and no
more, his difficult scornful lucidity. . . ."[130] Moreover, Yeats found
himself in easy agreement with the author of *Science and the Modern
World*. Here was a man who was fair to Berkeley, who mocked any

126. *An Outline of Philosophy* (London, 1927).
127. *Ibid.*, p. 126.
128. *Ibid.*, p. 149.
129. *Yeats and T. Sturge Moore*, p. 126.
130. *Letters*, p. 714.

mechanical theory of nature, and offered a concept of organism that seemed to Yeats to combine mind and sensation:

> He [Whitehead] seems to me among other things to give Ruskin's cat all the consideration it can reasonably expect. To Whitehead, as to Berkeley, there is no 'physical substratum,' no 'permanent possibility of sensation' behind the 'sense-data.' The point at issue, if it is at issue, is the independence of these 'sense-data' from 'mind.' The house cat and Ruskin's cat can lie down together in either case.[131]

They could also lie down together because Whitehead had returned the world to the poets, after it had languished for some centuries with the mechanists. Thus Yeats could write on the inside cover of his copy of *Science and the Modern World:* "Do we not get close to Berkeley, if as Whitehead advises we accept 'naive experience.' Do we not get a visible world which is the least common denominator of the imagined worlds of all individuals?"[132] How telling the phrase "imagined worlds" seems here. At last Yeats had found a modern thinker who agreed with him on final things; moreover, his aristocratic intellectual expression had seemed the parallel, Yeats thought, to his own imaginative suggestiveness.[133] Organic, concrete, and aesthetic, theirs was another faith from that of neorealism.

VII

Hence it may be right that our consideration of Yeats and Berkeley should conclude on the note of faith. Nor is there a more moving testimony to Yeats's faith than the following lines from "The Tower":

> I mock Plotinus' thought
> And cry in Plato's teeth,
> Death and life were not
> Till man made up the whole,

131. *Yeats and T. Sturge Moore*, p. 89.
132. *Science and the Modern World* (Cambridge, 1926).
133. *Letters*, pp. 712–14.

Made lock, stock and barrel
Out of his bitter soul,
Aye, sun and moon and star, all,
And further add to that
That, being dead, we rise,
Dream and so create
Translunar Paradise.
I have prepared my peace
With learned Italian things
And the proud stones of Greece,
Poet's imaginings
And memories of love,
Memories of the words of women,
All those things whereof
Man makes a superhuman
Mirror-resembling dream.

How satisfying it would be to claim the entire passage for Berkeley. But it is not his alone. In a note Yeats even admits that he had slighted Plotinus in declaring him on the side of sheer transcendence. The passage is, consequently, one of many echoes—including Plotinus, Boehme, Blake, Gentile, Croce, and even Vico.[134] But Yeats's special interpretation of Berkeley's thought is the key.

Yeats had opened Section VII of his Berkeley essay with a paraphrase of the following passage from the third of *The Three Dialogues between Hylas and Philonous*. Philonous is denying Hylas' point that according to Scriptures God created real things, not ideas:

> *Moses* mentions the sun, moon, and stars, earth and sea, plants and animals: that all these do really exist, and were in the beginning created by God, I make no question. If by *ideas*,

134. In his copy of Croce's *The Philosophy of Giambattista Vico*, trans. R. G. Collingwood (London, 1913), p. 29, Yeats marked this passage: "Man creates the human world, creates it by transforming himself into the facts of society: by thinking it he re-creates his own creations, traverses over again the paths he has already traversed, reconstructs the whole ideally, and thus knows it with full and true knowledge. Here is a real world; and of this world man is truly the God." Apparently Yeats read and annotated this volume in 1924 (Hone, p. 368).

you mean fictions and fancies of the mind, then these are no
ideas. If by *ideas,* you mean immediate objects of the understanding, or sensible things, which cannot exist unperceived, or
out of a mind, then these things are ideas. But whether you do,
or do not call them *ideas,* it matters little. The difference is only
about a name. . . . The creation therefore I allow to have been
a creation of things, of *real* things.[135]

A little later in the exchange, Philonous sums up his position in these
words:

When things are said to begin or end their existence, we do not
mean this with regard to God, but his creatures. All objects are
eternally known by God, or which is the same thing, have an
eternal existence in his mind: but when things before impercep-
tible to creatures, are by a decree of God, made perceptible to
them; then are they said to begin a relative existence, with
respect to created minds.[136]

In a similar passage, this time directed against the worship of matter,
Berkeley had written in the *Principles of Human Knowledge:*

The existence of matter, or bodies unperceived, has not only
been the main support of *Atheists* and *Fatalists,* but on the same
principle doth *Idolatry* likewise in all its various forms depend.
Did men but consider that the sun, moon, and stars, and every
other object of the senses, are only so many sensations in their
minds, which have no other existence but barely being perceived, doubtless they would never fall down, and worship their
own *ideas;* but rather address their homage to that Eternal
Invisible Mind which produces and sustains all things.[137]

If we extend Berkeley's belief about creation but one more step, as
Yeats put it, and acknowledge "that Man in so far as he is himself, in
so far as he is a personality, reflects the whole act of God," [138] then
Yeats's declaration of faith is also partly Berkeley's. In 1937, Yeats

135. *Works,* I, 203.
136. *Ibid.,* p. 204.
137. *Ibid.,* p. 71.
138. "Bishop Berkeley," *Essays and Introductions,* p. 408, n. 1.

set down Seven Propositions about ultimate things. The first two are
crucial here since they are diffused in their inchoate way throughout
these lines. They are also no less Berkeleian:

I

Reality is a timeless and spaceless community of Spirits which
perceive each other. Each Spirit is determined by and determines those it perceives, and each Spirit is unique.

II

When these Spirits reflect themselves in time and space they
still determine each other, and each Spirit sees the others as
thoughts, images, objects of sense. Time and space are unreal.[139]

Each man is thus a temporal example of a unique spirit. The real and
ideal are again one. So, the lines from "The Tower" give man the
power to create temporality, however embittering the experience may
be to the purity of his soul. The sun, moon, and stars may be said to
have their existence only on being perceived. Since death is but a portal
of creativity, life after death may be compared to a dream which is,
after all, the ultimate form of reality, if we use the language of those
who believe in an absolute external reality. Thus the poet, facing
death, makes his peace with the very building blocks of reality-
dream: the liberal concept of Unity of Being taken from the learning
of the Italian Renaissance; the beauty of classical Greece that also
incorporated measure and proportion; the ingredients of a traditional
literature that refused to separate the poet's imaginings from his
memories as a man. All these with their aesthetic overlay may seem
to be but fleeting appearances. But to Yeats, Berkeley, and Whitehead they are essential—the sounding and shining that make the
world real. So man both reflects and is reflected by what he creates.
His dream is superhuman because Yeats has solved the problem of
the continuity of perception by postulating an eternal community of
unique, perceiving and perceived spirits. Here then, in these lines

139. Cited by Virginia Moore, *The Unicorn*, pp. 378–79.

from "The Tower," as in his essay on Berkeley and his remarks to John Sparrow at Oxford, personality and the life of the spirit are what stir Yeats most. Man's uniqueness was incomprehensible to mechanical philosopher and Marxist theorist, for they rejected man as a living spirit, his society a living together.[140] However farfetched we may think Yeats's reliance on psychic research or the occult studies of Boehme, Swedenborg, and Blake, we must also recognize that his sometimes strained interpretation of Berkeley kept him tied, however tenuously, to a historic school of European philosophy which was a fitting counterpart to his own highly individual, imaginative kinship to European poetry since the time of Homer.[141]

140. Yeats turned down p. 40 in his copy of Croce's *Historical Materialism and the Economics of Karl Marx*, trans. C. M. Meredith (London, 1922), where the author inveighs against any "abstract and general science of *society*."

141. *Yeats and T. Sturge Moore*, p. 149.

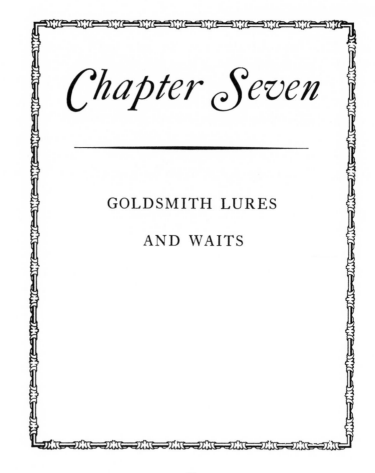

Chapter Seven

GOLDSMITH LURES

AND WAITS

I

WITH AN AIR of ebullience and anticipation Yeats once compared his attitude toward Goldsmith at the turn of the century with his attitude during the late twenties:

> I turned from Goldsmith and from Burke because they had come to seem a part of the English system. . . . But now I read Swift for months together, Burke and Berkeley less often but always with excitement, and Goldsmith lures and waits.[1]

1. *Wheels and Butterflies*, p. 7. In 1895, Yeats had written of eighteenth-century Ireland: "English-speaking Ireland . . . had no poetic voice, for

266

Despite this announced lure, one can only feel a marked disappointment in the meager interest shown the poet, essayist, dramatist, and novelist Goldsmith by the poet, essayist, dramatist, and novelist Yeats. Goldsmith did not go unread by Yeats, to be sure. His early Godolphin School Reports indicate that for one holiday task he was to memorize lines 113–237 of *The Deserted Village*.[2] He probably saw or read *The Good-Natured Man* produced at the Abbey Theatre in April 1920, and *She Stoops to Conquer* produced at the same theater in April 1923.[3] And he admits to having seen the latter play in Sweden in December 1923,[4] and refers to *The Citizen of the World* in his Introduction to *The Words Upon the Window-pane*, written in 1930–31. Yet in view of the close attention granted Swift, Berkeley, and Burke, Yeats can only be said to have neglected Goldsmith. As late as 1919 he condemned Goldsmith as "superficial and just suitable for an evening's entertainment." [5]

A closer inspection of the role played by Goldsmith in the work of Yeats, especially after he became associated in Yeats's mind with the golden age of the Irish eighteenth century, may provide some reason for this comparative neglect. Accordingly, first we shall explore the historical figure that Goldsmith cuts in Yeats's prose—with an eye to

---

Goldsmith had chosen to celebrate English scenery and manners" (Introduction, *A Book of Irish Verse* [London, 1895], pp. xii–xiii). In his notes to *The Deserted Village* in the same volume, Yeats called "the feeling and atmosphere of the poem . . . unmistakably English" (p. 250). An explanation of both these judgments may lie in a distinction Yeats made in 1891 regarding books for the Young Ireland League reading rooms: "Irish writers of equal or greater merit there have been whom I have not mentioned, because they did not make Ireland their subject matter, but united with the main stream of English literature. They have no special claim upon us, but must be read when, like Goldsmith, they are important enough to make a needful part of general knowledge. But those writers who have made Ireland their study have a peculiar claim on our affections" ("The Young Ireland League," *United Ireland*, 3 October 1891). See also "First Principles," *Samhain*, 1904, in *Explorations*, p. 159.

2. Godolphin School Reports in possession of Mrs. W. B. Yeats.
3. T. L. Dume, "William Butler Yeats: A survey of His Reading," unpublished dissertation (Temple University, 1950), p. 251.
4. *Autobiographies*, p. 557.
5. "The Abbey Theatre," *Irish Times*, 1 April 1919. Cf. "Irish Literature's Position," *Irish Times*, 9 November 1926.

the necessary distortions of history forced on Yeats in fitting Gold-smith into the company of Swift, Berkeley, and Burke—then touch on the poetic image that Yeats derived from his concept of Goldsmith.

II

In considering Yeats's portrait of Goldsmith, one notices that in most cases Yeats rhetorically exaggerates or depresses a side of Goldsmith in order to make him part of a greater persuasion, usually as sharer of a trait which Yeats has settled on Swift, Berkeley, and Burke together. For instance, Yeats could maintain that Swift, Berkeley, and Burke "found in England the opposite that stung their own thought into expression or made it lucid." [6] One is not surprised to find Goldsmith deriving his "opposite" from the same quarter by virtue of his "delight in the particulars of common life that shocked his contemporaries." [7] To reinforce this notion, Yeats added the following footnote on Goldsmith as a comment on the progress of the arts in Ireland during Berkeley's time: "He wrote that he had never laughed so much at Garrick's acting as at somebody in an Irish tavern mimicking a Quaker sermon." [8] As we may come to see, Yeats here of necessity simplified the personality of Goldsmith.

Perhaps the core of the matter lies in the fact that Yeats has rendered his footnote a trifle more purple than its actual source: "My present enjoyments may be more refined, but they are infinitely less pleasing. The pleasure Garrick gives me can no way compare to that I had received from a country wag who imitated a Quaker's sermon." [9] The words "more refined" suggest the predicament which Goldsmith found himself in and which Yeats neglected. The words indicate Goldsmith's admiration for the English middle classes, but the rest of the passage hints of his continued affection for what Yeats terms "common life." The story of this affection and the resulting dilemma

6. "Bishop Berkeley," *Essays and Introductions*, p. 402.
7. *Ibid.*
8. *Wheels and Butterflies*, p. 13, n. 1.
9. *The Bee*, No. II (13 October 1759), *The Works of Oliver Goldsmith*, ed. J. W. M. Gibbs (London, 1884–86), II, 334—hereafter *Works*.

of inveterate Irishry making up to the solemn and essentially static decorum of middle-class London has already been told.[10] For one thing this indecisiveness of mind in his early years allowed Goldsmith seemingly to contradict himself. When he wrote, for instance, to Mr. Ralph Griffiths, a bookseller, "What then has a gaol that is formidable, I shall at least have the society of wretches, and such is to me true society,"[11] his words are probably sincere (although he was heavily in debt to Griffiths and foolishly so). Yet he could at the same time write to Daniel Hodson a confession of his preference for a life different from that of the garrets: ". . . I eagerly long to embrace every opportunity of separating myself from the vulgar. . . ."[12] The self-contradictory Goldsmith simply would not do for Yeats. Thus to maintain Goldsmith in his role as a wise, childlike man, Yeats had to reduce measurably at least one complex relationship between Goldsmith and his own eighteenth-century world.

A second rallying point for at least four good Anglo-Irishmen of the eighteenth century was a hatred of abstraction.[13] By abstraction Yeats meant, as we have seen, some curtailment of the complete man or life, some drastic neglect of one activity for another.[14] And here precisely Goldsmith can be said to have satirized the abstraction sentimentalism in the drama, an abstraction variously related to the concept of universal benevolence, natural goodness, or cosmic optimism in his time.[15] But without disregarding Goldsmith's recorded disparagement of sentimental drama, and without denying the artistic intention as it unfolds in the opening scenes of *The Good-natured Man*, one is forced to deny any view of the total play as unsentimen-

10. See, for instance, Robert W. Seitz, "The Irish Background of Goldsmith's Social and Political Thought," *PMLA*, LII (June 1937), 405; Temple Scott, *Oliver Goldsmith Biographically and Bibliographically Considered* (New York, 1928), pp. 128–30; *Boswell's Life of Johnson*, ed. G. B. Hill, rev. L. F. Powell (Oxford, 1934), I, 411–17; and Sir Joshua Reynolds, *Portraits*, ed. Frederick W. Hilles (New York, 1952), p. 146.
11. *The Collected Letters of Oliver Goldsmith*, ed. Katharine C. Balderston (Cambridge, Mass., 1928), p. 67.
12. *Ibid.*, p. 52.
13. *Wheels and Butterflies*, p. 16.
14. *Autobiographies*, p. 190.
15. *Wheels and Butterflies*, p. 16.

tal.[16] Nor can *The Deserted Village* with its "picturesque, minute observation" fare much better as Yeats's proof of "an Irish hatred of abstraction." Actually the themes and feelings of the poem seldom rise above the commonplaces of eighteenth-century thought.[17] The hardships of the poor elicit our sympathy, but not our reverence. The rightfully generalized poetic diction remains a fitting vehicle only for an accepted sentiment. As James Sutherland has put it, "You do not feel that anyone in the village is quite adult."[18] In his various editions of *A Book of Irish Verse*, Yeats had included the famous "hounds and horns" section and some of the verses (lines 137–62) that he had been assigned at the Godolphin School. These last verses may have served him for evidence of Goldsmith's sharp eye, especially the account of the preacher's house "known to all the vagrant train." But that train—beggar, spendthrift, and broken soldier—is a singularly conventional one. If the description of the ale house comes closest to being a "picturesque, minute observation," still the walls, the floor, the clock, and the broken teacups are the trappings and kickshaws of any rural tavern of the time. As a matter of fact, the conventional, aphoristic tone of the poem almost requires that its persons and scene be oversimplified in order to answer the pastoral formula for turning the complex into the simple.

Much more arresting is Yeats's attempt to distinguish Goldsmith from the sentimental and logical English poets and dramatists

16. One wonders how strongly Yeats believed in the anti-sentimentalism of the play. Earlier, before his "return to the 18th century," he had written: "Sheridan and Goldsmith, when they restored comedy after an epoch of sentimentalities, had to apologise for their satiric genius by scenes of conventional love-making and sentimental domesticity that have set them outside the company of all—whether their genius be great or little—whose work is pure and whole" ("The Controversy over *The Playboy of the Western World*," *Explorations*, p. 225). The "dull places and unrealities" of the play, its technical inferiority to Molière, Yeats also readily admitted in his *Autobiographies*, p. 557. Most commentators now regard the play as sentimental. The exception is Robert B. Heilman, "The Sentimentalism of Goldsmith's *Good-Natured Man*," *Studies for William A. Read*, eds. Nathaniel M. Caffee and Thomas A. Kirby (Baton Rouge, 1940), pp. 237–53.

17. Wallace Cable Brown, *The Triumph of Form* (Chapel Hill, 1948), p. 154.

18. *A Preface to Eighteenth Century Poetry* (Oxford, 1948), p. 100.

around him. Yeats is also pitting Anglo-Irish Goldsmith against the collective manners and assumptions—argumentative, logical, and combative—of Johnson's circle. He is redressing Boswell's malicious distortions. Yeats's early version of the Quaker-sermon note is instructive here:

> I sometimes wonder if when Goldsmith "talked like poor Poll" he did not merely display how helpless could be a humourous narrator's dramatic talent in Dr. Johnson's litigious circle. He was said to frequent the society "of gamblers and venal beauties" who might have had a different tale to tell. He had himself said that much as he admired Garrick, he heard better comedy when somebody in an Irish tavern imitated a Quaker sermon. His conversation, like the Deserted Village & the notorious scene of the gambler in the Good-Natured Man, was in all probability low. Ireland the country still prevailed over the town. Swift [?termed] a litigious man as unfit for company as an inhabitant of bedlam and see "The Battle of the Books."[19]

But of equal importance is the role played by Goldsmith, who pricked abstractions and reveled in common life, in Yeats's scheme of national unity. Here part of an early essay by Yeats entitled "What is 'Popular Poetry'?" is illuminating; it describes the advent of the middle class:

> . . . people who have unlearned the unwritten tradition which binds the unlettered, so long as they are masters of themselves, to the beginning of time and to the foundation of the world, and who have not learned the written tradition which has been established upon the unwritten.[20]

Toward the end of the essay Yeats's attitude is unmistakable:

> . . . the counting-house had created a new class and a new art without breeding and without ancestry, and set this art and this class between the hut and the castle. . . .[21]

19. Large white vellum notebook begun 23 November 1930.
20. "What is 'Popular Poetry'?" *Essays and Introductions*, p. 6.
21. *Ibid.*, p. 10.

These well-known excerpts outline Goldsmith's position during the heyday of Yeats's enthusiasm for the Anglo-Irish eighteenth century. For during the twenties it was as solitary integrator of "the hut and the castle" that Goldsmith cleaved to Yeats's fourfold Anglo-Irish image. The low reality and crooked wisdom of common life available to Goldsmith thus rounded out the national vision that Yeats formulated from his interpretation of Swift's social, Berkeley's spiritual, and Burke's politically conservative leadership. "We wish to preserve an ancient ideal of life. Wherever its customs prevail, there you will find the folk song, the folk tale, the proverb and the charming manners that come from ancient culture." [22] These words, spoken during 1903–4 in New York, express the poetic mission which Yeats was to bestow on Goldsmith. Like Synge, whom Yeats considered a modern counterpart, Goldsmith became the singer of a traditional social life.[23]

This resemblance to Synge is important. While many critics have noticed the general similarity Yeats assumes, they have not seen his probable purpose. For one thing, the likeness puts Synge—so strange, wild, new, and anti-Irish to that first *Playboy* audience—in a tradition of sweetness and gentleness. For another, it showed the close touch with bedrock Ireland that was shared by both Synge and Yeats, heirs of a Protestant nation said to neglect peasant realities. In his contribution to a broadside, *Anglo-Irish Ballads*, Yeats not only speaks of Swift's political satires being sung in the Coombe as late as Sir Walter Scott's time but also notes that "Goldsmith while still at College wrote ballads for five shillings a-piece." [24] And in the same broadside, Yeats mentions Goldsmith's hearing "Barbara Allen" sung in the Midlands. The implication in both cases is that the wanderer Goldsmith had an ear for such hidden beauty.[25] Both he and Synge

---

22. TS. of speech given in New York, 1903–4.
23. Yeats classified Synge as one of "those who, like Wordsworth, like Coleridge, like Goldsmith, like Keats, have little personality, so far as the casual eye can see, little personal will, but fiery and brooding imagination" ("J. M. Synge and the Ireland of his Time," *Essays and Introductions*, p. 329).
24. "Anglo-Irish Ballads," *Broadsides* (Dublin, 1935), pp. ix–x.
25. *Ibid.*, p. ix.

heard and transmuted into art the wisdom and language of the people, whether found in Michael James's shebeen or in the village tavern of *The Deserted Village*. We are familiar enough with Yeats's meditations on Synge and his work, but here, in capsule, Yeats relates him historically to Goldsmith, makes him the solitary singer from Protestant Ireland, and puts him, like his vagrant eighteenth-century predecessors in Scotland and Ireland, Burns and Goldsmith, among the people:

> But who was Synge himself? . . . Like Lady Gregory he belonged to an old Irish Protestant family, a Dublin street is named after it, the Synge house in Dublin, now let as offices, is one of the show houses of Dublin; there were seven Bishops among his ancestors, one that Bishop who refused to ordain Oliver Goldsmith because Oliver Goldsmith wore red breeches. Sometimes, though a simple courteous man, he seemed to remember that past and became reserved and lonely. With just enough money to keep him from starvation and not always from half starvation, he had wandered about Europe . . . playing his fiddle to poor men on the road or in their cottages. He was the man that we needed because he was the only man I have ever known incapable of a political thought or of a humanitarian purpose. He could walk the roadside all day with some poor man without any desire to do him good or for any reason except that he liked him. He was to do for Ireland . . . what Robert Burns did for Scotland. When Scotland thought herself gloomy and religious Providence restored her imaginative spontaneity by raising up Robert Burns to commend drink and the Devil.[26]

To walk the roads, to sing of what he saw was also Goldsmith's way. Hence, Goldsmith, as tramp and poet, became partner to the uniqueness and moment of Berkeley's speculations through his own shocking and concrete observations. Thus the inclusion of "Irish tavern" and "the particulars of common life that shocked his contemporaries" is justified. They are no longer nugatory, no matter

26. *The Irish National Theatre* (Rome, 1934), pp. 7–8. See also *Autobiographies*, pp. 567–68.

how questionable historically, for they now merge with the thin air that Berkeley breathed, and at the same moment balance the aristocratic bias of Burke and bridge the social distance between Swift and mankind. A passage from *Stories of Michael Robartes and His Friends* demonstrates these connections; a little boy is described by Mary Bell to John Bond:

> "Everybody thinks he is so like his great-uncle, the famous Chancery lawyer, the friend of Goldsmith and of Burke, but you can judge for yourself, that is his portrait by Gainsborough." [27]

The virtue Yeats holds up is reflected in the friendship with Burke and Goldsmith, men of equal but different greatness. Thus in overemphasizing Goldsmith's vagabondage, loneliness, and simple directness, Yeats was able to revive further the image of eighteenth-century Protestant Ireland, refine it, and yet give it substance in the earth and the earthy. For that insistence, despite the brief mention of Goldsmith, Yeats's argument is a more telling and persuasive one.

III

Goldsmith is almost as rarely seen in Yeats's poetry as in his prose. But on the two occasions that he appears his presence is spectacular. In the second stanza of "Blood and the Moon," but one line is given Goldsmith while Swift, Berkeley, and Burke receive at least three or four apiece. Yet the conjunction in that one line of the momentarily homely and subjective attributes of Goldsmith, that Yeats had insisted upon in prose, makes it almost the equal in impact to any three or four other lines in the epithet-studded stanza: "Goldsmith deliberately sipping at the honey-pot of his mind." The line echoes passages from Goldsmith himself and descriptions of him made by his commentators. Take, for example, the passage from Lucretius which served as the motto for that ill-starred periodical, *The Bee: Floriferis ut in apes saltibus omnia libant;* or, possibly even more to the point,

27. *A Vision* (1956), p. 47.

Goldsmith's own words in his introduction to the first issue of *The Bee:*

> Like the Bee, which I had taken for the title of my paper, I would rove from flower to flower, with seeming inattention, but concealed choice, expatiate over all the beauties of the season, and make my industry my amusement.[28]

In the same way the following passages may be important:

> Fielding describes a class of men who feed upon their own hearts; who are egotists, as he says, the wrong way; and if Goldsmith was vain, it was the wrong way.[29]

and

> He [Goldsmith] could not live anywhere without attracting to himself a whole crowd of beggars. These honey-seeking bees must have scented afar off the perfume of this human flower.[30]

The point to be made is that the strength and conclusiveness of Yeats's line depend on the compression and packed suggestion that one feels deriving from not only Goldsmith's own life, but also that life abetted by the cunning argument and sense of history in Yeats himself. For if these quotations and Goldsmith's own words—"concealed choice"—are summoned up by the phrase "deliberately sipping," then just as powerful is our recall of Yeats's pot-house Goldsmith, with his aura of solitude and sweet particularity, in the phrase "honey-pot of his own mind." Finally, a good deal of the residual effect of the line derives from Yeats's slipping it between the reference to *blood,* tangible and warm, indicating Swift's basic humanity, and the haughtier *head* of Burke, who pondered states and royalty. The word "mind" prepares for "haughtier-headed," and, strengthening the span, "sipping at the honey-pot" retains the vascular and sensual connotations of Swift's "blood-sodden breast."

28. *Works,* II, 305–6.
29. John Foster, *Goldsmith, His Life and Times* (Boston, 1900), I, 11.
30. Temple Scott, *Oliver Goldsmith,* pp. 96–97. Writing to Oliver Elton of York Powell, J. B. Yeats once said, "The busy bee sunk in the heart of a flower is the true symbol of his intellect" (*Letters to his son W. B. Yeats and others 1869–1922,* ed. Joseph Hone [London, 1944], p. 86).

The mention of honey and the implied accent on choice in the word "deliberately" recall the ideal of the Protestant mind that we have considered more than once. They may also put us once again in the company of Synge, for the absence of any wish to reform or improve is also implied. To be sure, this gentle Goldsmith was, in part at least, the cherished memory of Yeats's father.[31] Still, Synge's example must not be denied. Once Yeats contrasted Goldsmith with the "churlish logicians" of his age whose way it was to argue everything. Unlike those spinners of argument, Goldsmith and Synge fed upon "that old Ireland which took its mould from the duellists and scholars of the eighteenth century and from generations older still." [32] And for a time at least Yeats highly praised "The Logicians Refuted" as Swift's, discovering only later that it was Goldsmith's imitation of Swift.[33] The choice exercised by Synge or Goldsmith was deliberate, but not rigidly deduced.

In "The Seven Sages" the Second Sage remarks:

> My great-grandfather shared
> A pot-house bench with Oliver Goldsmith once.

Here the line is remarkable for its casual assumption of Goldsmith's renown, along with his common touch. To have an ancestor who once shared a pot-house bench with Goldsmith steeps one in hereditary wisdom. Toward the end of the poem, the Second Sage asserts of Whiggery:

> Oliver Goldsmith sang what he had seen,
> Roads full of beggars, cattle in the fields,
> But never saw the trefoil stained with blood,
> The avenging leaf those fields raised up against it.

---

31. Goldsmith's gentleness and sympathy with the Irish poor were frequent themes of J. B. Yeats. See "Ireland out of the Dock," *United Irishman*, 10 October 1903, and *Early Memories* (Dundrum, 1923), p. 80.

32. "J. M. Synge and the Ireland of his Time," *Essays and Introductions*, p. 324.

33. Large white vellum notebook begun 23 November 1930. An unpublished portion in Yeats's 1930 Diary corrects an entry dated 17 October with the words " 'Dogma [sic] Refuted' is by Goldsmith. It was long attributed to Swift."

Perhaps most powerful are the last two lines. Even more than the first two, they suggest the limitations of Yeats's reading of *The Deserted Village;* yet how fortunate that he read it so! The key word is "trefoil." It charges the sense with heraldic and nationalistic significance in its emblematic blend of blood and shamrock. Yeats always abominated the word "shamrock," but "trefoil" solved his problem. For the trefoil's roots are in the low, enclosed Irish fields, which Goldsmith presumably saw and wrote about according to Yeats's version. The ambiguous use of "trefoil" also allows it the efficacy of an "avenging leaf," an honorific title. In like manner, Goldsmith, though rooted in common life like the trefoil, sets himself against Whiggery, sings against it, and augurs the strife to come. So once again Yeats has it both ways: Goldsmith, used elastically and imaginatively, sees beggars and cattle in those fields where Yeats hails the avenging clover leaf, the blood-stained trefoil of Ireland from 1798 on.

IV

From the sparkle and the rarity of Yeats's literary use of Goldsmith, one may arrive at a puzzling conclusion. Briefly, in celebrating Goldsmith, Yeats frequently represses in some arbitrary way aspects of Goldsmith's career which are considered endemic to him and to the eighteenth century. Yet despite his distortion of the historical Goldsmith, the éclat and excitement that ensue in Yeats's use of the man seem worth the damage to history. Thus he may abjure those personal and financial associations which align Goldsmith with the middle class; he may deny those literary habits which bind Goldsmith to sentimentalism and the so-called poetic diction of his day; he may even go so far as to use Goldsmith as a counter to the "external, sentimental and logical" side of the English eighteenth century which he as a modern Irish poet hated. On the other hand, when Yeats speaks of the concreteness of Goldsmith's observations, his disdain for abstractions, his delight in shocking details, his passivity and fiery imagination, these conclusions seem not so very far from Yeats's own poetic and dramatic practice.

However, in depicting him so very strikingly at variance with the eighteenth-century world he hated, Yeats, after all, clearly drags Goldsmith into his scheme by the heels. The strain is too much. The companion of Swift, Berkeley, and Burke continues to lure and wait. Others had tried to make something of the same connection between Goldsmith and Yeats himself with no more success. For instance, Goldsmith's lines

> And as the hare, whom hounds and horns pursue,
> Pants to the place from whence at first she flew,
> I still had hopes, my long vexations past,
> Here to return and die at home at last

simply do not apply to Yeats's final return and burial at Sligo, as Lennox Robinson thought they did.[34] No more does the analogy of Yeats's art to that of Goldsmith's apply, especially when the last is termed "wholly egocentric—man at the center of the world looking out at the universe." [35] No, Goldsmith was too much in the tradition of Pope, too much, for all his personal difference, Johnson's man for Yeats to assimilate. And Synge, for all of Yeats's devotion to his memory, was certainly a cat of a very different stripe from that of the gentle Goldsmith. Synge was altogether too tough, too rebellious, too commonsensical, and too outspoken for the solitary wanderer with his reed that Yeats would have us believe him.[36]

34. Lennox Robinson, "Journey's End," *Irish Literary Bulletin*, IX (October 1948), 166.

35. Sean O'Faolain, "AE and W.B.," *VQR*, XV (Winter 1937), 50.

36. See, for instance, Lady Gregory, "Synge," *English Review*, XIII (March 1913), 556–66, and Ann Saddlemyer, "Synge to MacKenna: the Mature Years," *Massachusetts Review*, V (Winter 1964), 279–96.

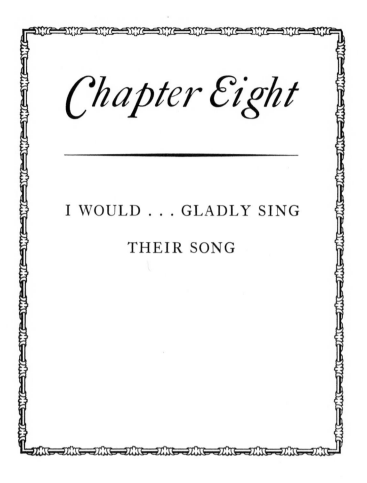

Chapter Eight

I WOULD . . . GLADLY SING

THEIR SONG

I

IN THIS CHAPTER it would be all too easy to drag in all things Augustan and Protestant from Yeats's poetry as blessed evidence of my preoccupations. But this would be to read Yeats as Yvor Winters has done, i.e., to read the poems as paraphrases of simple ideas.[1] Although such a reading might go some way to correct those critics who pass over the pictures in "Demon and Beast" as merely those of Irish worthies, who call "The Municipal

1. "The Poetry of W. B. Yeats," *The Dubliner*, No. 2, March 1962, pp. 7–33.

Gallery Revisited" too personal, or who find Robert Gregory's horsemanship adolescent, there is still another way of approaching the Augustan resonance of the verse. It was suggested by Yeats in an interview he granted the *Irish Times* when the announcement came that he had won the Nobel Prize. On the subject of Yeats's lyrics, the reporter recorded:

> Whenever he wrote a new poem, he said, he thought of it not only in relation to the [Anglo-Irish] literary movement, but also to his work as a whole. Sometimes he feels that his work needs a little more colour here, or a little more there; then he writes a poem to perfect the balance.
>
> For that reason, doubtless, Mr. Yeats never says that one of his lyrics is better than another. He thinks of his work as an artistic entity, which one suspects is not yet quite complete.
>
> The aim of all his work, he said, had been to perfect what he describes as the syntax of passionate speech. One ought to be able to declaim a lyric, he said, in a market square so that the people who heard it hardly would realise that they were not listening to prose. Wordsworth had broken new ground by his discovery of the vocabulary of such speech. Ernest Dowson, Lionel Johnson and himself—he, perhaps more consciously than the other two, for he was more of a philosopher—had striven to find its syntax.
>
> "Have you found it?" asked our representative. "Only within the last twelve or fourteen years," came the reply.[2]

The Georgian references, the Protestant point of view, the Anglo-Irish tone are frequently voiced in that syntax which we recognize as declamatory yet personal in poems like "The Tower" and "Blood and the Moon." But whether reference, point of view, or tone, this Augustan resonance is obviously a balancing part of Yeats's whole work from 1909–11 on. It may round out a single poem, it may join a number of poems in a single volume, or it may be a distinct element in the work as a whole. In any case, "the people to whom he belonged"—Yeats had thus described his Anglo-Irish background on

2. "Irish Poet Honoured," *Irish Times*, 15 November 1923.

the day of his Nobel Prize interview [3]—had not only a distinct patriotism but also a growing national importance in Yeats's verse, from the death of Synge on, second only to his devotion to the Irish folk.

Thus in blending his love of eighteenth-century Protestant Ireland with his many other passionate convictions, Yeats was also characteristically working from local, personal, subjective knowledge and feeling to something all men might understand. As he had early patterned his Sligo poems after the work of Allingham, the poet of Ballyshannon, so he could suggest to Belfastmen in 1931 that "if he were to see a Greek play in Belfast he would much sooner have it played with a good Belfast accent. Every man ought to feel, wherever he is, that his local idiom and his local interests are as good as any other idiom and any other interests." [4] The difficulty was that many of these Georgian references, like his local ones, might appear to be narrow or obscure to the reader outside Ireland. More than once we shall see Yeats generalizing or enlarging what was originally a highly local Protestant eighteenth-century reference from early drafts of his poetry. But if there is an occasional thrill of arrogance or pride in the public address of poems that ring out Yeats's Anglo-Irish patriotism, there is very little snobbery or condescension. One cannot imagine Yeats saying

> . . . there is an inexplicable gulf fixed between those of us who venerate the memory of King George the Fourth and those who hark farther back to King Laoghaire and his Dún.
>
> Politics or religion seem to have little or nothing to do with the nomenclature; it is rather a question of genteelness, a clinging to the memory of the old Castle days, those halcyon days when we had a Viceroy, not a President. [5]

Yet one can imagine Yeats looking back through Irish history in 1931 and even then recognizing the failure of the Anglo-Irish in the eighteenth century, their subsequent decline, and in the twentieth

---

3. " 'The Supernatural,' " *Irish Times*, 15 November 1923.
4. "Greek Play over Radio," *Irish Times*, 9 September 1931.
5. Lennox Robinson, *I Sometimes Think* (Dublin, 1956), p. 44.

century, after the Wyndham Land Act, their demise, yet nevertheless proclaiming:

> . . . their genius did not die out; they sent everywhere adminis-trators and military leaders, and now that their ruin has come—what resolute nation permits a strong alien class within its borders?—I would, remembering obscure ancestors that preached in their churches or fought beside their younger sons over half the world, and despite a famous passage of O'Grady's, gladly sing their song.[6]

This will be the sustaining note in Yeats's imaginative recall of a fading culture and its past glory. For all his fiercely critical use of the questioning Protestant mind that we have seen in scattered verses along the way so far, his final song of the Anglo-Irish nation is a melancholy one. If I had to sum up in a word the attitude or point of view that hovers over the predominant references to Georgian Ireland in Yeats's lyrics, the word would have to be elegiac.

II

Before the publication of *The Green Helmet and Other Poems* in 1910, Yeats had already come to use materials from eighteenth-century Ireland rather sparingly, yet in altogether characteristic ways. That is, he usually sentimentalizes Gaelic Ireland, say, a native priest, an old huntsman, or before him an Earl Paul, the survivor of Kinsale. At the same time, as suggested in Chapter One, there is often an air of ambiguity surrounding this material betokening his formal dislike of the English in the Ireland of that century, yet also something of a wistful admiration or covert liking for them.

In addition, his condemnation of his own class and its most illustrious period is seemingly all too visible in the unfinished novel "The Speckled Bird." Michael Hearne rejects the life of the Big House and even the beauty that so attracts him there. Again, in a later play, *Where There is Nothing*, Paul Ruttledge seeks desper-

6. *Wheels and Butterflies*, p. 14.

ately to escape from the "Colonel class," and so he does. In fact, the opening scenes are an outright attack on the Protestant and Unionist Ireland of the day, while the play itself is ultimately a call to a religion of the most disembodied sort. But Yeats took a decided dislike to the play and kept it out of his collected works. Its revised form, *The Unicorn from the Stars,* gives virtually no offense to Protestant Ireland. To what extent this change may be laid to Lady Gregory's influence is hard to say. However, Yeats once commented briefly on the difference by writing, "There is certainly much more of my own actual writing in *Where there is Nothing* [sic], but I feel that this new play belongs to my world and that it does not." [7]

Perhaps the best preparation for this uneasy hesitation in his poetry may be found as early as 1888 in Yeats's *John Sherman,* a novel he called his eighteenth-century romance.[8] While the narrative certainly plays over the nineteenth-century Sligo of his youth, the book is just as clearly about a town, or the memory of it, that still breathes the air of the eighteenth century. Howard the cleric and his friend John Sherman not only show Yeats's double nature but also his double view of Georgian Ireland. At one point, Howard, in Ballah (Sligo), asks Sherman: "Sherman, how do you stand this place? . . . Here everybody lives in the eighteenth century—the squalid century." [9] And yet it is to this life that Sherman vows to return from London. Yeats was even willing to make his character's identification more obvious in a letter to Katharine Tynan:

> Sherman belonged like Allingham to the small gentry who, in the West at any rate, love their native places without perhaps loving Ireland. They do not travel and are shut off from England by the whole breadth of Ireland, with the result that they are forced to make their native town their world.[10]

Beyond the hatred of London, all else in the book seemed confused to

7. *Letters,* p. 503.
8. *Ibid.,* p. 66.
9. *John Sherman, Collected Works in Verse & Prose* (Stratford-on-Avon, 1908), VII, 187.
10. *Letters,* p. 187.

Yeats. Yet, though the original of John Sherman was Henry Middleton, some of Sherman's confused love of Sligo is also a love of that which Yeats himself cannot clearly define. The squalid eighteenth century is somehow also part of an eighteenth-century romance.

"The Ballad of Father O'Hart" is a sentimental rendering of the good priest Father John done in by a Protestant shoneen to whom he had placed his lands in trust during Penal times. Undaunted, he goes his pious way, loved by all, until a saintly death overtakes him at the age of ninety-four. Even the birds mourn him. In a note to the poem Yeats remarked of the property taken from Father O'Hart, "These lines accurately record the tradition. No one who has held the stolen land has prospered. It has changed owners many times." [11] But Yeats's source, Father O'Rorke's account, directly contradicts him:

> The people have a notion that no family can prosper in Cloonamahon till the injustice done the bishop is repaired; but however one's sense of equity or of divine retribution may have started such an idea at first, when the evil-doer still held the ill-gotten goods, such an idea were only a vain imagination or silly superstition at the present day, when one hundred and fifty years have elapsed since the original wrong, and when the property has long passed, by fair and lawful process, into innocent hands.[12]

Yeats's clinging to a popular superstition, his refusal to name Father O'Hart an eventual bishop, and his added omission of the fact that the land was ultimately shared by, among others, the Coopers and the Ormsbys (distant relatives)—these are a poet's prerogatives. But in his later years, Yeats's reaching out for legends and myths of the eighteenth century will stay closer to fact and will tend to fix on the tragic, the brutal, and the unpopular. Still, even in this realm of the popular, Yeats makes it clear in another note that the incident of Father O'Hart's stolen lands was a rare instance of broken trust

11. *Variorum*, p. 93.

12. Rev. T. O'Rorke, *History, Antiquities, and Present State of the Parishes of Ballysadare and Kilvarnet* (Dublin, n.d.), pp. 209–10.

between eighteenth-century Protestants and Catholics in their efforts to circumvent the Penal code.[13] Yeats concedes to both sides.

Something of this vacillation between the popular opinion of the stranger and a less biased account may also be seen in the companion piece, "The Ballad of the Foxhunter." The poem is based on an incident from a sentimental novel, Kickham's *Knocknagow*, which Yeats came to dislike in later years. Our attention is drawn to the mournful death of an aged member of the gentry surrounded by his retainers, huntsman, and dogs. All too easily, a blind old hound, separated from the pack, holds a Wordsworthian "communion with his heart" and then howls out his master's moment of death. As Yeats presents this lingering reminder of the eighteenth century, the foxhunter might well be any ancient honored gentleman, Protestant or Catholic, whereas in Kickham's dreary novel, Old Somerfield, the master, as he is called, is a beloved Protestant landowner who is one of the few exceptions to Protestant villainy in the hamlet of Knocknagow. Yeats erases this distinction from his poem. On the other hand, the old man of the novel expires with his ugly granddaughters at his side; a sanctimonious prig from the Church of Ireland stands by to remind him that he is headed for "a better place," although the dying man expresses his doubts about that translation; and then a villainous son, Mr. Sam, gazes on his expiring parent with a look of pity and hatred. This bedeviler of the natives, we are told, had cleared the sunny hillside of its former worthy tenants. If that slope was pleasing to the dying man and his granddaughters, it was no less pleasing, we are assured, to the evicted tenants, the victims of Mr. Sam Somerfield's rapacity.[14] Protestant clergyman, grim son, and plain daughters also vanish in Yeats's ballad.

This matter of vacillation, which I am pushing rather hard, can also be seen on the other side. That is, native Gaelic Catholic Ireland can be shown in contrasting lights. In the much revised "Red

13. *Variorum*, p. 797.
14. *Knocknagow: or, The Homes of Tipperary* (Dublin, 1879), pp. 491–94.

Hanrahan's Song about Ireland," Yeats in later years declared he had rendered the fated tragic patriotism of peasant Ireland. In three stanzas we are faced with symbols from nature, respectively, a broken tree, thunder, and flood. These natural disasters are likened to the broken courage, the noisy feuds, and the emotional bondage to earth that have plagued the inherited patriotism of Celtic Ireland. Yet its confused adoration of the opposite ideals symbolized in the flame that withstands the wind, the calm and quiet composure, and the ethereal purity of Cathleen, the daughter of Houlihan, remains unchanged. Hanrahan, Yeats's own invention, was meant to represent this historical national character surviving into the eighteenth century.[15] On the other hand, "The Happy Townland," which first appeared almost ten years later than "Red Hanrahan's Song about Ireland," permits Yeats to expose more openly what seemed to him the flaw in that patriotism of the blood. He explained this poem, without making direct reference to that flaw, in 1926:

> What made Irish literature, as far as he could judge from what he had read, different from all others was just the way in which the other world overshadows it—sometimes Christian paradise and sometimes pagan paradise.
>
> He had always observed that songs that come from folk always went back to folk—it went back to the heart at once because it was pure emotion.
>
> The really overwhelming patriotism of Gaelic Catholic peasantry had been, he thought, sometimes influenced by thoughts of the other world, and that the thought of Ireland in a folk mind had got penetrated with an emotion that arose originally from what was perhaps the paradise of pagan Ireland, and was gradually changing into the paradise of Christian Ireland. To express this patriotism he read "The Song of Red Hanrahan."[16]

Yeats's hints on this occasion were to be the basis for outright admissions later on. The emphasis on emotion, the confusion of

15. "A Poet's Memories," *Freeman's Journal*, 26 January 1924.
16. "Plays and Poetry," *Irish Independent*, 25 February 1926.

paradises, and the mistaken pursuit of perfection in this world Yeats made explicit in 1937:

> As a child and as a young man I went into country cottages and heard stories of fairies and spirits. One woman told me that when she was in chapel a tall gray man sat beside her. She said "Where are you from?" and he said "From Tir-nan-ogue," which means the land of youth and is one of the names of fairyland. Many people are said to go to that land and never return. I describe such a journey in the poem which I am about to read. I called fairyland "the world's bane" because I thought of it as that ideal perfection which is the source of all hopeless longing and public tumult. I call the poem "The Happy Townland." [17]

He had long since found a more sophisticated idealism elsewhere.

III

In *The Green Helmet and Other Poems* and in *Responsibilities* the Gregory connection not only begins to assume an important role in Yeats's poetry but it presents a passionate protest and criticism that have the ring of indignation and scorn reminiscent of Swift. Much has been written of these two volumes. But we shall note this criticism and its source in the Gregory tradition only as preparatory to showing Yeats's later identification with eighteenth-century Anglo-Ireland.

First, the five poems in a cluster, "Upon a House shaken by the Land Agitation," "At the Abbey Theatre," "These are the Clouds," "At Galway Races," and "A Friend's Illness," deserve our attention. For each draws a subtle difference between the Gregorys or their kind and the average native patriot. The difference is one of the mind, specifically between the mind "Where passion and precision have been one," and the mind given to easy emotion. Not only does this line from the first poem mark the inhabitants of Coole House, it also

17. TS. of "My Own Poetry Again," BBC broadcast, 29 October 1937, 10.45–11.05 P.M. Even Yeats's note on the Country of the Young in his *Irish Fairy and Folk Tales* (Modern Library edition) associates it with "national trouble" (p. 214).

marks the aristocratic mind once accustomed to govern men and now to create "a written speech/Wrought of high laughter, loveliness and ease." The second poem defines this executive talent come to the aid of Irish literature as one capable of a high art which, nevertheless, is in touch with common things, an art able to mock common mockers also if need be. "These are the Clouds" puts the difference in terms of sun and clouds. The sun's flaring eye is fated to close as it drops to the horizon. The clouds will appear to obliterate it. They may well symbolize the Irish soul become vaporous with emotional national-ism, a soul Yeats described in *Estrangement*, XLV. But at that moment the diffused effulgence will give the sun—now that its race is run—its greatest majesty. The word "race" allows Yeats a pun by which to signify also aristocratic Anglo-Irish stock, exemplified by the Gregorys in general and Lady Gregory, her son and grandson, in particular. This concern with a dying race characterizes the tragic tone of many of Yeats's poems on Anglo-Ireland. Here a journal entry dated September 6, 1909, helps explain matters. It has already been quoted in another context:

> I thought of this house [Coole] slowly perpetuating itself & the life within it, in ever increasing intensity of labour, & then of its probably sinking away through courteous incompetence or rather sheer weakness of will for ability has not failed in young Gregory, and I said to myself 'Why is life a perpetual preparation for something that never happens?' Even as Odys-seus only seems a preparation to think of ruin or remembrance. Is it not always the tragedy of the great and the strong, that they see before the end the small & the weak, in friendship or in enmity, pushing them from their place, & marring what they have built, & doing one or the other in mere lightness of mind.[18]

Though the setting of the sun is inevitable, its departure may testify to its majesty. And so the Gregorys are attended in their going by the cloudy emotions of a weaker, humbler Ireland equated with the timorous commercial middle-class in "At Galway Races," Again,

18. Journal begun December 1908.

the contrast is between the "timid breath" of that class and the wild cry bursting from the Galway races and the horsemen for whom Yeats would prefer to write. They were part of the Gregory tradition; the art which "makes all of the one mind" would be Lady Gregory's and Yeats's continuation of that tradition. Perhaps Lady Gregory's soul in "A Friend's Illness" may then also have a familial dimension, though it is unstated, when Yeats weighs it against the world.

The critical tone, the syntax of personal address, the gaze into the past, the defiance of his contemporaries in these poems are sharpened in *Responsibilities*. There poems that look to Protestant Ireland have also a wider frame of reference. Yeats's touchstone includes not only the Gregory tradition but also Protestant names that had served Ireland from Wolfe Tone to Parnell, names in some cases touched by his own ancestral fortunes. Throughout these poems we are reminded of Yeats's anger at the methods employed to disparage Parnell, Synge, and Hugh Lane by their pious middle-class opponents. But these poems also contain severe criticisms of Protestant Ireland's diminished public spirit, perhaps more reason for Yeats's narrowing his enthusiasm to the eighteenth century. For at the height of the Gallery dispute, he was to remind the Irish aristocracy "that they had left the intellectual workers in Ireland to struggle alone." [19]

At any rate, in the opening poem of the volume, "Pardon, Old Fathers," Yeats almost self-consciously sorts out the princely virtues that have formed his art, all derived from merchants, scholars, soldiers, and irascible old men among his ancestors. His childhood imagination had summed them up in the phrase *"Only the wasteful virtues earn the sun."* The associations are telling. He names Jervis Yeats, trading from eighteenth-century Dublin and Galway; the Rev. John Yeats, Rector of Drumcliff and friend of Emmet; a Butler or Armstrong that fought at the Boyne; a Middleton given to instinctive acts recalling those of John Shawe-Taylor. Here, as with the Gregorys, Yeats has translated a tradition of heroic service into a tradition of literature: *"I have no child, I have nothing but a*

19. "Mr. G. B. Shaw and Cup Finals," *Manchester Guardian*, 15 July 1913, p. 10.

book,/Nothing but that to prove your blood and mine." The inference is that not only has Yeats's art opposed the new middle-class Ireland sprung up since Parnell's times, but that its blood source had always done so in times past.

That blood had been dishonored, so to speak, in the refusal of men like Sir Hutcheson Poë, Lord Ardilaun, and the Duke of Leinster to give more open-handedly towards the Gallery project. Hence "September 1913" holds up the Wild Geese, Fitzgerald, Emmet, and Tone as men "of a different kind" from those "born to pray and save" to whom modern Irish aristocrats had looked to decide their benefactions. However, the brunt of the attack is borne by those who fumbled for small change by the light of a holy candle, a class only recently come alive as a national force. The contrast between their leader, William Martin Murphy, and Hugh Lane is elaborated in the wider difference between, on the one hand, Catholic and Protestant patriots from Sarsfield to Emmet and, on the other, those modern patriots since the death of O'Leary. Delirious bravery confronts pious money-grubbing, romance is displaced by narrow sense, human magnanimity contrasts with animality, just as Lane's single-minded devotion to Irish art is set against Murphy's confused devotion to religion and business. Though Yeats grants Paudeen his reprieve in the poem "Paudeen," he does so in solitude and in God's eye.

These last are important, for already in "September 1913," Yeats had begun to broach the theme of Anglo-Irish solitude in the "loneliness and pain" surrounding the patriots of that poem. Then, "To a Friend whose Work has come to Nothing," a poem written to Lady Gregory about Hugh Lane, establishes a scornful incompatibility between the Gregory pursuit of honor and the middle-class Irish pursuit of success. Thus the Anglo-Irish ideal becomes one of difficult, secret, isolated exultation. Yeats was to call the Anglo-Irish the salt of the earth some years later; he would see the young Constance Gore-Booth as a bird poised for flight above an unruly sea; he would come to hail an ancient heroism resurrected among those who worked in the offices of converted grey Georgian houses. But here in the next poem, "To a Shade," these symbols—salt, sea bird, and grey Georgian house—maintain the attributes of another ghost of Protestant greatness, Parnell, happy not to contemplate his monument but

> To drink of that salt breath out of the sea
> When grey gulls flit about instead of men,
> And the gaunt houses put on majesty:
> Let these content you and be gone again
> For they are at their old tricks yet.

In the next lines the tie is made between Lane and Parnell. In their passionate service to the nation, in Lane's proffered gifts of sweetness and light—"loftier thought . . . sweeter emotion"—had lain Ireland's future, yet the pack had been set on both, leaving one a restive spirit, the other virtually exiled in disgrace. Solitude, isolation, rejection now begin to sharpen that difference between the two Irelands introduced in the *Green Helmet*.

Having opened this volume, however, with an ancestral tapestry of doughty Protestants, Yeats concludes with a poem flouting his self-described notoriety. In the poem "Friends" he had complimented Lady Gregory on her intellectual equanimity in the face of unceasing cares and troubles. Now he looks to Coole House. But in a companion poem, "An Appointment," he cleverly employs a wild squirrel to concentrate the verve, the proud and delighted boldness, the fierce presence of mind that he had discovered in Hugh Lane. Hence in the last poem, "While I, from that reed-throated whisperer," Yeats very nearly rusticates himself from urban Irish life in the midst of one of the famous woods of Coole, Kyle-na-no. This wood, noted for its squirrels, suggests their wild, instinctive passion for life and then its proper accompaniments—"A sterner conscience and a friendlier home"—beneath the roof at Coole. The tribute is fitting for an ancient house "Where passion and precision have been one." Thus far have Yeats's responsibilities to public events, family memories, and aristocratic friends taken him along the path to Georgian Ireland.

IV

A number of poems in *The Wild Swans at Coole* and *Michael Robartes and the Dancer* flash before the reader the lingering pertinence of that Georgian past. Perhaps the best example of this historical idealism generalized is found in "The Wild Swans at Coole." Beauty, passion, coldness, and conquest are gathered together in the symbol of the swans. They and the Gregorys, like a class set apart in nature, are the center of the world of earth, water, and sky now in its autumn and twilight. Moreover, as I have already pointed out, a mood—still, silent, mysterious—hangs over the scene and betokens a glimpse of a permanence that contrasts with the speaker's melancholy aging. In fact the poet may well be asking at the end not merely what manner of men will continue the traditions of Coole but also what depths of spirit, what lakes of the soul, and what astral reaches of imperishable dream will remain to sustain aristocratic patterns of wild and vigorous life. Passionate and cold, these masterful creatures may *choose* a different habitat.

This glorification of the Gregory tradition takes many human forms in these two volumes. Robert Gregory is the obvious example. "Reprisals" puts him in the Gregory line of improving, conscientious landlords lauded by Arthur Young. "In Memory of Major Robert Gregory" holds up the ideal Galway gentleman impaired only by the discourtesy of death. The added mention of art, Castle Taylor, and Roxborough also establishes the whole Gregory connection discussed in Chapter Two. His authority in architecture harks back to the eighteenth-century gentleman's gift long lost in our day. "Shepherd and Goatherd" had pointed to his solitude in country rounds. But to point up a quality of mind given special notice in these two volumes, a second look at "An Irish Airman Foresees his Death" is in order.

We have already seen Yeats use this poem as an example of the patriotism of Protestant Ireland. It was the element of choice, arising from an impulse of delight, rather than any law or duty that was the essence of Gregory's patriotism. But it is the relationship between

delight and election that is the ultimate eighteenth-century refinement of that patriotism. A passage from the Berkeley essay is the best
introduction to this point:

> In the *Commonplace Book* alone is Berkeley always sincere, and
> there I find in paragraph 639, 'Complacency seems rather
> to . . . constitute the essence of volition,' which seems what an
> Irish poet meant who sang to some girl 'A joy within guides
> you,' and what I meant when I wrote 'An aimless joy is a pure
> joy.' Berkeley must have been familiar with Archbishop King's
> *De Origine Mali* which makes all joy depend 'upon the act of
> the agent himself, and his election'; not upon an external object.
> The greater the purity the greater the joy.[20]

A great part of King's book is devoted to this relation between an
agent, election, and joy. Aside from Yeats's brief quotation, a passage
like the following is highly representative of King's theory that
happiness depends not upon external objects but on the agent's own
election, especially

> . . . in an *active* Power, the very Nature of which is to *make* an
> object agreeable to itself, *i.e.* good, by its own proper act. For
> here the Goodness of the Object does not precede the act of
> Election, so as to excite it, but Election makes the Goodness in
> the Object; that is, the thing is agreeable because chosen, and not
> chosen because agreeable: We cannot therefore justly enquire
> after any other cause of Election than the Power itself.[21]

Thus a fully considered choice between poised or balanced alterna-
tives marks the purity of the self-possessed, self-delighting mind.
Hence Yeats may write of Robert Gregory:

> I balanced all, brought all to mind,
> The years to come seemed waste of breath,
> A waste of breath the years behind
> In balance with this life, this death.

20. "Bishop Berkeley," *Essays and Introductions*, p. 408, n. 1. "An aimless
joy is a pure joy" is from the poem "Tom O'Roughley."
21. *An Essay on the Origin of Evil*, ed. Edmund Law, 2nd ed. (London,
1732), II, 279–80. Yeats liked to remember that his great-great-grandmother
had been a friend of Archbishop King (*Wheels and Butterflies*, p. 7).

Gregory's choice of a likely death that would engage his entire self—
as "an *active* Power"—made that death both good and joyous. For
Gregory the Anglo-Irishman, *dulce et decorum est pro patria mori*
did not exist before his election.

"The Fisherman" provides another human instance of several of
the wild swans' traits. Commenting on this poem much later, Yeats
said

> In later life I was not satisfied with these simple emotions
> [the emotions found in poems like "Down by the Salley
> Gardens" and "The Fiddler of Dooney"]—though I tried, and
> still try, to put the natural words in the natural order. I had
> founded Irish literary societies, an Irish Theatre, I had become
> associated with the projects of others, I had met much unreason-
> able opposition. To overcome it I had to make my thoughts
> modern. Modern thought is not simple; I became argumenta-
> tive, passionate, bitter; when I was very bitter I used to say to
> myself, 'I do not write for these people who attack everything
> that I value, not for those others who are lukewarm friends, I
> am writing for a man I have never seen.' I built up in my mind
> the picture of a man who lived in the country where I had lived,
> who fished in mountain streams where I had fished; I said to
> myself, 'I do not know whether he is born yet, but born or
> unborn it is for him I write.' I made this poem about him; it is
> called "The Fisherman.". . .[22]

For all of his freckles and Connemara cloth, this idealized sportsman
is certainly a racial portrait. In fact it stands opposed to the Ireland
that Yeats had to face. The opposition is caught in the lines "my own
race/And the reality." Such a man would appreciate the combination
of passion and coldness. Such a man stands as a living criticism of the
middle-class Irish nationalist that Yeats rejects. The Protestant
ability to choose or criticize freely is also implied in Yeats's scorn of
that other audience. But most important seems the fact that the
fisherman is such a man as would climb

22. "The Growth of a Poet," *The Spoken Word*, ed. Richard Church
(London, 1955), pp. 76–81. This *Listener* piece is dated 4 April 1934 at the
end of the text.

> . . . up to a place
> Where stone is dark under froth,
> And the down-turn of his wrist
> When the flies drop in the stream.

A man who climbs to a high place, where there is stone beneath froth, probably ascends very near the source of the stream, is attracted to truth rather than opinion, as Lane and Shawe-Taylor had been. His wrist also demonstrates control. And the cold stream is presumably his chosen element. This composite country figure in its isolation, command, and skill rebukes the city audience described as common, cowardly, drunken, ignorant, and insolent.

The vanishing of control, the denial of election, the refusal to fish the sources of life's stream, the sting of the common, bitter wind are lamented in these two volumes. "Easter 1916" finds lowly clerks through their sacrifices restoring glory to the "grey/Eighteenth-century houses" dwindled to offices. O'Connell's politics of mobs and comedy have transformed the nation only by becoming individual and tragic. Lacking wisdom, the revolutionists may be regarded as children yet they are also gloriously dead. But Yeats has most trouble with the heart of stone in the living stream and the excessive love of country that can addle men's wits. For heart of stone and vaporous soul go together. Both, of course, derive from that patriotism of fate, sought perfection, and pure emotion that Yeats had conferred on Gaelic Catholic Ireland in "Red Hanrahan's Song about Ireland." The beauty born is indeed terrible. No less, in "The Second Coming" a first image will show a loss of control and another a refusal of choice in the best men. Moreover, sixteen dead men may now be one with Lord Edward and Wolfe Tone, but a lady that lived went on to "conspire among the ignorant." She, Constance Markievicz, is pictured as a young beauty in a Georgian setting, a white bird above the mob—the stormy sea—in "On a Political Prisoner."

> When long ago I saw her ride
> Under Ben Bulben to the meet,
> The beauty of her country-side
> With all youth's lonely wildness stirred,

She seemed to have grown clean and sweet
Like any rock-bred, sea-borne bird:

Sea-borne, or balanced on the air
When first it sprang out of the nest
Upon some lofty rock to stare
Upon the cloudy canopy,
While under its storm-beaten breast
Cried out the hollows of the sea.

As Yeats once said of this poem: "In the lines of the poem which condemn her politics I was not thinking of her part in two rebellions but of other matters of quarrel." [23] Most likely the "other matters," as in "In Memory of Eva Gore-Booth and Con Markiewicz," are her desertion of that quality, visionary or intellectual or cultural, which Yeats describes in the young bird. She had forgotten that Anglo-Irish solitude, like the solitude of the student's lamp and the tomb in the next poem, "The Leaders of the Crowd." Or she may even be said to have forgotten that waterfall on the side of Ben Bulben, dear to Yeats in the next poem in the sequence, "Towards Break of Day." So far as one can make out, that waterfall finally ends in Lissadell as a beautiful stream which then takes its way to the sea. In a sense, then, and again I am looking ahead, Yeats may be suggesting in these three poems that Madame Markievicz turned her back on the source of that lofty stream, and refused to seek truth as did the fisherman and as will his poetical heirs in "The Tower." [24] Finally, one associates all that delirium, bewilderment, and indifference, that seemed to leave an incompleteness in the wake of the Rising, with the vaporous clouds and resounding hollows from which the bird stands aloof. To be balanced in the air, poised, bred in high place, and sweet-minded is to be much closer to the swans, airman, and fisherman who symbolize

23. TS. of "Poems about Women," BBC broadcast, 10 April 1932, 9.05–9.30 P.M.
24. See the description of that stream in Rev. T. O'Rorke, *History of Sligo: Town and County* (Dublin [1889]), II, 12–13.

the ideals of these volumes. So too Constance had seemed in the Georgian setting of Lissadell.

Yet even there a "raving autumn," like the "bitter wind" that threatened the shutters in the poem "In Memory of Major Robert Gregory," has forced a change: the revolutionary blast blights and destroys the delicate beauty of aristocratic culture. That same wind also blows over the stormy sea in "On a Political Prisoner," helps loose the anarchy of "The Second Coming," confounds and confuses in "Easter 1916," and presages the murderous years ahead in the poem that most animates the memory of Georgian Ireland in these two volumes, "A Prayer for my Daughter."

In "Demon and Beast" Yeats had characterized the mind freed from hatred and desire as at one with God: "I saw my freedom won/And all laugh in the sun." At such a moment personifications of the contending forces in Irish history seem to be resolved, understood, even blessed: Father Luke Wadding, a zealous partisan of the Gaelic Ireland defeated at Kinsale; the Ormondes, great Anglo-Irish bearers of the Butler name; and the Earl of Strafford, who virtually enslaved Ireland to save an English crown. The poet's "aimless joy" may win no momentary victories as did these Caesars of seventeenth-century Ireland but it can sympathetically comprehend their ambitions. Yeats's dearest thought in "Demon and Beast" is to protract such a sweetness. He finds his answer in the self-delighting denials of St. Anthony. But in "A Prayer for my Daughter" self-delight, while following upon a purgation of hatred, will be fostered by aristocratic custom and ceremony rather than the more negative tradition of religious asceticism. In making the continued beauty and innocence of the soul the object of his prayer, Yeats meditates courtesy, custom, ceremony, and tradition as divine safeguards against the world of 1919 in which the poem was written.

That world of social anarchy and personal willfulness had foreshadowed the coming of antichrist in "The Second Coming." Here, in Yeats's prayer against anarchy and willfulness, these forces combine in the symbolic "haystack- and roof-levelling wind/Bred on the Atlantic," that revolutionary wind which had begun to sweep the North Atlantic community at the end of the eighteenth century and passed into a greater storm after 1917. Yeats had questioned Johnson, a leader of the Irish labor movement, whether that wind, urban in origin, would split the Ireland of landlord and peasant, haystack and roof. The metaphoric opening of the poem also poses a tradition and an eminence—"Gregory's wood and one bare hill"—as the barriers to the revolutionary wind bred in murderous mobs and multitudes. In some sense, too, his daughter in her cradle must share something of the best of that tradition come from the rocking cradle of two thousand years before in "The Second Coming." In any case, that wood, the characteristic hardy reminder of the Protestant planters that protected delicate shrubs and greenery, cultivated earth and great house, is now symbolic of the tradition at Coole that might stand between those leveling winds of revolutionary doctrine and the mind of Anne Yeats. The wind also shrieks through the rest of the symbolic landscape, through a bridge, against the tower, among lesser trees, the elms that nevertheless stand above the flood. Hence, having established his landscape of good and evil spirits, Yeats is now free to picture the personal qualities of mind and person he would have bestowed on his daughter.

They are delicately Georgian. First he asks that a beauty be given her that will not hinder choice in herself or in him who might choose her. Helen and Aphrodite (Maud Gonne and Iseult?) had been incapacitated by their beauty. Yeats is setting beauty as an end in itself against beauty that adorns a mind human, courteous, magnanimous, ultimately joyous in its election. The Gregory wood and Coole itself allow the extended figure of the "flourishing hidden tree" or "green laurel/Rooted in one dear perpetual place." The personal and social ideals are joined, just as their opposites, leveling anarchy and hate-ridden, opinionated revolutionary, are joined in the figures of storm and "an old bellows full of angry wind."

The ideal of Protestant patriotism now takes a gentler form that seems no less inspired by Archbishop King and by Robert Gregory's example, for all the democratic overtones of Emerson's essay "Self-Reliance"[25] in the poem. Hatred absent, beauty and desire not ends in themselves, the soul's endeavors become God's, its choices free:

> Considering that, all hatred driven hence,
> The soul recovers radical innocence
> And learns at last that it is self-delighting,
> Self-appeasing, self-affrighting,
> And that its own sweet will is Heaven's will;
> She can, though every face should scowl
> And every windy quarter howl
> Or every bellows burst, be happy still.

This is an ideal. The only enemy becomes time. The last stanza envisions a bridegroom to lead his daughter "to a house/Where all's accustomed, ceremonious." Yeats's hope then turns to a future birth of "innocence and beauty," amid art and aristocracy. One such house and birth he was to recall was Lissadell, from which the "innocent and the beautiful" had departed to the premature ravages of time. Yet Anne had her father's wish, like Stella's words upon the window-pane, to remind her of the more enduring beauty of the heart, the mind, and the soul:

> You taught how I might youth prolong
> By knowing what is right and wrong;
> How from my heart to bring supplies
> Of lustre to my fading eyes;
> How soon a beauteous mind repairs
> The loss of chang'd or falling hairs;
> How wit and virtue from within
> Can spread a smoothness o'er the skin.

From very far away in time, then, a feminine ideal, a Protestant patriotism, and an intellectual nationalism shine out over the troubled world of 1919 from Coole, the Tower, and, later, from Lissadell.

25. I am indebted to my colleague Professor Harrison Hayford for this suggestion.

V

The Tower and *The Winding Stair and Other Poems* also stand together, for our purposes, as companion volumes. Here, more than in any other volumes, Yeats relies on Georgian or Norman memorials —the Tower, Coole, Lissadell, Swift's tomb—to embody his deepest feelings on almost every subject that gripped him: Ireland, art, the soul, old age, the afterlife, and so on. That master symbol, the Tower, is most important here. Yet the poem of that title has received almost no critical consideration.

Instead of the Freudian clichés or vague talk about the poet of Anglo-Ireland usually applied to this poem, a statement on a tower symbol by Yeats himself may be the best introduction to the kind of historical interpretation I have in mind:

> I don't think a man has any right to invent his own symbols.
> . . . Maeterlinck, for instance, takes a tower as a symbol of the
> spiritual nature, and he has people going up in the tower and
> falling out of it, and so forth. He invented that symbol. He did
> not take it from the life and traditions of the people. Wagner,
> on the other hand, draws his symbols,—as in 'Parsifal'—from
> things that have been in the very blood of Europe for centu-
> ries.[26]

Thus in "The Tower," perhaps as public, declarative, and proprietary a poem as Yeats ever wrote, we find "the mind looking outward upon men and things," as he once said of Shelley's towers.[27] Moreover, the poet's eye, gazing out over the past, present, and future days come to life before the Tower, virtually demands recognition of its Irish, ultimately its European, focus.

A Burke or De Burgo castle, the Tower was more than likely built during the fourteenth century. There is record of an Edmond Mc

26. Interview with Kate Carew, *The World* (New York), 22 November 1903, p. M3.
27. "The Philosophy of Shelley's Poetry," *Essays and Introductions*, p. 87.

Ulick Burke living in Castle Ballylee—Ballylee being the name of the townland in the parish and barony of Kiltartan—in 1585. His death in 1597 is recorded by the Four Masters. Richard, Earl of Clanrickarde, possessed the castle in 1617. Although we are not sure when it ceased to be a Burke residence, a Talbot was a Burke tenant there just prior to 1783—according to the Irish Registry of Deeds— the year the property became part of the Gregory estate. Patrick Carrig, more than likely the fabulous bankrupt, was the tenant of the castle in 1837.[28] It may have suited his extravagance, since a bailiff from Galway would almost surely have had to cross water—not permitted—in order to apprehend him. Yeats mentions his other dodges in notes to the poem. In any case, slightly before his time, Mrs. French, an O'Brien and grandmother of Sir Jonah Barrington, lived in near-by Peterswell. The dastardly deed of the clipped ears occurred in 1778.[29] Needless to say, Raftery and Mary Hines flourished later. The peasant beauty died in the 1840's, and the blind poet, born in 1784 at Killeadan, not far from Kiltimagh, Co. Mayo, died on Christmas Eve, 1835, and was buried at Killeenan, near Craughwell, Co. Galway.[30] Yeats, with Douglas Hyde, created the historical character Hanrahan and was once quoted as saying that he "had invented an 18th century Irish poet, who had lived in the most

28. See *The School Manuscripts* (in possession of the Irish Folklore Commission), XLVII, 89; Samuel Lewis, *A Topographical Dictionary of Ireland* (London, 1837), II, 211; "Letters . . . relative to the Antiquities of the County of Galway," *Ordnance Survey for 1839*, ed. the Rev. M. O'Flanagan (Bray, 1928), II, 95, 157, 208–10; Richard Griffith, "Union of Gort," *General Valuation of Rateable Property in Ireland* (Dublin, 1855), II (1856), 54; *The Compossicion Booke of Connought*, transcribed by A. Martin Freeman (Dublin, 1936), p. 31. See also Fahey, *The History and Antiquities of the Diocese of Kilmacduagh*, pp. 199,n. 4, 214, 247–48, 326, and 355.

29. Yeats took his account from the Every Irishman's Library volume, *Recollections of Jonah Barrington*, with an Introduction by George Birmingham (Dublin, n.d.), pp. 30–31. Mrs. Yeats read to him from this volume during the early 1920's. However, he first mentions the *Recollections* in *Irish Fairy and Folk Tales*, p. 351.

30. Douglas Hyde, *Songs Ascribed to Raftery* (Dublin, 1903), pp. 15–17, and Lady Gregory, *Poets and Dreamers* (Dublin, 1903), pp. 1–46. See also Lord Killanin, "Literary Tour of Connaught," *The Galway Reader*, I (Spring 1949), 20–21.

disreputable part of the town of Sligo at that time." [31] Later, of course, with Lady Gregory's aid, Hanrahan got translated to Galway. Yeats purchased Castle Ballylee from the Congested Districts Board in April 1917. He constructs his poetic tower from the universal force and energy latent in all these local facts.

Though Yeats chose to sound the Norman and Anglo-Irish names most in "The Tower," the poem still owes much of its lilt to the place given Raftery and Mary Hines of living memory in Galway. According to Gogarty, Yeats bought the Tower partly "because of its associations with the wandering blind man, the poet, Raftery, who wrote of that 'calm and easy woman, Mary Hines,' who lived beside it. He [Yeats] loved that line." [32] The tie between tragedy, beauty, art, and practical country affairs may also have overwhelmed Yeats in the stories that grew up about her. In one way, too, Yeats is about something of the same task that was the poet Raftery's, at least as Lady Gregory saw it in 1899 while describing Mary Hines: "She must have been beautiful, for her beauty is still remembered; but some say 'it was the poet that made her so handsome,' and some that 'whatever she was, he made twice as much of it.' " [33] Douglas Hyde's account of her makes the usual identification with Helen, mentions that a county gentleman fell in love with her, abandoned her, and left her to die in poverty just before the Famine. He adds that one old woman had said of her, "The sun nor the moon never saw anything as fine as she." [34] Of course this is much like Yeats's account. He himself had long meditated these native materials from as early as the time of his essay " 'Death hath closed Helen's Eye,' " which reads like a prose gloss to the lines devoted to Raftery and Mary Hines. However, the sentence that closed the 1900 version of this

31. "A Poet's Memories," *Freeman's Journal*, 26 January 1924. See also Wade, *A Bibliography of the Writings of W. B. Yeats*, 2nd rev. ed. (London, 1958), p. 72.

32. "Yeats: The Man and the Poet," *Irish Digest*, III (April 1939), 15–16.

33. Lady Gregory, "Raftery, the Poet of the Poor," *Tuam Herald*, 28 October 1899.

34. *Songs Ascribed to Raftery*, pp. 327, 329. In *Autobiographies*, p. 561, Yeats noted that she had been "the mistress of a small local landed proprietor."

piece is worth remembering: "It may be that in a few years Fable, who changes mortalities to immortalities in her cauldron, will have changed Mary Hynes and Raftery to perfect symbols of the sorrow of beauty and of the magnificence and penury of dreams." [35]

Earlier in the same essay Yeats made another connection between his art and the life around the Tower, when he wrote, "These poor countrymen and countrywomen in their beliefs, and in their emotions, are many years nearer to that old Greek world, *that set beauty beside the fountain of things,* than are our men of learning." [36] Thus, though we may seem to have wandered from the subject of Yeats and Georgian Ireland, we must see the poem as joining beauty and dream to sorrow and magnificence and, in no less degree, to the elemental behavior of men. This last, taken in its more intellectual, rigorous forms, usually means history, religion, and politics in Ireland. Discussing Raftery's songs, Lady Gregory shrewdly said of them: "It is hard to say where history ends in them and religion and politics begin; for history, religion, and politics grow on one stem in Ireland, an eternal trefoil." [37] "The Tower," then, would seem to come to this: Yeats relumes a fabulous Anglo-Irish past that is both the source and result of his own imagination. Then, looking to the future, he further solidifies this imaginative bond with the past, by writing out his will and declaring his faith, both derived from that past. Obviously past, present, and future become one, but so too do history, politics, and religion if one may call fable history, the pride of choice politics, and the identity of man's creativity with God's, religion. Moreover, although a trifle extended, the social world is essentially Anglo-Irish, usually Georgian. For, aside from the Norman men-at-arms, the society dreamed forth is that of Protestant patriot, flamboyant landlord, half-mounted gentry, wandering Gaelic poets, and peasant beauty in a world that came to an end in Ireland about the time Raftery died and Victoria took the throne. The laughing arrogance of Barrington, the cold pride of Burke and Grattan, the

35. *Mythologies,* p. 30.
36. *Ibid.,* p. 28. Italics mine.
37. *Poets and Dreamers* (London, 1903), p. 10.

power of choice given to Protestants, and the spiritual convictions of Berkeley imaginatively interpreted are mingled with the tragic beauty, song, and emotion of a depressed Gaelic Ireland, while both nations, the moon and sun become one, are held in the stony form and severity of the first Anglo-Irish, the Normans and their towers.

The great difficulty of the poem is its mesmeric effect. History and fable, Protestant Ireland and Catholic Ireland, thought and emotion, sun and moon, past and future, reality and imagination blend fantastically into each other. Yeats succeeds almost too well in making his reader delightfully mad. Once, apropos of Ballylee, he wrote in the margin of Bergson's *Matter and Memory:* "When I try to recall (say) Ballylee I find that the less abstract the forms are the more they have an *hallucinatory* element of form or colour. The hallucination must be Bergson's perception." [38] This observation had followed upon Bergson's statement:

> Our perceptions are undoubtedly interlaced with memories, and inversely, a memory, as we shall show later, only becomes actual by borrowing the body of some perception into which it slips. These two acts, perception and recollection, always interpenetrate each other. . . . they [psychologists] will have it that these mixed states, compounded, in unequal proportions, of pure perception and pure memory, are simple. And so we are condemned to an ignorance alike of pure memory and of pure perception; to knowing only a single kind of phenomenon. . . . [39]

Then, on the next page, Yeats underlined most of the following passage:

> But, for realism as for idealism, perceptions are 'veridical hallucinations,' states of the subject, projected outside himself; and the two doctrines differ merely in this: that in the one these states constitute reality, in the other they are sent forth to unite with it. [40]

38. Bergson, *Matter and Memory*, trans. Nancy Margaret Paul and W. Scott Palmer (London, 1912), p. 72.
39. *Ibid.*
40. *Ibid.*, p. 73.

Something like this blend of perception and memory marks the stream of verse in "The Tower." But the balance would seem to be Berkeley's in that realism and idealism combine content and form to effect an hallucination of subject and object, the poet's mind reaching out to the world outside the Tower.

The first section of the poem prepares us for Yeats's wildly imaginative summons to ear and eye by his pretending to abandon the poetic particulars of youth for the more proper philosophical abstractions of old age. If it is impossible to sum up this mocking but deadly serious stanza, a reader can nevertheless sense the irony of an introduction that promises abstract thought as the counter to the ravages of time only to find himself delivered instead into a highly imaginative world of tragedy, love, bloodshed, cunning, and personal testimony. Perhaps even more stupendous is the poem's concluding stanza; for once again Yeats's promises to refine his soul by "Compelling it to study/In a learned school." Yet everywhere else in the poem the soul has already triumphed through the imagination's substantial triumph over time.

Hence, in the second section, Yeats literally gazes out upon the stone foundations of the Tower and then upon a near-by tree and, imaginatively, upon the historical foundations: all those, from the Normans on, who had lived within sight or sound. He will question them all. As we have come to expect, the time is twilight, a time not only consistent with the poet's age and the decline of the Protestant Ireland that he represents but also with his wish to make moon and sunlight one, to madly defy that inexorable logic of old age, Protestant declension, and nature herself through art.

In the half-light of this substantial insubstantial Yeats first calls up Mrs. French. If we remember the source of her lines, the chapter "Irish Gentry and their Retainers" in Barrington's *Recollections*, the gist becomes more obvious. For the chapter purports to show "the numerous and remarkable instances . . . of mutual attachment between the Irish peasantry and their landlords in former times." [41] So deep in fact was the relationship, that a chance mention of a wish that

41. *Recollections of Jonah Barrington*, p. 29.

an insolent farmer have his ears docked was taken for an absolute command, the fancy resulted in the deed. Barrington's prose holds up an ideal of service and rapport that can take a lady's chance remark as a real command. However, Yeats, for all the jocularity of his stanza, offers us something more, a Mrs. French "gifted with so fine an ear." The pun refers to the bloody ears and also to her drunken servant's inner ear, so to speak. He can indeed "divine/That most respected lady's every wish," especially in the midst of emblazoned darkness—candlelight, silver, wine, and mahogany—the ritual of eighteenth-century life at its zenith, its moment of hospitality and service. This fantastic quality of imaginative service and fealty that can divine in the offhand remark what is nevertheless the *true* wish puts Yeats's lines a pace beyond his source. The real and the illusory are joined, perhaps drunkenly, brutally, even madly, but also divinely.

That power is conferred on Raftery in the next few stanzas. Here the imagination works on ear and eye. Like feudal loyalty, the song celebrating the peasant beauty, with the help of a bit of drink like the wine at Mrs. French's table, made men confuse sight and fancy, sun and moonlight as if they were mad. Hanrahan too pursued a phantom of desire and so gladly lost the world in his mad chase. These wasteful virtues—madness to mankind—include a bankruptcy which like a splendid lechery, enchanting song, or divine ear can rouse a man's wits to actions that grow fabulous in living memory. Like all the creatures mentioned so far—Mrs. French and her gifted servant, Raftery, Hanrahan—this figure right out of Jonah Barrington—"old, necessitous, half-mounted man" [42]—contests imaginatively

42. Well known is Barrington's description of the Irish gentry during the time of *Castle Rackrent*, beginning

In those days, then, the common people ideally separated the gentry of the country into three classes, and treated each class according to the relative degree of respect to which they considered it was entitled.
They generally divided them thus:—
1. *Half-mounted* gentlemen.
2. Gentlemen every *inch of them.*
3. Gentlemen to the *backbone* (*Recollections*, p. 90).

Barrington adds, in regard to the traditional duty of half-mounted gentlemen keeping order at public meetings: "A shout of merriment was always set up when

with the world as does Yeats, harried by old age rather than debts but no less a tormented dog:

> There's not a neighbour left to say
> When he finished his dog's day:
> An ancient bankrupt master of this house.

The last, the most ancient memories, are of armed men at their equally wasteful tasks, the Norman ghosts clad for warfare or violating sleeping eye and ear with their dicing. Then all are summoned, as if immured in the Tower walls themselves: arrogant, class-conscious gentry with their murderous servants; blind poet, his bewitching song and drowned victim; drunken, wandering, impulsive lecher and poet; cunning, ruined, artful ancient bankrupt; and legendary Norman soldiery and those fighting men come after them.

The question on old age requires no answer. Yeats then addresses his second question to Hanrahan, his epitome of Gaelic Ireland, now an authority on sexual love (did Yeats have the reaction to his Divorce Speech in mind?). Questioning Hanrahan, he questions himself. Hanrahan had turned from the challenge of Echtge; Yeats implies that he himself had also turned from such a woman. And now the thought can drive *him* mad. Thus this section ends with Yeats an heir, in the superior bewilderment of old age and lost love, to all those violent, maddened, tragic, harried creatures come faintly and impatiently from Anglo-Irish cultures of more turbulent ages. Raging against old age, he is imaginatively and sensuously one of them.

He is even more so intellectually, that is in matters of politics and religion, will and faith. For he wills the pride of choice and country he had discovered in the leaders of eighteenth-century Protestant Ireland to young men like his ideal fisherman. They too will go to the source of things. The image of pure impulsive delight, the leaping fountain, is augmented by the bursting dawn—signifying a

---

a half-mounted gentleman knocked down an interloper; and some of the *poets* present, if they had an opportunity, roared out their verses by way of a song to encourage the gentlemen" (p. 91). So, perhaps, Yeats sings his approval of his imaginative half-mounted predecessor.

hope not contained in the usual twilight dim of Protestant Ireland. There may even be a slight pun in the lines

> Drop their cast at the side
> Of dripping stone

since Yeats would hope that the ideal Protestant or heir to the choice of Protestant patriotism would drop any class exclusiveness in turning to the basic facts of Ireland's stream of history. In any case, Yeats offers such men a pride that follows upon that century and its leaders like Burke and Grattan who threw in their lot with Ireland. As is well known, a passage from his hated Divorce Speech points up that pride, that patriotism, and that tradition in Ireland. The tone is one of bitter disappointment, not snobbery:

> I think it is tragic that within three years of this country gaining its independence we should be discussing a measure which a minority of this nation considers to be grossly oppressive. I am proud to consider myself a typical man of that minority. We against whom you have done this thing are no petty people. We are one of the great stocks of Europe. We are the people of Burke; we are the people of Grattan; we are the people of Swift, the people of Emmet, the people of Parnell. We have created the most of the modern literature of this country. We have created the best of its political intelligence.[43]

Bound neither to England nor to the inherited cause of Gaelic Ireland, free to refuse either side, these gave for Ireland. There is a pride of Protestant intellect Yeats voices in his speech that is carefully amplified in the succeeding lines of this section of "The Tower." It is the pride of life, that of glorious morning, the gallantry of a lost cause, life-giving rain, the soul with its eye on eternity. Nor is this pride simply a matter of class; rather it denotes public service, family, and political voice, perhaps the voice of an appointed Senator in the parliament of a new state, a Senator looking back to Grattan's Parliament and expressing himself forthrightly on his pride of

43. *Senate Speeches*, p. 99.

position as did a member of that parliament whom Yeats had read. Here are Barrington's words:

> The day on which I first took my seat in the Irish Parliament for the city of Tuam I still reflect on as one of the most gratifying of my life. . . . I almost fancied, as I entered the House, that I could see my forefathers ranged upon those seats which they had so long and so honourably occupied in the senate of their country, welcoming their descendant to that post. . . . I felt myself an entirely independent representative of an equally independent nation—as a man assuming his proper station in society, not acquiring a new one.
>
> I confess I always had, and still continue to have, and to nourish, the pride which arises from having been born a gentleman. I am aware that wealth, and commerce, and perhaps talent, have in modern times occasioned family pride to be classed in the rank of follies, but I feel it, nevertheless, most strongly. . . . The sensations I experienced were, indeed, altogether delightful upon finding myself seated under that grand and solemn dome—I looked around me and saw the most dignified men of that day, the ablest orators of the period, many of the best bred courtiers, and some of the most unsophisticated patriots in the empire!
>
> . . . .
>
> I was very greatly moved and excited; but it was not excitement of an ephemeral or feverish character; on the contrary, my emotions had their source in a tranquil, deep-seated, perhaps proud satisfaction, impossible to be clearly described, and almost impossible to be felt by any but such as might be placed in circumstances precisely similar.[44]

Yeats's faith seems to me no less a part of the Protestant cultural heritage of that century. We have seen how his declaration is a compelling blend of his reading in philosophy, especially his highly individual reading of Berkeley. But in a wider context this faith includes the ability to confront old age and death with something more than Berkeley's immaterialism. It includes a breadth of culture

44. *Recollections*, pp. 112–13.

that marked a stunning age in Ireland, noted for its enthusiasm for the learning of Italy, the sculpture of Greece, the works of the great poets, and the world of romance. The literature of all these might be found, typically, in Lady Gregory's library at Coole.

The actions of the mother bird in the next stanza may refer partly to man's making "a superhuman/Mirror-resembling dream." Yet they almost certainly refer primarily to Yeats's own brooding over the faith and pride he has left to a new generation. His Tower had an empty room on top; to some extent Ireland seemed without the kind of leadership he desired and was thus hollow at the top; moreover, in one light, the poem has been an accumulation of twigs from the slow-growing tree of Irish history, if seen according to Burke's figure. Is it too much, then, to imagine Yeats the poet pondering or brooding—in his "sedentary trade"—over the towering wisdom of a Protestant past that he hopes to see reborn in the future?

To point to the irony of the last stanza of "The Tower" is not to explain it. In a very real sense Yeats has made his soul in the preceding verses, has offered its vision of history, politics, and faith as an ideal for the future. Ironically, then, his soul is already made or has stepped outside of time. Now, however, he may well be returning us to the approaching night, as it signals to eye and ear that he must await his old age and the demise of Georgian Ireland. In the poem "These are the Clouds," the coming of night in some way enhanced the glory of the setting sun. Here, at the end of "The Tower," we are told that the poet's tribulations and aging will be as nugatory as clouds and a "bird's sleepy cry" if his soul attend "a learned school" and batten on argument and abstraction. But, more tragically, more powerfully, the depletion of body and friends in gathering night is still very real and painful yet would seem to frame or focus even more brilliantly the soul already made, the imaginative outburst, the last blinding inextricable beam of sun and moon which old age, the surviving splendors of eighteenth-century culture, and the wresting of eternity by the forced enjambment of past, present, and future had accomplished. Clouds, sleepy cry, and deepening shades point up the contrasting miracle of the soul's clear, blinding declaration, but their oppression remains.

Before passing on to more Tower poems in this and the next volume, we ought to glance at two poems that follow immediately upon "The Tower" and extend its meaning.

The first is "Meditations in Time of Civil War," actually a series of closely related short poems. It too reflects the bitterness of the Tower poems, though it is shot through with reasoned pleas and passionate hopes. Again Yeats assumes as his vantage point a tower of intellect from which he takes the measure of murderous civil war. Thus the first poem in this long meditation, "Ancestral Houses," asks that the violence and bitterness of civil war be understood as the possible beginning of a new aristocratic order. In at least two stanzas Yeats looks back to comparable turbulent beginnings that saw the flowering of Ascendancy culture and beauty. Appropriately, the first and second stanzas depict the Georgian country house and its abundant, leisured life in the figure of the leaping fountain that may "choose whatever shape it wills" unhindered by ambition or social conformity. Springing "out of life's own self-delight," this life, like the mind of Robert Gregory and Anne Yeats, refuses ambitious calculation, outdoes itself in magnanimity, and leaps beyond any mechanical pattern. This image of election and joy is by now familiar, nor do its vague Georgian associations surprise us any more than does its inclusion in Homer's song. Yet this mounting thrust of shining talent, intelligence, and power has given way to another image in the second stanza. One must say most emphatically that Yeats is not rejecting the proper life of the rich when he offers as their modern symbol

> . . . some marvellous empty sea-shell flung
> Out of the obscure dark of the rich streams.

He is simply lamenting the fact that great ancestral country houses and their traditions in modern Ireland have been rejected (in fact often burned down) not only by the Irregulars but, in spirit, by the new democratic Ireland that was everywhere victorious. Most critics read these two stanzas as Yeats's own rejection of those houses and "the inherited glory of the rich." Nothing could be further from the truth. As we have heard him comment on the symbol of the "marvellous empty sea-shell" ten years later:

> In politics I have but one passion and one thought, rancour against all who, except under the most dire necessity, disturb public order, a conviction that public order cannot long persist without the rule of educated and able men. That order was everywhere their work, is still as much a part of their tradition as the *Iliad* or the Republic of Plato; their rule once gone, it lies an empty shell for the passing fool to kick in pieces.[45]

That same shell appears in the opening song of the highly political play, *Fighting the Waves;* that song best explains the transition between the second stanza and the rest of "Ancestral Houses":

> A strange, unserviceable thing,
> A fragile, exquisite, pale shell,
> That the vast troubled waters bring
> To the loud sands before day has broken.
> The storm arose and suddenly fell
> Amid the dark before day had broken.
> What death? what discipline?
> What bonds no man could unbind,
> Being imaged within
> The labyrinth of the mind,
> What pursuing or fleeing,
> What wounds, what bloody press,
> Dragged into being
> This loveliness?[46]

45. *Variorum*, p. 543. Writing of his audience with the Swedish royal family, Yeats could say, "I study the face of the old King, intelligent and friendly, like some country gentleman who can quote Horace and Catullus, and the face of the Princess Margaretha, full of subtle beauty, emotional and precise, and impassive with a still intensity *suggesting that final consummate strength which rounds the spiral of a shell*. One finds a similar beauty in wooden busts taken from Egyptian tombs of the Eighteenth Dynasty, and not again till Gainsborough paints" (*Autobiographies*, pp. 539–40). Italics mine.

46. *Variorum*, p. 784.

If we view the stormy sea here as we have seen it used in "On a Political Prisoner" and "A Prayer for my Daughter," it should not be hard to see that empty shell as another symbol of the Horn of Plenty undone by civil rancor and personal ill-breeding. However, the lament now is for the loss of power among the leisured, the propertied, and the educated.

Yet, as in the preceding lines, Yeats is willing to view the storm in Irish history that has flung that empty shell on the shore as also part of the storm and stress that might *create* new memorials that will again be graced by "the abounding glittering jet." Hence in the last three stanzas he recalls the origins of Coole, the Tudor manor house, Garsington, and, more than likely, a mansion similar to Carton or Castletown near Celbridge in Co. Kildare.[47] In all three stanzas, he asks that the magnificence symbolized by those houses accept the modern violence and bitterness of civil war in Ireland along with her continued greatness. For Yeats urges on us this thought: that the sweet clarity and elaborate beauty of country houses, which contrast with the "Asiatic folk wisdom" [48] of peasant cottages, might still be the vision of turbulent men as formerly with powerful owners, architects, or artists. From such men and times had come the beauty, gentility, and éclat of shadowed memorials that, bereft of living power, might nevertheless comprehend both destruction and its promise during civil war.

The third stanza contains a veiled glance at Coole. Yeats meditates, perhaps unfairly, on the likely end of such a house—though it is not clear if he is referring to Sir William Gregory, the great-grandson of the Gregory who bought Coole, or to Richard, Lady Gregory's grandson. Whatever the identification, the assumption is that such a house will rise again, a new sweetness will derive from ferocity. Similarly, his eye on Garsington, Yeats offers us the eighteenth-century personifications of Contemplation and Childhood, at ease and delighted, in a scene especially marked by Juno (Lady Ottoline?) and a peacock, a duo emblematic of beauty and control but

47. Information from Mrs. W. B. Yeats.
48. Rapallo Notebook II.

also known, upon the peacock's scream, to herald the breakdown of a civilization. The beauty of that garden would understand violence too. One might expect, then, the glories of eighteenth-century mansions like Carton and Castletown to be no less understanding of bitterness, since floors, galleries, portraits, and resplendent interiors mirrored an earlier greatness no less bitter in its ruthless seizure of power, property, and wealth. Carton, whose Fitzgeralds could look back to Strongbow's coming to Ireland in the twelfth century, had been rebuilt by the famous Richard Castle between 1739 and 1747 and became the seat of James, Duke of Leinster. Perhaps the greatest Irish country house, the nearby Castletown, begun in 1722, was owned by the wealthiest man in Ireland, Mr. Conolly, elected Speaker of the Irish House of Commons. Both houses were also joined by their associations with the aristocratic revolutionary, Lord Edward.

In somewhat the same manner, "My House" looks to the Norman beginnings of the Tower, and then to Yeats's own founding, both fraught with "befitting emblems of adversity," that marked the beleaguered Norman warrior and the mind sunk in Anglo-Irish solitude as like inhabitants of the same Tower and tradition. Looking back again in "My Descendants," Yeats thanks his Protestant ancestors for a vigor of mind that has flowered in his children, though he realizes that his stock might return to "common greenness," given a mistake in choice and the chance of a "natural declension of the soul." Whatever may happen, the Tower is a monument to that vigor, to his friendship with Lady Gregory, and his love for his wife. The quality of these exceptional people, all invested with the strength or love of Anglo-Ireland, is the norm with which Yeats judges the civil war and, in "The Stare's Nest by my Window," the very issue of the new state aborning.

That poem shows the method of the Tower poems at its simple best. Yeats explained it in a letter when he alluded to the "series of poems about this Tower and on the civil war at which I look (so remote one is here from all political excitement) *as if it were some*

314

phenomenon of nature." [49] So he had blended history into the landscape of "The Tower." However in this poem, "The Stare's Nest," his symbolic walls are loosening, nothing is clearly seen but formless chaos and murder, both sides have become murderous in their pursuit of abstractions:

> We had fed the heart on fantasies,
> The heart's grown brutal from the fare;
> More substance in our enmities
> Than in our love; O honey-bees,
> Come build in the empty house of the stare.

The wall becomes equivalent to the civil fabric or body politic rent by civil war. The call is for clarity, the sweetness and light Yeats always associated with the bee in Swift's *The Battle of the Books*. The grubs and flies, food for stares or starlings, we remember as the diet of Swift's spider. And rightly, for Yeats has used the raucous, strident character of the stare to figure forth the screaming, abstraction-ridden politicians on both sides. They have been sustained on base diets, the fantasies or grubby, fly-blown slogans of hatred that have coarsened the heart as the evidence of blood, fire, and two August weeks of intensive fighting attest. Swift's ideals might once again bind together the sundered masonry of the Irish nation.[50]

The first of these reflections on civil disturbance in Ireland catches something of the same destruction, makes the same diagnosis, and offers even less remedy or hope. In this poem, "Nineteen Hundred and Nineteen," placed right after "Meditations in Time of Civil

49. *Yeats and T. Sturge Moore*, p. 46. (Italics mine.) Yeats may have been describing something of the same method when commending Irish poetry from 1921 to 1924 at the Irish Academy House on Dawson Street: "During the last twenty years poems have grown very short, and instead of touching upon many topics, poets have celebrated life at its crisis when it seems caught up with what Patmore calls the integrity of fire.

"Irish poets had felt the general movement, and for the last three years they had suddenly freed themselves from historical prepossession, and written only out of themselves. It may prove in the end that they are not the less Irish because not obviously Irish at all" ("Laurel Crowns," *Freeman's Journal*, 11 August 1924).

50. See also Yeats's note on the poem in *Autobiographies*, pp. 579–80.

War," Yeats takes his sternest look at the spreading chaos of that year both in and out of Ireland.

The so-called world of that poem has been nearly altogether missed. However, all I would draw attention to is the relevance of the exalted Protestant ideal from eighteenth-century Ireland to the world of revolution in 1919, the year of his daughter's birth and the year of the poem "The Second Coming." In the poem concluding "Meditations," "I see Phantoms of Hatred and of the Heart's Fullness and of the Coming Emptiness," we viewed the future hatred in terms of class conflict in the eighteenth century. Contrasted with it was the poet's momentary "self-delighting reverie," a vision of aristocratic ladies, their hearts "full/Of their own sweetness, bodies of their loveliness." The image that replaces the best and worst of that century—the result of the nation in arms against itself—was the "indifferent multitude."

So had it been in 1919. Yeats opens "Nineteen Hundred and Nineteen" by pointing to those sacred and ornamental classical safeguards (for the multitude) whose modern counterparts—impartial law, humane habits, enlightened public opinion—have vanished. The wisdom of the high-minded few among the Protestant rulers of the Anglo-Irish eighteenth century also has its unpopular counterpart here in the continuing ideal of public service that had marked Irish, English, and European governments before the revolutions now come to a head in the year after the Great War's end. Oddly enough, the poem eulogizes dedicated men and rulers who had operated under law and, at the same time, mocks those Victorians and Edwardians for their undue optimism. This irony means, specifically, that Yeats can also look with some nostalgia at the idealism of Sinn Fein in 1912, with its nonviolent and nonpolitical objectives, and also at the development of a public opinion on both sides that could allow the passage of the third Home Rule Bill. Griffith's ideal had been Grattan's Parliament, an anathema to Connolly. So all is changed. There are bigots and incendiaries on both sides. Instead of Victoria's rule of law, there are the typical Black and Tan enormities around Gort that resulted in the wanton killing of Mrs. Ellen Quinn and the mutilation and murder of the Loughnane brothers.[51] We have seen how some of this material got into the poem "Reprisals" and into Yeats's roasting denunciation of English policy during the Oxford Union debate. Here in the poem, however, these horrendous deeds stand as mockeries of that tradition of disinterested service and, even more, of false optimism. In 1924, glancing back on those relatively halcyon days at the turn of the century, Yeats offered what might be called specific annotation for the first section of the poem:

> The nation is as it were a young man just entered upon his property, and of whom it is impossible to say whether he is a wise man or a fool, whether he will enlarge his estate, or [be] a mere spendthrift. He is celebrating his coming of age and asks the good will of his neighbour. Certainly he finds himself in a very difficult and troubled world. If Ireland had obtained freedom in the late Eighties when Gladstone brought in his first Home Rule Bill, he would have found himself in a much pleasanter world. While the fortune of Gladstone's Bill was undecided I spent certain days at Oxford copying for a publisher a Black Letter manuscript in the Bodleian. I stayed with a friend of my father's, and one evening a certain great scholar, Mr. Churton Collins, who is long dead, came to dinner. As a writer he was precise and matter of fact, but as a talker full of the vague dreams of the time. I remember his saying "Early in the Twentieth Century war will have come to an end, before the middle of the Twentieth Century there will be no more poverty." Everyone, certainly everyone who counted, everyone who influenced events believed that the world was growing better and better, and could not even help doing so owing to physical science and democratic politics, and that dream lasted for many years. A fortnight before the great war a friend of mine was standing beside an English Member of Parliament watching a Review in one of the London Parks. My friend said as the troops marched past "It is a fine sight." And the Member

51. For a full story of these brutalities, which Yeats knew well, see Brian Graney, "Days of Terror in South Galway," *Vexilla Regis* (Maynooth Laymen's Annual), 1954–55, pp. 85–98. See also "Local Heroes" and "Local Happenings," *The School Manuscripts*, XLVII, 133–35, 308–9.

of Parliament answered "It is a fine sight, but it is nothing else, there will never be another war."

"There will never be another war," that was our opium dream.[52]

At the end of the first section of the poem Yeats's reliance is once more on the solitary mind, this time the soul beyond the temptation of life's disappointments or the destroyers that no living man would admit existed. That soul, in the third section, Yeats likens to the swan, full of the pride of self-delight and playfulness, ready to surmount the leveling wind signaling civilization's end. The Gregory associations with swans, self-delight, and the winds foretelling night and winter seem strong enough. Then, after pointing to the idealistic politics in the Ireland, England, and Europe of 1912 in the fourth section, Yeats laments the fate of the "good, wise or great" unable to withstand that wind. In rapid succession he throws up images of increasing disorder that close his poem: violent horsemen or leaders running in circles or dispersed; then Herodias' daughters, self-seeking pettiness and opinionated emptiness adrift in the democratic wind; finally, the seductive inversion of mistress and man, the bewitched Lady Kytler and her insolent man, the succubus Robert Artisson. Yeats would seem to be mocking in her—and Ireland—the displacement of honor and truth, law and public service, dim ideals from the aristocratic past, by modern revolution. The poem's ending especially parallels another poem of that year, "The Second Coming." Nor are we done with the image of aristocracy in Ireland bewitched or seduced by the common. The play *Purgatory*, as we have seen, will place the event at the end of the eighteenth century.

These two poems, "Nineteen Hundred and Nineteen" and "Meditations in Time of Civil War," standing very close to "The Tower," so to speak, prepare us for the harsh reflection and castigation that shoot out from Yeats's position as heir to the intellect of Norman and Georgian Ireland. If the ideological crux of "The Tower" came from

52. TS. of "Speech for Tailteann Banquet, August 2, 1924."

the Divorce Speech, so did the thought behind the short poem "The Three Monuments," especially the lines that glorify intellect—in politics, literature, and philosophy—which Yeats saw as the great gift of the Protestant nation:

> . . . all the popular statesmen say
> That purity built up the State
> And after kept it from decay;
> Admonish us to cling to that
> And let all base ambition be,
> For intellect would make us proud
> And pride bring in impurity. . . .

But the grand intimation of "Blood and the Moon," a Tower poem from *The Winding Stair and Other Poems*, is that intellect actually brings purity, that pride of intellect counters the state's decay. In separate chapters we have already looked at the relevance of Swift, Goldsmith, Burke, Berkeley, and Kevin O'Higgins to the poem. Now, however, may be the time for a general comment, especially since "Blood and the Moon" mocks "a time/Half dead at the top."

A passage from *Per Amica Silentia Lunae* best sums up the poem's tripartite organization:

> There are two realities, the terrestrial and the condition of fire. All power is from the terrestrial condition, for there all opposites meet and there only is the extreme of choice possible, full freedom. And there the heterogeneous is, and evil, for evil is the strain one upon another of opposites; but in the condition of fire is all music and all rest. Between is the condition of air where images have but a borrowed life, that of memory or that reflected upon them when they symbolise colours and intensities of fire: the place of shades. . . .[53]

Thus "Blood and the Moon" contrasts the first two abodes and then reveals the third as a dim realm of memory that might have connected the two. After the first introductory section, the second identifies the wisdom of eighteenth-century Anglo-Ireland with the

53. *Mythologies*, pp. 356–57.

condition of fire; the third confronts the terrestrial condition of evil and bloodshed where imagination might have resolved those straining opposites; and the last introduces the condition of air where butterflies and moths, the souls of the dead and symbols of the wisdom of the Georgian past, go unheeded. Truth dies against the windows in a nation half dead at the top.

The introductory verses call Ballylee and the Tower blessed. The blessing is intellectual, a sense of form and a gift of forceful, purposive intelligence that had powerfully raised a tower expressive of superiority above the native cottages. Those conquering Normans had uttered and mastered that race, i.e., they had grafted a political and literary intelligence on Irish life for which the Tower is a symbol. Yeats had made something like that claim in his Divorce Speech. In the second section we have seen him make his boast specific by showing a second blessedness, an intellectual resurgence that took political and literary form in the eighteenth century. Passion and precision, blood and being, man and God pulse together in the epithets of "blood-sodden" (Swift), "honey-pot" (Goldsmith), "haughtier-headed" (Burke), and "God-appointed" (Berkeley). The last three lines of the section masterfully pull together what, imaginatively taken, these four might have done to bless modern Ireland:

> *Saeva Indignatio* and the labourer's hire,
> The strength that gives our blood and state magnanimity
>   of its own desire;
> Everything that is not God consumed with intellectual fire.

His driving hopes for social justice as Minister of Justice and his unfailing concern for the Irish workingman (as Kevin's Hour still testifies) make Kevin O'Higgins the logical embodiment of these gifts. His personal dignity, courtesy, and large-mindedness help round out the blessedness that Yeats confers on him from eighteenth-century Anglo-Ireland. For these lines summarize the Anglo-Irish ideals Yeats had enumerated: Swift's love of liberty; Goldsmith's eye for the particulars of ordinary life, and his defense of the oppressed rural laborer in the *Deserted Village,* after the example of Luke 10:7; the strength Burke saw in the slow growth of the nation that insured rulers of magnanimity and free choice; and Berkeley's immaterialism, a vision of the world beheld in God's eye. Had the nation imagination enough to make these beliefs part of public life, then all things not God might indeed have become like God, "consumed with intellectual fire." In less abstract terms, Yeats is probably saying that, with the free play of intellect, Irish life might come as close to being ideal as human life permits. Intellectual fire probably also includes the fire of love, the play of the "noblest of the elements, being a witness of the secrets of the heavens." [54] This last line is then a figurative quintessence of all those qualities seemingly come down from the world figures of eighteenth-century Ireland to Kevin O'Higgins—"the one strong intellect in Irish public life." O'Higgins' assassination had been a repudiation of those qualities.

The third section reveals to us the possible triumph of the intellectual imagination in the terrestrial realm, a continuous possibility despite the intermittent bloodshed and political roils since the Normans came in. That blood had been shed for a niggling wage, out of fanaticism, or from cowardice—all those opposites to the virtues listed in the second section. Yet moral imagination is capable of surmounting the differences that had spilled blood through seven hundred years in Ireland. And once again, with new blood spilt— "Odour of blood on the ancestral stair!"—men cry out for wisdom that will reconcile "the strain upon one another of opposites," to quote Yeats's words from *Per Amica* again, in the heterogeneous world of the terrestrial. The purging intellectual fire comes in the straight path of the arrow.

Ghostly wisdom from the past is, moreover, all about us yet unheeded. Or so the symbolic moths and butterflies suggest, recalling, as they do, Yeats's references to ultimate truths being "moth-like and fluttering," to wisdom being a butterfly, and to the fact that the souls of the dead are said to take the form of insects and butterflies.[55] In a

54. *Letters,* p. 263.
55. "The Message of the Folk-lorist," *The Speaker,* 19 August 1893.

note to the poem, Yeats had extended this meaning by observing that "Part of the symbolism of *Blood and the Moon* was suggested by the fact that Thoor Ballylee has a waste room at the top and that the butterflies come in through the loopholes and die against the window-panes." The imaginative wisdom from Georgian Ireland in the national memory has shared the fate of those moths and butterflies. Truth and wisdom die in an empty room, an act symptomatic in a nation lacking intellectual leadership and so "Half dead at the top."

Such is the wisdom, presented with less bitterness, of "The Seven Sages." It is also a composite poem. Since we have glanced before at the lines or images devoted to Swift, Burke, Berkeley, and Gold-smith, a consideration of the final enigmatic lines on the source of their wisdom is in order:

The Sixth. What schooling had these four?

The Seventh.   They walked the roads

> Mimicking what they heard, as children mimic;
> They understood that wisdom comes of beggary.

Apparently Yeats thought this process profoundly Irish.[56] For one thing, all four men are represented by song or verse: there is Burke's melody, Goldsmith's song, Swift's epitaph, and Berkeley's voice in gathering volume. For another, all are said to have acted out or mimicked "what they heard." Thus song, verse, or voice is based upon bedrock reality. Two statements by Yeats also help explain the process. The first is one we have seen applied to Synge as he wandered through Europe: ". . . he was the only man I have ever known incapable of a political thought or of a humanitarian purpose. He could walk the roadside all day with some poor man without any desire to do him good or for any reason except that he liked him."[57] Then, in *On the Boiler*, Yeats may also have illuminated these lines when he remarked that "Nature or reality as known to poets and tramps has no moment, no impression, no perception like another, everything is unique and nothing unique is measurable."[58] Conse-

56. Information from Mrs. W. B. Yeats.
57. *Autobiographies*, p. 567.
58. *On the Boiler*, p. 25.

quently, their education in wisdom was a direct, sensuous rendition of the unique experience of Ireland.[59] Their school was a "singing-school" of the road, not so terribly different from that of children heard singing their sums, alphabet, and prayers in Gaelic in the Irish national education of today. The method is also one dramatized in the opening stanza of "Among School Children" when the singing, ciphering, sewing, and reading Montessori children exemplify an education where mind and body are unified, where what a child senses, learns, and becomes are one. Though the carnal and the saintly are not precluded from this wisdom, one could not imagine "A levelling, rancorous, rational sort of mind" at that school.

The resounding echoes of these ancestral voices and melodies continue to break the stony silence of the Tower, then re-echo from other Georgian memorials joined to the Tower in fact and fancy, especially places so near as Coole and so distant as Lissadell. Though we have already heard many times of the Gore-Booth sisters, Yeats's disappointment in his and their folly and guilt is judged by sages very close in their loyalties, it would seem, to those in "The Seven Sages." Thus the poem "In Memory of Eva Gore-Booth and Con Markiewicz" offers another example of the elegiac tone, the social, and the historical symbolism that mark the theme of Georgian Ireland.

Once again the time is twilight, a moment and a mood befitting the decline of the Anglo-Irish aristocracy, and the time of year autumn, when the bloom and blossom of that culture have come to a historical close. One might even speculate that the mention of "Great windows open to the south" refers to both a physical fact and to the service that Lissadell in its decline had offered to the new Ireland. Yet the autumn had been a "raving" one. In one sense the reference is to the personal ravages that the conspiring or Utopia-dreaming mind can bring. In another, Yeats seems to have in mind that leveling wind or screaming storm beating against other eighteenth-century architectural mementos. For Lissadell too, in fact and imagination, had been built to withstand the storms off the Atlantic and those bred thereon.

59. *Per Amica Silentia Lunae, Mythologies*, p. 361.

Consequently, Yeats is probably holding up this role for Lissadell and its occupants—had both girls not departed from its traditions of protection, obligation, and local benefaction.[60] Perhaps Dante's lines paraphrased catch all these hints: ". . . Nobility of blood is a cloak soon shortened, for unless it be added to from day to day, Time goes around it with his shears" (*Paradiso*, XVI, 1–9). In any case, a long description of Lissadell, built between 1837 and 1839, a passage more than likely known by Yeats, is relevant here since it offers facts enough to suggest the symbolic role of a Georgian mansion and also the basis of the metaphors in "On a Political Prisoner" and "Towards Break of Day":

> With a fine southern aspect, with a rich soil and gently sloping surface down to the sea, and with magnificent views and surroundings, Lissadell is a most eligible site for a first-class mansion and demesne.
>
> The best view of the ground may be had from the strand, on the Rosses' side of the Drumcliff channel. When you look at Lissadell from this point, . . . you can't help finding a resemblance between the shape of the place, and that of the shells of the Cardium genus, which lie at your feet. . . .
>
> About the centre of the area, stands Lissadell House, or, as it is commonly called in the neighbourhood, Lissadell Court—a name which the stately pile well deserves for the magnitude of its proportions, the beauty and finish of its building material, which is Ballysadare limestone, and the simple but classic elegance of its design. Look at it from what side you will, and you are struck with the solemn and almost conscious dignity with which it reposes, and presides over the scene.
>
> · · · · · · · · · · · · ·
>
> . . . on visiting the place, it is found to contain a goodly proportion of open spaces, glades, and vistas. The plantations are numerous and thick for the purposes of shelter, which is greatly needed, as the winds tell with exceptional effect on the

60. O'Rorke, *History of Sligo*, II, 10–18, and Tadhg Kilgannon, *Sligo and Its Surroundings* (Sligo, 1926), pp. 218–19.

spot, owing to the exposed situation and the proximity to the Atlantic.

It was only by great skill and management these disadvantages could be overcome. But by planting the hardier species of trees over the sea, along the west border of the demesne, and on the higher knolls, and by planting them thick, a barrier was raised, on which the storm spends much of its force. . . . Still a contest goes always on between art and nature; and if the sickly hue of leaf, and shrivelled appearance of stem or trunk, which one observes, here and there, reminds one of the great principle, "Naturam repelles furca, tamen usque recurrit," on the other hand the flourishing state of most of the trees through the grounds, and in the plantations, the soft bloom of the flowers in the gardens, and the vivid green of the grass in the lawns, supply ample proof—that art, and outlay, and energy, can always go a good way in counteracting and neutralizing the most adverse condition of things.

And this observation applies to the Glen even more than to other parts of the demesne. The Glen is formed by a stream which runs down from Benbulben, and works its way on to the sea through Lissadell. In old times the stream was in bad odour . . . but by cleansing it and altering somewhat its channel; by turning into it an additional supply of water; by making several small cascades where the levels admitted them; and by planting its banks with fragrant shrubs and flowers; the Gore Booths have so altered its character, that it is now the gem of the demesne, and deserves the name of the Sparkling Sweet-scented Streamlet. Owing to the shelter and warmth of the deep glen, and to the running water, delicate exotics that would hardly live a day in most other parts of the neighbourhood, thrive there the whole year round, as in their native habitat.[61]

This last mention of "delicate exotics," so close to the figures in silk kimonos and the gazelle-like Eva, blends especially well with the added eulogy of innocence and beauty. All are rare dimensions of the

61. *History of Sligo*, II, 11–13.

central structure—"that old Georgian mansion"—and force the comparison between art and nature, or between an aristocratic tradition of service and a popular one, a Georgian ideal and a democratic one. The figurative contrast is between Lissadell and a "great gazebo," the one an embodiment of art, the other a golden dream stirred by the excited emotions of youth. The one leaves the innocent and beautiful at the mercy of nature or the attritions of time, the other is designed to protect rare lives from the storm.

This melancholy war between art and nature comes to its tragic end in "Coole Park, 1929," "Coole Park and Ballylee, 1931," and "The Black Tower," this last from among *Last Poems*.

In "Coole Park, 1929," night is already at hand for those symbolic, genealogical trees: by then Coole had already passed into government hands. However, Lady Gregory was still allowed to rent Coole. Thus, though the sun is setting, the cloud, the new order of Ireland, may still be said to be illuminated by the culture of Coole. The traditions of the house, still alive under Lady Gregory's hand and by her art and energy recalling to us the struggle at Lissadell, still contest with nature—"Great works constructed there in nature's spite." The artist—Hyde, Yeats, or Synge—found his place ideally, as he might have in Georgian Ireland, beside men of spirit and action, here "those/Impetuous men, Shawe-Taylor and Hugh Lane." In an earlier version of the poem, the circling return of the swallows found a like pattern in eighteenth-century dances, the waltz, Sir Roger de Coverley, and quadrille. The word "academy" also appeared for a moment to designate Lady Gregory's concerted efforts to bring new dignity to Ireland through a revival of the arts.[62] But these effects are seen much more subtly in such lines as "A dance-like glory that those walls begot" or "Found certainty upon the dreaming air," for both lines offer us the paradox that Yeats liked to evoke in voicing the combination of "passion and precision" at Coole. The social setting is also faintly Georgian—but no less contemporary—that finds "pride established in humility,/A scene well set and excellent company."

62. Jon Stallworthy, *Between the Lines* (Oxford, 1963), pp. 187–89.

These paradoxes heighten the prophecy of ruin in the last stanza, a ruin come all too exactly true. But what are we to make of the last three lines? I think we are meant to view the sun and shade, artfully commingled in the dim light of the poem's opening, as now symbolically separated in the future years. Perhaps Yeats is implying that the future sun will symbolize the light of intelligence, that the shade of a government forest afford but a pleasant physical relief from the sun and become the sun's symbolic opposite, the life of the emotions. As mind and emotion had been rendered one despite their natural separation in the first stanza, so they are glaringly parted in the world that will follow upon the demise of Coole and its mistress. He asks a future visitor to reject that separation momentarily for something better. For the last line holds us to her memory and to that former unity, especially in the final words, "that laurelled head." Here an individual intelligence and a leaf from that shade are joined in the commemoration not of nature but of art.

The second, an even more tragic poem, "Coole Park and Ballylee, 1931," is just as subtle. Yeats's own introduction to it in 1937 is valuable for its hint of this fact:

> From my twenty-seventh year until a few years ago all my public activities were associated with a famous country house in County Galway. In that house my dear friend, that woman of genius, Lady Gregory, gathered from time to time all men of talent, all profound men, in the intellectual life of modern Ireland. I have a house three or four miles from where her gate was, a mediaeval tower whose winding stair I am too old to climb. The river that passed my window sank into the earth in a round pool which the blind, or dark, poet Raftery called a cellar, then rose again and fell into a lake in Lady Gregory's park. The poem I am about to read was written shortly before Lady Gregory's death. It is typical of most of my recent poems, intricate in metaphor, the swan and water both emblems of the soul, not at all a dream, like my earlier poems, but a criticism of life. The poem is called "Coole [Park] and Ballylee, 1931." [63]

63. TS. of "My Own Poetry Again," BBC broadcast, 29 October 1937.

It is no longer autumn. Winter has come. All is over. With the image of the soul, the water that joins Ballylee to Coole in the first stanza, we are brought to the lake's edge in the second. The trees are not in their autumn beauty, they are "dry sticks under a wintry sun." The melancholy tone has become a tragic one. The mounting swan becomes a symbol of the inspiration [64] so many times triumphant at Coole. But in the third stanza it also becomes a symbol of the soul, and perhaps of the soul's departure, even the departure of an ideal of life at Coole—"so lovely that it sets to right/What knowledge or its lack had set awry." Perhaps a spot of ink could murder this concentration of the blessed mind and abode of the Gregory tradition; perhaps the ink on a paper that put Coole in government hands may well be said to have killed a swan. So water and swan have also embodied the poet's theme, "Traditional sanctity and loveliness."

Stanzas IV and V allow Yeats to touch his hat for the last time to the house and its mistress. Here too life is denoted by a stick. Although Lady Gregory took exception to this opening line, hating any reference to her illness,[65] Yeats is intent on showing her heroic leave-taking, her saying good-by to the house and its emblems. This fourth stanza is a succinct generalization of the cultured, traveled, inherited life of that Georgian house, a virtual summary of Lady Gregory's own description of the library, its books, pictures, and busts in *Coole*. Among the books that she gives special mention are Johnson's *Dictionary*, Clarendon's *History of the Rebellion*, and Evelyn's *Silva*; an Odyssey from Lord Wellesley; Murphy's *Tacitus* "in three volumes, dedicated to Edmund Burke." [66] She also points to "the portrait of Robert Gregory who built this Library, the friend of Burke and Fox, the host of Arthur Young." [67] Many of the books mentioned bear the binding and the care that went into bookbinding during the heyday of this art in eighteenth-century Dublin. A permanence marks these books as it does the gardens, trees, and

64. Hone, p. 425.
65. Information from Mrs. W. B. Yeats.
66. Lady Gregory, *Coole* (Dublin, 1931), p. 8.
67. *Ibid.*, p. 4.

alliances noted in the next stanza, all of them examples of choice, slow growth of ambition that looked beyond the caprice of fashions and fads. They—Yeats and Lady Gregory—were the last romantics if the word is used in the sense that it takes in the phrase "Romantic Ireland's dead and gone,/It's with O'Leary in the grave." This is literary romance that goes hand in hand with the heroic epic, that ties high meaning to plain expression, an especially appropriate combination at Coole, "where men and women are valued for their manhood and their charm, not for their opinions." [68]

In "The Black Tower" the wind is a roaring one and night has descended on the tomb where ancestors of the Tower's defenders stand buried. The poem remains an enigma, though the latest interpretations do a fine job in locating its source in O'Grady's *Finn and His Companions* and in showing how the sight of Roquebrune and the chapel of St. Pancras in Cap Martin may have stimulated the dying Yeats to recall his early reading and associations at Woburn Buildings.[69] Jon Stallworthy seems especially pertinent when he finds the poem embracing a number of defenses—"It is enough that we perceive that the Tower can be Yeats himself, Ireland, and a world threatened by the Third Reich"—yet also a promise of a new dawn for Ireland in the world.[70] But my preoccupations also suggest another dimension, however slight it may be. The Tower here is also Castle Ballylee; the roaring wind is in part that wind that had gained headway again in 1919. The banners or bribers would seem to represent many a propagandist that Yeats might rebuff: Nazi Germany, Communist Russia, liberal England. Yet the defenders are also "oath-bound men." Thus Yeats may also have in mind Irish politics, where, from the early thirties, Fianna Fail had been in power led by men who had taken the Oath in 1927 with mental reservations. That party and its leader had first abolished the system of appointed Senators and then, on May 29, 1936, abolished the Senate. To some

68. *Autobiographies*, p. 456.
69. Patrick Diskin, "A Source for Yeats's 'The Black Tower,'" *N&Q* (March 1961), pp. 107–8; and *Between the Lines*, p. 223.
70. *Between the Lines*, p. 242.

degree, Yeats may even be reflecting on the restoration of that Senate on very different lines under the rather opportunistically created *Bunreacht na hEireann* that took effect at the beginning of 1938. The appointed members of the original Senate had seemed to Yeats worthy of the Protestant Ireland they frequently represented, in particular the heritage of Grattan's Parliament which he wished to insinuate into so many of the Southern Unionist Senators. Thus if we grant the wider Irish origins of "The Black Tower," it may be just possible to see also in it the imaginative history, politics, and faith of "The Tower," of men—like their forefathers who could not be bribed or threatened to vote for the Union in Grattan's Parliament—that were Oath-bound, honor-bound, and unsatisfied with the new order in Ireland. Yeats in *Purgatory* and the completed though unpublished *On the Boiler* had put himself in that camp. In any case, this final coming of night, with perhaps a promise hinted for coming generations, has taken us to the last poem Yeats wrote, evidence enough that Castle Ballylee, the Tower of Norman and Georgian memory, lay powerfully enough on his mind to offer receptacle for all his heroic memories of resistance and refusal to the death.

VI

With this consideration of "The Black Tower," we have already reached ahead to *Last Poems*. But before continuing in that volume we ought to consider a poem from *A Full Moon in March*. This poem, "Parnell's Funeral," the first in the volume, acquaints us with the growing harshness that Yeats will borrow from his eighteenth-century figures to berate his own age. If one had to sum up the poem, he might well say that it sets Swift against modern Ireland.

However, the first section lays down the lines by directing Yeats's rage against the tradition of O'Connell, the man he once called the opposite of Emmet.[71] O'Connell's tomb is "the Great Comedian's tomb." Below it is the crowd or throng in all its animal blood, that

71. "Emmet the Apostle of Irish Liberty," *Gaelic American*, 5 March 1904, p. 5.

animal later identified as the rat. Above the tomb are the clouds, by now a familiar image of confusion, here described as an aimless "bundle of tempestuous cloud" driven by the wind. The contrast is the patch of clear sky where appears a shooting star—symbol of intellectual fire, the straight line of intellect, the image of man at his highest, saint or sage.[72] This vision come to the artist as sudden illumination Yeats elaborates by the figure of sacrifice, the beautiful woman, the shot arrow, and the boy of the next stanza explained in detail by his second note at the end of *Autobiographies*. That star also resembles the arrow-like beams of the moon in "Blood and the Moon" in that it is the mark of a political intelligence and behavior come from another century and other sacrifices, those of Emmet, Fitzgerald, Tone, and, ultimately, Swift. Never had Yeats contrasted so harshly the two Irish patriotisms.

But this opening section also demands that we make a distinction. England brought down those men. Parnell's own maddened countrymen brought him down and, Yeats seems to say, those who sacrificed Parnell did not gain by devouring his heart, since middle-class Catholic Ireland played no conscious role in the tragic drama of Irish history and thus could not profit by that sacrifice:

> None shared our guilt; nor did we play a part
> Upon a painted stage when we devoured his heart.

In the second section of the poem, as we shall discover, Yeats reconsiders, unsays, this sentence. However, the last stanza in this section allows him to take Swift's tone of savage indignation and give the lie to modern Ireland's patriotic delusions. In Yeats's disdain, Swift's satire joins the ancient Irish tradition of satire, which was reputed to be able to rhyme rats to death.[73] There is joy, not hatred in this stanza. It looks forward to this famous passage in a letter to Dorothy Wellesley:

> You say that we must not hate. You are right, but we may, and sometimes must, be indignant and speak it. Hate is a kind of

72. *Per Amica Silentia Lunae, Mythologies*, pp. 340, 361.
73. David Comyn, "Rats Were Rhymed to Death," *Irish Digest*, V (November 1939), 103–5.

'passive suffering,' but indignation is a kind of joy. 'When I am told that somebody is my brother Protestant,' said Swift, 'I remember that the rat is a fellow creature;' that seems to me a joyous saying. We that are joyous need not be afraid to denounce.[74]

Thus the difference between the two Irish patriotisms Yeats again declares a difference between art and nature, intelligence and emotion, man and animal. So may Parnell be judged—"let all men judge that *can*" (italics mine).

The second section admits that men in the comic tradition of Irish politics had also played their roles in a tragic drama. Yet they seem not to have heeded the wisdom available from the sacrifice of Parnell nor from Swift before him. In the French story of certain holy women, victims for an entire people, Yeats—we recall—had seen the fate of Swift: "One was victim for a whole country, another for such and such a village. Is not Swift the human soul in that dryness, is not that his tragedy and his genius? Perhaps every historical phase may have its victims. . . ."[75] Indeed, in this modern period after the fourth bell, Yeats seems to be pointing to the age's new victim, Kevin O'Higgins. Swift's had been a mind that chose in Anglo-Irish solitude according to the "bent and current" of a people, not according to the whim of the crowd. Modern Irish nationalism had started with him. Parnell had tasted the salubrious bitterness of Swift's mind. De Valera had not, nor had Cosgrave. Had they, there would not have been De Valera's fanatic appeal to the extreme Republicans nor the quibbling that caused the civil war. In the case of Cosgrave, one might even speculate that had he not reneged on Yeats's plan to get the Oath removed to bring the warring parties together in the Dail, no matter what the loss of face to his government, he might be said to have most certainly satisfied the land's imagination. That would have been Parnell's way. With more firmness, with more intelligence, Yeats seems to be saying, Cosgrave might have made O'Higgins' assassination less likely to have happened; and even

74. *Letters*, p. 876.
75. *Ibid.*, p. 819.

O'Duffy—but there, as Yeats hastily indicates, one must draw the line. No wonder Yeats could say of Parnell in the thirties, ". . . from that sacrificial victim I derive almost all that is living in the imagination of Ireland today." [76] None of these would have dared to voice the bitter wisdom Yeats later put in Parnell's mouth when addressing a cheering follower: "Ireland shall get her freedom and you still break stone." Moreover, Yeats knew it to be an actual saying of Parnell's.

There is a scattering of references, less oratorical, more rhetorical, to fighters for Irish freedom in the eighteenth century in "Three Songs to the Same Tune." But here they seem opportune rather than thoughtful. The first is all but a gallows song of '98. The second combines such of the renowned generations as those of Emmet and Parnell with those of O'Donnell and "both O'Neills." The third offers Burke's tree empty and blighted as a symbol of the nation bereft of the rule of its able and educated men.

Much more to our purpose is the poem "The Curse of Cromwell." In the same way that he used history to lash out at the ecclesiastic and political enemies of his ideals in Ireland, Yeats also used it to smite the barbarity of modern levelers, often of the left wing. Theirs is the modern version of Cromwell's curse. In his essay on Edmund Spenser, Yeats had written:

> . . . I doubt if anybody in Ireland could have understood . . . that the Anglo-Saxon nation was beginning to persecute in the service of ideas it believed to be the foundation of the State. I doubt if anybody in Ireland saw with certainty, till the Great Demagogue had come and turned the old house of the noble into 'the house of the Poor, the lonely house, the accursed house of Cromwell.' He came . . . with that great rabble who had overthrown the pageantry of Church and Court, but who turned towards him faces full of the sadness and docility of their long servitude, and the old individual, poetical life went down, as it seems, for ever.[77]

76. "Modern Ireland," *Massachusetts Review,* V (Winter 1964), 258.
77. "Edmund Spenser," *Essays and Introductions,* pp. 375–76.

In the year of the poem's publication, Yeats said of it: "Cromwell came to Ireland as a kind of Lenin. He destroyed a whole social order. There is not one of us, unless of a family imported by him or after him, that has not some memory of his tyranny and his cruelty."[78] Cromwell or Lenin, it made no difference: "money's rant is on." Like Swift who once wrote that his grandfather had suffered heavily from "the barbarity of Cromwell's hellish crew," Yeats is attacking the depredations of an intelligentsia, largely English communists, on what he thought to be the romantic and noble in life and letters.[79] To oppose this Whiggery, he conjures up a Gaelic poet, Egan O'Rahilly (1670–1726), and a great house—for the most part Leap Castle [80]—that had seen the nobility of both Irelands. As with Castle Dargan in another poem, or that "gallant gentleman," Casement, in yet another, Leap Castle admirably suited his purpose.

Built by the O'Carrolls in the twelfth century, Leap Castle is situated in the parish of Aghacon—"the Field of the Hound"—in Co. Offaly. In the seventeenth century it passed to the Darby family, whose representative, the "Wild Captain" Darby, fought against Cromwell in Ireland and died in 1648. This distinguished Anglo-Irish family occupied the castle into our century and included among their Christian names that of O'Carroll. One of the few mansions occupied continuously since Anglo-Norman times, Leap Castle was partly destroyed by fire in July 1922 by the Irregulars.[81] Yeats was especially impressed by its reputation as a haunted spot and by the fact that its windows were said to light up unexplainably at night with a red glow.[82] Thus Yeats probably makes the magnanimous spirit of those Gaelic and Anglo-Irish horsemen, swordsmen, ladies, and

78. TS. of "My Own Poetry," BBC broadcast, 3 July 1937.

79. *Letters on Poetry from W. B. Yeats to Dorothy Wellesley* (London, 1940), pp. 131, 135. See also H. W. Häusermann, "W. B. Yeats and W. J. Turner," *English Studies*, XL (1959), 233–39, and XLI (1960), 241–53.

80. Information from Mrs. W. B. Yeats.

81. James Fleming, "Historic Irish Mansions: No. 51: Leap Castle, Co. Offaly," *Irish Times*, 24 April 1937.

82. *Rolling Down the Lea* (London, 1950), pp. 30–31.

riders to hounds the haunting permanence of that half-ruined house. A left-wing intelligentsia—he had Stephen Spender among others in mind—so full of hatred and pity, not indignation and love,[83] and the fanatic wreckers and arsonists of 1922 come together with Cromwell and his crew and the howling wind. In talking with dogs and horses Yeats is still the servant of that nobility, ancient Gaelic or Georgian Irish. The enemy, today or yesterday, remains the same. More and more, then, among these ballads in *Last Poems*, Yeats takes the best of both Irelands in order to close ranks against a common enemy.

A fine example of this alliance is "Colonel Martin," perhaps as strange a poem as Yeats ever wrote. The legendary basis of the poem is glorious. The Colonel's story exists in many different forms. Yeats remarked to Edith Heald of the poem, "I have known from the start what I wanted to do, and yet the idea seemed to lie below the threshold of consciousness—and still lies. There is a chorus almost without meaning. . . ."[84] Yeats had spoken of the Colonel as early as March 1910 in a lecture, concluding his account of Tom and his master by saying: "That showed how the people delighted in a striking personality. It showed the mysterious love of that mysterious thing, human nature."[85] Yeats's source may well have been the "Galway shepherd" he cited in this lecture, but the details of his poem are much closer to Lady Gregory's version of the tale published in 1926.[86] The factual source of the story is probably contained in the account of a law case that came before Lord Kenyon, at the London Guildhall, reported in the *Connaught Telegraph* on December 22, 1791.[87] The action had been taken by Richard Martin of Dangan

83. *Letters*, pp. 875–76.

84. *Ibid.*, pp. 896–97.

85. Richard Ellmann, *The Identity of Yeats* (London, 1954), pp. 205–6. Yeats retold the story in 1919 and mentioned that Colonel Martin had died "sixty years ago" (Gerald Cumberland, "Some Dubliners," *Chronicle*, 1 February 1919). Here he probably confused the Colonel with his son Tom.

86. "At the Time of the Famine," *Kiltartan History Book* (London, 1926), pp. 80–83. The Colonel's son even had a legend attached to him ("Pithy Pars," *Tuam Herald*, 3 March 1906).

87. S. J. Maguire, "Notes. Martin v. Petrie," *The Galway Reader*, IV (Winter 1954), 122–23.

against John Petrie of Soho, who had met Martin's wife "casually at the scene of vice and luxury, Paris, there unprotected." The jury had returned a verdict against Petrie and ordered that he pay Martin ten thousand pounds.[88] The Irish Folklore Commission possesses two more accounts, one in English, another in Irish, which are closer to this factual account and show the fearsome Martin in a more murderous light, in one case tracking down his wife and her seducer and killing them both.[89]

The poem and its sources all stress that paradox which has made Colonel Richard Martin famous, for this fire-eater had always combined the strangest opposites in his personality, as his nicknames "Humanity Dick" and "Hair-Trigger Dick" testify. Born in 1784, the first child in his family to be educated as a Protestant, he became master of Dangan and Ballinahinch castles. Given the title Lord of Clare, for many years M.P. for Galway, J.P. and High Sheriff of the County in 1782, he was also Colonel of the Galway Volunteers and author of the Martin Act for the prevention of cruelty to animals. He made his first marriage in 1777, and his second (which is mentioned in Berry's tale) in 1796. Before his death in 1834 his notorious career as a duelist shone at its most memorable in a bloody fight with the no less formidable Fighting Fitzgerald. Martin was in truth the un-crowned King of Connemara.[90] These living opposites in the Colonel are voiced in his dialogue with Tom at the poem's end. They make up that mysterious attitude behind the recklessness that Yeats so enjoyed in eighteenth-century gentry and nobility. The voice is also the call or communication of the blood in "Hound Voice." It is also close to the consoling tone so dear to Yeats of God or saint in their "melancholy

88. *Ibid.*, p. 123.

89. TS. from James Berry, *Tales of the West. Recollections of Early Boyhood* (in possession of the Irish Folklore Commission), pp. 72–74; also "Tim O'Harte and Colonel Martin," in Seán Mac Giollarnáth, *Annála Beaga ó lorrus Aithneach* (Dublin, 1941), pp. 197–99. I am indebted to Dr. Thomas Wall of the Folklore Commission for translating this passage.

90. Archer E. S. Martin, *Genealogy of the Family of Martin of Ballinahinch Castle, in the County of Galway, Ireland* (Whinnipeg, 1890), n.p. See also Mary MacCarthy, *Fighting Fitzgerald and Other Papers* (London, 1930), pp. 185–219.

and apocalyptic cheerfulness." [91] Like that God who smiles in damning the lost or rewarding the good, the Colonel continues to go out sailing. In other words, the Colonel makes some judgment or takes some direct action in every stanza yet always goes his cheerful way. An intelligent man in the Irish sense of "clever," the Colonel accomplishes his revenge and the world goes on. His man obeys him to the letter—almost. Tom's first thought had been loyalty to the Colonel's command, yet by that command he might have thrown gold in his own pocket. However, the gold is gone, the moment past. A man may want yet he might also be rich. That is that. *"The Colonel went out sailing."* There may be human error, but both Irelands understand each other. "Colonel Martin" is a poem of love, not pity.

Catholic and Protestant Ireland join hands again in "The Municipal Gallery Revisited." There in Lord Charlemont's former town house, Yeats ties the heroics of the new Ireland of the past thirty years to the tradition of excellence at Coole. Quite properly, the opening stanza brings us images of pride and humility—such pictures by Lavery as "St. Patrick's Purgatory," "The Court of Criminal Appeal," "Arthur Griffith," "Kevin O'Higgins," and "The Blessing of the Colours" [92]—that accord with the artistic ideal of Synge, Yeats, and Lady Gregory: "Dream of the noble and the beggar-man." These are also images of the dignity Lady Gregory had worked to achieve for Ireland. They picture that dignity returned. Among the "permanent or impermanent images" Yeats moves towards the more lasting, those dead but permanent images of the Gregory connection. In doing so, he even puts his dislikes and physical ailments to work. He must seem for the moment to approve of the Mancini portrait, which he disliked, by passing off most of the compliment on John Synge. Suffering from a weak heart and stiff knees, Yeats puts these ills to metaphorical advantage by seeming to place himself in a kneeling position, or at least sinking down, before these pictures and,

91. Introduction, *Irish Fairy and Folk Tales*, p. xiii.
92. Arland Ussher, ed., *Yeats and the Municipal Gallery* (Dublin, 1959), n.p., has substantiated this selection of pictures.

in memory, at Coole. He is their servant. Both are also hallowed. The poem becomes a kind of prayer. As Yeats explained at a banquet in his honor on August 17, 1937, the poem was meant to describe

> Ireland not as she is displayed in guide book or history, but, Ireland seen because of the magnificent vitality of her painters, in the glory of her passions.
>
> For the moment I could think of nothing but that Ireland: that great pictured song. The next time I go, I shall stand once more in veneration before the work of the great Frenchmen. It is said that an Indian ascetic, when he has taken a certain initiation on a mountain in Tibet, is visited by all the Gods. In those rooms of the Municipal Gallery I saw Ireland in spiritual freedom, and the Corots, the Rodins, the Rousseaus were the visiting gods.[93]

This pride in the distinctive qualities of the two Irelands swells the benediction of "Under Ben Bulben." Though he charges future poets to sing first the peasantry and only thereafter "hard-riding country gentlemen," it is equally fitting that Yeats should consciously place himself in the Church of Ireland yet recall an earlier Yeats who had been Drumcliff's rector and placed there a Celtic cross. Though there is much in the poem, including the work of "Calvert and Wilson, Blake and Claude," that might be discussed here, these last lines are most pertinent to my conclusion on the Irish Georgian element in Yeats's verse. Although his was the first tombstone in the family since the eighteenth century,[94] Yeats's epitaph on it excites us most. It is Swiftian, very close in its challenge to that which fired Yeats in the epitaph and life of the Dean of St. Patrick. For all of Swift's contempt for the Irish, he defended their liberty. His own life or death became secondary to the defense of that liberty. Hence Yeats's initial dislike of what he took to be a mooning over death in Rilke's poetry was based on what he called an Irish trait. Rilke's giving death such emphasis was a theme alien to Irish literature.[95] Yeats's own

93. *Variorum*, pp. 839–40.
94. *Letters*, p. 915.
95. *Ibid.*, p. 917. See also William Rose, "A Letter from W. B. Yeats on Rilke," *German Life and Letters*, October 1961, pp. 68–70.

epitaph was his reaction. It expresses Swift's cool disregard for life as any permanent end in itself. It squares perfectly with that man Yeats called "the first great modern mind to deny the value of life." [96] Just as relevant is this capsule description from Yeats's essay on him: "Swift . . . a fakir-like contempt for all human desire; 'take from her,' Swift prayed for Stella in sickness, 'all violent desire whether of life or death.' " [97] And now Yeats too demands to be remembered for that hallmark of the eighteenth-century Protestant intellect, fearless choice in a world where passion and precision were not usually one, his eye cold in its passion for clarity. Like Swift's devotion to liberty, that eye looks beyond the self. If Yeats's immediate reaction had been against a sentimental and commonplace fear of death, just how contemptuous the equivalent love of life could make him is something that his last great testament in prose, verse, and drama, *On the Boiler*, can show.

96. "Modern Irish Literature," *Irish Times*, 18 February 1933.
97. *Wheels and Butterflies*, p. 25.

Chapter Nine

STUDY THAT HOUSE . . .

STUDY THAT TREE

I

YEATS MAKES A FULL STATEMENT of his last convictions in *On the Boiler*. The tone, the attack, and the brutality recall Yeats's legendary Swift in prophetic frenzy, especially the Swift of *A Modest Proposal* and the last book of *Gulliver's Travels*. These shockers are matched by *On the Boiler* since it too can offer not only aggressive material but aggressive form—that of the fighting pamphlet. Moreover, while Yeats's admitted antecedent was Ruskin's *Fors Clavigera*, his tradition obviously includes those many disquisitions on the state of Ireland written by Spenser, Molyneux, Swift, and

340

Berkeley. No less striking is the heroine of the symbolic drama to which the pamphlet builds, an eighteenth-century lady in the mold of Swift's "Injur'd Lady," Dark Rosaleen, or whatever woman—including Dervorgilla—one may choose to hold up as symbol of Ireland's shame. If at the time Yeats protested that he was finished with politics forever [1] and, in the very course of his writing, repudiated any one system of government, he could never be indifferent to the condition of Ireland. She was his politics and always had been. True, his nationalism had become one of the intellect,[2] as he had earlier described the nationalism of Swift and Berkeley. But now in *On the Boiler* it is subsumed under his pressing concern for the very tendance of the Irish soul.

Let us turn for the moment to Yeats's "Seven Propositions" of 1937. The first proposition—taken from Berkeley—is worth repeating since it comes close to being the basic assumption of *On the Boiler:* "Reality is a timeless and spaceless community of Spirits which perceive each other. Each Spirit is determined by and determines those it perceives, and each Spirit is unique." [3] Another document associated with these propositions is "A Race Philosophy," which in 1933 had momentarily borne the title "Irish Philosophy." [4] The emphasis in this series of assertions is on the necessary and continual struggle between the individual and the family. However, both the document and Yeats's private feelings at the time place the importance of the family first.[5] While the striving of the individual made for "intellectual initiative," the family insured the proper taste and habits most needed in Ireland: "Inherited wealth, privilege, precedence, have been created to preserve the family in its struggle." [6] His

1. *Letters*, pp. 881–82.
2. "A General Introduction for my Work," *Essays and Introductions*, p. 26.
3. Virginia Moore, *The Unicorn* (New York, 1954), p. 378.
4. Notebook beginning "On examining Michael's school reports. . . ."
5. Information from Mrs. W. B. Yeats. "A Race Philosophy" is available in Norman Jeffares, *W. B. Yeats: Man and Poet*, 2nd ed. (London, 1962), pp. 351–52.
6. *Ibid.*, p. 352.

political philosophy is more evolutionary than revolutionary.[7] Yeats is clearly beyond considerations of fascism and communism. This fact may explain the bitterness of *On the Boiler*. The best born were not ruling Ireland. The spiritual nature of the world, the crucial importance of the family, the desirable leadership from men of intellect seemed denied. The problem was Irish and European.

It was not new. Yeats had long been meditating it in his verse, prose, and plays. But here he is, almost for the first time, explicit. He also offers a conclusion which is a collective judgment, so to speak, taken from the men and the century under discussion. In charting the future of Ireland after the revolution he predicts, his eye is clearly on the eighteenth century and what he took to be its heirs in his lifetime:

> . . . although the Irish masses are vague and excitable because they have not yet been moulded and cast, we have as good blood as there is in Europe. Berkeley, Swift, Burke, Grattan, Parnell, Augusta Gregory, Synge, Kevin O'Higgins, are the true Irish people, and there is nothing too hard for such as these. If the Catholic names are few history will soon fill the gap. My imagination goes back to those Catholic exiled gentlemen of whom Swift said that their bravery exceeded that of all nations.[8]

Yeats has been accused of being concerned solely with a confused ideal of selective breeding derived from a late enthusiasm for eugenics and intelligence tests.[9] But like his eighteenth-century predecessors, and as his "Seven Propositions" and "A Race Philosophy" show, Yeats pondered the whole being of man, intelligence and character, body and soul alike. Some forty years before he wrote *On the Boiler*, the *Irish Homestead* reported him as saying:

> The end of all government, the end of all politics, the end of all movements was the making of character. The political move-

---

7. Ethel Mannin, *Privileged Spectator* (London, 1939), pp. 84–85.
8. *On the Boiler*, p. 30.
9. See Frank O'Connor, *Leinster, Munster and Connaught* (London, 1950), pp. 260–61, and "What Made Yeats a Great Poet," *Listener*, 15 May 1947, pp. 761–62.

ment, or the system of Government, was the best that made, when time had been given for its work to be done, the most men of high and stable character in a country, and certainly he could not imagine a movement that was more likely to make men of high and stable character than a movement that was teaching men to have confidence in one another; and to do their work by combining together instead of by opposing one another; and that was helping to end the suspicion of class for class; and that was giving men confidence in themselves by teaching them to do for themselves things they had been accustomed to have done for them.[10]

After urging that Ireland would regain her self-confidence in a future state founded on the soil and noble independence, Yeats had continued:

If we can do this we will take up again our ancient destiny, and our land will speak again among nations. We gave Christianity to Western Europe; we gave Johannes Scotus Erigena to philosophy. . . . We had a great lyric literature before Chaucer began the literature of England, and when disaster silenced our voice among nations we took up a cause [independence], which . . . we can agree to think a preparation for high labours, for it laid burdens on men, and taught them to bear them gladly.[11]

Able men, a unified Ireland, a country based on the soil, the intellectual and literary contributions of famous men—these familiar hopes and claims, with the names changed and the disaster pushed ahead about a hundred years, make *On the Boiler* the expression of a lifetime. But neither educator, logician, nor politician seemed able to point the future of the Irish race. Instead, the artist who looked to another age, who cast his eyes on other days, realized that "a single wrong choice may destroy a family, dissipating its tradition or its biological force, and the great sculptors, painters, and poets are there that instinct may find its lamp." [12]

10. Reported in the *Irish Homestead*, 6 November 1897, p. 742.
11. *Ibid.*
12. "If I were Four-and-Twenty," *Explorations*, p. 274.

Yeats, then, like the mad ship's carpenter who gave him the title for his pamphlet, will himself become the carpenter of the ship of state. Every bit of what he will say on these pages, whether in verse, prose, or drama, will point to the same theme, the enhancement of the Irish spirit or soul. In doing so, Yeats inundates us with references, examples, and personages to make and remake his point. Yet, his subject being modern Ireland or what it had become after the Union, is it surprising that the major corrective, the norm that he holds up, is one from Georgian Ireland? He turns his eye on that day and its wrong choice at the end of the century. This is not the only source of his curse. Heroic Ireland, the realm of King Arthur, the findings of eugenics, and no less the wisdom of Burton's *Anatomy of Melancholy* also serve him well in condemning that choice. Nevertheless, just as the play *Purgatory* forces upon us the connection between late eighteenth-century Ireland and the Ireland of Yeats's day, so too the theme of enhancement—or its lack—is fully and grimly informed by Swift, Burke, and Berkeley especially among his eighteenth-century masters. Yeats addresses himself to every class in Ireland, much as Swift had done in the *Modest Proposal*, and, like Swift, Yeats is saying what all his life he had said.[13]

II

To trace the eighteenth-century norm in intellect, art, and statesmanship that Yeats employs to criticize contemporary Ireland is to prepare ourselves for a reading of *Purgatory*, which is in itself not only a fittingly dramatic conclusion to *On the Boiler* but also to these

13. Gogarty, putting himself in the character of Ouseley, in his book *Going Native* (London, 1941), pictures Yeats in these years at sharp odds with Ireland: "Suddenly he turned in his chair, afire with vehement speech. 'Ouseley, you must go! You must leave this country! You cannot go on filled with bitterness or chilled with contempt for the little office-seekers and rude civil servants which is all that Ireland, left to itself, has made of its freedom. The Anglo-Irish are the salt of the earth. They are being persecuted. You must fly with the wild geese. You must go. To stand still is to sink in the bog' " (p. 9). Gogarty (Ouseley) then observes, "Here was a man confronted at the end of his days, not alone by the apparent failure of his ideals, but by their danger and menace to all that he held dear" (p. 10).

pages. In the *Boiler's* brief Preface and in the equally brief first section, "The Name," Yeats states the relevance of *Purgatory* and his scattered verses to his prose theme. He then recalls the mad antics of the great McCoy, who would harangue the Sligo populace for their wickedness from atop the boiler amid general execrations. We are prepared by Yeats's wild old man and his cunning relevance for the savage indignation that will follow.

And begin it does on the first page of the next section, "Preliminaries." Yeats sets out by lambasting Dublin's Mansion House and its inhabitant, the crowd-pleasing Lord Mayor, Alfred Byrne. Yeats condemns as symptomatic of the poor man's happy democratic vulgarity the stucco, the foolish porch, the vacant plate glass, and the superfluous grill work which are still hideously in view today. He holds up in contrast the Mansion House as it appeared in the eighteenth century—a red-brick building of two stories without a pediment, adorned with panels bearing figured subjects in relief above the cornice.[14] The pretentiously decked-out version on the Mayor's latest Christmas card compared just as unfavorably with a card more than likely bearing a Malton print that had preceded it.[15] The card, the house, and the inhabitant are summed up in this castigation:

> All Catholic Ireland, as it was before the National University and a victory in the field had swept the penal laws out of its bones, swells out in that pretentious front. Old historic bricks and window panes obliterated or destroyed, its porch invented when England was elaborating the architecture and interior decoration of the Gin Palace, its sole fitting inhabitant that cringing firbolg Tom Moore cast by some ironmonger—bronze costs money—now standing on the other side of Trinity College near the urinal.

The Mansion House was also symptomatic of the Mayor's desire for popularity, a desire he shared with the British Royal Family. Had he

14. This description is taken from the picture of the Lord Mayor's House in Brooking's Map of Dublin, 1728. I am indebted to Desmond Kennedy for this information.
15. Information from Mrs. W. B. Yeats.

been otherwise, he would have demanded a change or resigned, since "architectural taste is at present articulate only in the few." Aesthetic and political failures meet: "Try to be popular and you think another man's thought, sink into that slow, slothful, inanimate, semi-hypocritical thinking Dante symbolised by hoods and cloaks of lead."

Half-educated ignorance is the next target in Yeats's "Preliminaries." Specifically, he challenges compulsory education: "Forcing reading and writing on those who wanted neither was a worst part of the violence which for two centuries has been creating that hell wherein we suffer, unless indeed the spoilt priest in 'John Bull's Other Island' was right and the world itself is hell." Semi-literate ignorance hated books and literature and, as in the case of the Galway Library Committee of 1937, banned Shaw or, as Yeats implies, established an Irish censorship. Here again, Yeats's remarks on education also apply to politics, especially when he continues, echoing Burke: "Our representative system has given Ireland to the incompetent." For able appointed Senators he had known afford Yeats another contrast when set against "some typical elected man, emotional as a youthful chimpanzee, hot and vague, always disturbed, always hating something or other." The appointed ministers had seemed to need only travel and leisure to start the kind of aristocracy that Yeats hoped would date from the Post Office. Thus, quietly and cunningly, Yeats has suggested a time—two centuries earlier—to which those men might have truly looked.

These "Preliminaries" end on the same note. Ostensibly speaking of literary taste, Yeats muses over his former arrogant, ruling assertion—"Not what you want but what we want"—during his years with the Abbey Theatre. This attitude he links directly to the fact that the Abbey Players on tour "and Irish songs and novels, when they come from a deeper life than their nineteenth century predecessors, are taking the place of political speakers, political organizations, in holding together the twenty scattered millions conscious of their Irish blood." Recalling Yeats's comparison of the Abbey to Grattan's Parliament, this dictatorial attitude, the slighting of the nineteenth century, and the obvious Protestant leadership of the Abbey have a familiar political ring. Already, then, these supposedly innocent "Preliminaries" have subtly insinuated a norm of excellence we have seen before. We are also prepared for the framework and dogma of *Purgatory*.

The next section, "To-morrow's Revolution," maintains the burden of Yeats's argument for national enhancement through eugenics. Of course it is central to his plumping for both family and individual excellence. But at the risk of being greatly mistaken, I do not take this section as the main point of *On the Boiler*. It is true that he attended meetings of the Eugenics Society in the thirties. At one such meeting at 69 Eccleston Square, he is remembered to have asked pertinent and sympathetic questions on the subjects of population and eugenics.[16] Moreover, as a glance will show, many portions of this section were taken from Raymond B. Cattell's *The Fight for Our National Intelligence* and from a number of other sources, all acknowledged by Yeats in his footnotes.[17] Yet the first major quotation, a passage from Burton's *Anatomy of Melancholy*, is the important one in this section. It stresses man's degeneration, supposedly proved statistically by Cattell and Yeats's other sources.

The quotation starts with the words "So many different ways are we pledged and punished for our fathers' defaults" and ends with "we have many weak persons, both in body and mind, many feral diseases raging amongst us, crazed families, *parentes peremptores;* our fathers bad, and we are like to be worse." This is Yeats's subject: the general decay of Europe in the twentieth century. For democracy had put the weak in power. Probably only war would reverse the trend. He predicts it will start with the attempt of the educated minority to seize control of governments from the hands of the prolific masses. His call is for violence, war, and trauma that men's beliefs may be shaken. What more preparation do we need for the

16. Information in a letter to the author from Dr. C. P. Blacker, President of the Society.

17. Raymond B. Cattell, *The Fight for Our National Intelligence*, with Introductions by Lord Horder, Major Darwin, and F. P. Armitage (London, 1937).

degeneration of a family, murders, destruction, and, finally, the cold light of hatred at the end of *Purgatory?*

But "To-morrow's Revolution" also pertains to Ireland. The emphasis on human decay and diminution of mother-wit parallels Swift's most penetrating exposures of man. Every book of *Gulliver's Travels* points out the decline of man in one guise or another. However, Yeats defends Irish intellect itself. Interestingly enough, he saw that intelligence tests were meant for "a civilization dominated by towns, by their objectivity and curiosity." The Irish, in a different historical phase from the English, were also closer to the age of myth, were subjective where the English were objective. Berkeley begins to enter the argument, for Yeats goes on to set the Irish against the English, contrasting the mind strong on experience, tragedy, and reverie with that given to observation, pity, and psychology. Once again Berkeley seems to be answering Locke. We have seen how Yeats has customarily identified the worst of Irish life with English habits—democracy, vulgarity, compulsory education. Thus Berkeley has helped him extricate what he would call the true Irish mind from the utter degeneration suggested by test scores. To further, however, this idea of modern decay, Yeats sets "any notable eighteenth century orator" against Lloyd George, and then laments diminished Irish mother-wit—"co-ordination or a capacity for sustained purpose"—a gift very close to what he had considered the genius of eighteenth-century Protestant Ireland.

We now approach the heart of *On the Boiler*. It is the section labeled "Private Thoughts," with the parenthetical subtitle "(Should Be Skipped by Politicians and Journalists")" Needless to say our closest attention is solicited. But the truth divulged turns out to be an old one, the needed return to the heroic life, for the most part established or re-established in Ireland in the eighteenth century. Yeats takes us on a journey back to the Renaissance, a time that found Unity of Being—"mother-wit expressed in its perfection"—possible. Unity of Being came late, like the Renaissance, to Ireland. So that in Georgian Ireland there was still leisure, a hierarchical class structure, and an aristocracy that managed war, government, patronage, and the arts. Yet even by Swift's day the end was in sight. If Berkeley refused to aid Speaker Conolly in designing the front of Castletown, "he refused because too many country gentlemen were already at the task." After this came the specialist:

> Meanwhile a famous event happened with much notoriety; Sir Richard [sic] Temple and certain of his distinguished friends had affirmed the genuineness of the letters of Phalaris and the coarse, arrogant Bentley had proved them in the wrong; culture, unity of being, no longer sufficed, and the specialists were already there. Swift, when little more than a boy, satirised what "Gulliver" would satirise. . . .

Yeats then quotes in full the third stanza of Swift's "Ode to the Honourable Sir William Temple." He continues by massing Swift's and Berkeley's concrete thought against what he takes to have followed the rise of specialization, the mathematician's abstraction, the concept of the independence of space, getting its start at the end of the seventeenth century:

> Instead of hierarchical society, where all men are different, came democracy; instead of a science which had re-discovered Anima Mundi, its experiments and observations confirming the speculations of Henry More, came materialism: all that whiggish world Swift stared on till he became a raging man. The ancient foundations had scarcely dispersed when Swift's young acquaintance Berkeley destroyed the new, for all that would listen created modern philosophy and established for ever the subjectivity of space.

Looking backward and forward, Yeats continues in this section to speak of his own revolutionary times as might Burke: "Hegel's historical dialectic is, I am persuaded, false, and its falsehood has led to the rancid ill-temper of the typical communist and his incitements or condonations of murder." Goldsmith's sweetness is also part of that lost heroic life, for "Nature or reality as known to poets and tramps has no moment, no impression, no perception like another, everything is unique and nothing unique is measurable." Yeats then sums up his hopes for the future and his hatred of the seventeenth century in this sentence: "I detest the Renaissance because it made the human mind inorganic; I adore the Renaissance because it clarified form and created freedom." The implication is that Ireland had had the best of both: in the eighteenth century the Protestant Ascendancy gave form and freedom of the intellect to Ireland. At the same time, if Locke had rendered the mind mechanical, Berkeley had restored its totality, two facts for Ireland to remember in its coming counter-Renaissance.

That Ireland is outlined in "Ireland After the Revolution," a section where Yeats discusses education, armament, recognition of the crown, and religion. So far as the eighteenth century goes, the drift remains the same. The insistence on Greek partly duplicates the classical education of that century. A small, well-trained, heavily armed military "could throw back from our shores the disciplined uneducated masses of the commercial nations": this seems a military version of Berkeley's Salamis. No less, the minimum recognition of the crown Yeats calls for reflects his disdain for a royal family, deified by the middle class, that refused to aid Nicholas II for fear of the working-class reaction. Hence, Yeats can say, the "English mind, excited by its newspaper proprietors and its schoolmasters, has turned into a bed-hot harlot." So one may also choose to comment on the lady who marries a groom in *Purgatory*. However, this long section "Ireland After the Revolution" closes with a benediction which not only assures us of the relevance of that symbolic play, but also strikes at the so-called difference between this world and the next, as will the play: ". . . the whole nation must be convinced by some new argument that death is but passing from one room into another, for lacking that there can be no great lasting quality."

The remaining prose of *On the Boiler* is a critical exposition on Irish art in general and the Abbey Theatre in particular, in which Yeats slyly tells us how to read his play. This section, named "Other Matters," allows Yeats to inveigh against the increasingly vulgar whimsey of Irish drama and against the popularity of plays full of thought and bereft of action, both types examples of an urban and mechanical drama. But the second, with its slight claims to intellectuality and uniqueness, is the more meretricious, lacking as it does any hint of the body's pull on the unconscious, any magnanimity of style, or any real coherence. Out of this thin reduction of the drama had come one abortion, Flecker's *Hassan,* which had tried to flood the audience not with the ecstasy of tragedy but with low horror, the revolutionist's hatred of nobility, and a capricious, needless cruelty. Yeats's play will be the opposite:

> The arts are all the bridal chambers of joy. No tragedy is legitimate unless it leads some great character to his final joy. . . . Some Frenchman has said that farce is the struggle against a ridiculous object, comedy against a movable object, tragedy against an immovable; and because the will, or energy, is greatest in tragedy, tragedy is the more noble; but I add that "will or energy is eternal delight," and when its limit is reached it may become a pure, aimless joy, though the man, the shade, still mourns his lost object. It has, as it were, thrust up its arms towards those angels who have . . . returned into themselves in an eternal moment.

I call this the theory of *Purgatory,* the theory of the symbolic tragedy of the eighteenth century and its consequence for modern Ireland. Nor can we miss by now the joyous quality noted in the best Protestant minds by Yeats's account, nor the phrase from his Berkeley essay that Yeats uses to identify that joy in a tragic hero set against the immovable wall of history.

Last of all, Yeats explains the possible narrowness and, at the same time, the breadth of the play. The audience he seeks, for instance, must be small, know literature, and be knowledgeable in Irish affairs —"We, like all good poets, turn our backs on the heterogeneous, seek out our own kindred." Next Yeats turns to what literature may show us. Once again, the dream sequences mentioned in his Berkeley essay are cited to prove that "Events in time come upon us head-on like waves, each wave in some main character the opposite of its predecessor. But there are other events that lie side by side in space complements one of another." Opposite events in time will appear in the symbolic contentions between fathers and sons in the play;

complementary events in space will allow Yeats to dramatize the relevance of purgatorial suffering to the living. The consequences of ancient crimes may be made apparent to the living and the unborn through literature. Yet a play must keep before us what we know. The playwright must celebrate timeless Greek proportions, in order that sexual instinct may know its proper goal. That goal must never again be a groom who would destroy those proportions. Yeats had started by comparing the old with the new form of the Mansion House; now he offers a play illuminating the form and proportion lost from Irish life since the eighteenth century. The ghostly drama of a history an Irishman cannot help knowing will trace those lost lineaments in the ruinous generations that followed upon the French Revolution.

III

But before spelling out the cumulative disasters *Purgatory* links in a chain of guilt from that time to the present, let us examine the few poems interspersed in the prose just reviewed. For these poems hammer at the constant betrayal of promise and hope in Ireland and Europe by men and women born into former heroic roles. Their derelictions helped confirm the present decay. The opening eight lines of the first poem are instructive:

> Why should not old men be mad?
> Some have known a likely lad
> That had a sound fly fisher's wrist
> Turn to a drunken journalist;
> A girl that knew all Dante once
> Live to bear children to a dunce;
> A Helen of social welfare dream
> Climb on a wagonette to scream.

The theme of an old man's madness is just disguise enough here for the very sane Yeats to dig deep into his own career and point up wasted lives where most of Ireland would discover worldly or even ideal success. In one way or another his references have always been an open secret. For instance, the journalist was R. M. Smyllie, editor of the *Irish Times,* a native of Sligo, graduate of Trinity, and an enthusiastic defender of the Anglo-Irish.[18] A. N. Jeffares has correctly identified Iseult Stuart as the lady once learned in Dante. The Helen is equally obvious: Eva Gore-Booth. It may be readily argued that none of these are in fact the exaggerated failures that Yeats would have us believe. But in keeping with the anonymous, tentative identifications, Yeats can hold up any Irish journalist, traditionally hard drinkers if the Pearl Bar is any evidence, as a somewhat disappointing reader of his poetry compared to the ideal fisherman. Smyllie himself seems to have recognized the intent of Yeats's couplets, since he had little good to say thereafter of Yeats or even of his son Michael. Similarly, we have reviewed Yeats's disappointment in the course taken by Eva in her career. Her lines are particularly apt at this point since they also single out the social damage Yeats attributed to any scheme that would coddle the weak in the world. And no matter how he may have praised Francis Stuart as a novelist, he found the man personally a perplexing combination that was "typical of the new Ireland, at once so medieval and so sceptical." [19] Such a man probably had no business being married to a girl enamored of Dante; in any case, it is doubtful if Yeats ever approved of Iseult's marriage.

This poem "Why should not Old Men be Mad" despairs over the gifted and the beautiful, at least two of them denizens of the Sligo Yeats knew, one from a Georgian mansion, the other seemingly destined for the Anglo-Irish ideal of "The Fisherman." Yet both had gone astray in the sentimentalities of modern Ireland. The proper antidote was Crazy Jane's heroic disdain for George V of England, leader of a country supposedly the model for sentimental Ireland:

> A King had some beautiful cousins
> But where are they gone?
> Battered to death in a cellar
> And he stuck to his throne.

18. Information from Mrs. W. B. Yeats. See also "Meet R. M. Smyllie," *Bell,* III (December 1941), 180–88, and Brian Inglis, *West Briton* (London, 1962), pp. 46–58 and *passim.*

19. "Modern Ireland," *Massachusetts Review,* V (Winter 1964), 266.

These lines from Yeats's second poem (later called "Crazy Jane on the Mountain") show betrayal not merely by individuals but by a family and a nation. To abandon the Russian family to a revolution that stemmed from the same forces that had threatened in 1789 was to miss Burke's warning and once again forget aristocratic Europe.

Not surprisingly, the poem that both ends the prose discourse and introduces *Purgatory* incorporates all the betrayals mentioned so far. Perhaps we ought to fix our attention most carefully, then, on the second stanza of the poem later called "The Statesman's Holiday," for here Yeats points at the widespread irresponsibility of leaders in Ireland, England, and Europe. To try to name names here leaves one open to charges of wild speculation, since Yeats has left his exact meaning teasingly vague yet open to guesses from the kind of audience he had just finished touting in "Other Matters." Thus, while the singer in the poem is certainly Yeats himself, his disguise is especially relevant for this second stanza:

> Here in Monte Carlo, where I am writing, somebody talked of a man with a monkey and some sort of stringed instrument, and it has pleased me to imagine him a great politician. I will make him sing to the sort of tune that goes well with my early sentimental poems.

The irony of this introduction probably need not be pointed out. However, we ought to remember Yeats's description of the typical elected Senator as a chimp, and also acknowledge his pointed disgust with his own early sentimental verses. This same irony hovers over these lines from the second stanza, all lines of rejection:

> Am I a great Lord Chancellor
> That slept upon the Sack?
> Commanding officer that tore
> The khaki from his back?
> Or am I de Valéra,
> Or the King of Greece,
> Or the man that made the motors?
> Ach, call me what you please!

354

Here is more evidence that Yeats never forgave what he took to be De Valera's failure or irresponsibility in fomenting civil war in Ireland. This included the burning of many a great house and a later refusal to control the dissidents of the thirties. The King of Greece was probably George II, who had returned to Athens as king in November 1935 after a twelve-year absence and within a year appointed General Metaxas head of the government. Metaxas, in turn, established a Fascist dictatorship. Thus, another statesman had abdicated the responsibilities of his position. In the same way, Lord Nuffield, a self-made man whom Yeats admired, had mistakenly chosen to endow an Oxford College in the name of applied science and so accelerated the degeneration of education. He was "the man who made the motors," and Yeats had complained of his endowment in the section "To-morrow's Revolution." Striking closer to home, however, are the lines on the commanding officer. He may be General O'Duffy, but I think not, for his khaki shirt was ordered removed by De Valera. Whatever might be said against O'Duffy, his actions were not treasonable.

But Yeats might not have said the same of General Sir Hubert Gough, associated by family and name with Lough Cutra Castle, in modern times the very sinkhole of snobbish, anti-Irish Anglo-Ireland.[20] The first Viscount Gough of Lough Cutra had been a cousin of Sir Hubert's grandfather.[21] In any case, it is probably this Anglo-Irishman who is accused of dividing Ireland, the equivalent of treason in Yeats's eyes. For temporary Brigadier-General Hubert de la Poer Gough was the protagonist of the Mutiny at the Curragh or, as the English call it, the Curragh Incident. Loyal to Ulster, he accepted the choice of dismissal from the Army from fifty-seven of his cavalry officers on the 20th and 21st of March 1914. As commanding officer of the Third Cavalry Brigade based at the Curragh, he had been ordered to take up defensive positions in Belfast in the event

20. Vere R. T. Gregory, *The House of Gregory* (Dublin, 1943), pp. 91–95, and local information given to the author.

21. General Sir Hubert Gough, *Soldiering On* (London, 1954), p. 22, n. 1. For the official story of the Goughs and Lough Cutra, see Robert S. Rait, *The Story of an Irish Property* (Oxford, 1908).

that Ulster should reject the third Home Rule Bill, which was to become law in June. He himself refused the assignment, resigned, was dismissed from the service and then reinstated.[22] The rapid growth of the Southern Volunteers, the Easter Rising, and the civil war are in some senses the consequence. This must have seemed to Yeats Anglo-Irish dereliction with a vengeance.

In the same speculative vein, the sleepy Lord Chancellor could be Frederick Edwin Earl of Birkenhead. When known as Galloper Smith (F. E. Smith), he had been the government prosecutor at Casement's trial. As Lord Chancellor, he played a questionable role in the Treaty negotiations of 1921, since he is credited with having a hand in the final shaping of the disruptive Oath. And before these two events, he had worked with Carson to exclude Ulster from any Irish Home Rule settlement.[23] He had also personally guaranteed the authenticity of the Casement Diaries.[24] All these leaders and statesmen, whatever history may finally say of their actions, might well have seemed to Yeats to have contributed to the end of a Europe that was passing and was to pass absolutely away with World War II. And so to *Purgatory*.

22. See "Mutiny at the Curragh," *Irish Times*, 23 March 1914, and "The Debate," *Irish Times*, 24 March 1914. Also A. P. Ryan, *Mutiny at the Curragh* (London, 1956), Chapters X and XI; Sir James Fergusson, *The Curragh Incident* (London, 1964), *passim*; and General Sir Hubert Gough, *Soldiering On*, pp. 15–27, 98–112. The suggestion that Brigadier-General F. P. Crozier, who resigned his command of the Auxiliaries on 25 February 1921, might be the offending officer seems doubtful. He could hardly be called recreant to Ireland in removing himself from the Black and Tans. See his *Impressions and Recollections* (London, 1930), pp. 263–70, and *Ireland for Ever* (London, 1932), p. 180.

23. The Earl of Birkenhead, *Frederick Edwin Earl of Birkenhead* (London, 1935), I, 282–310, and II, 76, 161. For Gogarty's dislike of Birkenhead, see *It Isn't This Time of Year at All!* (New York, 1954), p. 202. There is the slight possibility that Yeats may have had Lord Glenavy in mind. Despite their mutual respect, Yeats may have remembered Glenavy's nodding during the Senate debate on divorce (*Senate Speeches*, p. 99). Churchill, whose name appears in an early manuscript version of the poem, is also a possible candidate.

24. William J. Maloney, *The Forged Casement Diaries* (Dublin and Cork, 1936), p. 108. After reading this book, Yeats had written his poem "Roger Casement" (*Variorum*, p. 581).

IV

The best way to open discussion of the play is to review Yeats's remarks prompted by its first performance. Strangely enough, those who have written with such confidence on *Purgatory* have paid no attention to these remarks. At the conclusion of the first Abbey performance on Wednesday night, August 10, 1938, Yeats had said, when called to the stage, that *Purgatory* contained his beliefs about this world and the next.[25] The next evening at a lecture on Yeats by F. R. Higgins during the Abbey Theatre Festival, the Rev. Terence L. Connolly, head of the English department at Boston College, asked the meaning of the play's symbolism and, amazingly, got no answer. On the 12th, Yeats was interviewed by a reporter from the *Irish Independent* on the puzzle. In this interview, Yeats elaborated on his original remarks:

> Father Connolly said that my plot is perfectly clear but that he does not understand my meaning. My plot is my meaning. I think the dead suffer remorse and re-create their old lives just as I have described. There are mediaeval Japanese plays about it, and much in the folklore of all countries.
>
> In my play, a spirit suffers because of its share, when alive, in the destruction of an honoured house; that destruction is taking place all over Ireland to-day. Sometimes it is the result of poverty, *but more often because a new individualistic generation has lost interest in the ancient sanctities.*
>
> I know of old houses, old pictures, old furniture that have been sold without apparent regret. In some few cases a house has been destroyed by a mesalliance. I have founded my play on this exceptional case, partly because of my interest in certain problems of eugenics, partly because it enables me to depict more vividly than would otherwise be possible the tragedy of the house.
>
> In Germany there is special legislation to enable old families

25. "Mr. W. B. Yeats's New Play," *Evening Mail*, 11 August 1938.

to go on living where their fathers lived. The problem is not Irish, but European, though it is perhaps more acute here than elsewhere.[26]

Quite clearly, then, it is life in this individualistic world that Yeats symbolizes. The relevance of the prose parts of *On the Boiler* decrying the loss of ancient wisdom must be evident. So too are those two prose tracts from these years, one a lecture, the other part of a book, in which Yeats theorizes on the development of modern Ireland after the flight of the Wild Geese. Both the lecture "Modern Ireland" and its ultimate form, the prose of Yeats's *Commentary on "A Parnellite at Parnell's Funeral,"* stress four periods, as discussed in Chapter Three, each going to the toll of a tragic bell: the Flight of the Earls; the Battle of the Boyne; the influence of the French Revolution; and the death of Parnell. Yeats claimed some knowledge of the last three. In the next to the last section of the lecture, Section VIII, Yeats sums up his meaning to that point and also helps us see how the main characters are meant to be taken in *Purgatory:*

> I have spoken of the three periods which have made the Irish nation. When a period is over, what it has created remains in the national character. The eighteenth-century governing class is still with us, though it [is] now Catholic and sometimes can speak Gaelic, and the second period still fights against it in our blood and against the third period with its bitter national self-knowledge and self-absorption.[27]

And at the end of this section, Yeats focuses on what he takes to be the most widespread view of Ireland held by modern Irish writers:

> Though I have classed Mr. Bernard Shaw with the writers of an earlier period, he has in the one play he wrote for the Abbey Theatre, *John Bull's Other Island,* displayed in the character of the spoilt priest Ireland as it appears to the Irish novelists and dramatists of today, and summed up what might be their final

26. "Dramatist's Answer to U. S. Priest's Query," *Irish Independent,* 13 August 1938. The italics are mine.
27. "Modern Ireland," *Massachusetts Review,* V, 267.

thought. Four years [ago], while ill in Italy, and not sure I would know active life again, I wrote in my diary the events of life and art that had most [moved] me, and I numbered the moralizing of the spoilt priest:

[. . . There is only one place of horror and torment known to my religion; and that place is hell. Therefore it is plain to me that this earth of ours must be hell, and that we are all here, as the Indian revealed to me—perhaps he was sent to reveal it to me—to expiate crimes committed by us in a former existence.] [28]

These comments and preoccupations, beyond the evidence of prose and poetry in *On the Boiler,* are added because modern Ireland, its past and future, is the essential material for *Purgatory.* From the destruction of a house, we see the decline of the family and the individual into the final spiritual anguish of souls in purgatory, while the Old Man lives in virtual hell on earth. Clearly I cannot agree with those who find the subject of Ireland somewhat beneath Yeats's talent. Equally obvious must be my indebtedness to interpretations of the play offered by Donald Pearce and John Heath-Stubbs.[29]

The action, immediately perceived, is curiously timeless. Yet if one contemplates it as present action, he can be said to meet an old pedlar —who had "lived among great houses"—and his son before the ruins of an ancient house. The Old Man had seen the house and the bare tree a year before. We are also told on the first page that he had seen it fifty years earlier, "before the thunderbolt had riven it." Presumably he would have seen it just before Parnell was rejected by his party in 1889, an act that split the nation. The scenario has the Old Man begotten some sixty-three years earlier than the time of the play. As I speculate, the scenario was written in early 1938. Thus the destruction of the house by his drunken father, when the Old Man was sixteen, would have occurred close to the death of Parnell in

28. *Ibid.,* pp. 267–68. The bracketed material is Shaw's, added by Curtis Bradford, the editor of Yeats's piece.

29. Donald R. Pearce, "Yeats's Last Plays: An Interpretation," *ELH,* XVIII (March 1951), 71–75; and John Heath-Stubbs, *On a Darkling Plain* (London, 1950), p. 205. Those who deny the importance of Ireland to the play may also be denying Yeats's intention of placing *Purgatory* at the end of *On the Boiler.*

October 1891. If we continue to believe the play contemporary, the Boy was born near August 10, 1922, by his own words: ". . . my age, sixteen years old/At the Puck Fair." One need not elaborate on the Saturnalia of those three days (9, 10, 11 August). The Fair, the beginning of the Free State, and the opening day of the play, August 10, 1938, all seem tied together. There is no reason to review the action that brings the Old Man to kill his son. However, as the Old Man discovers, that killing has not stopped his mother's purgatorial dream, for the consequences of her transgressions rest upon herself and her husband; thus "There is no help but in themselves/And in the mercy of God." She remains in her purgatory, her son the Old Man in his hell on earth. This double state is summed up in his final cry:

> O God
> Release my mother's soul from its dream!
> Mankind can do no more. Appease
> The misery of the living and the remorse of the dead.

Without turning the play into an allegory, which those with an historical interest like mine may tend to do, one can nevertheless see how the characters are nationally symbolic. Yeats himself had insisted in his statement to the Irish press that the play was to be read symbolically, not allegorically. Hence it does seem that Yeats's three periods of modern Irish history are dramatized in the characters.

Symbolically, the mother represents the second period, from the Battle of the Boyne to the French Revolution. As heir to the culture of that Protestant Ireland, she turned irresponsible to her tradition and married a groom. Seduced by his looks, she had married him and died in childbirth. These events seem to be shadowy parallels to the democratic seductions of the French Revolution and even to the popular seductions of schoolmaster and journalist that Yeats felt had turned "the English mind into a bed-hot harlot." In any case, Ireland's espousing the democratic politics of O'Connell—"the smile through the horse-collar"—seems perfectly symbolized in her choice of a groom.

Her son, the Old Man, is more complicated. He is the first consequence. His career appears representative of nineteenth-century Ireland under O'Connell, a nation in Yeats's eyes given to huckstering, denying its origins, hampered by ignorance, at best mourning over its lost heritage. The Old Man is close to being a very complete member of the Garrison, whose Catholic father later, drunk on piety and politics, burned the house down and destroyed the last vestige of that Protestant past in denying Parnell. To intrude on this neat scheme for a moment, one is also reminded of the equally relevant fanatic burning of Big Houses in 1922–23. As Yeats discovered many times from the *Playboy* days on, O'Connell's Ireland had lived on into the twentieth century and begot the Free State and those who fought it. But the difficulty—and it probably saves the Old Man from being considered allegorically—is that he suggests so much more. For one thing—and this is an important point—he is linked to both the second and the fourth periods, and seems to have all three warring within his blood. For another, as an Old Man, he also comes close to dramatizing many sides of Yeats himself: his love of the eighteenth century, his origins in the nineteenth, his helping establish an art and public opinion favorable to an independent Ireland, his increased hatred of O'Connell and those he took to be his heirs. Nor is there need to stop here. For many events of Yeats's life and memory crowd in and intensify the historical symbolism, not the least among them being Coole House itself, already marked for destruction in his mind. In fact, lines are actually used to describe the ruined house on the stage which he and Lady Gregory had used to describe Coole House:

> Great people lived and died in this house;
> Magistrates, colonels, members of Parliament,
> Captains and Governors, and long ago
> Men that had fought at Aughrim and the Boyne.
> Some that had gone on government work
> To London or to India came home to die,
> Or came from London every spring
> To look at the May-blossom in the park.

And then, in what is certainly Yeats's own voice:

>   . . . to kill a house
>   Where great men grew up, married, died,
>   I here declare a capital offence.[30]

Yet there is also much more of him in the play. After his death, Yeats felt, the woods of Coole would have his longest visits.[31] There was the ghost story he had heard in 1916 about a crime, a consequent haunting, and the degeneration of a family.[32] The fact of Edward Martyn's peasant background and the coarsening of George Moore's blood had not escaped his notice.[33] There is an accursed, ruined house and a pear tree that bears no fruit in *John Sherman*.[34] Yeats had also carefully noted the statement an old man once made to Synge: "The young people are of no use. . . . I am not as good a man as my father was and my son is growing up worse than I am." [35] Then, too, Yeats had written an early story, ghostly and cataclysmic, of Oona Hearne, a woman who had fallen in love with a rascal, Michael Creed, "through that love of strength which is deep in the heart of even the subtlest among them [women]." [36] Nor may the symbolic overtones of one more ruined house, empty at the top and marked with a bit of shell from a daw's nest, remain very far from the powerful images in poems like "The Stare's Nest by my Window" and "Blood and the Moon."

Perhaps the bastard Boy needs little comment at all. His few actions show him to be a sensation-seeking thief, a potential killer,

30. Lady Gregory had written, and Yeats had read and remembered, this passage in her *Journals* for 3 June 1922: "I have been out till after 9 o'c. Everything is beautiful, one must stand to look at blossoming tree after tree; the thorns in the Park that William used to come over from London to see at this time of the year best of all" (p. 22). According to Mrs. Yeats, W. B. thought such trips all too typical of Garrison responsibility to Ireland. See also *Variorum*, pp. 833–34.

31. *Autobiographies*, pp. 377–78.

32. Hone, pp. 284, 472.

33. *Autobiographies*, pp. 388, 402.

34. *Collected Works*, VII, 208, 279.

35. "The Great Blasket," *Spectator*, 2 June 1933, p. 798.

36. "Those Who Live in the Storm," *The Speaker*, 21 July 1894, pp. 74–75.

and a dull, embittered individualist. He refuses his father's wisdom, considers killing him, and openly admires his drunken forefather's success. How else consider right and wrong? Only before his death does he begin to see the light of his grandmother's purgatorial dream. Does Yeats hope that the sixteen-year-old Eire will also see its light? Yet the ignorant Boy helps *us* see how opposites meet in time, how dying is but a moving from one room to another, how we may embody truth without knowing it.

The stage settings intimate another dimension to the symbolism. The ruined great house offers to Ireland, Europe, and the world the ironic triumph of romantic individualism. That house, with its traveled men, library, administrators, and soldiers, is a memorial to what Swift, Berkeley, Burke, and Goldsmith had offered Ireland and, by 1938, Ireland had rejected. The Old Man's first words in the play are "Study that house." His next speech continues to claim our attention:

> The moonlight falls upon the path,
> The shadow of a cloud upon the house
> And that's symbolic; study that tree,
> What is it like?

And the Boy answers, "A silly old man." The meanings of the tree have been discussed previously. But now, seen together, the moon-light, path, cloud, and house—they remain unchanged throughout the play—are a composite image of eighteenth-century excellence fallen on evil days. A ruined house, ruined family, and ruined tree suggest individual, familial, and national failures. The house—"Its threshold gone to patch a pig-stye"—empty at the top, dark beneath a cloud or curse of vaporous patriotism from a "century disastrous to national intellect," flanked by a tree bathed in the light of hatred, symbolizes the haunted remains of Georgian Ireland. Other witnesses hover about in grim association. Specifically, there is Swift cursed with sibylline foresight and glaring over the wreckage to come; Burke in the tree stripped of its leaves and riven by the thunderbolt, and Burke who had fought the materialistic anarchy voiced by the

Boy and the leveling democracy that had seduced his grandmother; Berkeley who had proved the world of pigsties but a dream had man imagination and intellect enough to see everything in God's eye, and Berkeley who declared the subjectivity of space and time and so the uniqueness of all men whatever station they graced; and Goldsmith— yes, perhaps the path and the journey of the Old Man would have been otherwise in his company. Yet the Boy is also right. The tree *is* like a silly old man, his father, the Old Man, and, in the light of hatred, like Yeats. He rages under the cloud of emotional, Gaelic, Catholic, middle-class patriotism everywhere triumphant.

Tragic irony also gleams from this Georgian memorial. For the heart of this symbol of purpose and co-ordination, to re-echo Yeats's definitions of mother-wit, has at its center the Old Man's mother. The consequence of her act has been family degeneration, truly national degeneration, if we take her to symbolize that period beginning modern Ireland. Her transgression was to marry and pass on coarsened blood, a curse. Her crime, however, was really one of intellect, a wrong choice, a refusal of traditional sanctities, perhaps something like that of her original in paradise. But this fall is not fortunate, it is tragic. She had been seduced by commonness. In the face of destruction and murder the consequences must yet be played out. Hearing those eighteenth-century hoof beats on the drive of the house, must we not wonder at Yeats's words in *On the Boiler*,

> A woman's face, though she be lost or childless, may foretell a transformation of the people, be a more dire or beneficent omen than those trumpets heard by Etruscan seers in middle air,

especially since they explain a phrase describing the tragic complement of generations: ". . . each living the other's death, dying the other's life." The woman and her house had, for Yeats, the virtually sacred task of education Swift had assigned himself in *The Words Upon the Window-pane*. But here the scene of passion and the scene of remorse come together in one scene of tragic ecstasy for our edification.

Is this possible? I think so, for *Purgatory* points to the actual hell of the present. All is done. There is none to turn to except God. The limit has been reached: murder cannot dislodge historical consequence, though the Old Man mourns his lost mother and stretches his arms in supplication to God. Yeats has depicted a national genealogical tragedy in a manner that stresses action. He has recognized the awesome power of the body. His drama is based on what he takes to be true history. The end, however murderous, is not vulgar or morbid. The wicked are punished and the blame is fixed. One may imagine Yeats smiling joyously.

He may be terribly wrong, just as *On the Boiler* as a whole can be viewed as preposterous. But there is a truth expressed in the pamphlet and the play which all must feel even though it is felt in different ways. It is the truth of the purgatory all men experience from the errors inherent in the flesh during their strivings as individuals, members of families, and spirits in mortal coils. Like Swift, Yeats, and the mother of the Old Man, we are dragged down into mankind. Hence this inevitable tragedy may yet provide—and this is the great power of *Purgatory*—an aimless joy in allowing us to be the spectators of the ages. Yeats never forgot the story told him by Paddy Flynn of God's smiling at the last day both on those he rewards and those he sends to everlasting flames. One may imagine Yeats and those Augustan spirits—who shared his timeless indignation against the weaknesses of the flesh, the mind, and the society that might wreck a house or a country—happy, especially since reality was "a timeless and spaceless community of Spirits which perceive each other," and the pure joy of election still remained theirs.

Index

Abercorn, Duke of, 53
AE (George Russell), 9, 108, 111, 113, 143, 187n, 226, 227n
Aiken, Frank, 213
Ainslie, Douglas, 252n
Allgood, Sara, 250
Allingham, William, 6, 7, 281, 283
Alspach, Russell K., 4n
Anne, Queen, 133, 142
Antoinette, Marie, 171n, 209, 213, 214
Aquinas, St. Thomas, 223n, 242n, 249n
Ardilaun, Lord, 290
Armitage, F. P., 347n
Asquith, Mrs. H. H., 37
Atkinson, Dr., 11
Auden, W. H., 160
Austen, Jane, 212

Bagenal, Philip H., 97n
Bailey, William Frederick, 64, 65
Balderston, Katharine C., 269n
Balfour, Arthur James, Earl of, 21
Ball, F. Elrington, 121n
Balzac, Honoré de, 212, 244, 245
Bangs, Francis H., 217n
Banim, John, 29
Barlow, Jane, 5
Barrett, Richard, 182

Barrington, Sir Jonah, 37, 43, 44, 97n, 301, 303, 305–7, 309
Barry, James, 98, 154
Basterot, Comte de, 42
Baudelaire, Charles, 7
Beattie, Rev., 91, 92
Beauregard, Gen. P. G. T., 41
Beckett, Samuel, 109n
Behan, Brendan, 89n
Belloc, Hilaire, 199
Belton, Patrick, 157
Bennett, Arnold, 246n
Bentley, Richard, 132n, 134, 349
Bergson, Henri, 102, 235, 304
Berkeley, Bishop George, 21, 48, 86, 90, 99, 102, 105, 107, 108, 110, 111, 112, 122, 123, 125, 162, 163, 179, 193, 217n, 222–65, 266, 267, 268, 272, 273, 274, 275, 278, 293, 305, 309, 319–22, 341, 342, 344, 348, 349, 350, 351, 363, 364
Berry, James, 336
Birkenhead, F. E. Smith, Earl of, 356
Birmingham, George, 301n
Blacker, C. P., 347n
Blake, William, 6, 124, 186, 222, 223, 244, 245, 258, 262, 265
Blind, Rudolf, 95n
Blunt, Wilfrid Scawen, 244

Blythe, Ernest, 158n, 180n, 182n
Bodkin, Thomas, 61n, 75
Boehme, Jacob, 224, 262, 265
Bolingbroke, Henry St. John, Viscount, 127n, 132n, 133
Boswell, James, 271
Bowen, Elizabeth, 100, 101
Boyd, Ernest A., 190n
Bradford, Curtis, 359n
Bromage, Mary C., 155n
Brooke, Stopford A., 96n
Brophy, Liam, 110
Brown, S. L., 172
Brown, Wallace Cable, 270n
Browne, Mgr. Patrick, 126n
Browne, Sir Thomas, 4, 123, 124
Browning, Robert, 230, 244
Burke, Edmond Mc Ulick, 300–1
Burke, Edmund, 3, 21, 25, 38, 48, 60, 66, 78, 90, 99, 102, 105, 107, 108n, 110, 112, 116, 123, 162, 163, 168–221, 229, 232, 241, 242, 243, 255, 266, 267, 268, 272, 274, 275, 278, 303, 308, 310, 319–22, 328, 333, 342, 344, 346, 349, 354, 363
Burke, Oliver J., 97n
Burns, Robert, 273
Burton, Robert, 344, 347
Butler, Hubert, 96n
Butt, Isaac, 116
Byrne, Alfred, 345–46
Byrne, William, 126n
Byron, George Gordon, Lord, 230, 244

Cadogan, Lord, 144
Caffee, Nathaniel M., 270n
Calkins, Mary W., 225
Callanan, J. J., 21
Cambrensis, Giraldus, 118
Canfield, Curtis, 134n
Carew, Kate, 300n
Carleton, William, 5, 8, 9, 29, 30, 32
Carrig, Patrick, 301
Carson, Sir Edward, 81, 356
Casement, Sir Roger, 146, 334
Cassidy, Peter, 182
Castiglione, Baldassare, 99, 133
Castle, Richard, 100, 314
Castletown, Lord, 53, 115

Cattell, Raymond B., 347
Cecil, Lord David, 133
Charlemont, Lord, 98, 107, 337
Chesterfield, Lord, 254
Chesterton, G. K., 199
Church, Richard, 294n
Churchill, Sir Winston, 356n
Clanrickarde, Lord, 40, 46, 57
Clanrickarde, Richard, Earl of, 301
Clare, John Fitzgibbon, Earl of, 24, 110
Clarendon, Edward Hyde, Earl of, 328
Clark, David R., 134
Clarke, Austin, 126, 171n
Claudel, Paul, 201, 202
Clinton-Baddeley, V. C., 68n
Clive, Robert, 176n
Clonbrock, Lord, 53
Cole, W. L., 53
Coleridge, Samuel Taylor, 191n, 196n, 235n, 243n, 244n, 250, 272n
Collingwood, R. G., 262n
Collins, John Churton, 317
Collins, Michael, 155, 157, 175, 181, 182n
Comerford, Mr., 41
Comyn, David, 331n
Congreve, William, 21
Connolly, James, 189n, 218n, 316
Connolly, Rev. Terence L., 357
Conolly, William, 314, 349
Cooper, Bryan, 110, 111, 142, 175–79, 180n, 181, 213
Cooper, Mrs. Bryan, 175
Cooper, E. F. P., 175
Cooper, Joshua, 176
Corbet, Robert, 92, 93
Corcoran, Rev. Timothy, 143n
Corkery, Daniel, 20, 107, 108, 109
Cosgrave, William T., 80, 107, 158n, 159, 164, 165, 172, 179, 181, 182n, 207–8, 332
Costello, Miss, 207n
Coughlan, Col. P. J., 159n
Cowley, Abraham, 4, 244
Craig, Capt. C. C., 53
Croce, Benedetto, 217n, 252, 253, 262, 265n
Cromwell, Oliver, 203, 217, 333–35
Cronin, Commandant, 156
Cross, K. G. W., 252n

Crozier, Gen. F. P., 356n
Cumberland, Gerald, 335n
Curran, John Philpot, 100n
Curtin, Superintendent, 156

Dante, 324, 346, 352, 353
Darby, "Wild Captain," 334
Darwin, Major, 347
Davie, Donald, 230n
Davis, Thomas, 5, 8, 27, 29, 30, 31, 32, 52, 90, 124, 128n, 204
De Blacam, Aodh, 110–11
Delany, Patrick, 122n
Denham, Sir John, 21
Denson, Alan, 113n
Descartes, René, 236
Despard, Mrs. Charlotte, 211n
De Valera, Eamon, 128n, 147, 155, 156, 157, 158n, 160, 161, 164, 165, 332, 354, 355
Devane, James, 110
De Vere, Aubrey, 8
Devlin, Joseph, 45
Dickens, Charles, 212
Dickinson, Page L., 69n, 98n, 194n, 225
Dillon, John, 45, 52
Diskin, Patrick, 329n
Doherty, William, 55
Douglas, James, 172, 207n
Dowden, Edward, 10, 12, 13, 114
Dowson, Ernest, 280
Dryden, John, 114
Duffy, Sir Charles Gavan, 29, 124
Dume, T. L., 122n, 225n, 267n
Dunin-Markievicz, S., 185n, 190n
Dunraven, Earl of, 50, 53, 69n, 96n
Dwyer, Michael, 22

Edgeworth, Maria, 21, 152
Edgeworth, Richard Lovell, 96, 97
Edward VII, King, 15, 146n
Edwards, Oliver, 115n, 128, 129
Eglinton, John (William K. Magee), 89n, 171n, 217n
Eliot, George, 125n, 211
Eliot, T. S., 120, 121
Ellmann, Richard, 335
Elton, Oliver, 275n
Emerson, Ralph Waldo, 299

Emmet, Robert, 25, 26, 27, 62, 63, 79n, 90, 92, 95, 110, 116, 289, 290, 308, 330, 331, 333
Erigena, Johannes Scotus, 240n, 343
Ervine, St. John, 126n
Evelyn, John, 328
Eyre, Stratford, 37

Fahey, Mgr. Jerome, 39n, 57, 301n
Ferguson, Sir Samuel, 7, 8, 117
Fergusson, Sir James, 356n
Fielding, Henry, 92, 275
Fingall, Elizabeth, Countess of, 187n, 190n
Fisher, James, 182
Fitzgerald, Desmond, 158n, 161
Fitzgerald, Lord Edward, 63, 78, 79n, 81, 116, 290, 295, 331
Fitzgerald, George Robert (Fighting Fitzgerald), 22, 37, 336
Fleming, James, 334n
Fletcher, Ian, 65
Flitch, J. E. Crawford, 226n
Ford, Julia Ellsworth, 217n
Foster, John, 275n
Four Masters, The, 301
Fox, Charles James, 38, 328
Francini, Paul and Philip, 100
Freeman, A. Martin, 301n
French, Mrs., 301, 305–6
Freney, James (Freney the Robber), 22
Frobenius, Leo, 95n
Froude, James Anthony, 88n

Gaffney, John, 182
Gainsborough, Thomas, 92, 212, 312n
Gallagher, Frank, 79
Galsworthy, John, 246n
Gandon, James, 100
Gannon, Rev. P. J., 147n
Gardner, Edmund G, 99n
Garrick, David, 268, 271
Gentile, Giovanni, 252, 253, 262
George II, King, 98
George II, King (of Greece), 355
George IV, King, 15, 26, 281
George V, King, 215, 353
George, David Lloyd, 348
Gibbon, Monk, 110n, 147, 187n, 198n

Gibbs, J. W. M., 268n
Gladstone, William Ewart, 317
Glenavy, Lord, 172n, 356n
Gogarty, Oliver St. John, 73, 75, 83, 88n, 94, 95, 96, 98, 100, 122, 126n, 135n, 149, 213, 302, 334n, 344n, 356
Goldsmith, Oliver, 3, 21, 91, 92, 99, 108n, 123, 169, 179, 229, 242, 243, 266–78, 319–22, 349, 363, 364
Gonne, Iseult (Mrs. Francis Stuart), 298, 353
Gordon, D. J., 65
Gore-Booth, Eva, 184, 185, 186, 187, 190, 323–26, 353
Gore-Booth, Gabrielle, 185n
Gore-Booth, Sir Henry, 185
Gough, Viscount, 355
Gough, Guy, 71
Gough, Mrs. Guy (Margaret Gregory), 66, 71, 74
Gough, Gen. Sir Hubert, 355–56
Granard, Lord, 173
Graney, Brian, 317n
Grattan, Henry, 24, 25, 32, 39, 48, 61, 62, 78, 86, 87, 90, 91, 96, 99, 104, 105, 107, 110, 113, 116, 118, 128n, 163, 169, 171n, 172, 175, 176, 181, 202, 204, 303, 308, 316, 330, 342, 346
Gray, Thomas, 114
Greene, David H., 88n, 89n
Gregory, Lady Isabella Augusta, 15n, 17n, 25n, 34n, 36, 37, 38, 39, 40, 42n, 43n, 46n, 47n, 50, 57n, 58, 59, 60n, 61n, 62n, 65, 66, 67, 68, 69–81, 82, 83, 86, 91, 104n, 107, 108, 109, 117n, 121, 123, 141n, 143, 144n, 149n, 152, 153, 180n, 190n, 191n, 200, 209, 212n, 227, 273, 278n, 288, 289, 290–91, 301n, 302, 303, 310, 313, 314, 326–29, 335, 337, 342, 361, 362n
Gregory, Richard, 38
Gregory, Major Richard, 74, 313
Gregory, Robert (of Coole), 37, 38, 42, 328
Gregory, Vere R. T., 66n, 79n, 355n
Gregory, Sir William, 38, 40, 41, 42, 43, 313, 362n
Gregory, William (Under-Secretary of Ireland), 38n, 39, 40, 298

Gregory, Major William Robert, 38, 64–69, 74, 82, 83, 125, 292–94, 311
Grenville, Lord, 173n
Griffith, Arthur, 155, 157, 175, 182n, 316
Griffith, Richard, 301n
Guinness, Henry Seymour, 173
Gwynn, Denis, 50n
Gwynn, Stephen L., 52, 97n, 112n, 121n, 129n, 178n

Hales, Sean, 182
Hallinan, John, 43n
Hamilton, Sir William Rowan, 95
Harrison, Miss S. C., 61n
Hart, Ruth, 92
Hastings, Warren, 169n
Häusermann, H. W., 334n
Hayford, Harrison, 299n
Hayward, John, 121n
Heald, Edith, 335
Healy, Timothy M., 123
Heath-Stubbs, John, 359
Hegel, George W. F., 217, 228, 230, 235, 349
Heilman, Robert B., 270n
Hemingway, Ernest, 244
Henderson, W. A., 28n, 77n
Henn, T. R., 82, 242
Henry II, King, 118
Higgins, F. R., 357
Hill, G. B., 269n
Hilles, Frederick W., 269n
Hines, Mary, 301–3
Hinkson, Pamela, 187n, 190n
Hinton, Jack, 97n
Hitler, Adolph, 154, 162
Hobbes, Thomas, 239, 242, 255, 256
Hoby, Sir Thomas, 73n
Hogan, J. J., 97n
Hogan, Patrick J., 182n, 207
Hogarth, William, 92
Holloway, Joseph, 64n, 70n, 77n, 146n, 152n, 209n, 240n
Homer, 251, 265, 311
Hone, Joseph M., 18n, 42n, 45n, 66n, 75, 90, 91n, 108, 111, 116, 119n, 121n, 126n, 128n, 129n, 166, 172, 185n, 187n, 195n, 225, 226, 227, 231, 238n, 262n, 275n, 328n, 362n

Hopper, Nora, 9
Horder, Lord, 347
Hugo, Victor-Marie, 220, 230
Hume, David, 252
Huysmans, Joris Karl, 244
Hyde, Douglas, 52, 53, 301, 302, 326

Inglis, Brian, 353n
Ireland, Denis, 89

Jackson, Aunt, 187
James, Henry, 212
Jameson, Sir Andrew, 172, 178n
Jarrell, Mackie L., 121n
Jeffares, A. Norman, 145n, 205, 225n, 226n, 249, 252, 341, 353
Jessop, T. E., 238n
John, Augustus, 127n, 153
Johnson, Esther (Stella), 135, 137, 138, 139, 299, 339
Johnson, Lionel, 9, 34n, 62, 93, 96n, 280
Johnson, Maurice, 121n
Johnson, Samuel, 92, 114, 122n, 254, 271, 278, 328
Johnson, Thomas, 216, 217, 298
Johnston, G. A., 225n, 234n, 239
Joyce, James, 44, 122, 128n, 230, 245, 246
Joyce, R. D., 8

Kant Immanuel, 230, 242n
Keane, Sir John, 173
Keats, John, 82, 83, 244, 272n
Kelleher, D. L., 122
Kelly, Gerald, 60n
Kelly, R. J., 45n
Kelly, Thomas, 53
Kennedy, Desmond, 345n
Kennedy, Patrick, 57n
Kenyon, Lord, 335
Kickham, Charles, 29, 30, 79n, 285
Kiernan, T. J., 73, 75n
Kilgannon, Tadhg, 324n
Killanin, Lord, 301n
Kilpatrick, Mary, 135n
King, Richard Ashe, 122, 124, 125n
King, Archbishop William, 91, 129, 293–94, 298

Kirby, Thomas A., 270n
Kropotkin, Prince, 195

Laird, Lady, 75
Lamb, Charles, 92
Lane, Sir Hugh Percy, 26, 36, 47, 58–64, 65, 68, 69, 75, 77, 82, 116, 146, 173, 194, 204, 289, 290–91, 295, 326
Larkin, James, 184
Latham, James, 228
Lattery, Mr., 43n
Law, Edmund, 293n
Law, Hugh A., 87, 88
Lecky, W. E. H., 10, 15, 88n, 114, 122n
Leinster, Duke of, 290
Leinster, James Fitzgerald, Duke of, 314
Lenin, V. I., 189, 217, 218, 334
Leslie, Sir Shane, 122, 171n
Leventhal, A. J., 109n
Lever, Charles James, 22
Lewis, Samuel, 301n
Lewis, Wyndham 124
Linnane, Eoin, 43n, 46n, 65n
Locke, John, 227, 229, 230, 236, 237, 242, 248, 249, 251, 253, 254, 255, 256, 259, 348, 350
Londonderry, Lord, 53
Loughnane, Henry and Patrick, 79, 317
Lover, Samuel, 22
Luce, A. A., 225n, 233, 235, 236, 238n, 249n
Lucretius, 274
Lutyens, Sir Edward, 61, 204
Lynd, Robert, 94n
Lyons, F. S. L., 50n, 204

MacBride, Madame Maud Gonne, 8, 186, 190, 298
MacBride, Sean, 218
McCartan, Patrick, 126, 145n, 207–8
MacCarthy, Mary, 336n
McCracken, Henry Joy, 180
McCullough, Denis, 207n
MacDermott, Frank, 158n
MacDonald, J. Ramsay, 208n
McDowell, R. B., 96n
MacEntee, Sean, 214
Mac Giollarnáth, Séan, 336n
MacGreevy, Thomas, 99

McKelvey, Joseph, 182
Macken, Mary M., 97n
MacKenna, Stephen, 278n
MacManus, Capt. D. A., 154n, 161, 162n, 219
MacManus, M. J., 159n
MacNeill, Mrs. Josephine, 133
MacSwiney, Mary, 207n
Madariaga, Salvador de, 226n
Madden, Daniel Owen, 113n
Magee, D'Arcy, 29
Maguire, Bryan, 22
Maguire, S. F., 39n, 335n
Mahaffy, John Pentland, 10, 18
Maloney, W. J. M., 208n, 356n
Malton, James, 345
Mancini, A., 337
Mangan, James Clarence, 7, 8, 29
Mannin, Ethel, 66n, 83n, 219, 342n
Marat, Jean Paul, 138
Margaretha, Princess, 312n
Markievicz, Countess Constance, 184–90, 213, 290, 295–97, 323–26
Marlborough, Duke of, 135n
Martin, Alec, 98
Martin, E. S., 336n
Martin, Richard (Humanity Dick/Hair-Trigger Dick), 37, 335–37
Martyn, Edward, 42, 362
Marx, Karl, 194, 214, 217n, 218n, 249, 251, 252–55, 265
Masefield, John, 70
Maurras, Charles, 202
Maxwell, Constantia, 118n
Maxwell, W. H., 69n, 96n
Mellows, Liam, 182
Meredith, C. M., 217n, 265n
Metaxas, Gen. Joannes, 355
Miles, Alfred H., 7n
Mill, J. S., 201
Milton, John, 17, 114, 173, 186
Mirsky, Prince, 255
Mitchel, John, 30, 52, 79n, 218n
Mitchell, Susan L., 47n
Molière, 270n
Molyneux, William, 78, 128n, 163, 340
Montague, William Pepperell, 258n
Montesquieu, Charles Louis, 173
Moore, G. E., 256, 257

Moore, George, 10n, 362
Moore, T. Sturge, 226, 256–61
Moore, Thomas, 5, 21, 29, 33, 99, 212, 345
Moore, Virginia, 256, 264, 341
Moran, D. P., 212
More, Henry, 349
Morrell, Lady Ottoline, 313
Morris, William, 216
Murphy, William Martin, 62, 290–91
Mussolini, Benito, 137n, 154, 155, 158n, 162, 180n, 202

Newton, Sir Isaac, 236, 237, 239, 241, 242, 251, 252, 255, 256
Nichevo, 180n
Nicholas II, Czar, 215, 350
Nolan, Sebastian, 54
Norbury, John Toler, Earl of, 110
Nordau, Max Simon, 124
Nuffield, Lord, 355

O'Brien, William, 45n, 171n
O'Casey, Sean, 128, 130, 153n, 187n, 214, 248
O'Connell, Daniel, 25, 26, 27, 28, 31, 32, 33, 34, 40, 41, 79n, 81, 86, 102, 106, 162, 163, 295, 330, 360–61
O'Connell, Rev. Jephson Byrne, 222, 223
O'Connell, Mrs. Morgan John, 20n
O'Connell, Norreys, 62
O'Connor, Frank, 75, 107, 122, 155n, 342n
O'Connor, Rory, 181, 182
O'Donnell, Peadar, 211n, 218, 219
O'Donnell, Red Hugh, 333
O'Duffy, Gen. Eoin, 154–65, 219, 333, 355
O'Faolain, Sean, 153n, 190, 278
O'Flaherty, Liam, 152
O'Flanagan, Rev. M., 301n
O'Grady, Standish James, 8, 14, 34n, 45, 105, 123, 128n, 225, 282, 329
O'Heffernan the Blind, 19
O'Hegarty, P. S., 122, 128n
O'Higgins, Kevin, 155, 156, 157, 165, 175, 179–84, 207, 319–21, 332, 342
O'Higgins, Mrs. Kevin, 144, 180–81, 183
O'Higgins, Thomas, 156

O'Leary, John, 26n, 28, 63, 97n, 108n, 129, 148, 213, 290, 329
Oliver, F. S., 122n
O'Neill, Eoin, 180n
O'Neill, Hugh, 333
O'Neill, James J., 104n
O'Neill, Owen Roe, 333
O'Rahilly, Egan, 334
O'Reilly, Hugh, 158n
Ormond, James Butler, Duke of, 133
O'Rorke, Rev. T., 176n, 178n, 284, 296n, 324–25
Orrery, John Boyle, Earl of, 121n, 132–33, 137
O'Sullivan, Donal, 147, 158n
O'Sullivan the Gaelic, 19
O'Sullivan the Red, 19

Paine, Thomas, 197
Palmer, W. Scott, 304n
Pankhurst, Miss Sylvia, 189n
Parnell, Charles Stewart, 5, 6, 32, 33, 34, 42, 45, 52, 62, 63, 77, 90, 102, 104, 105, 116, 146, 162, 165, 173, 212, 289, 290, 291, 308, 330–33, 342, 358, 359, 361
Parnell, Thomas, 21, 112
Pater, Walter, 7
Patmore, Coventry, 315n
Paul, Nancy Margaret, 304n
Payne, Basil, 126n
Pearce, Donald, 359
Pearse, Padraic, 44, 114
Peel, Sir Robert, 40
Péguy, Charles, 201, 202
Percy, Bishop Thomas, 92
Persse, Dean Dudley, 39
Persse, Dudley, 43n
Persse, Elizabeth, 44
Persse, Henry (the elder), 39
Persse, Henry (the younger), 39, 41
Persse, Robert Parsons, 39
Persse, William, 39
Petrie, Flinders, 105
Petrie, John, 336
Pitt, William (the younger), 214
Plato, 241
Plotinus, 262
Plunkett, George Noble, Count, 47
Plunkett, Sir Horace, 49, 52, 53

Poe, Edgar Allan, 7
Poë, Sir William Hutcheson, 290
Pope, Alexander, 20, 114, 278
Pound, Ezra, 204, 230, 245, 246
Powell, L. F., 269n
Powell, York, 275n
Power, Albert, 83, 84
Power, Pat (Power of Dargle), 22
Prior, James, 169n, 170n, 202
Proust, Marcel, 230
Purser, Sarah, 185

Quinn, Mrs. Ellen, 76, 316
Quinn, John, 20n, 29n

Raftery, 301–3, 306, 327
Rait, Robert S., 355n
Raleigh, Walter, 73n
Redmond, John, 52, 53, 81, 206
Reeves, James, 247n
Reynolds, Horace, 18n, 88n
Reynolds, Sir Joshua, 269n
Richardson, Samuel, 212
Ricketts, Charles, 65
Rilke, Rainer Maria, 338
Robinson, Lennox, 75n, 79n, 108, 109n, 111, 112, 144, 176n, 179n, 225, 278, 281
Roche, Tiger, 22
Rockingham, Charles Watson Wentworth, Marquess of, 38, 172
Rolleston, T. W., 96n
Roosevelt, Theodore, 54, 202
Roper, Esther, 189n
Roscommon, Wentworth Dillon, Earl of, 21
Rose, William, 338n
Rossi, Mario M., 121n, 126n, 127, 129n, 225, 226, 227, 331
Rothenstein, Sir William, 70, 128n, 137n
Rousseau, Jean Jacques, 114, 138, 204, 205, 217
Ruddock, Margot (Margot Collis), 68n
Ruskin, John, 220, 256–58, 340
Russell, Bertrand, 217n, 251, 252, 256–61
Russell, Lord John, 41
Ryan, Miss, 207n
Ryan, A. P., 356n

Ryan, Col. J., 156
Ryan, Mark F., 25n

Saddlemyer, Ann, 278n
Sadleir, Thomas Ulick, 66n, 69n, 98n, 100n
Salisbury, Lord, 116
Salkeld, Cecil, 250
Schneider, Hermann, 105
Scott, Temple, 269n
Scott, Sir Walter, 122n, 272
Seitz, Robert W., 269n
Shakespeare, Olivia, 137n, 193
Shakespeare, William, 17, 136, 250
Shaw, G. B., 68, 76, 89, 90, 102, 162, 216, 227n, 358–59
Shawe-Taylor, Frank, 57
Shawe-Taylor, Mrs. Frank, 57
Shawe-Taylor, John, 36, 44–57, 58, 59, 65, 68, 69, 82, 89, 289, 295, 326
Shawe-Taylor, Mrs. John, 56
Shawe-Taylor, Walter, 43n, 44, 46
Shawe-Taylor, Walter Michael, 56
Sheehy-Skeffington, Mrs. Hanna, 190n
Shelley, Percy Bysshe, 6, 229, 230
Sheridan, Richard Brinsley, 21, 270n
Sheridan, Thomas, 121n, 129
Sherlock, Lord Mayor, 60
Shorter, Clement, 78
Simms, J. G., 37n
Simon, Collyns, 225
Sinclair, Arthur, 77
Sirr, Major Henry Charles, 92, 110, 113
Smart, Christopher, 4
Smyllie, R. M., 352–53
Sophocles, 251
Sparrow, John, 225, 265
Spender, Stephen, 335
Spenser, Edmund, 6, 333, 340
Spinoza, Baruch, 228
Stalin, Joseph, 154
Stallworthy, Jon, 214n, 326n, 329
Stanford, W. B., 98n, 169n
Stendhal, 230, 244, 245
Stephens, Edward M., 88n
Sterne, Laurence, 21
Stevenson, R. L., 20
Stock, A. G., 126n
Strafford, Thomas Wentworth, Earl of, 297

Strindberg, August, 123
Strong, L. A. G., 129n, 147
Strongbow (Richard FitzGilbert de Clare, Earl of Pembroke), 118
Stuart, Francis, 250, 353
Sullivan, T. D., 182n
Sutherland, James, 270
Swedenborg, Emanuel, 265
Swift, Jonathan, 3, 21, 34, 60, 78, 86, 87, 88, 90, 91, 102, 105, 106, 107, 108, 110, 111, 112, 114, 116, 120–67, 169, 172, 179, 180n, 196n, 222, 223, 226, 229, 240, 241, 242, 243, 266, 267, 268, 271, 272, 274, 275, 276, 278, 287, 300, 308, 315, 319–22, 330–32, 338–39, 340–41, 342, 348, 349, 363, 364, 365
Swords, L. F. K., 126n
Symons, Arthur, 75
Synge, Archbishop Edward, 88
Synge, John Millington, 26, 30, 31, 34n, 76, 80, 82, 86, 94, 107, 108, 117, 143, 146n, 200, 272, 273, 276, 278, 289, 322, 326, 337, 342, 362

Taylor, Sir John, 56
Taylor, John F., 129, 204
Temple, Sir William, 129, 140, 349
Tennyson, Alfred, 244
Téry, Simone, 181n, 182n
Tierney, Michael, 147n
Todhunter, John, 8
Tone, Theobald Wolfe, 25, 26, 63, 79n, 90, 189n, 289, 290, 295, 331
Tree, Sir Herbert Beerbohm, 15
Trevelyan, George M., 128
Turner, W. J., 246, 334n
Twohig, Richard, 182
Tynan, Katharine, 7, 283
Tyrrell, G. N. M., 136n, 247
Tyrrell, R. Y., 10

Unamuno, Miguel de, 226n
Unterecker, John, 247n
Ussher, Archbishop James, 21
Ussher, Percy Arland, 114, 122n, 165, 337n

Valois, Ninette de, 213n
Vanhomrigh, Esther (Vanessa), 137–39

Index

Vaughn, Capt., 40
Verelst, Governor, 176n
Vico, Giambattista, 134, 137n, 262
Victoria, Queen, 14, 15, 115, 144
Voisin, Mary, 91, 129
Voltaire, 204

Wadding, Father Luke, 297
Wade, Allan, 302n
Wall, Thomas, 336
Wallace, William, 234n
Walsh, Ernest R., 45n, 60n, 66n, 109n
Walsh, John Edward, 22
Washington, George, 39
Wellesley, Lord, 328
Wellesley, Lady Gerald (Dorothy), 146n, 331
Wellington, Duke of, 100, 178n
Wesley, John, 204
Whaley, Thomas (Buck Whaley), 23, 94, 97n, 99
White, Terence de Vere, 180n, 181n
Whitehead, Alfred North, 260, 261, 265
Wilde, Oscar, 94, 95
William III, King, 132–33
Williams, Sir Harold, 121, 128
Williamson, Dr., 83
Wilson, Rev. David R., 128n
Wilson, Mrs. H., 172
Winters, Yvor, 112n, 279
Witt, Marion, 16n, 144n
Woolf, Virginia, 245
Wordsworth, William, 230, 272n, 280
Wyndham, George, 50
Wynn, Maud, 190n

Yeats, Anne Butler, 297–99, 311
Yeats, Benjamin, 91
Yeats, Elizabeth C. (Lolly), 103
Yeats, Dr. Francis Butler, 90n
Yeats, Jervis, 289
Yeats, John Butler, 12, 13, 61, 75, 90n, 92, 93, 128, 275n, 276
Yeats, Michael Butler, 107, 353
Yeats, Susan Mary (Lily), 91
Yeats, Rev. William Butler, 91, 289
Yeats, William Butler:
    Published works cited:
    "The Academic Class and the Agrarian

Yeats, William Butler (*Continued*)
    Revolution," 11; "An Acre of Grass," 245; "Among School Children," 200, 252, 323; "Ancestral Houses," 83, 311; "Anglo-Irish Ballads," 272; "An Appointment," 291; "At the Abbey Theatre," 287; "At Galway Races," 287, 288, 289; *Autobiographies*, 13, 21n, 23, 31, 32n, 33n, 34n, 35n, 44, 72n, 80n, 88, 91n, 92n, 93n, 94n, 105n, 115–16, 117n, 127n, 200, 203n, 204, 205, 206n, 211, 213, 218, 232, 267n, 269n, 270n, 273n, 302n, 315n, 322, 329, 331, 362n
"The Ballad of Father O'Hart," 284, 285; "The Ballad of the Foxhunter," 285; *Beltaine*, 105n; "The Best Books from Ireland," 21n, 169n; "Bishop Berkeley," 125, 191n, 222–65, 268; "The Black Tower," 326, 329, 330; "Blood and the Moon," 100, 125, 179–80, 191, 235–37, 242, 258, 274–76, 280, 319–22, 331, 362; *A Book of Irish Verse* (1895), 19, 21; *The Bounty of Sweden*, 198
"A Canonical Book," 24n; "Carleton as an Irish Historian," 25n, 32n; *Cathleen Ni Houlihan*, 25, 79, 190; "The Celtic Element in Literature," 19n; "The Censorship and St. Thomas Aquinas," 151; "The Child and the State," 112, 238; "Church and State," 164n; "Clarence Mangan," 7n; "Colonel Martin," 335; *Commentary on "A Parnellite at Parnell's Funeral,"* 102, 358; "Compulsory Gaelic," 95n; "The Controversy over *The Playboy of the Western World*," 270n; "Coole Park, 1929," 83, 326–27; "Coole Park and Ballylee, 1931," 83, 326–29; *The Countess Cathleen*, 31, 143, 146; "The Cradles of Gold," 72; "Crazy Jane on the Mountain," 353–54; "The Curse of Cromwell," 333–35
"The De-Anglicising of Ireland," 5n, 15n; " 'Death hath closed Helen's Eye,' " 302–3; "A Defense of the Abbey Theatre," 110n; "Demon and Beast," 279, 297; "Divorce: An Un-

375

Yeats, William Butler (*Continued*)
delivered Speech," 150; "Dr. Todhunter's Irish Poems," 21; "Down by
the Salley Gardens," 294; *The Dreaming of the Bones*, 113; "Dublin Fanaticism," 145–46; "Dublin Scholasticism
and Trinity College," 11

"Easter 1916," 187, 213, 295, 297;
"Edmund Spenser," 333; "Ellen
O'Leary," 7; "Emmet the Apostle of
Irish Liberty," 24–25; *Estrangement*,
288; "The Evangel of Folklore," 29n

"The Fiddler of Dooney," 294; *Fighting
the Waves*, 312; "First Principles," 16,
30n, 267n; "The Fisherman," 294–95,
353; "Fragments," 254; "The Freedom
of the Press in Ireland," 144;
"Friends," 291, "A Friend's Illness,"
287, 289; *A Full Moon in March*, 330

"A General Introduction for my Work,"
95n, 127, 129n, 140n, 196n, 249n,
341; "*Gods and Fighting Men*," 18,
24; "The Great Blasket," 362n; *The
Green Helmet and Other Poems*, 282,
287, 291; "The Growth of a Poet,"
294

"The Happy Townland," 33, 286–87;
"High Crosses of Ireland," 224; "The
Holy Mountain," 218n; "Hopes and
Fears for Irish Literature," 6n; "Hound
Voice," 336

"If I were Four-and-Twenty," 115, 198,
205, 217, 218n, 343; "*An Indian
Monk*," 17n; "In Memory of Eva
Gore-Booth and Con Markiewicz," 185,
187, 188, 189, 296, 297, 323–26; "In
Memory of Major Robert Gregory," 68,
292, 297; "Introduction" to *A Book of
Irish Verse* (1895), 267n; "Introduction" to *Essays and Introductions*, 199n,
249; "Introduction" to *Fighting the
Waves*, 205n, 242, 243, 245; "Introduction" to *The Resurrection*, 215n;
"Introduction" to *The Words upon the
Window-pane*, 1, 2, 3, 4, 90, 93, 94,
101n, 106, 121, 122, 128, 129, 132,
134, 137n, 138, 141, 142, 159, 169n,
174, 175, 197, 254, 266, 267, 268,
269n, 282, 293n, 339; "Ireland,

Yeats, William Butler (*Continued*)
1921–1931," 85n, 86–87, 118, 222;
"An Irish Airman Foresees his Death,"
67–69, 130, 292–94; "The Irish Cen-
sorship," 151; *Irish Fairy and Folk
Tales* (Modern Library Edition), 19,
287n, 336–37; "The Irish Intellectual
Capital: Where Is It?" 5n; "The Irish
Literary Theatre (14 January 1899),"
18n; "Irish Literature," 13n, 21n;
"Irish Literature. A Poet we have
Neglected," 7n; "Irish National Litera-
ture," 5n, 8n, 13, 21; *The Irish
National Theatre* (Rome), 80, 273;
"The Irish National Theatre and Three
Sorts of Ignorance," 35; "An Irish
Patriot," 18, 29, 117; "I see Phantoms
of Hatred and of the Heart's Fullness
and of the Coming Emptiness," 316

"J. M. Synge and the Ireland of his
Time," 30n, 33, 94, 203, 272n, 276;
"John Eglinton," 217n; "John Shawe-
Taylor," 47–48; *John Sherman*, 283–
84, 362n

"The King's Visit," 16

The Land of Heart's Desire, 185; "The
Last Gleeman," 21n; *Last Poems*, 326,
330, 335; "The Leaders of the Crowd,"
296; "Leda and the Swan," 109; "A
Letter from W. B. Yeats," 83; "Letter
to *The Leader*," 212; *The Letters of
W. B. Yeats*, 5, 7n, 17, 20n, 21n, 22n,
26n, 28, 32n, 78, 83, 84, 91, 111,
117n, 125, 126, 127, 128n, 129n, 132n,
134n, 135n, 137n, 140, 143n, 144n,
146n, 150n, 153, 155, 159, 160, 183,
184, 193, 195n, 196n, 200, 205, 211,
213n, 218, 219, 232, 239, 240, 247,
260, 261n, 283, 321, 331–32, 335,
338n, 341n; *Letters on Poetry from
W. B. Yeats to Dorothy Wellesley*,
216n, 334; *Letters to the New Island*,
18n, 20, 21n, 22n; "The Life of Patrick
Sarsfield," 19n, 29n; "Lionel Johnson," 96n; "Louis Lambert," 142,
197n, 241, 242, 244

"Major Robert Gregory," 68n; "Meditations in Time of Civil War," 311,
315–16, 318; "The Message of the

Yeats, William Butler (*Continued*)

Folk-lorist," 4n, 321n; *Michael Robartes and the Dancer*, 292; "'The Midnight Court,'" 122n; "Mr. John O'Leary," 28; "Mr. Standish O'Grady's 'Flight of the Eagle,'" 19n; "Modern Ireland," 71, 333, 353, 358–59; "Modern Irish Poetry," 9, 10; "The Municipal Gallery Revisited," 279–80, 337–38; "My Descendants," 314; "My House," 314

"The National Publishing Company," 29n; "Nationality and Literature," 192; "The Need for Audacity of Thought," 153n, 240n; "The New Irish Library," 124; "The New 'Speranza,'" 8n; "Nineteen Hundred and Nineteen," 315–18; "The Nineteenth Century and After," 246; "Noble and Ignoble Loyalties," 15

On the Boiler, 114n, 134, 172n, 183n, 196n, 205, 220, 221, 253–54, 322, 330, 339, 340–65; "On a Political Prisoner," 187, 295–97, 313, 324; "Oscar Wilde's Last Book," 94n

Pages from a Diary Written in Nineteen Hundred and Thirty, 107n, 122n, 123, 127n, 129n, 131, 132, 137n, 141, 149n, 168, 181n, 182n, 191, 194, 196n, 197, 198, 201n, 217n, 224, 231n, 234n, 236, 239, 241, 246n, 248, 250n, 254; "Pardon, Old Fathers," 289–90; "Parnell," 333; "Parnell's Funeral," 165, 330–33; "Paudeen," 290; "A People's Theatre," 210, 249; *Per Amica Silentia Lunae*, 242, 319, 321, 323, 331n; "The Philosophy of Shelley's Poetry," 300; *Plays and Controversies*, 169n; "Plays by an Irish Poet," 21n; "The Poetry of Sir Samuel Ferguson (9 October 1886)," 8; "The Poetry of Sir Samuel Ferguson (November 1886)," 8n, 13n, 14; "The Poetry of R. D. Joyce," 8; "Poetry and Tradition," 104n, 204; "A Postscript (*Ideals in Ireland*)," 24; "A Prayer for my Daughter," 297–99, 313; "Preface to the First Edition of John M. Synge's *Poems and Translations*, 140n; "Preface" to *Selections from the*

Yeats, William Butler (*Continued*)

Writings of Lord Dunsany, 33–34; "Preface" to *Wild Apples*, 125–26; "Professor Dowden and Irish Literature," 13n, 32n; "*Prometheus Unbound*," 241; *Purgatory*, 220, 221, 318, 330, 344, 345, 347, 348, 350, 351, 352, 354, 357–65

"A Race Philosophy," 341, 342; "A Reckless Century. Irish Rakes and Duellists," 22–23; "Red Hanrahan's Song about Ireland," 66, 67, 285–86, 295; "Reprisals," 69, 292, 317; *Responsibilities*, 287, 289; "Roger Casement," 356n; "Rosa Alchemica," 100n

Samhain, 95n; "Sean O'Casey's Story," 153n; "The Second Coming," 214–15, 216, 219, 295, 297, 298, 316, 318; *The Senate Speeches of W. B. Yeats*, 90, 112n, 113, 150n, 169, 174, 175, 191, 193, 194n, 197, 199, 218n, 240n, 250, 255; "September 1913," 63, 290; "Seven Propositions," 341–42; "The Seven Sages," 133, 142, 201, 251, 252, 276, 277, 322–23; "Shepherd and Goatherd," 83, 292; "The Silenced Sister," 29, 123; "Some Irish National Books," 29n; "Some New Letters from W. B. Yeats to Lady Gregory," 18n, 26n, 31n, 32n, 66n, 123n, 204; "The Stare's Nest by my Window," 215, 314–15, 362; "The Statesman's Holiday," 354–56; "Statistics," 246–47; *Stories of Michael Robartes and His Friends*, 274; "Swift's Epitaph," 123, 141; "Symbols," 247, 250

"The Tables of the Law," 127n; "These are the Clouds," 287–88, 310; "The Thirty Best Irish Books," 88n; "Those Who Live in the Storm," 362; "Three Irish Poets," 9; "The Three Monuments," 319; "Three Movements," 245, 246; "Three Songs to the Same Tune," 333; "To a Friend whose Work has come to Nothing," 63, 290; "To Ireland in the Coming Times," 6; "To a Shade," 63, 291; "To a Wealthy Man . . . ," 63; "Tom O'Roughley," 293n; *To-morrow*, 109, 146, 250, 251;

Yeats, William Butler (*Continued*)
"Towards Break of Day," 296, 324;
"The Tower," 66, 261–65, 280, 296,
300–11, 315, 318, 330; "The Treasure
of the Humble," 223–24; *Tribute to
Thomas Davis,* 27
"Under Ben Bulben," 113, 338–39; *The
Unicorn from the Stars,* 283; "The
Union of the Gael," 25; "Upon a
House shaken by the Land Agitation,"
287–88
*The Variorum Edition of the Poems of
W. B. Yeats,* 26, 30n, 100n, 141n,
147n, 160, 161, 164, 172, 173, 219,
284, 285n, 312, 338, 362n; *A Vision*
(1925), 212n; *A Vision* (1956), 74n,
105, 106, 131, 132n, 137n, 139n, 231,
241, 274
*W. B. Yeats and T. Sturge Moore: Their
Correspondence 1901–1937,* 95n, 124n,
140n, 153n, 226, 256–61, 265n,
314–15; "What is 'Popular Poetry'?"
271; *Where There is Nothing,* 282–83;
"While I, from that reed-throated whis-
perer," 291; "Why should not Old
Men be Mad?" 221, 352–53; *The
Wild Swans at Coole* 292; "The Wild
Swans at Coole," 73, 292; "William
Allingham" 7; "William Carleton," 9,
20, 22, 223; *The Winding Stair and
Other Poems,* 319; "A Woman's Beauty
is like a white frail Bird," 312; *The
Words upon the Window-pane,* 121,
131, 134–40
"Young Ireland," 30, 31; "The Young
Ireland League," 6n, 267n
Unpublished Works Cited:
"Autobiography," 17n, 72, 123, 185–87,
206n, 232
The Death of Lady Gregory, 71, 74, 75,
76, 80n, 83n; Diary of Thought, begun
23 September 1928, 139n, 180–81
Fragment beginning "and what has Ire-

Yeats, William Butler (*Continued*)
land to do with internationalism
. . . ," 195
Journal begun December 1908, 32, 75n,
76, 82, 91, 204; Journal begun Decem-
ber 1912, 213n
Large white vellum notebook begun 23
November 1930, 140, 154, 155, 219n,
232, 244, 255, 271; Letter to Clement
Shorter, 28 March 1917, 78; Letter to
Ethel Mannin, 1 February 1934, 66n,
83n; Letter to Joseph Hone, 2 Septem-
ber 1932, 133; Letter to Lady Gregory,
December 1928, 133
Manuscript book begun 7 April 1921, 114n
1930 Diary, 136, 153, 154, 237, 276n;
Notebook beginning "On examining
Michael's school reports . . . ," 161,
163, 166, 341
Political Organization, 162
Rapallo Notebook II, 141n, 313
The Speckled Bird, 282
TS. of "Congratulatory Address from the
RSL to the RDS on the occasion of the
BCC," 241n; TS. of "Introduction" to
Fighting the Waves, 137n, 242n, 249;
TS. of letter to Commissioner Bailey,
23 June 1915, 64–65; TS. of "Modern
Poetry," BBC broadcast, 95, 244, 246;
TS. of "My Own Poetry," BBC broad-
cast, 68n, 287, 334; TS. of "My Own
Poetry Again," BBC broadcast, 72n,
327; TS. of "Poems about Women,"
BBC broadcast, 185n, 188, 296; TS. of
"Speech for Tailteann Banquet, August
2, 1924," 317–18; TS. of Speech given
in New York, 1903–4, 4, 5, 9, 193,
272
Yeats, Mrs. W. B., 16n, 18n, 33n, 50n, 59n,
75n, 98n, 114n, 121n, 137n, 150n, 152,
169n, 172n, 180n, 198n, 207, 214n,
217n, 223n, 313n, 314, 322, 328n, 334n,
341n, 345n, 353, 362n
Young, Arthur, 38, 107, 114, 292, 328

95601

DATE DUE